THE LAST TREK
OF THE INDIANS

BY GRANT FOREMAN

THE UNIVERSITY OF CHICAGO PRESS · CHICAGO

THE LAST TREK
OF THE INDIANS

TO CAROLYN

THE UNIVERSITY OF CHICAGO PRESS · CHICAGO 37

Agent: CAMBRIDGE UNIVERSITY PRESS · LONDON

COPYRIGHT 1946 BY THE UNIVERSITY OF CHICAGO. ALL RIGHTS
RESERVED. PUBLISHED 1946. SECOND IMPRESSION 1946. COMPOSED
AND PRINTED BY THE UNIVERSITY OF CHICAGO PRESS
CHICAGO, ILLINOIS, U.S.A.

PREFACE

FROM the time the first European set foot on the American continent, conflict of interests was the normal attitude between the Indian and the white man. In early Colonial days hostilities between them yielded to or integrated with commercial activities; the principal interest of the European in the American Indian related to trade, as the Indian garnered for the white man the American harvest of furs and at the same time created a market for the manufactured output of the European.

To protect and nourish the interests of the Englishman in this field, the British government set up an arm of administration over its American dominion. For a long time preceding the Revolution there were two principal superintendencies that exercised supervision over Indian relations in the British colonies. That known as the Southern District of America was under the jurisdiction of John Stuart, and the Northern District was supervised by Sir William Johnson. They both reported to their chiefs, the Lords Commissioners of Trade and Plantations in London. The result is an extensive collection of manuscript material in the form of letters, journals, reports of expeditions, treaty councils, and such, all of great historical interest and value to the student of United States and Indian history. These documents, identified as "Colonial Office 5" or "C.O. 5," were to be seen before the present war in the Public Record Office in Chancery Lane in London, where, it is hoped, they have escaped the fury of the Germans. Fortunately, the authorities of the Library of Congress had the foresight a number of years ago to copy most of these records, and the transcripts are now available for examination in the Manuscript Division of our great library in Washington.

After the Colonies had won their independence and the United States came into being, the Indians continued of general concern; and the federal government, conceiving the subject to be a matter of national importance, created a department of Indian affairs which functioned for years as a branch of the War Department. In order to extend the authority of the government into every area where Indian relations required it, agencies were created where they could maintain contact with the Indians and perform locally all the functions delegated to them by the government in Washington. In this exercise of authority a prodigious amount of correspondence was carried on between the Department of Indian Affairs and the superintendencies and agencies. A large amount of this correspondence derived from treaty conferences and negotiations which lay at the foundation of the more than three hundred treaties negotiated with the tribes and from the interminable uprooting and moving of the Indians from one place to another.

The story of the removal of the Indians is to be found, in the main, in tens of thousands of pages of manuscript material formerly in the Department of Indian Affairs but now on deposit in the National Archives in Washington.

The author has made full use of this material, necessarily reduced to the form in which it is presented here. In addition, he has examined voluminous correspondence of army officers relating to Indian affairs, now preserved in the National Archives. He has also examined extensive correspondence covering this subject in the archives of the State Historical Society of Wisconsin, the Indiana Historical Society, the Indiana State Library, Indiana University, Ohio State University, the Ayer Collection in the Newberry Library in Chicago, the Oklahoma Historical Society, the Kansas State Historical Society, and the New York State Library in Albany. Contemporary newspapers preserved interesting accounts of the movements of these Indians, and their files have been examined with profit in the most important newspaper collections in the country: the Library of Congress, the State Historical Society of Wisconsin, the University of Texas, the Oklahoma Historical Society, the State Historical Society of Missouri, the Missouri Historical Society, and the Mercantile Library in St. Louis.

Outside Washington, the most extensive collection of Indian manuscripts in the country is to be seen in the Oklahoma Historical Society; made up of official correspondence and reports garnered from many Indian agencies of Oklahoma by authority of an act of Congress, this collection has yielded much material essential to this work.

The source which lent itself with the greatest facility and reward to this volume was the printed editions of matter currently relating to the administration of Indian affairs. Of first importance in this category are the annual reports, from 1824 to 1907, of the Commissioner of Indian Affairs. Each contains in great detail reports from the local

Indian agents, giving accounts of the current movements and developments in the different agencies.

These reports were published with the reports of the War Department as a part of the documents (annual departmental reports) accompanying the *Message from the President of the United States to Both Houses of Congress at the Commencement of the Session of the Congress*, which was usually issued as a numbered document of both House and Senate. Reports were also issued separately during this period, the earliest one in the Library of Congress being for the year 1837-38. Thus for this early period there were at least three printings or editions. After 1848 these reports appeared in editions that varied at different times, the imprints usually bearing the dates of the reports, sometimes as part of the report of the Secretary of the Interior, sometimes as separates having no relation to any other report.

Reference to the reports of the Commissioner of Indian Affairs herein will be to the pages appearing in the editions most available and familiar to the student, which is usually that edition appearing with the report of the Secretary of War or (since 1848) the Secretary of the Interior, where the pagination is that of the secretary's report. Occasionally the commissioner's report appeared as an independent document and was paged accordingly.

Perhaps the most fruitful source of material touching federal administration of Indian affairs and related Indian history is the series of congressional documents published throughout the life of Congress. Pending bills, resolutions, recommendations by the executive branch, and memorials reaching Congress directly or by way of the Indian office from the Indians and other sources invoked congressional committee hearings that developed reams of evidence, sometimes consuming scores, hundreds, and even thousands of pages when Congress directed it to be printed, which was the usual course. Hundreds of such congressional documents with their rich historical content have been consulted in the preparation of this book.

Indian removal had been under way for some time under Jackson's Removal Bill of 1830, when the United States House of Representatives, solicitous about the expenditure involved, on January 27, 1832, adopted a resolution calling for information on the subject. President Jackson thereupon, on March 15, supplied correspondence compiled by the Secretary of War; this material, as published by authority of Congress, extended to ninety-one printed pages (*House Doc. 171* [22d Cong., 1st sess.]).

Later, the Senate, also concerned with the element of expense, on December 27, 1833, adopted a resolution calling for information. Accordingly, the commissary-general of subsistence compiled the desired records, which were published by authority of Congress as *Senate Document 512* (23d Cong., 1st sess.) comprising five volumes under the title *Correspondence on the Subject of the Emigration of Indians between the 30th November, 1831, and 27th December, 1833, with Abstracts of Expenditures by Disbursing Agents, in the Removal and Subsistence of Indians, &c., &c., Furnished in Answer to a Resolution of the Senate, of 27th December, 1833, by the Commissary General of Subsistence.* The 4,271 printed pages contained in this document include reports, journals, and correspondence touching every phase of the subject and, therefore, constitute a priceless and indispensable source of information concerning Indian removal for that period. The title is so long that, for brevity, reference hereafter will be made to *"Document"* or *"Doc."*

The two volumes known as the *Handbook of American Indians*, edited by Frederick Webb Hodge (Bull. 30 [Washington: Bureau of American Ethnology, 1912]), are useful and convenient books of reference concerning the Indians discussed. For ease of reference, this work will be cited as merely *"Handbook."*

The *United States Statutes at Large* contain a rich and indispensable source of Indian history, for they contain not only every Indian treaty ratified by Congress or the Senate but every statute enacted by Congress relating to the Indians. Indian treaties are to be found also in Kappler's edition of *Laws and Treaties*, Volume II (Senate Doc. 452 [57th Cong., 1st sess.]).

Emigration of the five great tribes of southern Indians between 1830 and 1840 to the present Oklahoma is a chapter unsurpassed in pathos and absorbing interest in American history. This dramatic story is now available to the student (Grant Foreman, *Indian Removal*). Almost obscured in the shadow of this great exodus was the emigration of numerous smaller detachments of Indians living farther north. These fragments of once powerful and colorful Indian nations, whose names were written large across the pages of American history, had come to rest temporarily in Ohio, Indiana, and Illinois. And as the white man settled the prairies of those states, he demanded the land on which the Indians lived, and the latter, oppressed and discouraged by the influence and pressure of their new neighbors, were induced to enter into treaties by which they gave up their homes and agreed to remove again farther west, where they were assured they need never fear that their lands would again be coveted by the whites. The experiences of these Indians and others are recorded herein.

The author began collecting material for this book long before the creation of the National Archives, and he therefore consulted and copied the essential manuscripts while they were still located in their early repositories in the Department of Indian Affairs and various branches of the War Department, where his labors were facilitated by the uniform courtesies of the custodians of those files, a number of whom have since been retired from service by death. Since the organization of the National Archives, these files have been removed there for better preservation, and the author has pleasure in expressing his appreciation for the co-operation of those in charge and particularly for the valuable assistance and courtesy of Mr. P. M. Hamer, director of reference service. The author is indebted to many persons in scores of libraries and archives over the country, but particularly to Mrs. Rella L. Looney, archivist of the Oklahoma Historical Society, whose services have placed the archives of that association on a high plane of usefulness. Mrs. Margaret H. Anderson, of the Indiana State Library, and Mrs. C. M. Whaley, of Muskogee, have been most helpful to the author. But, above all, he wishes to register deep obligation to his wife, Carolyn Thomas Foreman, for her long-sustained and sustaining interest and encouragement. For years she has shared with him all the labors of research, copying and arranging of notes for the writing of this book, and reading and criticizing the manuscript at all stages. The maps in this book were adapted by the author from the originals in the Bureau of American Ethnology and were drafted by A. H. Hansen of Muskogee.

G. F.

MUSKOGEE, OKLAHOMA
November 1945

TABLE OF CONTENTS

INTRODUCTION

THE state of Oklahoma was aptly named: in congressional discussions[1] it was said to mean "Home of the Red Man," a name born of the fact that it is the home of many Indians. At the present time Oklahoma contains nearly a third of the Indian population of the United States—more than are to be found in any other state of the Union. At least fifty-five tribes are represented in Oklahoma—the remnants and descendants of once powerful Indian nations who, in their days of pristine strength and freedom, bulked large in American history.

Less than a half-dozen of Oklahoma's Indian tribes are indigenous. The movement of the immigrant Indians to their present and final home is a vital and poignant story in American history.[2] From where did they come? And when and how? The questions suggest an interesting study.

From the time the first white settlements were made along the Atlantic Coast the lands of the aborigines were appropriated by the newcomers, who forced the Indians to yield possession. By degrees over many years the red men were compelled to retire before the growing might of the colonists. They were put upon and pushed around until ultimately they were forced across the Mississippi River to find a home on remote lands which, it was thought, the white man would never want and where, it was believed, the Indian could live undisturbed and perhaps develop a civilization along lines that the "White Father" thought would be good for him—there in the "Home of the Red Man" to end his days in the process of extirpation or amalgamation with the white race.

The Indians living south of the Ohio River—the Cherokee, Creek, Choctaw, Chickasaw, and Seminole, who became known as the "Five Civilized Tribes"—occupied contiguous territory and were more or less homogeneous; that is to say, in their history, their permanence on the soil where they lived, their tribal organization, and their customs and contacts with the whites they had much in common. The removal of their sixty thousand individuals westward was achieved under federal organization and substantially as one huge operation over a period of a decade or two. Their displacement was handled by tribal units, thereby lending itself to a comparatively simple narration, which has already been written.[3]

This book is an account of the removal, in the main, of the Indians from north of the Ohio River, a more complicated undertaking entailing a much more involved narrative. They had not preserved their tribal integrity as the southern Indians did, and there was little homogeneity among them. Their removal was haphazard, not coordinated, and wholly unsystematized.

To attain an approximately accurate picture of the Indians dealt with in this book, it may be necessary to revise preconceptions of them. The uninformed, if he has any impressions at all, is likely to think of Indian tribes as permanent organizations with fixed limits and populations. On the contrary, many of the tribes north of the Ohio were permanent neither in their homes nor in their tribal organizations and territorial limits. Outstanding in this particular were the Shawnee and the Delawares, who, in historical times, had been buffeted about so much by the fortunes of intertribal war, and by the white man, that they had been broken up into fractions scattered over a large part of eastern United States. Thus it is difficult to say where their home was at any given time until early in the eighteenth century, when the major parts of these tribes became residents of the areas north of the Ohio River. Factions of these and other tribes often left the main body for various reasons: to find better hunting or better maple-sugar groves or huckleberry country; to flee from an epidemic; or to follow the fortunes of a rival chief or medicine man. These factions would take up their homes in remote places or, influenced by friendship or intermarriage, attach themselves to some other tribe. These tribal divisions and mutations are more particularly indicated hereafter in their appropriate place.

In the confused congeries that passed for Indian administration, few of the men who negotiated with the Indians knew any of their history. These men were often vague and misleading in their reports; and, as these reports frequently furnish us our only access to the facts, it is often difficult to identify satisfactorily the areas and particular Indians involved, to determine a logical sequence of events, and to classify other details the reader would like to know. And, when reference is made to a tribe, the official recorder sometimes fails to tell us whether he is speaking of the whole tribe or of only a band or faction, and, if so, what faction. The removal of fifty tribes of Indians to what is now Oklahoma, under pressure of different state and national governments, conformed in no phase or degree to any pattern. There was an infinite variety of methods, experiences, and details.

Most of the Indians dealt with at the turn of the eighteenth century were residents of Ohio, Indiana, Illinois, and New York. These Indians were the Delawares, Shawnee, Ottawa, Wyandots, Kickapoo, Potawatomi, Peoria, Kaskaskia, Piankashaw, Sauk and Foxes, Cayuga, and Seneca. They had become more or less permanent residents of areas indicated on the maps herein.

The government undertook Indian removal without plan or experience. With candor or guile, by arguments, threats, or cajolery, by appealing to the cupidity of corruptible chiefs, by gorging the Indians at councils with food and drink—whatever the exigencies suggested to agents, inexperienced and often poorly qualified, as calculated to break down the resistance of the Indians was employed. The tribes or parts of tribes most accessible and susceptible to the approach of agents and the first to yield were first to start on their way westward. There was no system and no order; some bands would yield more easily than others and were sooner on the march. Those who resisted came when they, too, surrendered later.

In some instances, where a whole tribe could not be induced to remove, a band or faction under the influence of a leader would surrender and start west—sometimes with a faction of another tribe to which it was bound by ties of friendship or intermarriage or allegiance to a petty chief or medicine man or other leader. Where a faction was thus removed, the reader of current reports might be confused, thinking that the whole tribe had emigrated. The records thus made were fortuitous and defiant of efforts to discover any logical order of removal, association of tribes, or, sometimes, positive identification of Indians involved.

One of the problems confronting the historian writing of the American Indian and relying on contemporary records is the various, contradictory, and often capricious spelling of Indian names. Officials were not in agreement, and even acts of Congress employed spellings which emphasized the lack of settled rules. The Bureau of American Ethnology in recent years has undertaken to standardize the spelling of Indian names, and, while this suffices for current discussions, it does not reconcile divergent spellings in historic times and exposes the writer to suspicion of carelessness in his contemporaneous spelling of names.

NOTES

1. *Senate Report 131* (41st Cong., 2d sess.).
2. Grant Foreman, *Indian Removal: The Emigration of the Five Civilized Tribes.*
3. *Ibid.*

THE LAST COUNCIL OF THE POTTAWATOMIES, 1833

Courtesy of the Chicago Historical Society

THE POTAWATOMI COUNCIL HELD IN CHICAGO IN 1833

PART I

CHAPTER I

EARLY INDIAN TREATIES

IN TREATING the subject of Indian removal to Oklahoma, there is no very obvious sequence to guide one. Chronology alone does not avail, for there were other and conflicting elements, such as tribal relationships and ethnic groupings, geographical divisions, chronological disparities, varying degrees and phases of regional and official pressure, local developments, and other influences that defy any certain order or pattern of treatment.

History, however, seems to single out the Delaware Indians to introduce the discussion, for it was this tribe with which our infant government in 1778 made its first Indian treaty.[1] We were at war with Great Britain and desperately in need of help. At Fort Pitt we entered into a covenant with the Delawares by which an Indian confederation was proposed that would have representation in Congress. The underlying purpose of the treaty, however, was to give the United States certain rights of access into the Indian country in order to facilitate our operations against the British forts and outposts.

The Delaware Indians, a confederacy of Algonquian stock, formerly occupied the entire basin of the Delaware River in eastern Pennsylvania, southeastern New York, and most of New Jersey and Delaware. The Lenape, or Delaware proper, included three principal tribes—the Munsee, Unami, and Unalachtigo. Their first treaty was made with William Penn in 1682, when their great chief, Tamenend, from whom the Tammany Society takes its name, was identified with the affairs of the tribe.

The aggressions of the Iroquois forced the Delawares westward from time to time; and in 1751, by invitation of the Huron (Wyandot), they began to form settlements in eastern Ohio. About 1770 the Delawares received permission from the Miami and Piankashaw to occupy the country between the Ohio and White rivers of Indiana, where at one time they had six villages.[2] In 1789, by consent of the Spanish government, a part of them removed to Missouri, and afterward to Arkansas, with a band of Shawnee. Successive treaties detailed hereinafter, made by the Delawares and their associates with the United States, marked their retirement westward before the advance of the white pioneer.

Of the numerous tribes living in the Northwest Territory, the Shawnee were perhaps more closely associated with the Delawares in interests and experiences than any other. In their early history the Shawnee were found in South Carolina, where they were known also as Savannahs. They were a wandering people and in their movements became identified from time to time with Tennessee, Pennsylvania, Virginia, Kentucky, and Alabama. When the first treaty was made with them by the United States in 1786,[3] most of the United Tribe of Shawnee Indians were found within the present limits of Ohio.

Congress recognized a federal responsibility for dealing with the American Indian when, on August 7, 1789, it created the War Department and, among other things, assigned to it certain duties relating to Indian affairs. The principal concerns of the government in connection with the Indians then were the suppression of hostilities and the regulation of Indian-white trade.

Soon after the close of the Revolutionary War the United States made a number of treaties with the Indians north of the Ohio River, in which tribal domain, boundaries, and other matters affecting the Northwest Territory were defined. In 1785 a treaty was negotiated with the Wyandot, Delaware, Chippewa, and Ottawa in Ohio[4] by George Rogers Clark, who entered into another treaty in 1786 with the Shawnee Nation of Ohio.[5] The treaty of 1789 was negotiated at Fort Harmer (Ohio) by Arthur St. Clair, "governor of the Territory of the United States, northwest of the River Ohio," with the Wyandot, Delaware, Ottawa, Chippewa, Potawatomi, and Sauk nations.[6]

Compliance with the terms of these three treaties was prevented by the continued hostilities of the Indians. Indian warfare was finally terminated on August 20, 1794, by their overwhelming defeat on the banks of the Maumee at the hands of General "Mad Anthony" Wayne in what has become known as the "Battle of Fallen Timbers." Under the influence of this defeat, General Wayne, on August 3, 1795, concluded an important treaty of peace with these tribes[7] and thus opened the state of Ohio to white settlement. The Indians involved in this treaty were the Wyandots, Delawares, Shawnee, Ottawa, Chippewa, Potawatomi of Huron, Miami, Eel River, Wea, Kickapoo, Piankashaw, and Kaskaskia. In this treaty, with the exception of certain tracts of land ceded by the Indians, the United States acknowledged the Indians' title to all land east of the Mississippi and west of the Cayahoga (Cuyahoga) River and east and south of other prescribed boundaries in Ohio; so that these Indians thereby became recognized owners of most of the present Ohio, Indiana, and Illinois.

When James Monroe became president in 1817, the tide of western emigration had already resulted in a considerable white population in what are now Ohio, Indiana, and Illinois, accompanied by a growing sentiment for removal of the Indians from that region. This situation presented problems of concern common to a number of tribes who were to be forced to cross the Mississippi River and find their ultimate home in Oklahoma. These Indians included the Delawares, Shawnee, Ottawa, Wyandots, Seneca, Kickapoo, Potawatomi, Peoria, Kaskaskia, Wea, Piankashaw, Sauk, and Foxes. As they were more or less allied in warfare, removal, and other activities, they are logically associated in this account. A brief preliminary notice of these Indian tribes up to the time that President Monroe's removal policy was inaugurated will make for a better understanding. From that point some of them may be considered separately, though others will continue to be associated in their confederacies and common experiences.

Early in the eighteenth century the Illini or Illinois Nation of Indians was more numerous than any other that inhabited the country now included within Illinois and Missouri and consisted of the tribes of Mascoutin, Miami, Peoria, Michigamea, Cahokia, Kaskaskia, and Tamaroa. The Mascoutin were settled in the northern part of what is now Illinois and the southern part of Wisconsin; the Miami near the site of Chicago; the Peoria on the borders of Lake Peoria; the Michigamea on the right bank of the Mississippi River where St. Louis was later built; the Cahokia on the left bank of that river, opposite St. Louis; the Kaskaskia on the Kaskaskia River about twelve miles above its confluence with the Mississippi; and the Tamaroa on the Kaskaskia River thirty miles above the village of the Kaskaskia Indians. Though separated by a considerable distance, these tribes were held together by a general confederacy, making common cause in all the wars in which they were engaged against their enemies north and south of them. Notwithstanding the formidable adversaries who continually assailed them on every side, says Chouteau, they would have maintained their ground had it not been for the introduction of ardent spirits among them by the white people, in which they indulged to such excess as in a great measure to contribute to their destruction physically and morally and impair their ability to contend efficiently with their many powerful enemies.[8] In time, however, the Mascoutin and the Miami, being the most exposed, were so constantly engaged in conflicts with their neighbors, and were so harassed by bloody incursions, that for self-protection they removed to a river in the state of Ohio, which from that time became known as the Miami (Maumee) River.[9]

Encouraged and emboldened by the emigration of these tribes, the northern barbarians, including the Sauk and Foxes, united their strength and, redoubling their efforts, waged a relentless war against the Peoria and the remainder of the Illinois Confederacy. The murder of Pontiac at Cahokia by a Kaskaskia Indian about 1769 provoked the vengeance of the Lake Tribes[10] on the Illinois Indians, and a war of extermination followed, which in a few years reduced them to a small number. These, weakened by the defection of the Miami and Mascoutin and discouraged by repeated disasters, fled south to the mouth of the Illinois River and settled.

But even here their vindictive enemies pursued them; and, eventually abandoning all their settlements on the beautiful Illinois and its tributaries, they fled farther south and took refuge with the French settlers at Kaskaskia, while the aggressors—Sauk, Foxes, Kickapoo, and Potawatomi—took possession of their country. In the southern Illinois country the Peoria, Michigamea, and Cahokia, combining their strength, built a strong fort and, having three thousand warriors, were able for a time successfully to oppose their enemies, who, notwithstanding, continued to harass them. Through change of situation they avoided the tomahawk of their former foes but acquired greater facility for obtaining ardent spirits, which proved still more injurious; for, besides the diseases arising from unlimited indulgence in the use of liquor, infuriated by it, they frequently fell upon and killed one another .

Owing to this cause principally, the warriors of these tribes were reduced in 1763 to about one thousand; and in 1780, when they numbered about two hundred, they crossed the Mississippi River and located at Ste Genevieve, where they made their village and lived for many years.[11]

The Kaskaskia and Tamaroa, having been subject to these influences, were nearly destroyed in the same way; so that, soon after the Louisiana Purchase, with the exception of the Mascoutin and Miami, there remained of the once powerful nation of Illinois Indians only about seventy persons, including men, women, and children, living near Kaskaskia, and a few straggling Peoria in their village of Ste Genevieve. There was, however, a tradition among these Indians that, before they had ever seen a white man, a band of their nation had previously settled at the Saline near Ste Genevieve, where they had a large village, and later had moved southwest to the Washita country.[12]

While negotiations for the Louisiana Purchase were in progress, President Jefferson directed General William Henry Harrison to hold himself in readiness to negotiate with such Indian nations as the President might later indicate, with a view to acquiring their lands in the vicinity of the Kaskaskia Indians and the adjoining lands on the Mississippi and Ohio rivers.[13] There resulted a series of treaties divesting the Indians of their lands lying north of the Ohio River, through Ohio, Indiana, and Illinois.

At the time of the Revolution the Indians of the Illinois Confederacy had been recognized as owners of a vast area of what were known vaguely as "Illinois Lands" lying on both sides of the Mississippi. In 1773 William Murray, a trader in the Illinois country, for himself and others undertook the purchase of a large tract of "Illinois Lands." In June of that year he held a conference with representatives of several tribes of Illinois Indians at Kaskaskia, which was then a British settlement and military station. These conferences were attended by the inhabitants of the place as well as by several military officers of the British government. On July 5 the Indians agreed to the sale, and an instrument was executed by which Tamaroa and other Kaskaskia and Cahokia chiefs purported to convey to the Illinois Land Company a large part of the present southern Illinois. They conveyed also another tract, one boundary of which began on the eastern bank of the Mississippi, opposite the mouth of the Missouri, and followed the Illinois River upward to "Chicagou or Garlick creek." The further course of this boundary is expressed in idiom and description that are impossible of assimilation with present features of the country.

The grantors acknowledged receipt of the consideration consisting of five shillings in cash, 260 strouds, 250 blankets, 350 shirts, 150 pairs of stroud and half-thick stockings, 150 stroud breechcloths, 500 pounds of gunpowder, 4,000 pounds of lead, one gross of knives, 30 pounds of vermilion, 2,000 gun flints, 200 pounds of brass kettles, 200 pounds of tobacco, 36 gilt looking-glasses, one gross of gun-worms, two gross of awls, one gross of fire-steels, 72 garterings, 10,000 pounds of flour, 500 bushels of Indian corn, 12 horses, 12 horned cattle, 20 bushels of salt, and 20 guns.

In September, 1775, Murray negotiated with the chiefs and sachems of the Piankashaw tribe at Post St. Vincent's, or Vincennes, on the Wabash, then a military post under the British government. Here a deed was executed on October 18, conveying to the agent, Louis Viviat, "John Earl of Dunmore, governor of Virginia," John Murray, and other Englishmen another tract of land extending across the Wabash River and into the present Indiana. The deed recited receipt of the following consideration: 400 blankets, 22 pieces of stroud, 250 shirts, twelve gross of star garterings, 120 pieces of ribbon, 24 pounds of vermilion, 18 pairs of velvet-laced housings, a piece of malton, 52 fusees, 300 large buckhorn-handled knives, 480 *couteaux*, 500 pounds of brass kettles, 10,000 gun flints, 600 pounds of gunpowder, 2,000 pounds of lead, 400 pounds of tobacco, 40 bushels of salt, 3,000 pounds of flour, 3 horses, and the following quantities of silverware: 11 very large armbands, 40 wristbands, 6 whole moons, 6 half-moons, 9 earwheels, 46 large crosses, 29 hairpipes, 60 pairs of earbobs, 240 small crosses, 240 nose crosses, and 1,320 brooches. These deeds were recorded at Kaskaskia in September, 1773, and December, 1775. After the ceded country became part of the United States, the grantees named in these two conveyances solicited the executive offices of the government and the Congress of the United States to ratify these sales and confirm their titles to the land described. As late as December, 1810, the deeds were again submitted to Congress in a lengthy memorial, urging their validity and proposing a compromise under which they solicited favorable action. Confirmation of these deeds was opposed in Congress on several counts: that it was against public policy to permit the sale of Indian land to private individuals without a treaty; that the second deed was made since the Revolution while Congress had an agent for Indian affairs residing at Fort Pitt who had no notice of the purchase; that the lands had been since ceded by the Indians to the United States for a valuable consideration; and that the lands had been sold and the proceeds applied on the discharge of the public debt.[14]

Most of General Harrison's treaties were negotiated at Fort Wayne and Vincennes. Among the earliest were the treaties with the Illinois Indians who were indigenous to the area that is now the state of Illinois, though some of them had already crossed the Mississippi and had begun the movement that was to carry the remnants of all these northern tribes to the West.

The first treaty under Harrison's instructions was negotiated at Fort Wayne on June 7, 1803,[15] with the Delawares, Shawnee, Potawatomi, Miami, Eel River, Wea, Kickapoo, Piankashaw, and Kaskaskia. The principal object of this treaty was the better definition of boundaries previously indicated by the French and British, which were to determine the holdings of the United States surrounding the settlements at Vincennes. The terms of the treaty acknowledged the area within the prescribed boundaries, amounting to 1,634,058 acres, of which 336,128 acres lay within the limits of the state of Illinois, to belong to the United States.

The first treaty of cession, however, under direction of the President, was that made by General Harrison with the Kaskaskia Indians on August 13, 1803.[16] In this the treaty-makers were described as "head chiefs and warriors of the Kaskaskia Tribe of Indians so called, but which tribe is the remains and rightfully represents all the tribes of the Illinois Indians, originally called the Kaskaskia, Mitchigamia, Cahokia and Tamaroi."

Section 1 of this treaty ceded to the United States all their land in the present limits of Illinois, comprising more than eight million acres, except about three hundred and fifty acres at their town of Kaskaskia.[17] The ceded area extended from the confluence of the Ohio and the Mississippi rivers northward nearly to the Kankakee River and was bounded on the west by a line from its northerly point to the mouth of the Illinois.

President Jefferson, in October, submitted this treaty to the Senate for confirmation.[18] In his third annual message to Congress, on October 17, 1803,[19] he referred to the securing of it as an achievement of much importance, comparable in a small way, one might suppose, to the Louisiana Purchase: "Another important acquisition of territory has also been made since the last session of Congress. The friendly tribe of Kaskaskia Indians, with which we have never had a difference, reduced by the wars and wants of savage life to a few individuals unable to defend themselves against the neighboring tribes, has transferred its country to the United States, reserving only for its members what is sufficient to maintain them in an agricultural way." The treaty provided further that the annuity accruing to these Indians should thereafter be paid to them at Vincennes, Fort Massac, or Kaskaskia.

By this treaty with the Kaskaskia the United States had for the first time acquired from the Indians title to a definite area of land in what is now Illinois. As there were several hundred white settlers in the southern part, and as other whites wished to make their homes in this section of the public domain, Congress, on March 26, 1804, directed the survey of the area and the establishment of a land office at Kaskaskia for the disposition of the country lying within its boundaries. Provision was made in this act for all persons claiming land within said area by virtue of any grant made by the French government prior to the Treaty of Paris on February 10, 1763, under any local grant made by the British government subsequently to said treaty and prior to the treaty of peace between the United States and Great Britain, September 3, 1783, or by any act or resolution of Congress after that date to deliver to the land office at Kaskaskia his evidence of title for record and proof.[20]

General Harrison was accustomed to call the Indians into conference at "Grouseland," his home near Vincennes, whenever necessary. Here he again summoned representatives of the Delaware and, on August 18, 1804, negotiated another treaty in which they yielded to the United States a large tract of land lying between the Ohio and Wabash rivers, adjoining the Vincennes tract.[21] Permission to live on this land had been secured by the Delaware from the Miami, who were later to deny their right to cede it to the United States; and interminable controversy was to revolve around this troublesome subject for many years. Still at his home, Harrison negotiated with the Piankashaw on August 27, 1804, for the relinquishment of any claims they might have to the lands just ceded by the Delaware in Indiana.[22]

In view of the Louisana Purchase and its effect on the neighboring territory and of recent developments east of the Mississippi, it was considered important to possess at least a color of title to the lands in Illinois bordering that river. For this purpose the Sauk and Foxes appeared as the most convenient agency. These people, who claimed the country along the Mississippi from Portage des Sioux north to the Wisconsin River, had had an interesting and turbulent career and, at the time of the Louisiana Purchase, were particularly identified with the upper part of the Illinois country, which they, with the Kickapoo and the Potawatomi, occupied after driving the Illinois Indians from their old home.

Five members of the Sauk band known as the Missouri River Sauk were induced to come to St. Louis, where, on November 3, 1804, General Harrison persuaded them to enter into a treaty purporting to bind the united tribes of Sauk and Fox Indians.[23] In this treaty the Indians undertook to cede to the United States a vast area, bounded on the west in part by the Mississippi River, on the east and south by the Illinois and Fox rivers, and on the north by the Wisconsin, extending from the southern end of the present Calhoun County, Illinois, north into Wisconsin.[24] A part of this cession lay on the west side of the Mississippi. The area thus ceded was estimated at fourteen million acres, of which six million lay along the Illinois River, south of a line running due west from the south end of Lake Michigan to the Mississippi. That part of the cession lying north of this line, estimated at five million acres, was dealt with in later treaties.

Harrison called the Indians into council at "Grouseland," where he negotiated another treaty[25] with the Delaware by which he undertook to adjust their title to the lands acquired from the Miami. This treaty included representatives of the Miami, Eel River, and Wea, reciting that they "were formerly, and still consider themselves as one nation," and held their lands as joint owners. They ceded to the United States a large area in the southern part of Indiana along the Ohio River, extending from the Wabash east to New Albany. They acknowledged the right of the Delawares to cede their lands according to the terms of the treaty of 1804, which tract, according to Harrison's recital in the treaty "was given by the Piankashaws to the Delawares about thirty-seven years ago." But as to the Miami land, it was quite different; the members of that tribe said that it was never their intention to give the Delawares anything more than a right of occupancy, subject to the pleasure of the grantors. The Delawares accordingly abandoned their claim to the land and released the United States from certain reciprocal obligations.

The Piankashaw were formerly a subtribe of the Miami but later were a separate people. Their ancient village was on the Wabash River at the junction with the Vermilion. In order to round out the public lands in southern Illinois, soon after the establishment of the land office at Kaskaskia, the Piankashaw were induced by Governor Harrison at Vincennes, on December 30, 1805, to convey to the United States an area of more than twenty-six thousand acres contiguous to the Wabash River, being all the land owned by them east of the Mississippi.[26] President Jefferson submitted this treaty to the United States Senate on February 7, 1806, with the remark that it completed the entire consolidation of "our possessions on the north bank of the Ohio."[27] The treaty reserved to this tribe a tract of two square miles and also the privilege of hunting over the country ceded by them. This they enjoyed for a few years until, in 1814, they crossed the Mississippi and settled with the Peoria Indians at Ste Genevieve.

Harrison again assembled his Indian friends at Fort Wayne on September 30, 1809,[28] where the Delawares, Potawatomi, Miami, and Eel River Miami explicitly acknowledged the equal right of the Delawares with themselves to the country watered by the White River and entered into a treaty ceding to the United States two tracts of land—one on the west side of Indiana, adjoining the Vincennes reservation, and one on the east side, adjoining the Ohio line, amounting in all to 2,685,000 acres. A month later, at Vincennes, this cession was concurred in by the Wea.[29]

Continued Indian hostilities in what are now Illinois, Indiana, and Ohio; the example and influence of the Shawnee chief, Tecumseh, and his abortive attempt at a great Indian confederacy, followed by his defeat at the Battle of Tippecanoe on November 7, 1811; the advice and persuasion of Tecumseh's brother, the Prophet; and other events and influences created in the Indians an inflamed state of mind against the Americans, so that when Congress declared war against Great Britain on June 18, 1812, Indians of many tribes north of the Ohio River were found arrayed on the side of the British.[30]

Of the Indian nations that in later years were to become residents of Oklahoma, the Iowa, Kickapoo, Potawatomi, Piankashaw, Osage, Sauk and Foxes, Kansas, Ottawa, Shawnee, Wyandots, Miami, Delawares, Seneca, Wea, Oto, Ponca, and Pawnee, in whole or in part, sided with Great Britain during the War of 1812. Less than two months after the declaration of war, the garrison at Chicago received orders to evacuate that post and retire to Detroit. On August 15, the troops, numbering about fifty men, accompanied by some women and children, marched from Fort Dearborn. They had proceeded but a short distance when they were attacked by a host of savages, mostly Potawatomi, inspired by the war whoops of the ferocious chief Waubunsee. A determined resistance was made for some time, but the number of Indians proved too great for any hope of success, and Captain Heald, the commander, consented to surrender on the promise of protection. The survivors of this little band, however, had no sooner given up their arms than they were brutally massacred. Twenty-six of the regulars and all of the militia were killed, with two women and twelve children.[31] Reprisals by the Americans included the destruction of Kickapoo villages on the Sangamon River, of Kickapoo and Miami villages at the head of Lake Peoria, and of the

French and Indian village of Peoria at the lower end of the lake, whose inhabitants were carried far down the Illinois River.[32]

Negotiations to end the war were entered into at Ghent, Belgium, where the British commissioners arrived August 4, 1814, to meet the American commissioners, who had preceded them. The latter included Albert Gallatin, Henry Clay, and John Quincy Adams. At the first meeting, two days later, the British commissioners submitted the basis of peace discussion, consisting of three principal points. Two of these, the first and third, dealt with the subject of seizure of mariners on board merchant vessels and the revision of the boundary between the United States and Canada. The second was to introduce a subject of great interest and novelty in our Indian relations. This point read as follows: "The Indian allies of Great Britain [are] to be included in the pacification, and a boundary [is] to be settled between the dominions of the Indians and those of the United States. Both parts of this point are considered by the British government as a *sine qua non* to the conclusion of the treaty." The American commissioners were astounded at the proposals. They protested that the Indians were not proper parties and that they had no authority to include them in the treaty discussion.[33]

Nevertheless, the British commissioners persisted in their demands, which, they said, were based on instructions from London, from which there could be no departure. They expressed an obligation not to abandon their Indian allies, and through months of negotiation they reiterated their contention in various forms. In a letter of October 8 they offered as their ultimatum an article intended to cover the controversial point. The American plenipotentiaries finally, to end the deadlock, decided to accept the British terms and incorporated their proposition as article 9 in a draft of a proposed treaty submitted November 10 to the British commissioners. Working from this tentative basis, negotiations continued until December 24, 1814, when the treaty was signed.[34]

President Madison submitted the treaty to the Senate on February 15, 1815, and two days later it was ratified—more than a month after the Battle of New Orleans. The alacrity with which the United States proceeded to carry out its engagements with Great Britain expressed in the treaty is startling. Article 9 reads in part as follows: "The United States of America engage to put an end immediately after the ratification of the present treaty to hostilities with all the tribes or nations of Indians with whom they may be at war at the time of such ratification, and forthwith to restore to such tribes or nations respectively all the possessions, rights and privileges which they may have enjoyed or been entitled to in 1811, previous to such hostilities."

Less than a month after the Treaty of Ghent was ratified, Secretary of War James Monroe, on March 11, notified Governor William Clark of Missouri, Governor Ninian Edwards of Illinois, and Auguste Chouteau of St. Louis that they had been constituted by the President a commission to carry into effect the provisions of article 9 of the treaty by calling into council the Indians concerned and entering into appropriate treaties with them. They were directed to confine their efforts to the one subject insisted upon by the British. The secretary told them that it was incumbent on the United States to execute every article of the treaty in perfect good faith but that the government wished to be particularly exact in the execution of article 9.[35]

The commissioners were instructed to give immediate notice to all tribes with which the United States had been at war on the Mississippi and its waters of the peace concluded with Great Britain and of the stipulations concerning them. They were to invite the tribes to send deputations to meet with them for the purpose of concluding the proposed treaties of peace and friendship.

When the commissioners organized, they decided to hold the peace conference at Portage des Sioux, a little French village on the Missouri side of the Mississippi River, about five miles below the mouth of the Illinois River. Here they established themselves on July 6, 1815.

A military guard was provided for the commissioners, and a great brush arbor was erected, with rude seats of puncheons, for the accommodation of the negotiators. Twenty thousand dollars' worth of goods of all sorts were provided as presents for the thousands of Indians who attended during the summer; and their camps around the council grounds presented a picturesque and animated scene.[36]

Indians in attendance could be identified by their handiwork displayed in scores of canoes tied up at the water's edge or resting on the shore. The Reverend Timothy Flint witnessed this interesting assemblage and wrote of what he saw: "Their squaws and children accompanied them. . . . . I remarked their different modes of constructing their watercraft. Those from the lakes and the high points of the Mississippi had beautiful canoes or rather large skiffs of white birch bark. Those from the lower Mississippi and from the Missouri had pirogues or canoes hollowed out of a large tree. Some tribes covered their tents with bear-skins. Those from far up the Mississippi had beautiful cone-shaped tents, made very neatly with rush matting. Those from the upper regions of the Missouri had tents of tanned buffalo robes, marked on the inside with scarlet lines, and they were of an elliptical form. In some instances, we saw marks of savage progress in refinement and taste, in covering the earth under their tents with rush or skin carpeting." As Reverend Mr. Flint walked about through the habitations of the thousands of Indians present, he noted the young dogs impaled on spits before the fires, tended by squaws and children, and Indians engaged in gambling. "The tribes from the Upper Mississippi and the Lakes, that is, from the vicinity of the British settlements, gambled with our playing cards. They put their rations, their skins, their rifles, their dogs, and sometimes, we were told, their squaws, at stake on the issue of these games. The Missouri Indians gambled with a circular parchment box, having a bottom and shaped like a small drum. From this they cast up a number of small shells or pebbles, waving the palms of their hands horizontally between the falling pebbles and the box, at the same time blowing on the falling pebbles with their mouth."[37]

In compliance with instructions to the commissioners, each of the treaties presented was entitled "A Treaty of Peace and Friendship." They were nearly all uniform in their provisions, covering only points mentioned in article 9 of the Treaty of Ghent. They contained only three articles besides the preamble and attestation. The first treaty was made July 18 with the Potawatomi of the Illinois River. A small band of Piankashaw who were prisoners of war signed up the same day. On the nineteenth, four tribes from high up the Mississippi and Missouri agreed to the terms of as many treaties. The Maha concurred on the twentieth, but others could not be induced to come to terms until the Kickapoo signed on September 2. Through that month the Osage, Sauk and Foxes, and Iowa also signed the treaties of peace and friendship. After the Kansas Indians made a treaty on October 28, no more could be secured until the following May.[38]

In order fully to comply with the obligations assumed in article 9, General William Henry Harrison, General Duncan McArthur, and John Graham, on June 9, 1816, were named a commission to negotiate at Fort Wayne with other tribes in Indiana, Ohio, and Michigan who had been associated with Great Britain in the war. The tribes who thus by treaty signalized their abandonment of fealty to Great Britain and announced their loyalty to the United States were: Wyandots, Delawares, Shawnee, Seneca, Miami, Potawatomi of Illinois River,

Piankashaw, Tetoni, Sioux, Yancton, Maha, Kickapoo, Chippewa, Ottawa, Great and Little Osage, the Sauk of Missouri River, Foxes, Iowa, and Kans. The treaties thus secured with these Indians were submitted by President Monroe on December 18 to the United States Senate for ratification.[39] The securing of treaties with the remaining tribes, necessary for a full compliance with the terms of the Treaty of Ghent, was not completed until the summer of 1818. Representatives of the Sauk of Rock River, various bands of Sioux, Winnebago, Wea and Kickapoo, Ottawa, Chippewa, and Potawatomi living on the Illinois and Milwaukee rivers, and the Menominee, Oto, and Ponca and four branches of the Pawnee tribe—making a total of thirty-four tribes or parts of tribes of American Indians previously fighting with Great Britain against the United States—had agreed to the terms of these treaties and signalized their fealty to the United States. This concluded one of the most remarkable episodes in our history—one in which our domestic Indian policy was dictated by our diplomatic relations with a foreign government.

While the treaty conference at Portage des Sioux was in session, the Sauk Indians of Missouri River entered into an agreement on September 13, 1815,[40] assenting to the cession of November 3, 1804, and this was confirmed by the Sauk of Rock River on May 13, 1816,[41] at the council held at St. Louis by Clark, Chouteau, and Edwards.

The Indians in the region adjacent to the Great Lakes had suffered devastating losses of population from the War of 1812, not so much in battle as from hunger and disease occasioned by the fugitive and irregular life they were driven into by the conflict. Whole villages were depopulated or reduced to a few souls. Henry R. Schoolcraft related, some years later, that he had passed over the ancient sites of towns, populous in 1812, "which are now overgrown with grass and brambles, where not a single soul dwells to repeat the tale of their sufferings."[42] He charged the British traders with responsibility for their condition, for it was they, he said, who persuaded the Indians to take up arms against the United States so as to promote their mercenary schemes for controlling the Indian trade in peltries taken south of the Canadian border.

NOTES

1. 7 *U.S. Stat.* 13.
2. Frederick W. Hodge (ed.), *Handbook of American Indians*, I, 385.
3. 7 *U.S. Stat.* 26. Colonel John Johnston, for many years Indian agent in Ohio, wrote in 1819: "The Shawnese have been established in Ohio about sixty-five years. They came here from west Florida, and the adjacent country. They formerly resided on

Suwaney River, near the sea. Black Hoof, who is eighty-five years of age, was born there and remembers bathing in the salt water when a boy. 'Suwaney' River was doubtless named after the Shawnese, 'Suwaney' being a corruption of the Shawnese" (John Johnston, *Recollections of Sixty Years*, p. 57; Jedidiah Morse, *A Report on Indian Affairs*, Appendix, p. 90).

4. 7 *U.S. Stat.* 16.

5. *Ibid.*, p. 26.

6. *Ibid.*, p. 28.

7. *Ibid.*, p. 49.

8. See Chouteau's "Notes" below.

9. Chouteau's "Notes." Chiefs of the Kaskaskia, Cahokia, and Piankashaw tribes had lately, in 1773 and 1775, executed to a company of Englishmen deeds purporting to convey a large part of what is now Illinois. After the ceded country became part of the United States, the grantees named in the deeds repeatedly, but vainly, endeavored to have these deeds ratified by responsible authority of the government (*American State Papers*, "Public Lands," II, 108, 119). Shortly after Laclede founded St. Louis, February 15, 1764, a band of Peoria Indians under their chief, Little Turkey, received permission to build a village near by, on the site of the present city.

10. The term "Lake Tribes" refers to the Indians living along the southern margins of the Great Lakes.

11. Chouteau's "Notes."

12. *Ibid.*

13. *American State Papers*, "Indian Affairs," I, 701.

14. *American State Papers*, "Public Lands," II, 108, 119.

15. 7 *U.S. Stat.* 74. See Chouteau's "Notes," p. 34. The first legal provision for an exchange of lands with the Indians, and for their removal and settlement beyond the Mississippi, is contained in the fifteenth section of the Act of March 26, 1804, "erecting Louisiana into two territories and providing for the temporary government thereof." This act appropriated $15,000 to enable President Jefferson to effect these objects. The earliest intimation of this policy may be found in a confidential message of the President to both houses of Congress, dated January 18, 1803. The inducements to the passage of the act of 1804 are stated in two reports from the Committee on Public Lands in the Senate of January 9, 1817, and December 1, 1818 (see James D. Richardson, *Messages of the Presidents*, I, 352).

16. 7 *U.S. Stat.* 78.

17. The areas of these cessions are to be seen in a volume entitled *Indian Treaties and Laws and Regulations Relating to Indian Affairs, to Which Is Added an Appendix Containing the Proceedings of the Old Congress, and Other Important State Papers, in Relation to Indian Affairs, Compiled and Published under Orders of the Department of War of the 9th February, and 8th October, 1825* (Washington: Way & Gordon, 1826).

The areas referred to, compiled by the General Land Office on June 23, 1826, are shown in the *Abstract of Indian Treaties*, pp. 492-505. Charts of those areas are to be seen in the volume of *Indian Land Cessions in the United States*, compiled by Charles C. Royce (*Eighteenth Annual Report of the Bureau of American Ethnology, 1896-97*, Part II).

18. *American State Papers*, "Indian Affairs," I, 687.

19. Richardson, *op. cit.*, p. 359.

20. 2 *U.S. Stat.* 277; *American State Papers*, "Public Lands," II, 123 ff.

21. 7 *U.S. Stat.* 81.

22. *Ibid.*, p. 83.

23. *Ibid.*, p. 84.

24. Grant Foreman, *Illinois and Her Indians* ("Papers in Illinois History" [1940]), pp. 93, 94.

25. Of August 21, 1805 (7 *U.S. Stat.* 91).

26. *Ibid.*, p. 100.

27. Foreman, *op. cit.*, p. 76; *American State Papers*, "Indian Affairs," I, 794. A treaty was negotiated November 25, 1808, at Detroit, with the Wyandots, Shawnee, Potawatomi, Chippewa, and Ottawa, whereby they ceded to the United States a right of way for a

road running across Ohio to Connecticut (7 *U.S. Stat.* 112). A delegation of these Indians then, on the invitation of President Jefferson, visited him in Washington. In January, 1809, he made them a friendly talk full of good advice and admonitions for their benefit, assuring them of the white man's friendship. (This talk appears in full in *The Territorial Papers of the United States*, X, 258.)

28. 7 *U.S. Stat.* 113.

29. *Ibid.*, p. 116.

30. Foreman, *op. cit.*, p. 76.

31. *Ibid.* and authorities there cited.

32. *Ibid.*

33. *Ibid.* The United States, however, had already entered upon negotiations with her Indians, but with other ends in view. General William Henry Harrison, Governor Isaac Shelby of Kentucky, and Governor Lewis Cass of Michigan Territory were appointed a commission to negotiate a treaty of peace with these Indians, and on their arrival at Greenville, Ohio, July 3, 1814, they found three thousand Indians of the Wyandot, Seneca, Delaware, Eel River, and Wea tribes awaiting them. Councils were held daily, when speeches were made by the commissioners and by the chiefs and principal men of the Wyandots, Seneca, Delawares, Shawnee, Miami, Eel River, Wea, Potawatomi, Ottawa, and Kickapoo. The council was held on the identical spot where the famous treaty of 1795 between General Wayne and the northwestern Indians was held. It resulted in a treaty of peace and friendship between Commissioners Harrison and Cass for the United States and representatives of the Wyandots, Delawares, Shawnee, Seneca, and Miami, dated July 22, 1814 (*American State Papers*, "Indian Affairs," I, 836). This treaty on July 23 was forwarded by the commissioners to the Secretary of War, ratified by the Senate on December 13, 1814, and proclaimed December 21, three days before the signing of the Treaty of Ghent (7 *U.S. Stat.* 118).

34. *American State Papers*, "Foreign Affairs," III, 695–748.

35. Foreman, *op. cit.*

36. *Ibid.*

37. Timothy Flint, *Recollections of the Last Ten Years*, p. 142.

38. Foreman, *op. cit.*; *American State Papers*, "Indian Affairs," II, 1–25; 7 *U.S. Stat.* 123 ff.

39. Foreman, *op. cit.*

40. 7 *U.S. Stat.* 134.

41. *Ibid.*, p. 141.

42. *Report of the Commissioner of Indian Affairs, 1838* (Senate Executive Doc. 2 [25th Cong., 3d sess.]), p. 458.

CHAPTER II

MONROE'S ADMINISTRATION

DURING the administration of President Monroe (1817–25) a policy was inaugurated looking to increased westward emigration of Indians from east of the Mississippi. This new policy in a measure had its genesis in conditions and preceding events, reference to which will be necessary. Early in Monroe's administration an important council was convened at Fort Meigs at the foot of the Rapids of the Miami in the autumn of 1817. Here Commissioners Lewis Cass and Duncan McArthur met a large number of Chippewa,

Potawatomi, Wyandot, Delaware, Shawnee, Seneca, and Ottawa Indians.

After negotiations, prolonged for seven weeks by the fact that fourteen interpreters were required repetitiously, tediously, and laboriously to translate the proceedings into many tongues so that all could understand, on September 29 a long and detailed treaty was executed by nearly a hundred "sachems, chiefs and warriors" of the tribes represented.[1] By this agreement the Wyandots ceded to the United States more than four and a half million acres in Ohio, Indiana, and Michigan, including most of the northwest quarter of the state of Ohio south of the Miami (Maumee) River; the Potawatomi, Ottawa, and Chippewa relinquished the major part of the present Williams and Defiance counties lying north of that river. The Indians were given small restricted areas and individual allotments.

President Monroe, in his first annual message to Congress, December 2, 1817, felicitated that body that, "with moderate reservations," the whole of the state of Ohio and parts of Indiana and Michigan had been ceded by the Indians to the United States.[2] Under the auspices of the favor with which these activities were regarded by the administration and the pressure of white sentiment, movements were promoted in 1818 to secure further cessions of lands from the Indians in these states.

Representatives of all the tribes of these areas were induced to assemble at St. Mary's near Wapakoneta in the autumn of 1818. Here the commissioners negotiated treaties of cession with the Wyandots, Seneca, Shawnee, and Ottawa on September 17, 1818;[3] with the Wyandots on September 20;[4] with the Potawatomi on October 2;[5] with the Wea on October 2;[6] with the Delawares on October 3;[7] and with the Miami on October 6. These treaties all dealt with the lands of the Indians. In the case of the lands in Ohio, terms were employed for revised definitions of the small reservations remaining to the Indians; but the Wyandots relinquished their two small reservations in Michigan, receiving in lieu thereof others still smaller. The Potawatomi granted lands in Indiana lying on the Wabash River, and the Wea and Miami ceded other lands in Indiana. Reservations were made to the Miami tribe on the Wabash River, with special tracts within the reservation assigned to the chief, Jean Baptiste Richardville, and to a large number of other prominent members of the tribe.[8] Among the Wea a reservation was made to Christmas Dagnet. Emigration of the

Indians represented at St. Mary's was not mentioned in the treaties, though it was the ultimate object of the negotiations.

The winter of 1814 and the spring of 1815 found these Indians reduced in numbers and in spirit and beggared in means of subsistence. Corrupted by the use of whiskey, they were sadly in debt to the traders and welcomed the possibility of selling their land in order to cancel their obligations and buy food and clothing for their families.[9]

Beginning with the general treaty of 1818 and during the succeeding twenty years, the Indians of that region alienated all their possessions in Ohio, Indiana, and Illinois with trifling reservations. By the proceeds of these sales the failure of the chase was in a measure compensated, their families clothed and fed, and to some extent their debts paid.

To understand current and future activities and the development of Monroe's Indian policy, it is necessary to refer briefly to the earlier and more or less voluntary westward emigration of the Indians.

The Kickapoo, Shawnee, and Delaware tribes were well represented in the West at an early date by roving bands who had left their eastern homes and made their way to the future Indian Territory, quite apart from any organized emigration. These Indians were found along the Red and Canadian rivers, where they had more or less permanent settlements, whence they carried on trading and hunting expeditions among the wild tribes.

Soon after the Revolution there was a considerable migration of the Shawnee tribe on hunting expeditions. A large body of them located on a tract of land twenty-five miles square near Cape Girardeau, Missouri, under a grant made by the Spanish governor, Baron Carondelet, on January 4, 1793, duly recorded in the office of the recorder of titles at St. Louis. Bounded on the east by the Mississippi River, it included most of the present Cape Girardeau and Perry counties. A band of Delaware Indians who later joined the Shawnee on the Spanish grant remained until about 1815, when some of them moved farther southwest.

Bands of Delawares and Shawnee in the West became closely associated with the Cherokee living in Arkansas at an early date; and in the year 1795 they applied to the Quapaw for leave to hunt in their country, which then comprised a vast domain lying north of the Arkansas River. When this request was refused, the governor of Orleans directed the commandant of Arkansas Post to permit the Cherokee to settle and to hunt on the St. Francis River and the Delawares on the White River.[10]

After the defeat of the British in the War of 1812, some of their Shawnee allies came to the future Oklahoma to live in seclusion, as they thought, far from the Americans whom they had opposed, in a country made known to them through the expeditions of their hunters. Bands of these Indians and their Delaware allies who had separated from their tribe frequented the Red River country on their hunting expeditions. Attracted by its many advantages, some of them located in Texas near Nacogdoches with the Caddo and Cherokee already residing there on land claimed by the latter, where they engaged in agricultural pursuits and were living a life of peace and comparative comfort.

A delegation of Cherokee Indians from Arkansas in 1818 requested the Secretary of War to permit the Delawares and Shawnee of the Cape Girardeau settlement to remove and join the Cherokee on the Arkansas River for their better protection against the Osage.[11] Secretary Calhoun thereupon, on May 8, 1818, directed Superintendent of Indian Affairs General William Clark, at St. Louis, to expedite the change if the Indians desired to go.[12] Some of them did so remove, and in 1820 Cherokee, Delawares, and Shawnee were found in the present Pope County, Arkansas.

Another tribe of Indians whose early removal west of the Mississippi was noticed by the authorities was the Piankashaw. General Clark wrote on March 27, 1819, to the Secretary of War: "During the late war with England a tribe of Indians (the only remains of the Piankashaw Nation of 180 persons) moved from their country on the Waubashaw River, to the west of the Mississippi and settled on the Missouri where they remained at peace until compelled by hostile tribes of the Mississippi to join them in War against the Frontiers of this territory. Their establishment was destroyed & this Tribe brought to this place by a detachment of Militia & the Indians under the orders of the General Commanding this department at that time. I sent those retched people to the edge of the Mississippi Swamp west of the mouth of the Ohio and near the St. Francis River where they have remained since, living on scanty subsistence obtained principally from Game out of the Swamps and an annuity of about $800 in merchandise. Previously to their Capture they cultivated the earth and obtained a subsistence principally from that source. The tribe expressed some anxiety to apply themselves to labor and industrious pursuits, having requested of me with much solicitude to assist them with the articles mentioned in the enclosed Invoice, which I beg leave to refer to you."[13]

Congress, on May 6, 1812, had directed that two million acres of land in Illinois be surveyed in townships, sections, and quarter-sections and made available for the location of bounty claims by non-commissioned officers and privates, under legislation enacted for raising troops during the War of 1812. The land designated for this purpose, and which became known as "military lands," was included in the cession made by the Sauk and Foxes in 1804, lying east of the Mississippi and north and west of the Illinois River as high as the Wisconsin River. Because of the continued hostilities of these Indians, the survey was not attempted at once; and, when it was got under way in 1815, there was much objection by the Potawatomi of the Illinois River, who said that they had not previously heard of the action of the Sauk. They claimed it as their home, their hunting ground, and their land, in spite of the deal with the Sauk and Foxes, whose right to it they denied. To adjust this situation, the Secretary of War, on May 7, 1816, instructed Commissioners William Clark, Ninian Edwards, and Auguste Chouteau to negotiate for a release of their claims and, in so doing, to extend the cession of the Potawatomi as far east and north as the shores of Lake Michigan if possible.[14]

The "Prairie Pottawatomi," or Illinois band of that tribe, were living on the Illinois River with some of their kinsmen, the Ottawa and Chippewa, with whom, for mutual protection, they had long been united in a confederacy. They claimed the land from the Indiana line west to Rock River, south as far as Peoria, and north into Wisconsin, though the northern boundary was not well defined. But their friendly relations with the Chippewa made that a matter of small importance.[15]

Authority to treat with the Indians of "The Illinois [Country]" and other Indians was intrusted to Governor William Clark, Governor Ninian Edwards, and Auguste Chouteau in a commission issued to them by the Secretary of War on March 11, 1815.[16] Their services resulted in the famous previously mentioned "Treaties with Twenty-one Tribes" required by article 9 of the recent Treaty of Ghent.[17] In the negotiations at Portage des Sioux and St. Louis[18] it developed that there was much disagreement and controversy among some of the tribes concerning the ownership of lands in "The Illinois." Auguste Chouteau was intimately acquainted with the aborigines of the region, and, when the question arose as to the extent of the holdings of the Illinois Indians, there was no one better qualified than he to explore the history and holdings of these people and to make his knowledge a matter of record for the benefit of the government in its subsequent effort to negotiate treaties of cession with the lawful Indian owners of the respective areas in question. This information he incorporated in a manuscript entitled "Notes," later deposited in the Office of Indian Affairs.[19] This document of thirteen large pages is probably the most important contribution of its time touching the history and holdings of many tribes of Indians.

The powers of the commissioners were enlarged the next June 11 so as to embrace new subjects. In an effort to adjust the discontent of these Indians and secure a relinquishment from them of the lands conveyed by the Sauk and Foxes and of additional lands, representatives of the confederated Potawatomi band were induced to attend a council in St. Louis, where, on August 24, 1816, they entered into a treaty[20] with Clark, Edwards, and Chouteau by which they relinquished to the United States that part of the land ceded by the Sauk and Foxes lying south of a line running from the southern extremity of Lake Michigan due west to the Mississippi River near Rock Island. In return, they were guaranteed title to land lying north of this line amounting to about five million acres.[21] By this treaty the Indians conveyed also to the United States another tract, including the present southern half of Cook County, Illinois, extending south and west to the Illinois River.[22]

During these negotiations another treaty was made September 25, 1818, at Edwardsville, Illinois, by Ninian Edwards and Auguste Chouteau with the Peoria, Kaskaskia, Michigamea, Cahokia, and Tamaroa tribes,[23] looking to their removal west of the Mississippi, with the annuity due the Peoria to be thereafter delivered at their village near Ste Genevieve, Missouri, where some of the Wea and Peoria had resided for many years. In the treaty of October 3, 1818, the Delawares ceded all claim to lands in Indiana;[24] and in return the United States agreed to provide a home for them on the west side of the Mississippi and to furnish them horses and boats for transport, together with sufficient provisions to sustain them on the way, though at the time no place was designated and no authority delegated to direct their migration.

In the treaty of September 25, 1818, with the Peoria Indians, the United States agreed to confirm their title to 640 acres of land in Missouri on Blackwater River near Ste Genevieve, which, it was said, they had had in possession since before the Revolutionary War, and an annuity of three hundred dollars for twelve years. By another treaty the Miami, on October 6, 1818, ceded to the United States a large area lying in the center of Indiana, extending almost across the state from east to west, and nearly as far north and south, amounting to more than 6,700,000 acres, in addition to 297,000 acres in Ohio.[25]

The Kickapoo, a branch of the Algonquian group, were first known in southern Wisconsin. On the destruction of the Illinois Confederacy about 1765 by the combined forces of the tribes north of them, the conquered country was partitioned among the victors, the Sauk and Foxes moving down to Rock River; while the Kickapoo went farther south, fixing their headquarters for a time at Peoria. They appear gradually to have extended their range, a portion centering about Sangamon River, while another part pressed toward the east, establishing themselves on the waters of the Wabash despite the opposition of the Miami and Piankashaw.[26] The western contingent became known as the "Prairie band," while the others were denominated the "Vermilion band" from their residence on the river of that name. The Secretary of War, in 1816, reported four hundred warriors, or a total of sixteen hundred individual Indians, of the Kickapoo tribe living at the headwaters of the Kaskaskia. Throughout years of negotiation they jealously maintained their claim to the lands on the Vermilion River.[27]

At the beginning of the century the Kickapoo then living in the Wabash country in Illinois and Indiana was a large and powerful tribe but divided into two bands. One of these bands went southwest into the Indian Territory in those early days,[28] and it will be discussed in its proper chronology. The other band remained in the "Wabash country." About 1820 a band of Potawatomi came among the Kickapoo to see and worship their celebrated prophet, Kenekuk, and, under his influence, to live and intermarry with them.

At Edwardsville, Illinois, on July 30, 1819, Auguste Chouteau and Benjamin Stephenson, commissioners for the United States, made a treaty with the Kickapoo[29] by which the latter conveyed their lands between the Illinois and Wabash rivers, amounting to more than thirteen million acres. In return the United States gave them a tract in southwestern Missouri on the Osage River near the Delaware reservation, including substantial parts of the present St. Clair, Cedar, Polk, Dade, and Greene counties.[30] The United States agreed to pay an annuity of two thousand dollars for fifteen years and to furnish them two boats well manned to transport their property from any point they should designate on the Illinois River.

A month later the Kickapoo of the Vermilion in Illinois, at Fort Harrison, made a treaty ceding to the United States all the land claimed by them on the Wabash and its tributaries.[31] Article 4 recited that, "as the said tribe are now about leaving their settlements on the Wabash," the location for the payment of future annuities would have to be determined later. Another treaty was made with them on September 5, 1820, at Vincennes,[32] by which, "as said tribe [were] about leaving their settlements on the Wabash," Commissioner Benjamin Parke gave them two thousand dollars in full of their annuity for 1821 to defray their expenses.

Thus, in this casual manner Indian removal at that time was contemplated. The Indians were supposed to make their journey the best way they could. The results were what could be expected.

After the execution with the Kickapoo of the treaty of July 30, 1819, the commissioners, Chouteau and Stephenson, sent the secretary of the commission, Paschal Cerré, to attempt the removal of the Kickapoo to the country on the Osage River designated in the treaty as their new home. After an absence of three months Cerré returned to St. Louis and made a report. The country ceded by the Kickapoo included a great part of the best land in central Illinois, extending from the Illinois River east and across the Wabash into Indiana. Their principal towns were on the Sangamon River and Peoria Lake.

When Cerré arrived at their main village on the Illinois River, he learned that the majority of the Kickapoo, in small parties, had left and were scattered "through the woods," determined not to go to the Osage River. They were driven to this course by threats of the Potawatomi of personal violence and death, and loss of their horses, if they acquiesced in the wishes of the whites. Part of the tribe, however, under their war chief, Waw-pee-ko-ny-a ("Blue Eyes"), was ready and anxious to get started. Cerré guided them across the Illinois, Mississippi, and Missouri rivers and through the white settlements, where the Indians feared to go because of a report heard originating with the Potawatomi that the government agents planned to lure them that far, where the white settlers would kill them. The influence of the Potawatomi on the prejudice and fears of the Kickapoo made Cerré's undertaking a difficult one. They traveled slowly "and apparently with the greatest repugnance (for they threatened to winter at every navigable stream we came to)." He succeeded in getting them as far as "the grande Batture, nine miles up the Osage River," where they stopped, to remain through the hunting season; and they declined to go to their assigned reservation before the next spring. They then asked Cerré to return to St. Louis and request Chouteau to send them subsistence for the ensuing spring and summer at their new home. On the journey Cerré's familiarity with the use of firearms had enabled them to subsist on game.[33]

During the following year (1820), Chouteau proceeded to the Kickapoo country to attempt the removal of the remainder of the tribe, who had left their villages ostensibly to proceed to the Osage River; but, reluctant to leave their old home, they soon changed their minds and bent their course toward the Rock River where the "Sakias" (Sauk Indians) told them they might remain through the winter and make a corn crop the next year. When Chouteau found them, they complained of the treaty inasmuch as it implied that they had sold their land in Illinois; whereas, from fear of the Potawatomi, and some imagined security in a change of verbiage, they desired the treaty to say that they had merely *exchanged* it for land on the Osage River. Chouteau then called Stephenson into another conference at St. Louis, with a delegation of the Indians headed by their chief Pemoatain, where a purported amendment to the treaty was agreed upon that contained the language desired by the Indians, who were in deadly fear of the Potawatomi and Sauk. They said that they were yet detained in Illinois by the fact that many of their people were "scattered in the eastern and western part of the woods" of Illinois. Loath to leave their old home, they had many excuses for not going; one was the necessity of a treaty with the Osage before settling near them. "We are anxious to entertain with them a friendly intercourse," they said, though "not by fear of them; you well know that the Kickapoos are the bravest among the brave, and you will surely recollect our wars with the Cherokees, but we sincerely wish a solid peace with our Indian neighbors, because our great father of America wishes sincerely the peace among his red children."[34]

While the Indians were in St. Louis they begged for the annuities promised in their treaty of the preceding year, but which Chouteau was unauthorized to give them in the absence of Indian Superintendent William Clark. Soon after Pemoatain and his band left St. Louis to rejoin their people on the Illinois River, Blue Eyes and a hundred and thirty of his warriors came from the Osage River to St. Louis to ratify the amendment to their treaty and solicit promised annuities now long past due.

In the summer of 1821 Indian Agent Graham at St. Louis was preparing to make the desired treaty between the Kickapoo and Osage, who were coming to St. Louis to meet ninety lodges of Kickapoo still living in Illinois. The latter were having trouble with whites, who were introducing whiskey among them. In 1823 many of the Kickapoo of Illinois still refused to leave their homes, which they denied they had sold. Clark thought that their attitude was influenced by the British of Canada, who continued to send them "presents." In February, 1824, he sent a Kickapoo chief to prepare the Illinois band for removal to the Osage River.

Pierre Menard at Kaskaskia, Illinois, was subagent for the Illinois Indians, the Delawares, Shawnee, and others who came within his jurisdiction. Indians of Illinois, Indiana, and Ohio who prepared to emigrate directed their course toward Kaskaskia, where Menard was to issue rations to them, provide for their crossing of the "Great River," and perform other services that came within his province.[35] Menard had been issuing rations to the Peoria and Piankashaw Indians near Ste Genevieve until they moved; and, in 1819, by orders of the Secretary of War, he conducted them to the new location of the towns of the two tribes 150 miles west of Ste Genevieve.[36]

In the summer of 1820, Indiana Delawares emigrating from Whitewater River in the southeastern corner of that state and a band of Shawnee began arriving at Kaskaskia and calling on Menard for assistance. Thus his accounts show payment for ferriage across the Kaskaskia and Mississippi rivers for one party of 70 Indian families and their 75 horses, and another of 41 families and 56 horses. In November, 1820, he paid for ferrying 1,346 Delawares and their 1,499 horses across the Mississippi.[37]

Purchases were made for these emigrants of 17,600 pounds of flour, 22,226 pounds of beef, 462 bushels of corn, 700 bushels of salt, 672 pounds of powder, 288 pounds of lead, 368 pounds of tobacco, 1,700 gun flints, and many other necessities. Disbursements were made for repairing their rifles and for the pursuit of white horse thieves who had stolen thirteen horses from the Delawares.[38]

The Delawares had no definite plans, though they intended tentatively to continue to some point on the Arkansas River where the hunting was good and remain until the government should indicate the reservation on which it was proposed to locate them, which was made in southwestern Missouri on the beautiful James Fork and White Rivers, adjoining the lands later given the Kickapoo and embracing the present counties of Barry, Stone, and parts of Taney, Christian, Lawrence, and Greene.[39] While camped about Kaskaskia in the autumn of 1820 these Indians visited the village frequently in connection with their calls on Agent Menard. On one occasion curiosity led some of them into the shop of a gunsmith who had taken from the forge a rifle barrel which, unknown to the smith, contained a charge of powder and ball. At the instant an Indian was going out the door the charge in the barrel exploded, and the ball entered his back. The Indian soon died, and, as he was prominent in the Delaware tribe, his death created some excitement until the whites convinced the chief that the tragedy was an accident. Officers of a detachment of troops stationed at Kaskaskia accompanied the burial of the Indian with honors of war; at this mark of distinction the red men expressed their thanks and entire reconciliation to the accident.[40]

The Delawares were detained here and along their route by thieving whites who stole their most cherished possession—their horses—at every opportunity. In addition to the Indians' own horses, the government had given them some good animals with which to begin their journey. While organizing their departure from the Whitewater River in June, 1820, the whites stole a number of the best horses the Indians had obtained from the government; others were taken from them along their route; and still more were stolen while they were camped in the Mississippi bottom near Kaskaskia. Detachments of the Indians were detained for days and weeks in vain search for the stolen property. These outrages entailed much hardship and inconvenience on the Indians and on the government officials, who were later required to assemble evidence in connection with efforts to make restitution to the unfortunate emigrants.[41]

In the summer and autumn of 1820, payments were made for emigrating Kickapoo who were removing to Castor Hill under the leadership of Peter Cadue, Kickapoo interpreter.[42] Flour was furnished to 186 emigrants, and disbursements were made for repairs to rifles; for thirty sights, one side plate, bushing, rifling, breaching, repairing and stocking barrels, repairing locks, splicing stocks, bullet molds, steeling fifteen axes, repairing brass kettles, one bell, four beaver spears, plows, hoes, felling axes, mattocks, iron wedges, trace chains; and for many other items needed by the Kickapoo. An interpreter was sent in March to the Osage villages to notify them that the Kickapoo were coming and were about to become their neighbors. He was paid sixty dollars for his long ride and service.[43]

Since there was much sickness among the Indians, progress was slow, and the winter of 1820 found the Delawares in camps on the Current River in the present Carter and Shannon counties, Missouri. Here they spent several miserable and unhappy months. In the spring they planted about a hundred acres of corn, which looked promising until an early frost killed it, leaving them without hope for a crop. They had no energy to resume their march and remained here another winter, while they were furnished food by Menard from his agency at Kaskaskia. Their venerable chief, Anderson, was ill but extremely anxious to get on to their new home, as he wished his people to be settled before he should die.

The interpreter, Wilson, was sent back to Indiana in June, 1821, to start the remainder of the Delawares on White River so as to reach the Current before winter. However, many of them became sick and remained a long time in camp, naked and starving, on the Embarrass River in eastern Illinois near Vincennes and did not reach the Mississippi until wintertime.

Indian Agent Richard Graham was directed in 1821 to locate emigrating Shawnee, Delawares, Kickapoo, Miami, Piankashaw, and Wea in Missouri as far west as possible, next to the Osage. Unfortunately, the land assigned to the Delawares contained a valuable lead mine coveted by white people, who, in 1822, were moving in from Boone's Lick County and operating it under an old Spanish grant. The whites upon the land menaced and annoyed the Indians. Menard said that their neighbors, the Kickapoo, bore with fortitude their afflictions, for fever had carried off three of their principal chiefs and had so reduced the survivors that they had become objects of pity and charity.[44]

Graham endeavored to secure the attendance of the Indians at a peace conference with the Osage, who were resentful at the intrusion of the Delawares and other immigrant Indians in their country.[45] The theft of nearly all their horses had seriously incapacitated the Delawares in securing game to feed their families. In February, 1824, the head chief, William Anderson, Black Beaver, Natcoming, and other Delawares addressed a pathetic letter to General Clark:

"Last summer a number of our people died just for want of something to live on. . . . . We have got in a country where we do not find all as stated to us when we was asked to swap lands with you and we do not get as much as was promised us at the treaty of St. Mary's

[Ohio] neither. . . . . Father—we did not think That big man[46] would tell us things that was not true. We have found a poor stony country and the worst of all no game to be found on it to live on. Last summer our corn looked very well until a heavy rain came on for 3 or 4 days and raised the waters so high that we could just see the tops of our corn in some of the fields, and it destroyed the greatest part of our corn, punkins and beans and a great many more of my people coming on and we had to divide our little stock with them. Last summer there was a few deere here and we had a few hogs but we was obliged to kill all of them and some that was not our own but this summer there are no game nor no hogs and my old people and children must suffer. Father—you know it is hard to be hungry, if you do not know it we poor Indians know it. Father—if we go a great way off we may find some deere but if we do that we cannot make any corn and we must still suffer. Father—we are obliged to call on you once more for assistance in the name of God. . . . . Father—we expect a great many more of our people here this spring to make corn . . . . we wish to gether all of my people onst more to Gether coss I know I cant live always; Father— if you will give us any help you will please let us know as soon as possible by writing to our friend Pierre Menard, if you do not we cannot make much corn this summer."[47]

The Delaware, Shawnee, Kickapoo, and Piankashaw immigrants were in constant trouble with their Osage neighbors to the west. As they were rapidly depleting the game in Missouri, the Indian hunters were obliged to make long excursions far to the southwest across the present Oklahoma.[48] The Osage, former occupants of the country, claimed the exclusive right to hunt over it and bitterly resented the newcomers, who, for self-defense, traveled in large bodies as far as the Red River. Collisions were frequent and bloody. In one of these encounters, in 1824, on Upper Red River, a son of the venerable Delaware chief, William Anderson, was killed. This and numerous other killings called for reprisal, and the immigrant Indians planned large-scale operations against the Osage.[49]

The Cherokee living in Arkansas were eager to participate, and messengers were sent to the Sauk and Foxes to secure recruits. The movement assumed such proportions that P. L. Chouteau, Osage agent, Richard Graham, Delaware agent, and General Arbuckle at Fort Gibson were exerting every effort to assemble the warring factions in peace councils and to put an end to the excitement and unrest in the country in which the government was trying to locate the immigrants from the East. Graham wrote to General Clark, on May 29, 1826, of his arrival at the Delaware agency on White River, where he found the chiefs all drunk. He talked with Anderson, who finally consented to call a council of the Indians in the neighborhood, which was attended by Delawares, Kickapoo, Piankashaw, Peoria, and Wea. They were determined on revenge against the Osage and positively refused the agent's request for peace, which he tried to convince them was essential in order to encourage emigration of their friends from the East.[50]

Throughout all this turmoil some of the Indians urged the government agents to furnish them a home where they could live a more peaceful life. Accordingly, steps were taken to accommodate them by measures then under way to remove them and other Indians from Missouri to the present Kansas.

NOTES

1. 7 *U.S. Stat.* 160. Colonel John Johnston, agent for the Ohio Indians and the Delawares of Indiana, collected seven thousand whom he conducted to the treaty ground. The proceedings were delayed by the Indians, who insisted on stopping on the way to perform certain religious rites without which they could not engage in such important business as the government planned (John Johnston, *Recollections of Sixty Years,* p. 45).

2. Richardson, *Messages of the Presidents,* II, 16.

3. 7 *U.S. Stat.* 178.

4. *Ibid.,* p. 180.

5. *Ibid.,* p. 185.

6. *Ibid.,* p. 186.

7. *Ibid.,* pp. 188-89.

8. Jean Baptiste Richardville was the English name of a Miami chief whose Indian name was Peshewah ("The Lynx"). He was born on St. Mary's River, Indiana, near the present Fort Wayne, about 1761. After the death of Little Turtle the chieftainship fell to Peshewah. Inheriting noble French blood on his father's side, his abilities were such, it is said, as well adapted him to direct the affairs of the Miami. He spoke French and English fluently as well as his native tongue; and for many years his house on the bank of St. Mary's River, about four miles from Fort Wayne, was known as the abode of hospitality. At the time of his death, April 13, 1841, Peshewah was about eighty years of age and was regarded as the wealthiest Indian in North America, his property, it is said, being valued at more than a million dollars. The town of Russiaville, Indiana, takes its name, in corrupted form, from him (*Handbook,* II, 235).

9. Henry R. Schoolcraft, *Report of the Commissioner of Indian Affairs, 1838,* p. 458.

10. Grant Foreman, *Indians and Pioneers* (2d ed.), p. 189.

11. Charles C. Royce, *The Cherokee Nation of Indians: Fifth Annual Report of the Bureau of American Ethnology,* p. 221.

12. For accounts of the Cherokee living on the Arkansas River at this time see Grant Foreman, *Pioneer Days in the Early Southwest, Indians and Pioneers* (2d ed.), and *Indian Removal: The Emigration of the Five Civilized Tribes.*

13. General William Clark to Secretary of War, March 27, 1819, Records of the War Department, Office of the Secretary of War (National Archives); Foreman, *Indians and Pioneers* (2d ed.).

14. Foreman, *Illinois and Her Indians,* p. 93; *American State Papers,* "Indian Affairs," II, 97.

15. Foreman, *Illinois and Her Indians.*

16. *American State Papers*, "Indian Affairs," II, 6.

17. *Ibid.*, p. 1.

18. Foreman, *Illinois and Her Indians.*

19. This manuscript document is to be seen in the Records of the Department of the Interior, Office of Indian Affairs, "Ancient and Miscellaneous Surveys," Vol. IV: "A. Chouteau's Notes," in the National Archives in Washington. Published with introduction and footnotes by Grant Foreman in "Glimpses of the Past," *Missouri Historical Society Publications*, October-December, 1940.

20. 7 *U.S. Stat.* 146.

21. Which they were permitted to hold only a few years, when they conveyed it all to the United States. The land ceded by the Indians amounted to nine million acres, lying mostly on the west side of the Illinois River and on both sides of the Mississippi.

22. Through the length of which a canal was constructed to connect Lake Michigan with the Illinois River.

23. 7 *U.S. Stat.* 181.

24. *Ibid.*, p. 188.

25. *Ibid.*, p. 189.

26. Chouteau's "Notes."

27. *Ibid.*

28. *Report of the Commissioner of Indian Affairs, 1859.*

29. 7 *U.S. Stat.* 200.

30. Charles C. Royce (comp.), *Indian Land Cessions in the United States.*

31. 7 *U.S. Stat.* 200, 202.

32. *Ibid.*, p. 210.

33. Cerré to Auguste Chouteau and Ben Stephenson, commissioners, December 6, 1819, inclosed with "Report" of Chouteau to Calhoun, February, 1820, Records of the War Department, Office of the Secretary of War (National Archives). In 1828 Pierre Chouteau, as agent of the American Fur Company, secured a license to trade with the Kickapoo on a tributary of the Osage River.

34. Auguste Chouteau to Secretary of War, September 11, 1820, Records of the War Department, Office of the Secretary of War (National Archives).

35. *American State Papers*, "Indian Affairs," II, 287 ff.

36. June 15, 1820, "Frost Papers" (Missouri Historical Society, St. Louis).

37. *American State Papers*, "Indian Affairs," II, 301 ff. Many other disbursements by Menard were recorded here.

38. *Ibid.*

39. See Royce (comp.), *op. cit.*, maps and text. As early as November, 1818, Schoolcraft found on the "Osage Fork of the Merrimack" several villages of Osage and Delaware Indians engaged in hunting (Henry R. Schoolcraft, *Journal of a Tour of the Interior of Missouri and Arkansas in 1818 and 1819*).

40. *Edwardsville* (Ill.) *Spectator*, October 24, 1820, p. 2, col. 2.

41. "Clark Papers" (Kansas Historical Society, Topeka), pp. 2-3, 100.

42. Castor Hill, near Castor (Beaver) Pond, where General Clark negotiated a number of Indian treaties, was near his home within the present limits of northwestern St. Louis, about seven miles west of the St. Louis of that time. On September 21, 1838, Henry R. Schoolcraft noted in his memoirs: "The St. Louis papers are dressed in mourning, on account of the death of Gen. William Clark. Few men have acted a more distinguished part in the Indian history of the country. He was widely known and respected by Indians on the prairies, who sent in their delegations to him with all the pomp and pride of so many eastern Rajahs" (*Thirty Years with the Indian Tribes*, p. 608). Cadue, a native of Detroit, was United States interpreter for the Kickapoo Indians, with whom he lived until his death in 1860 (*Senate Executive Doc. I* [36th Cong., 2d sess.], p. 325). See Kickapoo treaties (7 *U.S. Stat.* 208, 391).

43. *American State Papers*, "Indian Affairs," II, 290. Other items furnished these emigrating Indians were catfish hooks, shirts, blankets, sugar, scissors, sheet-iron kettles, tin cups, snuff boxes, gartering, nails, tomahawks, bed cords, rope, jews'-harps, ivory combs, ridding combs, tin pans, and scores of others.

44. Foreman, *Indians and Pioneers* (2d ed.), p. 36.

45. Graham to Menard, November 12, 1821 (Missouri Historical Society); "Frost Papers," October 23, 1822, *ibid.* Soon after their arrival the Delawares and Shawnee negotiated a treaty of peace with their new neighbors, the Osage (Foreman, *Indians and Pioneers* [2d ed.] p. 187).

46. In the recent treaty of October 3, 1819, at St. Mary's, Ohio, with the Delawares (7 *U.S. Stat.* 188) the United States was represented by Jonathan Jennings, Lewis-Cass, and Benjamin Parks. Which of these was "that big man" who made representations to the Indians and actually negotiated the treaty it is impossible to say (Foreman, *Indians and Pioneers* [2d ed.], p. 197). Delaware Chief William Anderson, or Kithtuwheland, stood high in the annals of early Ohio and in the esteem of his contemporaries. During the War of 1812 he and his people resided at Piqua. He was one of the signers of the treaty at the rapids of the Miami in 1817 and of the treaty the next year at St. Mary's. The Indian agent, John Johnston, wrote of him that "he was a half breed, the son of Mr. Anderson by a Delaware woman, who resided prior to the Revolutionary War, below Harrisburg on the Susquehanna, and gave name to the ferry, long within my remembrance, called 'Anderson's Ferry.' This chief was a very dignified man in character and appearance, upwards of six feet high, well proportioned; a man of great benevolence and goodness; of excellent understanding, but not a public speaker; was greatly beloved by his people. In 1823 he must have been about sixty years old" (Johnston, *op. cit.*, p. 9).

47. Foreman, *Indians and Pioneers* (2d ed.).

48. The Delaware hunters took the precaution to secure a passport from General Matthew Arbuckle at Fort Gibson, dated October 29, 1825, permitting them to hunt between the Arkansas and Red rivers ("Clark Papers" [Kansas Historical Society], Letter Book 2-3, p. 144).

49. Osage Agent P. L. Chouteau vigorously defended his Indians. He said that during the recent year he had "spent with the Osages, no Delaware or Kickapoo scalps have been danced, heard of, or even seen in that nation" (Chouteau to General Clark, June 10, 1826, Office of Indian Affairs [National Archives]). Troops were ordered out by Colonel James B. Many from Fort Jesup to cope with the threatened aggression of Delaware, Shawnee, and Kickapoo reported to be menacing the Caddo agency (*Natchitoches Courier*, August 7, 1826, p. 2, cols. 1 and 2).

50. R. Graham to General Clark, May 29, 1826, Office of Indian Affairs (National Archives); Grant Foreman, *Indians and Pioneers* (2d ed.), p. 231.

CHAPTER III

MONROE'S INDIAN POLICY

PRESIDENT MONROE and Congress viewed the Indians with growing concern and from time to time enacted needed legislation. In 1819 the administration took a forward step when, "for the purpose of providing against the further decline and final extinction of the Indian tribes, adjoining the frontier settlements of the United States, and for introducing among them the habits and arts of civilization," it made the munificent appropriation of ten thousand dollars annually,[1] which was expended principally for sending missionaries to the Osage and to the Cherokee and other immigrant tribes west of the Mississippi River.

Other legislation was enacted relating principally to federal trading establishments, which, however, were abolished in 1822, when it appeared that the influence of the federal arm through these agencies was no longer needed to counteract that of British traders. In 1824 a bureau of Indian affairs in the War Department was organized, headed by Thomas L. McKenney, largely responsible in connection with Indian affairs since April 2, 1816. Under McKenney, Indian administration expanded to comprehend the ambitious plans of Monroe and his secretary of war, John C. Calhoun.

Because of the continued occupation of their country by white people, many of the Ohio Indians were seriously considering leaving their old homes and removing west of the Mississippi to join their tribesmen—the Shawnee, Delawares, and the Cherokee—who had settled in that region. The latter tribes, frequently involved in hostilities with the neighboring Osage, had a conception of an alliance with the Indians from the East that would make it possible to drive the Osage out of the country. For several years the eastern and western tribes had been carrying on a correspondence by means of wampum on the subject of the removal of the eastern tribes to the west of the Mississippi.

Captain Lewis (John Lewis or Quitewepea) was an influential member of the Shawnee tribe and one of the signers of the treaty of September 29, 1817, at Fort Meigs, by which the Shawnee gave up most of their land in Ohio. In that treaty, by the name of "Colonel" Lewis, he was given a large tract of land. It was perhaps by reason of this that he fell into disrepute with his people, as a result of which he removed west of the Mississippi to live with members of the tribe who had preceded him and with whom he discussed plans for inducing the Indians remaining in Ohio to remove west and join them.

A council was held in 1823 in the Cherokee settlements in Arkansas by representatives of the immigrant Indians—the Cherokee, Delawares, Shawnee, Wea, Kickapoo, Piankashaw, and Peoria tribes. The Cherokee chief, Takatoka, and Captain Lewis dominated the council, which decided to extend to their red brethern in the East a formal invitation to remove west of the Mississippi and to unite with them in the proposed confederacy.[2] Lewis was deputized to carry the white wampum to his tribe in Ohio and, with it, to deliver the invitation of the western council and to explain the benefits to be derived from such a union and the attractions of the western country. He carried also a request that the eastern Indians arrange a council at the Wapakoneta council ground where deputations from the western Indians could meet with representatives of the Shawnee, Wyandots, Ottawa, Miami, and Tuscarora, explain to them the purpose and benefits of the proposed confederacy, and extend to them a formal invitation to join it. On his journey to Ohio, Captain Lewis stopped at St. Louis, where he visited General William Clark, Indian superintendent, and explained the purpose of his mission.

General Clark, impressed with the importance of the project, immediately communicated the information to the Secretary of War. The reasons which had led to the call for this great council, as explained to General Clark by the Indians, were, "first, the Indian settlements in Indiana, Ohio and New York had become surrounded and hemmed in by a dense white population, leaving no lands to hunt on, and affording too great a facility for the introduction of ardent spirits, so destructive to the Indians; and secondly, to give the Indians forming the council a settlement by which they might enact and enforce their own laws and regulations to promote an agricultural life, which they were extremely anxious to exchange for that of hunters which was become a precarious dependence; and thirdly, to receive among them teachers, and husbandmen to prepare themselves in every way to enjoy the same blessings which they see industry and agriculture extended to the white man, and endeavor to enjoy those blessings themselves and extend them to other nations under their influence."[3]

The plans of the Indians so nearly coincided with the wishes of Monroe's administration and of the white settlers in Ohio that every encouragement was given them. Major Graham, Indian agent, was directed by General Clark to accompany Lewis and his delegation to Ohio, where he would unite with them in explaining to the Shawnee the purpose of the mission and its indorsement by the government.

A strong advocate of the movement was Takatoka, the Cherokee war chief, who had visited a number of southwestern tribes in a successful effort to win their approval and co-operation. His renown as an Indian warrior and statesman had extended far and wide, and the Ohio Indians were greatly interested and impressed by Lewis' information that Takatoka would accompany the visiting delegation to Wapakoneta.

Takatoka endeavored to make the journey during 1823, but he was delayed by difficulties between his tribe and the Osage. In the following spring, as the Cherokee had not appeared in Ohio according to their agreement, the Seneca and Shawnee sent messengers to St. Louis to ascertain whether they had been deceived by the promises of Captain Lewis. Trouble with the Osage again delayed departure until October, 1824, when a formal commission in writing was issued to Takatoka, the "Beloved Man," in the name of the Cherokee Nation, to assist in the council, because, they said, the Cherokee Nation "felt a deep solicitude for the success of the negotiations as being intimately connected with the happiness and prosperity of numerous Indian tribes." The commission authorized Takatoka to meet with the delegations of Shawnee, Delawares, Kickapoo, Peoria, Piankashaw, and Miami living east of the Mississippi River and to accompany them to Washington "for the purpose of aiding .... them in negotiating .... for an exchange of lands" owned by them east of the Mississippi for lands on the west side of that river. The commission was authorized in council and signed by Chief John Jolly (Ahuludegi) and eleven others. It directed that Spring Frog and five others accompany Takatoka, besides John Drew, who was to act as his interpreter.[4]

The Cherokee deputation left in October, 1824, for Kaskaskia, to meet representatives of the Ohio tribes there anxiously awaiting them; but upon arrival at this place the venerable "beloved man," Takatoka, fell sick and died.[5] However, so insistent was he on the success of his undertaking that on his deathbed he urged his followers to continue. They accordingly proceeded to St. Louis and reported to General Clark, who authorized Indian Agent Pierre Menard to accompany them with Captain Lewis and a Sandusky chief to Washington to lay their plans before President Monroe. The delegation, numbering seventeen persons mounted on horseback, proceeded to the council at Wapakoneta and from there on to Washington, where they arrived February 19, 1825.[6]

While the Cherokee and Shawnee delegation was on the way to Washington, the President, on January 27, 1825, submitted to the United States Senate a special message[7] in which he announced a new policy for dealing with the Indians. He proposed removal of all Indian tribes from the lands they then occupied within the limits of several states and territories to the country lying west and north thereof.

With a view to this important object, he recommended that Congress adopt "by solemn declaration certain fundamental principals" for the protection of the Indians thus to be removed and provide for the appointment of commissioners to visit the several tribes of Indians to explain to them the object of the government and to make with them suitable arrangements for their removal.[8]

The President's recommendation was supported by a report submitted to him on January 24 by Secretary of War Calhoun, with statistics and information concerning the Indians in contemplation of the new policy. Calhoun's letter, probably inspired by Senator Benton of Missouri, contained the suggestion that, in order to find room for the Indians proposed to be emigrated, it was desirable to secure cessions of their lands from the Osage and Kansas and on the land thus acquired to allot a portion to each of the eastern tribes and to commence the work of removal. The first to be emigrated, thought Calhoun, should be the Cherokee, Piankashaw, Wea, Shawnee, Kickapoo, and Delawares, then occupying different tracts of country in the northwestern part of Arkansas Territory and southwestern Missouri. The kindred tribes of Ohio and Indiana, including the Wyandots, the Seneca, the Miami, and the Eel River Indians in those states and the Kaskaskia in Illinois, would be quite willing, he thought, to join those of southwestern Missouri as soon as they were established on their location west of that state.[9]

After remaining in the capital a month and finding their efforts indorsed by the president, the Indian deputation departed on March 21 and returned to Wapakoneta, Ohio, where a council was begun on May 11. Governor Lewis Cass, representing the War Department, was present, but he did not arrive in time to prevent much adverse influence by designing white men upon the Indians present, who made the most of Captain Lewis' unpopularity with his tribe; and, in spite of the foundation that had been laid to induce their removal west, few of the Indians present agreed to go.

The delegates then returned to St. Louis, where another council was held with General Clark on November 10. A Cherokee chief spoke and showed General Clark the wampum that was sent to them at the meeting at Wapakoneta. As he displayed the wampum, he said: "This is from the Mingoes, this the Wyandotte, this the Delewares, this the Senecas, this the Oneidas, this the Ontarios, and this from the women begging us to pursue in our undertaking and not to give it up. This large wampum of white is a strand from each of the tribes mentioned to make the road clear. . . . ."

Captain Lewis of the Shawnee spoke and said: "I shall move over the Mississippi for my people now with me will not return—those who are not on their way will soon commence their journey..... The Prophet was invited to attend the Great Council, supposing he had learned some sense by this time, and have a wish with the other Indians to live altogether..... We have a large party of Shawnees and Senecas with us; We will make our fires for the present and enter the swamps near the Mississippi and try to sustain ourselves until we hear from you. I hope you will take pity on us and afford us some aid, in corn, lead and powder this winter."[10]

In the meantime, the prospect of more Indians coming from the East and locating among them was not pleasing to the people of Missouri. For a number of years these emigrants had been drifting into southwestern Missouri under various influences, some under treaty arrangements and others voluntarily, hopeful of joining their old neighbors from the East. By 1824 there were said to be eight thousand of them, with the prospect of the number increasing. A proposition to extinguish the Indian title to land in Missouri and move the Indians farther west was promoted by Senator Benton of the Senate Committee on Indian Affairs, responsive to a message from the President communicating a memorial of the joint assembly of the state of Missouri on the subject.[11]

These sources and Secretary of War Calhoun listed the Indians referred to as follows: 1,800 Delawares and 1,383 Shawnee living near Cape Girardeau and at the head of the Current River; remnants of the Delaware on the headwaters of the White River; 2,200 Kickapoo on the Osage River; Piankashaw on the headwaters of the Black River; Peoria on the headwaters of the St. Francis River; 327 Wea; and parts of the Osage on Osage River.[12]

These Indians had removed to Missouri by authority of treaties previously mentioned. The Delawares, Calhoun said, moved from Indiana to Missouri under the treaty of October 3, 1818; a few went from Ohio and joined the others. The Kickapoo went from Indiana and Illinois under the treaties of July 30 and August 30, 1819. The Shawnee emigrated from Ohio of their own accord to Missouri to join their brothers, late of Cape Girardeau.[13] The Wea went from Indiana and Illinois under the treaty of August 11, 1820.[14] The Piankashaw—a few over two hundred—migrated voluntarily from Indiana and Illinois.[15]

Senator Benton, for his Senate committee, on May 14, 1824, recommended legislation looking to the removal of these Indians from Missouri to some place west of that state.[16] The committee report cited the fact that the red men had previously retired before the advance of white civilization and were now again overtaken and "threatened to be swallowed by it."[17] However, the only legislation evoked immediately by this committee report was a bill passed May 25, 1824, which provided merely for making treaties of trade and friendship with the tribes beyond the Mississippi.[18]

In order to provide a home for these Indians, steps were taken to secure lands farther west. Under instructions from Washington, Clark convened representatives of the Kansas and the Great and Little Osage at Castor Hill near his home at St. Louis, where, on June 2, 1825, the Osage entered into a treaty by which they conveyed a great tract of land, including approximately the present Benton County, Arkansas; the western tier of counties of Missouri south of the Missouri River; the northern half of Oklahoma; and a band of country nearly fifty miles wide extending east and west through Kansas.[19] The next day they secured from representatives of the Kansas tribe a cession covering most of the present state of Kansas lying north of the Osage, in addition to other lands.[20] Reserved from this cession, however, were tracts for the Osage children of Colonel A. P. Chouteau, located along the Grand River in the present Oklahoma. These reservists were Chouteau's children by Osage women who lived with him, and were thus the grandchildren of Pierre or Peter Chouteau, A. P. Chouteau's father.[21]

By these treaties most of the future Kansas was cleared of its Indian title and population and made available for Indians living in Missouri and other states whom it was desired to remove west.

Urged by the white people in the East and anxious to realize the advantages of a western home free from the irritating contacts with the whites and curious to see what the West had to offer them, parties of Indians organized from time to time to make the change. Thus the *Western Sun* of Vincennes reported on December 13, 1826, that "500 men, women and children of the Shawnee tribe passed through Vincennes from their reservation at Wapakeneta on the way to cross the Mississippi. The celebrated Indian Prophet and a son of Tecumseh were in the company."[22] However, of this party only 255 Shawnee from Wapakoneta and one Seneca family succeeded in reaching the Mississippi by January, 1827. As their horses were unable to travel farther, the Indians spent the winter in the "Big Bottom" twenty miles below Kaskaskia.[23]

When, about 1815, the Missouri Shawnee removed from the Cape

Girardeau location on assurance of receiving other lands in exchange, they left valuable and permanent improvements which were appropriated by white people. Under a promise by the federal government to indemnify them for losses occasioned by these events, Indian Superintendent Clark, at St. Louis on November 7, 1825, entered into a treaty[24] with the Shawnee of Missouri known as the Black Bob Band, whereby they ceded to the United States all their lands at Cape Girardeau lying between the "River St. Come and Cape Geredeau," bounded on the east by the Mississippi and on the west by the Whitewater. In exchange the United States gave to the Missouri Shawnee for themselves and for the Shawnee of Ohio who might elect to emigrate west of the Mississippi and join them, part of the Osage cession.

It was described as "a tract of land equal to fifty miles square, situate west of the State of Missouri, and within the purchase lately made from the Osages by treaty bearing date the second day of June, 1825, and within the following boundaries: Commencing at a point two miles northwest of the southwest corner of the State of Missouri; from thence north twenty-five miles; thence west one hundred miles; thence south twenty-five miles; thence east one hundred miles to the place of beginning."[25]

As this land proved unsatisfactory to the Shawnee, another area in the Kansas cession was given them in place of it. It was a strip about twenty miles wide, bounded on the north by the Kansas River, and extending from the Missouri River west about one hundred and twenty miles, including all, or substantial parts, of what are now the counties of Olathe, Johnson, Douglas, Osage, Wabaunsee, and Shawnee.

The Delawares of Missouri and recent emigrants from Ohio, who were consolidated on the James Fork of White River, having consented to remove from Missouri to other lands selected for them by the government, a treaty was made September 24, 1829,[26] at James' Fork, designating for the occupancy of the whole tribe part of the Kansas cession adjoining on the north the lands of their friends, the Shawnee. This tract was described as lying in the fork of the Kansas and Missouri rivers, extending up the Kansas to the Kansas line, and up the Missouri to "Camp Leavenworth"; and thence by a line drawn westwardly, leaving a space ten miles wide north of the Kansas boundary for an outlet. This indefinite description would include approximately the present Wyandotte, Leavenworth, Jefferson, Jackson, Pottawatomie, and parts of adjoining counties of Kansas. The boundaries were surveyed in the autumn of 1830 by the Reverend Isaac McCoy. On the way to begin his labors, accompanied by the Delaware representative, Chief Captain John Quick, he passed through the Shawnee settlements, where he found the recent immigrants engaged in a "talk" with thirty Kansas principal men. Here McCoy embraced the opportunity to explain to all of them the significance of his survey and the changes taking place in the western country. He and his party reached Fort Leavenworth on August 28, 1830, where they were provided a small military escort. After some delay they reached the Kansas land and began the survey on September 16. McCoy reported the area of the Delaware reservation as 1,444 square miles, or 924,160 acres.[27] The western extension or outlet, reaching as far as Solomon River, added enough to make a total of 2,808,000 acres.[28]

The treaty provided that the United States would aid the Indians in removing by furnishing them forty horses, the use of six wagons and ox teams, farming utensils, and provisions during removal and for one year thereafter.[29] But so anxious were the Delawares to remove that some of them could not wait for the promised assistance and proceeded at their own expense. As soon as they heard that McCoy was on the way to survey their country, they hastened preparations to remove thither. The venerable Delaware chief, William Anderson, with a hundred of his people, set out and arrived in their new home in the autumn of 1830, before McCoy had completed the survey. The remainder of the tribe were on the way from Missouri, except for a few who had gone on a hunting expedition and planned to rejoin their people in the spring. Chief Anderson told McCoy that he "felt peculiar gratification that now, in his old age, he had the pleasure, before his death, of seeing his people settled in their own country, where they were to remain—a country with which they were all well pleased."[30]

McCoy said that the Delawares were greatly in need of the provisions promised them. Their neighbors, the previously arrived Shawnee, McCoy continued, were "improving in agriculture and kindred arts promisingly. Their neat log cabins, fields, etc., appear little inferior to most new settlements of white people on our frontier."

Soon after McCoy left, Anderson died, but with the satisfaction of seeing his people established in what he ardently believed was their permanent home.[31] He had sent his peace wampum to his neighbors, the Pawnee, by their agent, John Dougherty; but he died before Dougherty could return in October, 1831, to report to the aged chief that his gesture of peace was well received by the Pawnee and that they would be glad to become acquainted with the new arrivals.[32] Anderson was survived by four stalwart sons, who became known to frontier fame as Captains Shounack, Secondyan, Pushkies, and Sacacoxy.[33] The first two served as guides for General John C. Frémont and other explorers.

A deputation of the principal chiefs of the Delawares and Seneca remaining in Ohio went to Detroit in June, 1829, and in a formal council with Lewis Cass stated the wish of their people to cede their land in Ohio to the United States and remove west of the Mississippi. Captain Pipe, a Delaware spokesman, said that for a long time the whites had been harassing them to move west and join the Delawares already there. When their agent pressed them on the subject, they agreed to remove but said that they would require assistance from the government, as they were very poor. Walking Stick, another chief, declared that their game was all gone and that there was no inducement to remain. The Seneca, however, were divided on the subject of emigrating.[34]

The red people could not yet bring themselves to leave their loved homes. The government did nothing to organize the emigration, assuming the Indians themselves would prepare to start. Naturally, nothing came of it. The agent, John McElvain, thought he was doing everything in his power to get them on the way by his lecturing that the sooner they removed the better it would be for them. He had sent one of the interpreters to Canada to stir up the Delawares living there, who had expressed a wish to accompany their brethren in Ohio to the western country.[35]

Some progress was made, however, and the diligent Pierre Menard reported from his post at Kaskaskia on October 8, 1830, to General Clark that at least 456 Shawnee and Seneca from Ohio were expected by him during the fall and winter and must be provided for. In addition, there would be 500 Miami from Massisineway and Stone Eaters Town in Indiana. They would, as usual, require provisions sent them, even before reaching Kaskaskia and during their stay there, in addition, to those sufficient to last them all the way to Kansas; for these necessities he would require $7,025. Besides, he would need $1,500 to purchase clothing for some of the poorest women and children, who were likely to arrive practically naked; without these provisions their suffering would be intense during the ensuing winter months before reaching their destination. For ferriage across the Kaskaskia and Mississippi rivers he would need an additional $520.[36]

NOTES

1. 3 *U.S. Stat.* 516.
2. Grant Foreman, *Indians and Pioneers* (2d ed.), p. 189; *Daily National Journal* (Washington, D.C.), February 8, 1825, p. 3, col. 4.
3. Foreman, *op. cit.*, and references cited there; Clark to Calhoun, September 5, 1823, "Graham Papers" (Missouri Historical Society).
4. A copy of this commission is to be seen in "Clark Papers" (Kansas Historical Society), Letter Book 2-3, p. 81.
5. Foreman, *op. cit.*, p. 193.
6. *Ibid.*, p. 194; *Missouri Republican* (St. Louis), March 7, 1825, p. 3, col. 3.
7. *House Doc. 64* (18th Cong., 2d sess.); Richardson, *Messages of the Presidents*, II, 282.
8. *American State Papers*, "Indian Affairs," II, 541; *Senate Report 218* (18th Cong., 2d sess.).
9. Henry R. Schoolcraft, *Historical and Statistical Information Respecting the History, Conditions and Prospects of the Indian Tribes of the United States*, III, 573. In Illinois at this time (1824), Potawatomi bands were living and hunting on the north fork of the Sangamon and on the Macoupin, Kickapoo on the south fork of the Sangamon and on the Kaskaskia, Delawares on the latter stream, and 300 Miami on the Wabash—all of whom most of the few white people in the county wished removed, though they were opposed by other whites engaged in vending whiskey to the Indians (Graham to Clark, January 15, 1825, Office of Indian Affairs [National Archives]).
10. Foreman, *op. cit.*, p. 197.
11. *American State Papers*, "Indian Affairs," II, 512.
12. *Ibid.*
13. Who, pursuant to the later treaty of November 7, 1825, the next year were to move from this district to Kansas.
14. Commissioner Thomas L. McKenney stated that the number of Wea removed to Missouri was 1,400 (*House Doc. 233* [20th Cong., 1st sess.]).
15. *Ibid.*, Schoolcraft, *op. cit.*, p. 585.
16. *Senate Report 211* (18th Cong., 1st sess.).
17. *American State Papers*, "Indian Affairs," II, 512; *Missouri Intelligencer* (Franklin) June 12, 1824, p. 2, cols. 3 and 4.
18. 4 *U.S. Stat.* 35.
19. 7 *U.S. Stat.* 240.
20. *Ibid.*, p. 244.
21. Sometimes called "Jeane Pierre" or "Major" Chouteau, but who invariably appeared in government documents as "Peter" or "P." Chouteau (Foreman, *Pioneer Days in the Early Southwest*, pp. 259 ff.).
22. Copied in *Missouri Intelligencer*, January 25, 1827, p. 3, col. 1. The Prophet and his twin brother, Tecumseh, and a third brother, who died at birth, were triplet children of a Shawnee woman. After the War of 1812, the Prophet lived in Canada near Malden, where he was supported by the British. Though he had lost the sight of one eye, he was pleasant and jocular in his old age. He died on the Osage reservation in Kansas in 1835 ("Draper Manuscripts" [Wisconsin Historical Society, Madison]).
23. Menard to Graham, January 17, 1827, "Graham Collection" (Missouri Historical Society).
24. 7 *U.S. Stat.* 284.
25. *Ibid.*; *Doc.*, II, 705. See also *Doc.*, III, 408; 7 *U.S. Stat.* 937. Shawnee Mission was established in 1829 by the Reverend Thomas Johnson in the present Johnson County, Kansas; in 1839 it was removed to a point two miles southwest of Westport, Missouri.
26. 7 *U.S. Stat.* 327.

27. In April, 1830 (*Doc.*, II, 430). Six months after the organization of the Mormon church, on April 6, 1830, Parley Parker Pratt and other missionaries of the church visited some of the New York and Ohio Indians and continued to Kansas. Here they interviewed William Anderson, Delaware chief, to whom they explained the Book of Mormon. After much persuasion, he was induced to call the council into session, to whom the missionary, Oliver Cowdery, made an address. The Delaware chieftain, as spokesman for his tribe, promised to build a council house in which the Mormons might instruct his people. According to the account by Elder Pratt in the archives of the Mormon church in Salt Lake City, considerable interest was manifested by the members of the tribe; but, when news of this interest reached the frontier settlements in Missouri, the Indian agent ordered the Mormons out of the country. They then moved across the line into Jackson County, Missouri, and began their labors among the whites (Grant Foreman, *Missionaries of the Latter Day Saints in Indian Territory* ["Chronicles of Oklahoma," Vol. XIII], p. 196).

28. *Senate Doc. 512* (23d Cong., 1st sess.), II, 432.

29. 7 *U.S. Stat.* 327.

30. Isaac McCoy to Secretary of War, April, 1831 (*Doc.*, II, 439). Desiring to unite the scattered segments of the Delaware tribe, Chief Anderson had dispatched wampum to the faction living in Canada called the "Moravian Town" as distinguished from the Pagans, who remained in Ohio; in order to facilitate Anderson's invitation, Secretary of War John H. Eaton caused the wampum to be delivered to the Delawares in Canada (Menard to Clark, November 2, 1830, "Clark Papers" [Kansas Historical Society], VI, 65; *Doc.*, II, 57). Menard said that Anderson and some of his people started for the Kansas River before the middle of October, 1830. Some of them had gone "to the Swamp" (Marais des Cygnes), but the greater part of the tribe had started out for the Arkansas River to spend the fall in hunting, to return and winter on the Neosho River and in the spring to join Anderson's people on the Kansas River.

31. Anderson wrote to the Secretary of War, September 22, 1831, a few days before his death, that he hoped "the balance of my nation, who are now scattered, some on the Red River and some in the Spanish country, will all come" and settle with his people in their new home. He hoped that the government would grant a pension of $100 annually to each of his four sons in lieu of other obligations previously assumed by the government and not performed (*Doc.*, II, 599).

32. *Ibid.*, p. 721.

33. *Ibid.*, p. 599.

34. "1829 Delaware and Senecas in Ohio (Emigration) Gov. Lewis Cass," Office of Indian Affairs (National Archives).

35. McElvain to McKenney, Columbus, Ohio, May 27, 1830, "1830 Delawares of Ohio (Emigration), John McElvain *accounts* of removal" (Office of Indian Affairs [National Archives]).

36. "Kaskaskia (Sub-Agency)," Office of Indian Affairs (National Archives).

CHAPTER IV

JACKSON'S ADMINISTRATION

THE subject of removal of the Indians from the states east of the Mississippi, and particularly from the southern states, quickened in interest when Andrew Jackson made it a presidential campaign issue that enlisted wide public concern. Jackson was elected in 1829, and one of the first measures he urged following his inauguration was what became known as the "Indian Removal Bill." After one of the bitterest debates in the history of Congress, this bill was enacted into law on May 28, 1830.[1] It did not itself authorize the enforced removal of the Indians, but it announced a federal policy favorable to removal and placed in the hands of President Jackson the means to initiate steps to secure the removal of any tribe "residing within the limits of the states or otherwise."

After enactment of the Removal Bill, commissioners were sent among the eastern tribes to negotiate treaties with them providing for their emigration westward. As fast as Indians could be induced to enter into these treaties, plans for their removal were prepared and the actual emigration begun. While the Indians of the southern states were the primary concern of Jackson's administration, officials in due time reached those north of the Ohio.

The Indian Removal Bill did not implement the government with all needed facilities, and, under the influence of Jackson, Congress enacted much important Indian legislation for effectuating the new policy. Besides numerous other bills, mentioned hereafter, a measure was enacted on July 9, 1832, providing for the appointment of a commissioner of Indian affairs, to serve in the War Department.

Essential legislation was also enacted by Congress, not only to direct the emigration of the Indians, but to set up an arm of administration in the West to carry into effect the treaty promises made to them and to regulate the activities of all Indians, intrusive as well as those indigenous to the western soil. To this end it was particularly essential that some branch of the Indian service should maintain contact with the movements of the Indians and report on the execution of federal laws and regulations among them. The necessity was realized also for some federal authority in the Indian country to consider and adjust many problems connected with that new subject which the officials at Washington were unable to administer efficiently from the distant seat of government. Accordingly, a commission was created by Congress, to which the President, on July 14, 1832, appointed Governor Montfort Stokes of North Carolina, Henry Ellsworth, of Hartford, Connecticut, and the Reverend John F. Schermerhorn, of Utica, New York. This commission dealt principally with the Five Civilized Tribes removed from the Gulf States, though on occasion their duties took them to Kansas and involved negotiations also with numerous tribes indigenous to the West.

On June 30, 1834, Congress adopted a measure entitled "An Act to regulate trade and intercourse with the Indian tribes, and to preserve peace on the frontiers," which established the area west of the Mississippi River—and west of Missouri and Louisiana and Arkansas Territory—as the "Indian Country." Another bill was enacted on the same date supplementing the act of 1832, creating a department of Indian affairs and defining the many functions committed to it.[2]

Regulations prescribed by the Secretary of War were to be enforced by local superintendents and agents. Two superintendents were to function in the Indian country, one of whom, established at the Choctaw agency in 1834, at the termination of the service of the Stokes Commission, had supervision over the Five Civilized Tribes. The other, established at St. Louis, supervised the immigrant Indians in Kansas and adjoining areas.

While the Missouri or the Black Bob Band of Shawnee had agreed in their treaty of 1825 to accept and move upon the tract on the Kansas River, they later changed their minds, as they were bitterly opposed to joining the Shawnee lately removed from Ohio. Instead they located on White River in Arkansas, later moving to southwestern Missouri on Cow Skin River near the Seneca in present northeastern Oklahoma. The neighboring whites in Missouri vigorously objected to their presence, and efforts were made to dislodge them.[3]

On November 20, 1831, a delegation of Shawnee Indians at St. Louis, representing the four hundred members of the Black Bob Band, addressed a memorial to the President. These Indians, formerly of the Cape Girardeau settlement, represented that they had lived in Missouri for forty years, entirely distinct from the portion of the Shawnee who were living on the Kansas River. While the latter were ranged on the side of Great Britain in the war against the United States, the former were peaceably engaged in farming and other domestic occupations. So long a time had elapsed since their separation, they said, that very few ties of blood or friendship remained. They were then living on the White River near where it crosses the line from Missouri into Arkansas. They said that the climate was cold there and that they were being surrounded by white strangers. They had been invited by the Creeks to locate near them, they continued, and they wished to accept the invitation to live where they believed it would be warmer than upon the lands assigned them near the Kansas River. They therefore asked to be given a tract of land on the Verdigris or Six Bulls River in exchange for such land as they were entitled to on the Kansas River. Part of their people, they said, were already living on the Verdigris; and many of their relatives, among the Shawnee of Ohio, agreed to join them on that stream if they could procure land there.[4] However, as this land belonged to the Cherokee by virtue of their treaty of 1828, their request was denied.

These Shawnee, broken up into bands, were living in Arkansas and the present eastern Oklahoma, engaged in hunting. They refused to remove to their new home on the Kansas River, and in March, 1833, the government threatened to remove them by force if they did not voluntarily proceed to the country allotted them in their late treaty and join the other faction of the tribe. A number of Shawnee, Seneca, Piankashaw, and Cherokee, in 1835, were living near New Madrid, Missouri, and, as the whites were trying to get rid of them, they appealed to the government for help in removing.[5]

The Kickapoo Indians living on their reservation in southwestern Missouri were crowded by white squatters who harassed them continually. In order to secure relief from this intolerable situation, the Kickapoo proposed to General Clark an exchange of their lands for others above the Kansas River.[6] Receiving no response to their proposition, some of the chiefs went to St. Louis to see the Indian superintendent. Clark reported their visit and condition to the Secretary of War; he feared trouble, unless corrective measures were taken, between the Indians and the whites who were encroaching on them.[7] Still nothing was done, the unfortunate situation being allowed to continue without redress for nearly a year and a half, when Clark again called it to the attention of his superiors in Washington.

Clark reported on September 22, 1831, that the Kickapoo possessed a tract of country assigned them, in the treaty of 1816, of sixty miles square on the Osage and Pomme de Terre rivers on which white people were trespassing; that difficulties between them occurred every day; and that, in order to avoid further trouble, the Indians had begged Clark to effect an exchange of their holdings in this beautiful country for other lands near Fort Leavenworth. Clark favored this solution and requested authority to negotiate with the Indians on the subject.[8]

The confederacy known as the Illinois Indians, now reduced to a weak remnant of formerly powerful tribes, after their emigration to southwestern Missouri were usually spoken of as the Kaskaskia and Peoria Indians. Remnants also of the Wea and Piankashaw, formerly living on the Wabash River, were located as their neighbors in Missouri.

In the effort to rid Missouri of Indians, some of these had been induced to move across the line into what is now Kansas, on land which the government promised to grant them. Here the Illinois Indians had established themselves in a village on the Osage River, and the Wea and Piankashaw had two villages—all of them in the vicinity of the present Paola, Kansas. Before the government conveyed this land to them, there was much complaint by the Indians during the summer of 1830 of conditions in their new home. They said that their women were prevented from gathering pecans by the Osage, who claimed the land and who came among the newcomers and frightened the women. The Kansas Indians stole the bells from their horses. Their interpreter, Baptiste Paoli, wrote that they were much in need of oxen; for lack of them the women had been obliged to carry rails on their shoulders until they were almost worn out. They needed farming implements and other facilities to enable them to get settled.[9]

Adjustment of these vexatious problems was permitted to hang fire in Washington indefinitely. As a step in the direction of the much-desired solution, on July 9, 1832, a measure was passed by Congress, appropriating funds for negotiating treaties with the Indians to extinguish their title to lands in Illinois, Indiana, and Michigan.[10]

On the fourteenth a bill was passed authorizing the making of treaties providing for the transfer to the United States of the title of the Kickapoo, Shawnee, and Delawares of Cape Girardeau to lands lying in the state of Missouri and of the Piankashaw, Wea, Peoria, and Kaskaskia in Illinois; for the expense of treating with, removing, and subsisting for one year of these Indians; and for dealing with the Shawnee and Menominee.[11]

After the enactment of this legislation runners were sent out with messages to the tribes interested, with the result that late in October, 1832, representatives of these tribes assembled at "Castor Hill," the home of General Clark, where consultations were begun. In attendance were two hundred and fifty members of the Prophet's band of Kickapoo Indians from the Vermilion River of Illinois and a few Potawatomi attached to that group. But they were not quite ready to agree before they could examine the country it was proposed to assign them. General Clark and the other commissioners reported that the treaty council was suddenly broken up by an alarm of cholera, general prevalence of which in St. Louis "and the fact of the existence of several well-authenticated cases in the country, together with the appearance of the usual premonitory symptoms in several persons attached to the commission, rendered an adjournment positively necessary."[12]

In their haste to get away, the Kickapoo on October 24 signed a preliminary treaty[13] which, after a delegation visited the proposed reservation, was ratified by another at Fort Leavenworth on November 26.[14] By the terms of this treaty the Indians ceded to the United States all their lands in southwestern Missouri granted them by the treaties of Edwardsville, July 30, 1819, and July 19, 1820, and agreed to accept in exchange as their new home, and to remove to, a tract on the Missouri River of about twelve hundred square miles near Fort Leavenworth adjoining the Delawares, including much of the present Atchison, Doniphan, and Brown counties, Kansas. This new treaty contained the familiar guaranty that the new cession was to be "their permanent place of residence as long as they remain a tribe."

Two days later a second treaty[15] was negotiated with the Black Bob Shawnee and Delawares lately living on the Spanish grant at Cape Girardeau, by which they relinquished to the United States all claims to lands ceded them by Spain in 1793. In exchange for this relinquishment and for improvements necessarily abandoned by the Delawares when they left the Spanish grant in 1815, the government promised compensation and agreed to aid both tribes in removing to their new reservations in Kansas, assigned them in treaties of 1825 and 1829, respectively.

In the third treaty, that of October 27, the Kaskaskia, Peoria, Michigamia, Cahokia, and Tamaroa bands announced their union as one tribe and agreed to the cession to the United States of all their lands in Illinois and Missouri. The government gave them 250 sections of land, "to include the present Peoria village on the Osage River," bounded on the east by the western line of Missouri, and on the north by the Shawnee reservation, comprising approximately the northern half of the present Miami County, Kansas. The western 150 sections, which contained their town on the Osage River, was designated as the home of the Kaskaskia and Peoria Indians; the remaining 100 sections, which contained their two villages, were reserved for the Piankashaw and Wea.

The remaining treaty at "Castor Hill," made on the twenty-ninth, was with the Wea and Piankashaw, who ceded to the United States all claim to land in Illinois and Missouri and received in exchange a home within the reservation just made to the Illinois Indians and a promise to the Piankashaw of compensation for the improvements abandoned and horses lost while removing.[16]

The signing of the treaties looking to the removal of the Indians from Missouri and Illinois was followed by intense activity in connection therewith. During the autumn of 1832, as disclosed by the accounts submitted to the auditor, General Clark, and other commissioners, considerable sums were expended in purchasing supplies to facilitate the attendance of the Shawnee, Delaware, Wea, Peoria, Piankashaw, and Kickapoo delegates at the treaty council in St. Louis and in the subsequent removal of these tribes from Missouri and Illinois to Fort Leavenworth. Messengers were sent to these Indians to secure their attendance at the councils. Small bodies of Delawares and Miami were among those who came by St. Louis on their way west. Numerous parties of Shawnee, Kickapoo, Seneca, and Delawares were furnished provisions and other necessary facilities at St. Louis. Companies of Indians crossed the Mississippi River at Kaskaskia, where they were outfitted and sent on their way.[17]

In the summer of 1833 James Kennerly, an Indian agent, conducted from their old home in Missouri 375 Kickapoo Indians and 119 Potawatomi who lived with them to the new reservation on the Missouri River six miles above Fort Leavenworth.[18] However, one band of Kickapoo headed by Kishko, a war chief, refused to settle on the tract assigned them, claiming the lands were not so good as they had been represented. Because of misunderstanding, Governor Montfort Stokes of the Indian commission at Fort Gibson came to confer with the disaffected Indians in an effort to compose their discontent.[19]

When President Jackson's Removal Bill was enacted in 1830, there were living in Ohio bands of Seneca, Shawnee, Ottawa, Delawares, and other Indians, former lords of a great domain in the East. These Indians had been crowded and put upon by the constantly increasing white population until life was all but intolerable. In treaties previously noted herein they had been induced from time to time to cede to the United States most of their holdings, and in 1830 they were living on much diminished and scattered reservations; but the whites were still clamoring for the government to remove their red neighbors. After Jackson's bill became law, special agents were sent to Canada to interview the Delawares there about joining the Ohio Delawares in a general westward migration.

Some progress was registered with the band of Delawares living on a tract three miles square adjoining the Wyandot reservation on the Sandusky River, reserved to them in the treaty of the "Rapids of the Maumee" on September 29, 1817. On August 3, 1829, at Little Sandusky, McElvain induced the Delawares to enter into a treaty ceding this, their last remaining land in Ohio, to the United States and agreeing to remove to the lands assigned for their occupancy west of the Mississippi by the first of the following January.

The chiefs of this band told the agent that they would assemble their people at Wapakoneta, one of the western outpost settlements, and remain here until time to leave. The crowding by whites had made the Indians so unhappy that some of them were not only willing but anxious to leave for the remote country in the West where they could escape contact with the white man. But, reluctant to depart, they all lingered in their old homeland. And, before they completed their journey, their destination was changed from Missouri to the future Kansas by the making of the previously mentioned treaty on September 24, 1829, on James Fork of the White River, with the Delaware Indians then living in Missouri, by which they gave up the beautiful country occupied by them there in exchange for an area in the fork of the Kansas and Missouri rivers.

In March, 1831, the President commissioned Colonel James B. Gardner of Ohio to confer with the Indians of his state and to explain to them the necessity for removing from their homes and departing to the country west of the Mississippi.[20] He was urged to be discreet and, if possible, to create in the minds of the Indians a conviction that they could never be happy again in their old country and that the only hope for them lay in westward migration. He was enjoined to secure a removal of all the Indians at once if possible and was vested with authority to agree with them on the terms of the treaties it was expected he would negotiate, with particular reference to the exchange of their present holdings for others in the West.

The Indians to be affected by his mission were 500 Wyandots, 600

Shawnee, 200 Seneca, and 300 Ottawa, who owned 370,000 acres of land in Ohio. He was authorized to offer them 1,500 blankets, besides 150 each of plows, hoes, axes, and guns; to pay the expense of the removal—all at an estimated thirty dollars a head.

The Seneca of Sandusky were so discontented with their situation that they needed no urging, and at the first opportunity a delegation had made a treaty in Washington[21] with Gardner, February 28, 1831, by which the chiefs and warriors of the Seneca tribe living on Sandusky River exchanged their holdings in the present Seneca and Sandusky counties, Ohio, where they had lived for more than fifty years, for a tract of 67,000 acres in the future Indian Territory, immediately north of the Cherokee country and east of the Neosho River. They were thus to become the pioneers of the several small bands of Indian immigrants in that part of the present Oklahoma. The other Ohio Indians were offered the choice of locating near the Seneca or near the reservations of other immigrant tribes in eastern Kansas who subsequently removed to the Indian Territory.

Gardner returned to Ohio and at Lewiston negotiated a treaty of removal with the band of consolidated Seneca and Shawnee of Lewiston, July 20, 1831, by which they gave up their land on the Great Miami River in Logan County, estimated to be 39,681 acres, reserved to them in their treaties of 1817 and 1818;[22] with the Shawnee living at Wapakoneta and Hog Creek on August 8, when they ceded their homeland in Allen County,[23] and with the Ottawa on August 30, by which they surrendered several tracts secured to them by former treaties.[24] In each of the current treaties secured by Gardner the Indians agreed to move west. Instructions were then given by the Secretary of War on September 6 to John McElvain to begin the removal of the Seneca, who had made the first treaty.

The Seneca are New York Indians, most of whom still reside in that state. As early as 1824 some members of this tribe joined the confederacy in Arkansas, headed by the Cherokee chief, Takatoka, for warfare on the Osage Indians. A band of them, located in Ohio on the Sandusky River, headed by Mesomea or Civil John, by the treaties of 1817 and 1818 were assigned a tract of 40,000 acres of choice land on that river in Seneca and Sandusky counties, previously given them by their friends, the Wyandots. While called "Seneca" Indians, the ethnological history and identity of this people have been subject to some doubt; while some authorities think that they were descendants of the Erie,[25] it has been claimed by others that the majority of them were Cayuga Indians. The fact is that there were Cayuga Indians among them at an early date and that part of that tribe from Canada followed them in later years to the Indian Territory.

Migration was to have begun by September 1, 1831, so that it would be completed before winter. Soon after the execution of the first Seneca treaty, preparations were begun to carry it into effect. For a time the Indians put off the dread undertaking; later in June they promised to be ready at "roasting-ear time"—after the middle of August. When August arrived, Civil John and other Seneca chiefs were visiting their tribesmen in New York, to whom, on the eve of long separation, they surrendered the belt of wampum that theretofore had symbolically bound them together.[26]

At the beginning the government ordered made for them by George W. Tryon, a rifle manufacturer of Philadelphia, one hundred rifles, to be furnished with flintlocks, with barrels three feet four inches long, and with a half-inch bore, to cost $12.50 each. It was autumn before the Indians could arrange their affairs and make ready to begin removal. In October they were all vaccinated, and twenty-seven men with wagons and teams were employed to go to the homes of the Indians, collect their baggage, and remove them to Dayton, Ohio.

When the time came to start, the Indians were desolated by the impending prospect of leaving their homes forever. Their resolution failed them, and they were strongly inclined to back out. Some favored joining their friends in New York; some proposed going to Canada, others to Green Bay. It took much persuasion by their agent, John McElvain, to get the first family to load their cherished possessions, mount their ponies, and depart.[27] When the first were on the way, others were prevailed on, one or two at a time, to move forward a little, until nearly the whole land party was scattered along the road for seventy-five or eighty miles. Their journey from the Seneca village near Sandusky to Dayton, where they arrived on November 5, was one of extreme suffering, reported their conductor, Henry C. Brish. They were exposed to almost incessant rain and severe cold; on some days they were unable to struggle more than four or five miles over the bad roads. About 110 Seneca and 58 Delawares who had been afraid and unwilling to trust themselves on an Ohio River steamboat made their way to St. Louis on horseback.[28]

The remainder of the Seneca, numbering 231, with their baggage, were conveyed by canal boat from Dayton to Cincinnati, where they were placed on board the steamboat *Ben Franklin*. On November 16

Brish landed his Indians and their voluminous personal effects on the levee at St. Louis, while he took steps to make them comfortable. The weather was excessively cold, and the Indians were sent out about seven miles to camp while Brish assembled sixteen wagons and other equipment necessary for their overland journey. The agent in Ohio had failed to provide the blankets and other effects promised in their treaty, and, as they were suffering from the cold, Superintendent Clark secured and issued a blanket to each one, along with twenty heavy flintlock rifles, fifty axes, fifty hoes, and some of the plows promised them, which the Indians were eager to have before leaving for their wilderness home.[29]

The red men contemplated change to the remote Indian Territory with misgivings, aversion, and anxiety and were loath to leave behind any of the possessions that would make their future life more comfortable and relieve it of the strangeness and hardship they dreaded. They were a foresighted and provident people and took pains in their preparations for making a home in a strange environment. Many of the families had large boxes filled with adzes, augers, saws, chisels, and broadaxes. Some had bags and barrels of sweet corn and beans. They took sacks of peach stones and seeds of other kinds, with which they planned to make their prospective home fruitful, so as to be re-mindful of the cherished places they were sorrowfully leaving forever. These, with trunks of clothing, bedding, and household goods, presented an appalling spectacle to General William Clark, superintendent of Indian affairs at St. Louis, who saw them almost fill two rooms of a large warehouse on the river front.[30]

In addition to this, said General Clark, the Indians who had money derived from the sale of their improvements in Ohio laid out a great deal of it in comfortable clothing and in various cooking utensils. When the time arrived for loading the plows, hoes, axes, rifles, and blankets issued to them at St. Louis under the terms of their treaty, in addition to a dozen barrels of pork, flour, and salt to be used in the event they were unable to purchase provisions along the route, it was necessary, in order to accommodate the old and infirm, as well as the women whose children were too young to walk, to employ more teams than those authorized by the Indian department at Washington.[31]

When preparations were completed for the overland journey, they set out from St. Louis early in December on foot, horseback, and with wagons, together with their precious personal property. They had not gone far before they encountered inclement weather and a number became ill. At St. Charles, where they crossed the Missouri River, fourteen were too ill to go farther and were left, one woman dying there. The remainder continued to within five miles of Troy, county seat of Lincoln County, fifty-five miles from St. Louis. By now the whole party was ailing in various degrees, and two more died. It was so cold that neither the Indians nor the teams could proceed.[32] A number of children suffered from frozen hands and feet, and some of the teamsters were similarly afflicted. Many were ill with measles and some dying, and the whole party was greatly depressed, despondent, and terrified. Conductor Brish, finding it impossible to continue, camped his party here, where they remained during the winter. His expense account includes payment for a large number of coffins during this detention and $201.25 for the services of Doctors English and Woolfolk, of Troy, for attendance on the stricken Indians through the autumn, winter, and spring.[33] David and Samuel Baily, contractors for removing the Indians, were likewise laid low by illness at Troy.[34]

The overland party also had a difficult time from sickness and bad weather. By December 10 they had progressed no farther than Muncietown, Indiana. Four had died, including two children—Wippingstick's youngest child, who died at St. Mary's, and Cayuga Jim's eldest child. Eighteen of their horses had died. They were out of food for themselves and their horses and had gone into camp about ten miles northeast of Muncie, where they proposed to remain until spring should bring better weather and roads. Some of them were restrained from endeavoring to return to their old homes only by their helpless condition. Here Small Cloud Spicer, Seneca John, and other members of the party addressed a letter to the President, telling him of their plight and reporting that their conductor had abandoned them, leaving them without funds except such as they could borrow from their interpreter. They also sent greetings to the party ahead. The venerable Delaware, Captain Pipe, one of the signers of the treaty of 1778, was with the party, with twenty-six other Delawares.[35]

They sent a small delegation to overtake the advance party and report their dire situation. After their arrival, Brish reported on December 14, 1831: "The Seneca chiefs have requested me in the most importunate manner, either to go myself, or send some person, to ascertain the situation of their friends who started from Ohio some time in September last."[36] As they were apparently in great distress, and as there was fear that they would wander back to Ohio, Brish asked General Clark for permission to return to Indiana to see what could be done for them.

Brish left his Indians at Troy and returned to Indiana to urge the Indians stopping at Muncie to continue.[37] In the spring Brish brought the land party from Muncie to join those at Troy. When he returned to Troy, he found more than a hundred sick of various diseases, principally measles. Most of them were too ill to walk or ride horseback, and he was obliged to secure six more wagons in addition to the twenty-four already in use; but these thirty wagons were not enough to satisfy the pleadings of the Indians for relief from their hardship and suffering. The immense quantity of baggage taken by these people, he said, left little room for the stricken in the wagons; and there were times during the journey when the sick, the dying, and the dead were unavoidably crowded together in the same vehicle. When they departed from Troy, they left behind six Indians who were expected to die. So much time had been lost that the conductor insisted on continuing on their unhappy way.

The journey was a sad and miserable experience. They were detained five days in crossing the Missouri River at Jefferson City.[38] There was only one ferryboat—a boat so small that but one wagon without the team could be taken at a time—and the crossing required many trips. Much difficulty was caused by continued friction between the Seneca and Cayuga in the party; constantly quarreling, they gave Brish much anxiety and trouble.

They traveled through frequent rains. The roads were deep and heavy in mud all the way across Missouri, and they were unable to average more than six miles a day. They often had to contend with high water. In some places they could cross a stream only by putting the loads on top of the wagon beds high above the water; in others they had to make bridges. In many places where there were no ferries they were obliged to wait for the water to run down, after which the mud was so deep that much labor was required to prepare the banks before the wagons could descend into the streams and ascend again. The difficulty in crossing wet bottom prairies, Brish said, could scarcely be imagined. They could negotiate them only by disengaging the oxen and horses from half the wagons and adding them to the other half, and then the whole to those left. This procedure was resorted to many times, day after day. In addition to these difficulties, in the last part of the journey the flies attacked the horses and oxen in such swarms that they could travel only during the night. This severe work, he said, ruined many fine animals.

The second auditor of the Treasury Department, with little under-standing of the situation or sympathy for the suffering Indians, wrote several waspish letters to General Clark about the expense and delay involved in the emigration. He refused to accept the explanations offered by Clark and Brish. The latter, with deep regret, said that he felt condemned for having forced these unfortunate people on at a time when a few days' delay might have prevented some deaths and rendered the sickness of others less severe. But he was compelled by the rules of his employment to push on as rapidly as possible.

They were nearly a month reaching Harmony Mission on the Marais des Cygnes River in southwestern Missouri. Here they buried an Indian woman and a number of children. After waiting several days for the river to fall so that they could cross, they left June 13, 1832. During the next three weeks, while they were making the inter-vening ninety or one hundred miles to their reservation, four more adults and five children died of measles, which had continued with them ever since they left Troy. The Christians, Brish said, required time to perform the burial services as they understood them; and such as were pagans solicited the privilege of performing their rites. Neither could be interfered with, and much time was necessarily consumed in this way.[39]

In addition to these difficulties and to that of securing provisions along the road, the Seneca and Cayuga in Brish's party continued their quarreling. Finally, on July 4, 1832, after more than six months of travel, Brish and his reduced company, now numbering 352, arrived at their new home in the Indian Territory. Their first encampment was on Cowskin (or Elk) River, which they at first proposed to call Seneca River. The area assigned them here, the first in the future Oklahoma granted to any of the northeastern Indians, was described in their treaty as "adjacent to the northern boundary of the lands heretofore granted to the Cherokee Nation of Indians, and adjoining the bound-ary of the State of Missouri; which tract shall extend fifteen miles from east to west, and seven miles from north to south, containing about sixty-seven thousand acres."

Next in turn to emigrate was the mixed band of Seneca and Shaw-nee, numbering about three hundred, who lived on a small reservation of sixty-two square miles at Lewiston, lying in the western part of the present Logan County and extending over into Shelby and Auglaize counties, Ohio. Gardner's treaty with them, of July 20, 1831,[40] has been mentioned. By it they ceded this tract to the United States and took in exchange a reservation of 60,000 acres lying west of that granted to the Seneca of Sandusky and just north of the Cherokee boundary. The United States further agreed in the treaty to remove this band of Indians to their new home in the West.

A band of four hundred Shawnee Indians occupied a reservation of about 125 square miles at Wapakoneta and Hog Creek, including parts of the present Auglaize and Allen counties,[41] which, by their treaty with Gardner,[42] they ceded to the United States; in consideration they were given 100,000 acres within the fifty-mile-square tract in the present Kansas ceded to the Shawnee of Missouri by the treaty of November 7, 1825.

By Gardner's fourth treaty, that of August 30, 1831, with bands of Ottawa Indians living on four small, scattered reservations in northwestern Ohio, they ceded their lands amounting to about 50,000 acres. These tracts lay on Blanchard's Fork of the Great Auglaize River, at Oquanoxa's village on the Little Auglaize River, Roche de Boeuf, and Wolf Rapids on the Miami of the Lake (the Maumee) River.[43] In consideration the United States agreed to emigrate the two hundred Indians of Blanchard's Fork and Oquanoxa's village and give them a tract of 34,000 acres on the fifty-mile-square tract in Kansas assigned the Shawnee Indians of Missouri and Ohio in the treaty of November 7, 1825; to give the adjoining 40,000 acres to the Ottawa of Roche de Boeuf and Wolf Rapids; and remove them whenever they should accept the grant.

With the approach of spring, 1832, these Ohio Indians were restless to know when the removal contemplated by their treaties was to begin. As no information on the subject had been vouchsafed them, they were in a state of confusion and anxiety; if they were not to be removed, it was a matter of great importance to them to plant crops so that they would have something to eat during the year. Some of them had sold their homes and property in preparation for leaving and were bewildered by their situation. Those known as Lewiston Indians, living near Bellefontaine, were particularly importunate to be on their way, so that there would be an opportunity to raise a crop on their new location before the end of the year. Having received no information from Washington by the middle of March, John McElvain, their agent, was obliged to write to the Secretary of War, calling attention to the situation of his Indians and urging that their removal be expedited.

However, after an unaccountable delay of more than six months, it was April 6, 1832, before the treaties were ratified by the Senate, and it was May 17 before the President appointed James B. Gardner as special agent to inaugurate and superintend the removal of the Indians. Gardner was required to notify them to prepare for migration and to assemble at a designated rendezvous; to determine on the route to be followed and the point where they should board boats; to make suitable division of the Indians into companies; and to attend to many other necessary details.[44]

On the twenty-fourth the Secretary of War commissioned Lieutenant Jeremiah Lane of Columbus, Ohio, to assist and superintend the preparation for removal of the Seneca and Shawnee of Lewiston, to aid them in selecting and arranging the property they were to take with them, and to supervise them in advertising and selling all property that they could not take. A similar commission was issued to William H. Woodward, of Dayton, for the Ottawa Indians and to Benjamin Briggs, of Newark, for the Shawnee.

The treaties provided that the Indians should be removed in a convenient and comfortable manner. Accordingly, they unanimously and earnestly requested to go by land, said Gardner. "They are more allied to their ancient customs than any other people on earth. They scarcely ever change a trail when once made, however crooked or circuitous, and they now wish to travel 'in the manner of their fathers.' They know nothing about steamboats. They do not wish to 'move by fire,' nor to be scalded 'like the white man cleans his hog' [evidently thinking of the horrors of boiler explosions].[45] Some of their little children might be drowned. Their native modesty revolts at the use of the only convenience on board a boat to obey the calls of nature. They have many horses, too, from which they could not be induced to part for any consideration whatever. These and many other arguments they use, in the most forcible and importunate manner, in favor of selecting the route by land." They had five hundred horses, said Gardner, which they would not sell, and they recalled how the Seneca who emigrated the year before by water were compelled to dispose of their beloved horses at a shameless sacrifice when they were brought to Dayton to board the boats on the Miami Canal.[46]

These considerations convinced Gardner that the Indians ought to be permitted to travel by land. But the authorities at Washington overruled him, largely for reasons of economy, water transportation being not only much faster but less expensive. Some apprehension was felt in Washington that, in passing through Illinois, the emigrant tribes might in some manner become involved with the Sauk and Fox Indians who were engaged in the Black Hawk War. But Gardner said that there was not the slightest danger; that the Indians of Ohio, with a very few exceptions among the Wyandots of Sandusky and the Ottawa of Maumee Bay, were sincerely attached to the American government and, if called upon, would rally under the American flag against any other tribe or foreign foe. The Ottawa of the Maumee, however, were not on good terms with those of the Great and Little Auglaize, and Gardner feared that there might be trouble between them on the road.

Gardner again wrote to General Gibson, commissary-general, that the Indians preferred to go by land, and he requested leave to send someone to select a route all the way to the Mississippi River. He also desired permission to divide his charges into separate detachments, so as to avoid strife and disorder between the Shawnee of Wapakoneta and those of Hog Creek. Gibson informed him on June 5 that his requests would not be granted, that the movement would be by water, and that the Indians must all travel together.

The summer was passing, and the Indians were restless and demoralized; they had planted no crops and were exhausting their resources. Unprincipled white men were employing familiar artifices to entice from them the little money they had received from the sale of their improvements.

The chiefs of Wapakoneta and Lewiston unanimously and vigorously urged the government to take the necessary measures to have all their people vaccinated before setting out on their journey.[47] This was not attended to for more than two months, and it was late in August before the vaccination began. The business had progressed to the point where the Indians were directed to assemble at Lewiston, Logan County. Here a number of them were vaccinated and received their rations. They then returned to their homes to recover from the vaccination and await the day of departure. But they were not ready to start, being still torn by fear and dissension on the subject of traveling by steamboat. Civil John, the venerable chief of the Seneca, and other head men met to consider this momentous subject. After much counseling and persuasion, they finally agreed that they were ready to carry out their agreement to leave their homes for the West but that they positively refused to travel by boat. They quoted their old and infirm women as saying:

"We will not go on steamboats, nor will we go in wagons; but we will go on horseback; it is the most agreeable manner for us; and if we are not allowed to go so, we can and will remain here and die and be buried with our relatives; it will be but a short time before we leave this world anyway, and let us avert from our heads as much unnecessary pain and sorrow as possible."

Dissension continued and preparations for their departure progressed slowly. The Indians were now alarmed by reports of cholera on the steamboats on the lakes and rivers, and some of them declared they would postpone their emigration to the next year rather than risk death from cholera on steamboats.[48] The next few days they spent at home selling their personal property, settling their affairs, and shoeing their horses in preparation for departure. On Sunday night, the second day of September, they celebrated the "Feast of Death." In ceremonies of this kind they commemorated the good and worthy qualities and deeds of some deceased member of the tribe and extravagantly mourned his death with tears and lamentation. They adopted some person in his place for the purpose of perpetuating his name and the memorial of his life and virtues.[49]

The next day they assembled to receive their blankets, tents, and rifles, with which they were well pleased. They were also rejoiced to learn that the President had at last yielded to their prejudice and had said that they might make the journey by land on the condition that the cost should not exceed twenty dollars per person. They then agreed to be ready to start on September 17, 1832.

While they waited they were constantly beset by white men seeking to involve the Indians in obligations for the purchase of articles for which they had no use and to induce them to waste the funds they were about to receive from the sale of their effects but which they would greatly need to make homes on the raw land on which they were about to locate. Liquor was constantly employed by this class of white men, but Gardner said that he was using every means and persuasion in his power to "counteract the destroying influence which heartless avarice is throwing around our poor savages, for the purpose of filching from them the last dollar for which they have sold their heritage amongst us, and the 'graves of their fathers.'"

The departure was a ragged and haphazard movement.[50] The mercenary whites who used their influence to detain the Indians as long as they had money to spend found an influence to serve their purpose in the sudden death of Mrs. McPherson, wife of the conductor of the Logan County Indians. She was much loved by the Indians among whom she had been reared, and they deeply mourned her death. Some heartless villains, said Gardner, who wished the Indians to remain longer for the sake of robbing them of the few dollars they had just received, "are trying to make them believe that we brought the cholera here and killed her, and will kill them too."[51] That disease was then raging in the Mississippi Valley, and the Indians were greatly alarmed by the prospect. The funeral of Mrs. McPherson on September 18 was attended by a large number of mourning Indians whose cup of desolation at leaving their old homes was already filled to overflowing.

At last, on September 19, they finally began to move. They had received the annuity promised in their treaty and some of the pay for their improvements. They were nearly all mounted on their ponies—men, women, boys, and girls, with babies on the backs of their mothers. It was a scene of sorrow and apprehension as these people turned their backs on old homes and the first detachment proceeded ten miles along the road, where they made their first camp. The government wagons, drawn by the slow-moving oxen, had preceded them and now waited at the camping place for the Indians to come up, claim their rations, make campfires, and prepare the evening meal. For old people—some of them women more than one hundred years old—space was reserved in the wagons if they should tire of the backs of their ponies.

The Indians left their rendezvous near Piqua[52] in detachments; the Seneca and Shawnee first; then, twenty miles back, the Ottawa; and, after an interval of a day's march, the Shawnee of Wapakoneta.[53] Some of them camped at Hardin, some at Greenville, and others at Richmond, Indiana. At the latter place many of them came into town, some to see the sights, some to trade, and some to buy whiskey. It was four days later before they could be induced to leave the place; as it had rained heavily, travel was difficult and progress slow—only ten to fifteen miles daily.

Near Richmond one camp presented a martial appearance. For 258 persons there were but fifty tents. Guns, tomahawks, and scalping knives were scattered about the ground. The Indians were annoyed by curious white people who had come to stare at them.[54]

Gardner reported on October 1 at Richmond, Indiana,[55] that the

Indians were in the vicinity. "The Lewiston detachment arrived here on Thursday last. They started on the 19th ultimo, leaving many loitering in the rear, came seven miles to the crossing of the Great Miami and encamped. Next day I took charge of them in person, and sent back the conductor and an assistant to bring on the balance. On the 20th they encamped on Turtle creek in Shelby county, and in the course of the next day were joined by most of the band. A few went through the white settlements to Fort Wayne, and promised to join the main body at Indianapolis. On the 22d. they left the Turtle creek, and traveled by way of Greenville to White Water, four miles east of this place, where they remained by my order until yesterday, awaiting while I could collect and organize the Shawnees and Ottaways, and bring them within half a day's march of the Lewiston band. That band moved yesterday from their encampment to a creek two miles west of this place, and started again this afternoon towards Indianapolis.

"The Shawnees of Wappaughkonetta have almost exhausted our patience. They forfeited their promises and abused every kindness. It seemed impossible to get them to make the least movement towards preparation. They were furnished with everything promised, and much more. We *lent* them twenty-five horses, and supplied three light 2-horse wagons for their baggage. They abused the horses, rode them off to the neighboring towns, kept in a state of intoxication for several days together, until nature sunk under their beastly intemperance. During this time I was laboriously engaged in preparing the Lewiston band, with whom I had much trouble, owing more to the intrigues and frauds of the whites around them than to any other cause. At length I was compelled to go back from Turtle creek to Wappaughkonetta myself, and send forward the Senecas under their conductor; I found the Shawnees in a most wretched condition. Many sick, some wounded, their own horses all astray, and all that could, still drinking whisky, women as well as men, though half-crazy and enfuriated. I will not attempt to describe the exertion necessary to bring anything like order out of this human chaos. I succeeded, however, in getting them on by dozens to Turtle creek, distant twenty-two miles, until the main body of them assembled and prepared for the march.

"The whites beset us again with their barrels and kegs of whisky, *hid out in the woods*, and three days were consumed in almost fruitless efforts to remedy the serious evil inflicted by our own citizens. I found the Ottaways, about one hundred, also near Wappaughkonetta. Many were drunk and the chiefs highly incensed at not having received their annuities. I had sent an express to Colonel McElvain to meet me at Hardin, on Turtle creek, and there to pay the $370 sent on by Governor Porter; of this I informed the chiefs, coaxed, flattered, scolded and threatened; and finally they followed me to Hardin, received their annuities, guns, blankets, sheeting, twenty-five United States horses, twelve saddles, and two wagons to carry their baggage; since then they have behaved as well as could be expected from them.

"On Friday last the Shawnees and Ottaways set out on the march from Turtle creek to this place—about sixty miles—keeping a few miles apart. We had all sorts of trouble to get thus far; fortunately, I have the confidence of the chiefs and head-men of both bands, and, when present, can govern them. The several assistants, to whom they at first paid little attention (I know not from what cause) are now gaining the proper authority over them, and able to manage them in my absence. With one or two exceptions, no inexperienced man could be more efficient than the gentlemen associated with me. They are zealous, active and energetic and fear neither weather nor hard work to facilitate my operations. I hope we shall now do well. We are getting away from the old haunts and associations of the Indians. I would to God I could say we were also away from those miserable, mean wretches who, for a paltry gain, carry disorder, mutiny, and distraction into our ranks as we pass along the road, and into our camps at midnight. No human vigilance can guard against them. We have done all, everything we could think of, to check and prevent it. The evil has abated, to be sure, since they left Greenville, in Darke County; but even in *this* moral and enlightened community, composed principally of members of the Society of Friends, wretches are found to waylay the miserable Indians with a keg or jug, prostrate him by the roadside, or in the street, and filch away his last penny. We have now organized a corps of sober Indians to guard the camp, and the experiment, so far, has proved salutary.

"This rapid sketch is all I have been able to write you since I set out. I can truly say I have not slept three hours in any night for two weeks, and in the day time I am incessantly and most arduously engaged. I have not found it possible to take time to make out my estimate to the Commissary General for funds, but will do so as soon as practicable. I must keep all three detachments moving. We fail if we *stop three days between this and the Mississippi.*"

Gardner wrote again from Richmond, October 3, that the Lewiston

Indians were about forty miles ahead on the road to Indianapolis and doing well.[56] They were traveling on the National (or Cumberland) Road. The Shawnee and Ottawa detachments passed through Richmond that day, and Gardner's room had been crowded with the Indians. Many of them were sick and others obstinate and refractory from the use of whiskey and the influence of whites. The eight hundred Indians were traveling in five detachments that extended for eighty-five miles along the highway, causing much difficulty in issuing rations to them. Provisions were deposited for delivery to the Indians every thirty miles; at one point bacon; at another, beef; at another, flour.[57] On October 5 the advance party camped within two miles of Indianapolis, while they waited for the Ottawa to come up and join them.[58]

Gardner said that he could never learn while on the march the precise number of Indians in his charge. For convenience he marched them at intervals of ten to twenty miles apart. But the Indians were constantly visiting each other for days at a time, and this intercourse between the parties, and their habit of scattering along the line of march, made it difficult for him to count them.[59] Most of the Indians, said Gardner, rode their five hundred horses. A few had carriages and wagons of their own. The sick, the aged, and the decrepit were carried in the public baggage wagons.

Until they arrived at Indianapolis the Indians were supplied with rations by contract, but from there on they were furnished in bulk on the orders of the respective conductors. Flour and meal were procured in bags and barrels and beef and pork on foot. The Indians butchered the cattle, receiving the hide and tallow for their labor, with which they purchased coffee, sugar, spices, and other articles.[60]

Gardner wrote to Gibson on October 6, 1832, at Belleville,[61] Indiana, twenty miles west of Indianapolis, that many of the Indians had funds from the sale of their property and that the whites knew about it and were selling them whiskey and trying in every way to get their money. "They are alarmed by reports of cholera at St. Louis. The mixed bands of Shawnees and Senecas, which, for sake of convenience we call the Lewiston detachment, will encamp eight or ten miles west of this village tonight. The Ottawas now precede the Shawnees of Wapaughkonetta in consequence of the indolence and dissipation of the latter. They will encamp in this immediate neighborhood this evening. There has been much sickness among them. There is a small band of sober, industrious and highly meritorious Indians called the 'Hog Creek Shawnees,' about forty-five in number, who at first refused to start this fall because of the drunkenness and quarrelsome habits of the brethren of Wapaughkonetta. They have their own wagons and teams, and ask no assistance in their transportation except a few sets of horse gears, two or three wagon covers, and two or three horses. Some days after the departure of the Shawnees of Wapaughkonetta, the Hog Creek people agreed to migrate, and will come on in charge of Judge Shelby.

"We dare not stop for any purpose whatever, if it is possible to travel. Delay would be the death to our prospects of getting there this year. The Shawnees, however, if permitted or if able to defeat our plans by either stratagem or mutiny, would gladly halt anywhere and frolic or hunt until spring. Their chiefs, with a solitary exception, are indifferent to expense incurred by the Government or the interests of their people.

"The weather has been very inclement most of the time, and the roads extremely bad. At Richmond we changed the transportation from light two-horse wagons to heavy four-horse teams. Still it is with great difficulty we can make from twelve to fifteen miles per day. We have been shamefully imposed on in the cost of rations by a settled plan of extortion, connived at by the disbursing agent and his relatives."

On October 12 the head of the column reached the Wabash River, which they crossed the next day at Clinton, Indiana. The horses were made to ford the river, while most of the women and children were taken across in ferryboats. On the fifteenth, getting an early start and traveling rapidly, they made the unusual distance of twenty-seven miles in Illinois. This was necessary, as there was no water or nearer camping place. The next few days were uneventful except that some of the horses wandered from the camps at night and entailed delay. Heavy rains fell, and they found it necessary to remain in camp until the tents dried.

Beyond Indianapolis they traveled in three detachments. There were five hundred horses in the party belonging to the Indians and seventy-five which had been purchased by the government. The later were badly selected, some of them incurably diseased, and most of them too poor and old for such service. Many of them died or broke down on the road, though fed grain and hay; the Indians' ponies, nourished only on the pasturage along the way, with a few exceptions completed the journey in good shape.

The first detachment reached Shelbyville, Illinois, on October 20. The other contingents, fifteen miles apart, were following in good order. Gardner rode ahead to Vandalia, where he wrote of conditions.[62] On October 23 the Indians were within six miles of that town, and later they stopped while a messenger went ahead to ascertain the cholera situation in St. Louis. The camp was removed from the highway, so that travelers from that city might not come among the Indians and bring the disease into camp.

The first detachment reached Hickory Grove in Bond County, Illinois, forty miles from St. Louis, on October 24, 1832, after twenty-eight days of actual travel, said Gardner, "supported principally on money borrowed from the Indians themselves."[63] Here they remained several days to rest the horses, receive instructions from General Clark at St. Louis concerning the remainder of the journey, and await the arrival of seventy or eighty Hog Creek Shawnee who had remained at Wapakoneta after the main body had left the rendezvous at Piqua.[64]

Gardner reported from Hickory Grove, October 25, to General Clark that he had eight hundred migrating Indians, Seneca, Shawnee, and Ottawa, in three detachments. "The first detachment of 250, two-thirds Senecas and one-third Shawnees, now camped on the east fork of Shoal Creek two and a half miles east of here. The Ottawas, numbering 100 arrived today. The Shawnees of Wapaughkonetta and Hog Creek, numbering 450, will be here tomorrow or next day."

With few exceptions, he said, the Indians were on horseback or in their own wagons and carriages. "We have about 600 horses in the party. At least half of the emigrants are women and children. Several of the former are aged and infirm, and many of the latter are helpless infants. A few deaths from cholera infantum, bad colds, etc., but there was an equal number of births.[65]

"On the river at Vandalia I stopped to receive instructions from the War Department as to my future movements. Have not received a single word." Gardner requested directions about crossing the Mississippi River and concerning the route to Neosho River. He also asked for a physician, saying that he had two hundred dollars' worth of badly selected medicine which he did not know how to use. Here, on October 29, because of a feud between Disbursing Agent Lieutenant J. F. Lane and Gardner, and consequent confusion, mismanagement, and delay, Colonel J. J. Abert of the Army arrived to assume charge of the emigration in an effort to get the Indians to their destination before cold weather. The rear detachment arrived on the twenty-eighth, and the next day the emigrants separated, the Shawnee of Wapakoneta and the Ottawa departing for Alton and the Kansas River.[66]

The same day General Daniel M. Workman, in charge of about two hundred of the mixed band of Seneca and Shawnee, including the Lewiston Indians,[67] departed on the road to Kaskaskia, a French village near the mouth of the Kaskaskia River, where they were to cross the Mississippi. There was some delay occasioned by men loitering and the necessity of hunting horses that had wandered away from camp. On Sunday, the fourth of November, having arrived within four miles of the ferry, the conductor of the party rode to Kaskaskia to see Colonel Pierre Menard and to secure information concerning the route and assistance in crossing the Mississippi.[68] Two days later they reached the ferry, but the wind was blowing so hard that the ferryman refused to cross. The next day, near Ste Genevieve, in rowboats, about two-thirds of the emigrants were taken over before dark, and on the eighth the remainder crossed. They remained in camp another day while horses were shod, and on the thirteenth they reached Mine-a-Burton, where they had the remainder of the horses shod and the squaws had an opportunity to wash their clothing and blankets. Owing to rains, snow, and excessive cold and the straying of their horses from camp, the progress was slow for several days. A child died on November 20. On the twenty-ninth they reached Gasconade River and afterward crossed a number of other flooded streams.

On December 2, more than two hundred miles from Ste Genevieve, Lieutenant J. F. Lane, the disbursing agent, reported that he had added two wagons to carry provisions, as there was no flour forty miles west of the Mississippi, and that he found corn meal at only two watermills along the road. Houses were twenty-five to forty miles apart. The day he wrote they had traveled only eight miles and in that distance had forded one stream six times where the water was near swimming depth.[69] The next day Lieutenant Lane gave the Indians a keg of powder and one hundred pounds of lead. They were now in a fine game country, and the Indians were required to hunt game for food with which to pay for the ammunition. On December 7 they reached White River, and the next day crossed Gibson's Fork of the Neosho. On the thirteenth they reached the Seneca agency in the Indian Territory, where Lane delivered the Indians to Major Augustine Kennerly, Seneca agent.

They camped on the lands of the Seneca while their conductor and some of the chiefs departed to examine the country assigned them on the west side of Grand River. Unable to cross the river, and receiving unfavorable reports concerning the land beyond the stream, they refused to accept it. Their principal objection was its alleged lack of good timber.

Henry L. Ellsworth and John F. Schermerhorn of the Indian commission at Fort Gibson arrived on December 26, 1832, and convened the recent arrivals and the Seneca in council in an effort to compose their discontent; three days later the Indians entered into a treaty with the United States and with each other by which they surrendered the land on the west side of the Neosho or Grand River in exchange for an equal extent—60,000 acres—on the east side, lying north of and contiguous to that of the Seneca Indians of Sandusky; and in which they announced that they and the Seneca who had arrived the year before had united in a confederacy by which they called themselves the "United Nation of Senecas and Shawnees."[70]

The returns made by Lieutenant J. Van Horne, disbursing agent at the Seneca agency, showed 275 Seneca of Sandusky and 258 of the band called Seneca and Shawnee. There was some confusion[71] about the count of these Indians, but this was later adjusted.[72] There were a few white families (principally horse thieves, said Van Horne) living about sixteen miles distant in the corner of Arkansas.[73]

The next summer, long after the season for plowing, these Indians, through their disbursing agent, were beseeching the War Department for the plows, grist mill, and other implements promised them in their treaty, to facilitate the beginning of their new life in the West. They also begged that steps be taken to suppress the sale of whiskey by white people on adjoining lands in Missouri, who were also destroying the fine timber on the Indian land.[74]

When the emigrants separated at Hickory Grove, the detachment composed of Shawnee of Wapakoneta and the Ottawa, numbering about five hundred, left October 30 and on November 1 and 2 crossed the Mississippi River at Alton, Illinois. From here Gardner took his departure for home. The emigrants, in charge of Colonel Abert, continued on their way to the lands assigned them on the Kansas River. On November 9 they reached Lutz Creek, ninety miles from St. Louis. Excessive use of poor brandy during a three-day debauch had killed an old Ottawa chief, and two others were in a critical condition.[75] This had given rise to a rumor of cholera, and the Indians were much alarmed, as cholera was raging in St. Louis and other places on the road.[76] A postmaster along the route refused to receive in his house mail from St. Louis and had resigned his office. This had caused great inconvenience to the officers conducting the emigration.

On November 12 and 14 the emigrants passed through Columbia, Missouri. The *Missouri Intelligencer* contained an account saying that there were 420 Shawnee and 100 Ottawa Indians, and among the former were two women, a hundred and two and a hundred and twelve years old, respectively, who had ridden their ponies all the way.[77] "They did not travel in a compact body, but in detached companies of five, ten or fifteen, but all in sight of each other—and it was half a day before they had all passed through Columbia. A number of wagons accompanied them, with baggage and children. Many of these sons of the forest exhibited a fantastic appearance, their clothing and ornaments being of almost every color and description; but they all appeared to be comfortably clad and well provided. Nearly all were on horses." Two days later a hundred Ottawa Indians passed through Columbia, and after four days the company was camped in the river bottom ten miles above Franklin. Cholera still raised a wall of hostility against the emigrants. "You would laugh to see how we are frequently received on the road," said Colonel Abert; "doors are slammed in our faces, yet some are bold enough to peep at us through the windows. However, as long as they do not stop our progress, we don't care; and yet some of these whites will continue to sell whisky to our Indians. About twenty of our Ottaways were as drunk as David's sow yesterday. When sober, these are by far the most orderly and manageable of the whole detachment. But drunk, sober, or sick, we will move them along."[78]

Some of the Indians were ferried across the Missouri River at Arrow Rock near Franklin,[79] but, on the eighteenth, Abert reported that they were still on the riverbank, "confined by a storm, or we should have gained ten miles today. It has been a violent storm both yesterday and today, wind, rain, sleet and now snow. These poor devils suffer considerably but we cannot help it. The weather is not of our making. The Ottaways are in a warm bottom on the east bank, ready to cross so soon as the Shawnees give them room. The Ottaway camp still continues healthy, but I should not be surprised if some of these Shawnees were found frozen to death tomorrow, as, on passing through their camp I found some of them rather drunk; they are a sort of overgrown children, and require continual care. The agents are very clever and attentive and the Indians are all anxious to shove ahead. Ah! this weather, this weather—they should have been at their homes before this, and would have been if the business had been properly managed from the start."[80]

After five anxious days the Indians were all ferried across the Missouri River and resumed their journey. They arrived at the new one-hundred-thousand-acre home of the Shawnee twenty miles west of the town of Independence, on November 30, 1832. The land provided for the Ottawa was about forty miles distant among strangers, and they were invited by the Shawnee to remain with them until spring. This band of Ottawa was connected by marriage with the Shawnee of Wapakoneta and looked upon them as an "elder brother."[81]

Abert reported a total of 72 Ottawa immigrants delivered by him on their western reservation. The Shawnee Indians from Hog Creek and Wapakoneta numbered 334. The latter had been furnished only sixteen felling axes and two cross-cut saws, and the Ottawa ten felling axes, with which to erect houses, and they were in great need of more tools and farming implements; their blacksmith had made them some frows, iron wedges, and axes, but he was unable to meet the demands of so many Indians, discontented and indignant at the failure of the government to furnish them needed facilities for establishing themselves on their land as promised in the treaty.[82]

By 1835 a total of 251 Seneca from Sandusky and 211 of the Seneca and Shawnee band had been moved to the tract between the western boundary of Missouri and the eastern boundary of the Cherokee Nation.

NOTES

1. 7 *U.S. Stat.* 411.
2. These measures are to be seen in 4 *U.S. Stat.* 564, 595, 725, and 729.
3. *Doc.*, II, 705; *Doc.*, III, 635; *Doc.*, IV, 745; Clark to Superintendent of Indian Affairs, December 2, 1829, "Clark Papers" (Kansas Historical Society), IV, 67.
4. *Doc.*, III, 634.
5. Moseley to Clark, July 4, 1835, "OIA St. Louis (Emig.) Gen. Wm. Clark" (National Archives); Grant Foreman, *Indians and Pioneers.*
6. *Doc.*, II, 584; Clark to Superintendent of Indian Affairs, December 2, 1829, "Clark Papers" (Kansas Historical Society), IV, 67.
7. Clark to Secretary of War, April 6, 1830, *ibid.*, p. 94.
8. *Doc.*, II, 584; "Clark Papers," IV, 209.
9. *Doc.*, II, 115, 118, 119.
10. 4 *U.S. Stat.* 564.
11. *Doc.*, II, 869; 4 *U.S. Stat.* 594. See Grant Foreman, *Indian Removal: The Emigration of the Five Civilized Tribes* and *Pioneer Days in the Early Southwest.*
12. Doc., III, 511.
13. 7 *U.S. Stat.* 391.
14. *Ibid.*, p. 393.
15. *Ibid.*, p. 397.
16. *Ibid.*, p. 410. A band of Shawnee living on Crooked Creek, Arkansas, were

brought by way of Ste Genevieve to this treaty council, but it does not appear that they were parties to any treaty negotiated there that summer (*Doc.*, V, 48).

17. *Doc.*, I, 644; *Doc.*, III, 640. Indian Superintendent Clark reported the issuing of supplies to the Indians being removed from Missouri to Kansas: agricultural implements to Miami and Wea, merchandise to Peoria, Piankashaw, Kickapoo, Delawares, and Kaskaskia. The Shawnee were accustomed to manufacturing clothing in their homes, and they required spinning-wheels and wool and cotton cards, before going into the wilds of Kansas (*Doc.*, V, 58). Three six-horse teams and wagons were promised the Delawares to remove their possessions (*ibid.*). On April 22, 1833, John Dougherty also landed at Fort Leavenworth a number of Kickapoo he brought from St. Louis (*Maximilian's Travels* ["Thwaite's Western Travels," Vol. XXII], p. 253; see also "Thwaite's Western Travels," XXVIII, 131-41).

18. *Doc.*, I, 644.

19. Grant Foreman, *Pioneer Days in the Early Southwest*, p. 214.

20. *Doc.*, II, 270.

21. 7 *U.S. Stat.* 348.

22. *Ibid.*, p. 351. Having much intermarried, these Seneca and Shawnee had united as one band or tribe.

23. *Ibid.*, p. 355.

24. *Ibid.*, p. 359.

25. See *Handbook of American Indians.*

26. *Doc.*, II, 471; *Doc.*, V, 122.

27. Much of their personal property was sold at public auction, September 22-28, at the home of Small Cloud Spicer and at their council house on Green Creek (*Doc.*, II, 597).

28. *Doc.*, II, 692. Indian Agent John McElvain reported on November 15, 1831, that the Seneca recently departed for the West numbered 340, including a few individuals from other tribes, 230 of whom went by water and the remainder by land. Fifty-eight Delawares, the majority of those living in Ohio, had also started. The remaining 20 Delawares, who were blood relations of the Wyandots, could not be induced to leave their friends and remained to emigrate with them (*Doc.*, II, 684).

29. "Clark Papers" (Kansas Historical Society), IV, 319; *Doc.*, II, 722. McElvain sought to excuse his failure to provide the Seneca with blankets by the statement that they had recently received a large supply from the British agent at Malden, who was still trying to keep these Indians under British influence (*Doc.*, II, 685).

30. General Clark to U.S. Auditor, November 18, 1833 (*Doc.*, V, 112).

31. Brish to Clark, December 13, 1831 (*ibid.*, p. 115).

32. *Doc.*, II, 722-24.

33. *Ibid.*, p. 705.

34. *Doc.*, V, 116, 117.

35. *Doc.*, II, 691, 705, 722, 725; "Clark Papers" (Kansas Historical Society), IV, 321, 330.

36. *Doc.*, II, 724.

37. *Doc.*, V, 116. He then reported from Fort Ball, Ohio (Brish to Secretary of War, February 28, 1832, Office of Indian Affairs, "Senecas in Ohio, Shawnees—Ottawas [Emigration] J. B. Gardner, Special Agent [Misc. Letters]" [National Archives]).

38. When within fifteen miles of Jefferson City, Brish was visited by two young Seneca representing a party of 42 members of that tribe who had been living "for some years past" near Ste Genevieve, who wished to join the emigrants and live with them in their Kansas home. Brish referred their request to General Clark (*Doc.*, V, 117).

39. Brish to Clark, July 16, 1832 (*ibid.*, p. 119).

40. 7 *U.S. Stat.* 351.

41. This area the Shawnee Indians held under Section 6 of the treaty they made at the foot of the rapids of Miami River on September 29, 1817. There were two tracts—one of ten miles square surrounding their council house at Wapakoneta and adjoining, and another of twenty-five miles square, including the Seneca settlement on Hog Creek (now Ottawa River), all duly conveyed to them by a government deed dated April 20,

1821. They held an additional tract of 12,800 acres adjoining the east line of the first, conveyed by Section 2 of the treaty of St. Mary's in Ohio on September 7, 1818.

42. Of August 8, 1831 (7 *U.S. Stat.* 335) previously mentioned.

43. *Ibid.*, p. 359. Early government writers and treaty negotiators introduced some confusion into the nomenclature of the field when they spoke of the Miami of the Lake, the Miami of Lake Erie, and the Miami Bay of Lake Erie, which they later indicated as synonymous with Maumee. The fact is that when these treaties were being negotiated there were two Miami rivers in Ohio. In General Anthony Wayne's treaty of 1795 he noted a portage connecting the "Miami of the Ohio with St. Mary's river which is a branch of the Miami which runs into Lake Erie." That emptying into the Ohio was, and still is, the Miami River; the other Miami River, which emptied into Lake Erie, for distinction was called the Miami of the Lake, etc. This river in later years became and still is known as the Maumee.

44. *Doc.*, V, 101. A small party of Indians, impatient of delay, left in April from Dayton for Cincinnati by canal boat and proceeded to St. Louis by the steamboat *Charleston*.

45. *Doc.*, I, 687, 690.

46. *Ibid.*, p. 690.

47. *Ibid.*, p. 692.

48. *Doc.*, IV, 113.

49. Workman's "Journal of Occurrences" (*ibid.*, pp. 78, 111, 117).

50. *Ibid.*, pp. 78, 111, 117, 745.

51. *Doc.*, I, 702.

52. Piqua, named for the Shawnee chief Peckuwe, later known as Old Chillicothe (for Cha-lah-gaw-the, another Shawnee chief) (Thomas Wildcat Alford, *Civilization*, p. 201; but see *Handbook of American Indians*).

53. *Doc.*, I, 704; "Journal of Occurrences" (*Doc.*, IV, 78, 111 ff.). A party of two or three hundred Seneca and Shawnee Indians of this emigration encamped near New Paris in Ohio on their way west. Among them was a white woman a hundred and five years of age who had resided more than a century among these Indians. She had been taken captive when five years old in Green Briar, Virginia, and knew nothing of her former name or relatives (*St. Louis Beacon*, November 15, 1832, p. 1, col. 5).

54. The Dunihue correspondence of 1832, published in the *Indiana Magazine of History*, XXXV, No. 4 (December, 1939), 408-26, contains a number of letters relating to this subject, written by people connected with it; in particular by Daniel R. Dunihue to his brother, Alexander H. Dunihue.

55. *Doc.*, III, 478.

56. *Doc.*, I, 703.

57. *Ibid.*, p. 732.

58. *Ibid.*, p. 704.

59. *Ibid.*, p. 732. In visiting and consoling with each other and getting drunk, the Indians sought a measure of solace and forgetfulness of their sorrow at leaving their homes.

60. They were several days passing through Indianapolis, said the *Democrat* of that city. Detachments had been camped in the vicinity. "Most of them were sober, discreet men, but a few turbulent fellows. A number of the Ottawas went into Canada in preference to going west—influenced by British traders" (*Columbus Sentinel*, October 25, 1832, p. 1, col. 6).

61. *Doc.*, I., 704.

62. *Doc.*, III, 504.

63. *Doc.*, IV, 115.

64. *Ibid.*

65. *Ibid.*, p. 117.

66. There was a lamentable lack of co-ordination between Conductor Gardner and Disbursing Officer Lane, who charged the former with being in a constant state of drunkenness and inattention to duty and said that he was overbearing and inefficient.

Each was incessantly bombarding his superiors in Washington with charges and recriminations against the other that added measurably to the bulk of *Document 512.*

67. *Doc.,* I, 392.

68. *Doc.,* II, 82.

69. *Doc.,* I, 738; Office of Indian Affairs, "Ohio (Emigration) *Accounts,*" Lieut. J. F. Lane, Disbursing Officer (National Archives).

70. *Doc.,* I, 739; Kappler (ed.), *Laws and Treaties,* II, 281.

71. When confronted with an obvious exaggeration of the number entitled to rations, Disbursing Agent Lieutenant Van Horne said: "They looked at each other and laughed and assured me that at the time of their arrival, while in camp, Major Brish directed them to hand in the numbers composing their families at his tent, by notches cut on small sticks, in order to know for how many to obtain provisions. Before doing so, he said, 'we counselled together, and, as our treaty stated our number is about four hundred, we agreed to add to the number composing each of our families as many altogether as would make about 400' " (*Doc.,* I, 928).

72. *Ibid.,* p. 310.

73. *Ibid.,* p. 925. Dr. John T. Fulton, special agent for the removal and subsistence of the Indians, visited the new Seneca country, but Brish's Indians had not yet arrived. However, he later met them thirty-five miles from their destination. He reported that there were 352 Indians in the party after the death of 30 from measles. Another detachment of 48 from Indiana was expected. He was present when 50 Osage warriors convened in council with the new arrivals and pledges of friendship were exchanged (Fulton to Brown, Little Rock, July 15, 1832, Office of Indian Affairs, "1832 (Emigration) Dr. John T. Fulton" [National Archives]).

74. Van Horne to Cass, June 27, 1833, and August 1, 1833, Office of Indian Affairs, "1833 Senecas, West, Lt. J. Van Horne" (National Archives).

75. *Doc.,* I, 397.

76. *Ibid.*

77. *Missouri Intelligencer,* November 12, 1832, p. 2, col. 3; *Arkansas Gazette,* December 12, 1832, p. 3, col. 2.

78. *Doc.,* I, 399.

79. Arrow Rock is southeast of Marshall on the west side of the Missouri River at a narrow place where two ferryboats operated. From here the Osage Trace ran west to Fort Osage. Two months earlier Washington Irving had crossed here on his way to Fort Gibson.

80. *Doc.,* I, 399. Here at Arrow Rock, Abert issued to the Shawnee twenty-three new rifles promised in their treaty.

81. Abert to Cass, January 5, 1833 (*Doc.,* IV, 4-10). How arduous and necessarily infrequent were the contacts between Washington administration and the Indian objects of concern in remote sections are illustrated by the experiences of Colonel J. J. Abert, who left Washington on October 4, 1832, and, traveling by stagecoach, reached Urbana, Ohio, a week later. As the Indians had departed and were not traveling on a stage road, he was obliged to pursue them on horseback. Leaving Urbana on October 13, and traveling as fast as his horse could go, it was twelve days later, on October 25, or three weeks from Washington, that he overtook the emigrants at Hickory Grove, Illinois. His duties performed, he started on his return from the Mississippi River, and after another long and difficult journey he arrived back in Washington on December 30, where he prepared a detailed and illuminating report of that part of the emigration that came within his observation (*ibid.*).

82. Another party of 84 Shawnee left Ohio early in June to travel with their conductor, Joseph Parks, by way of St. Louis, to their western home (*Doc.,* III, 698).

CHAPTER V

OHIO INDIANS

OTTAWA

THE Ottawa Indians at an early date were broken up into a number of bands, dispersed through Ohio, Michigan, and Illinois, and treaties of cession were made by these bands in connection with other tribes with whom they emigrated to the West. Those confederated with the Potawatomi and Chippewa who ceded their lands at the Chicago treaty of 1833 are dealt with in this book elsewhere, as are those who were emigrated in 1832 under James B. Gardner. Other bands removed to Canada, their former home, where their descendants long survived them.

Another branch of the tribe settled on a reservation of thirty-four square miles at the mouth of the Maumee River, whence they became known as the Ottawa of the Maumee, set apart to them by the treaty of September 29, 1817.[1] Directly after the passage of Jackson's Indian Removal Bill, a number of white landowners living in the vicinity of the Ottawa reservation joined in a petition to Lewis Cass to take steps for the purchase of this land and removal of the Indians therefrom, on the ground that it occupied a key position on the river and stood in the way of commercial enterprise of the whites.[2]

However, nothing was attempted immediately with them, though during the next two years four treaties were negotiated with the other Indians of Ohio looking to their removal west of the Mississippi. The treaty of August 30, 1831, related to the Ottawa living on Blanchard's Fork of the Great Auglaize, and those of the Little Auglaize at Oquanoxa's village. It was not until July 4, 1832, that Secretary of War Lewis Cass directed George S. Porter, governor of Michigan Territory, to select a suitable person to visit the Ottawa of the Maumee and confer with them on the subject of selling their lands and removing westward. Pursuant to this authority and further directions from Washington, Governor Porter convened the chiefs and principal men of that band at Maumee on September 21.[3]

At this conference there was considerable sparring and maneuvering for advantage between the Indians and Governor Porter. The Indians were reluctant to say whether they would remove or not until Governor Porter indicated some of the terms to be considered. Porter declined to mention any conditions until the Indians would answer yes or no as to whether they would remove in any event. His attitude, he reported to Secretary of War Cass, was based on the belief that he might drive a sharper bargain with the Indians if he could get them first to say that they would remove. Finally, the governor prevailed, and the Indians said that they would go, under terms to be discussed later and incorporated in the treaty which it was proposed to make with them.

The Indians, however, did establish a few tentative preliminary understandings concerning reservations to be made to individuals of the tribe who wished to remain in Ohio, including an area of a mile and a half square for the members of the Navarre family on Presque Isle lying in the mouth of the Maumee River. Another reservation they insisted on was a piece of land containing the graves of their people, which was to be reserved in the name of Peter Menard, or Yellow Hair. When they emigrated, they wanted this land left in the custody of Menard, that "he might preserve for them the bones of their fathers."[4]

Finally, on February 18, 1833, the Indians were convened at Maumee by Governor Porter, who negotiated with them a treaty of that date[5] in which they gave up the last of their holdings in Ohio and agreed to remove therefrom, though no future home was indicated.

No steps were taken either by the Indians or by the government to remove them from the reservation until September, 1834, when Lieutenant I. P. Simonton was directed to begin their removal. He was not to temporize with the Indians by agreeing to send an exploring party but was supposed to be able to start them from their homes by the simple order to leave. These Indians were not so easily handled as that; and when Simonton came from Detroit to confer with them, they gave the customary answer that they would not go until some of their number could visit the western country where it was proposed to move them. They were much opposed to leaving their homes under any circumstances, and Simonton, who knew their disposition better than the Secretary, conceding the reasonableness of their request, agreed to accompany an exploring party to the West which would return and report to the remaining five hundred members of the tribe. The exploring party, made up of a half-dozen of their leading men, accompanied by Simonton, departed from their home on September 15, 1834.[6] They went by way of Fort Wayne, resting two days at Logansport at the Indian agency. Passing Vandalia on September 29, they reached St. Louis on October 2 and St. Charles three days later. They crossed the Missouri River at Arrow Rock, arrived at Independence on October 13, and at the agency, sixteen miles from Independence, the next day. After ten days in the West, they returned to Maumee, where Simonton reported that the Indians took little interest in their mission and were not inclined to examine the land closely. They were opposed to leaving their homes and were reluctant to comply with any request made by the government.

The attitude of the government assumed that the Indians would pack up and remove to Canada, their earlier habitat, or west of the Mississippi of their own volition, than which nothing was less likely. They continued in their attachment to the old home place; and three years later on April 3, 1837, the Commissioner of Indian Affairs directed Henry R. Schoolcraft, Michigan superintendent of Indian affairs, to interview these Indians on the subject of removal to lands "west of the Mississippi and south of the Missouri," pursuant to their treaty. After conferring with the Indians, Schoolcraft, on April 28, 1837, notified the Commissioner of Indian Affairs that the Ottawa had agreed to emigrate. In the following June, John McElvain was employed to take charge of their movement.

The annuity roll showed that these Indians numbered less than four hundred souls in 1836. In charge of McElvain, two hundred of them departed from Maumee by steamer on August 31, 1837. They were transferred from lake steamer to canal boats at Cleveland, whence they traveled through the Ohio Canal by way of Columbus to Portsmouth on the Ohio River. Here they boarded a large steamer which descended the Ohio and ascended the Mississippi River, arriving at St. Louis on September 22. The journey was completed on a Missouri River steamer, which deposited the party at Chouteau's Landing near Westport, Missouri, and by an overland trip from this point to the Indian lands in the Osage River subagency, which was reached on October 11, 1837.[7] The muster roll submitted by McElvain on November 22 shows 170 emigrants of this party who arrived at the agency. One hundred and fifty or more of the tribe remained in Ohio on public lands in the Maumee Valley, where they were destined for destruction; some, said their agent, went to Canada, where they would eventually freeze and starve to death.

However, the remainder of the tribe, numbering 105, who were amenable to efforts of the government, were placed aboard the steamer *Commodore Perry*, which landed them at Cleveland in July, 1839.[8]

From here they were taken to the Ohio River and placed aboard the *Monsoon*, from whch they debarked at St. Louis on August 14. They then departed overland to the headwaters of the Osage River to join the Ottawa who had preceded them.[9] But, owing to hardships and loss of horses and equipment, they went only as far as the Shawnee agency, where, with permission of their friends, the Shawnee chiefs, they spent the winter before proceeding to their reservation.[10]

Agent Henry R. Schoolcraft reported that a few score of stragglers, uprooted from the soil, had become wanderers on the country which they had formerly owned, in the northwestern angle of Ohio. Here, said the agent, they were likely to perish from intemperance and idleness. At this stage of the business, the people of Ohio felicitated themselves that they were now rid of all the Indians but those who were the next concern of government—the Wyandots.

WYANDOTS

Over a long period at different times the Wyandot (Huron) Indians ceded to the national government their lands in Illinois, Michigan, Indiana, and Ohio. On September 29, 1817, they joined in the treaty of Fort Meigs,[11] by which they surrendered almost the whole of the northwest quarter of the state of Ohio, retaining only four relatively small reservations.

After the passage of Jackson's Indian Removal Bill in 1830, Commissioner James B. Gardner approached them on the subject of giving up the remainder of their land in Ohio on which they were living and emigrating to the West. As they were becoming crowded and oppressed by the white people, some were inclined to comply. First, however, they induced the government to defray the expense of an exploring party to the western country. The party consisted of five Wyandots, conducted by William Walker, an intermarried white citizen of the tribe. They traveled by water, and on October 27, 1831, left Cincinnati aboard the steamboat *New Jersey* for Louisville, and thence proceeded by another steamboat to St. Louis.[12]

During the succeeding winter they examined the country in the northeastern part of Kansas,[13] where they had much sport hunting bear. On their return they made an unfavorable report to the chiefs of the tribe. Their principal indictment of the western country was that it possessed almost no sugar-maple trees which, in Ohio, they had found essential to their sustenance and happiness. The proposed new home of these Indians was objectionable for other reasons: "Fugitives from justice from Virginia, Kentucky, Tennessee and other southern states, the most abandoned, dissolute and wicked class of people they ever saw, formed most of the white population on the border; their country would become an asylum and sanctuary for runaway and vagrant slaves; their neighbor, Missouri, a slave state, would be unfriendly to the Indians as Georgia has been." Slaveholders, they said, "had proved themselves the most merciless oppressors the Indians ever met with among the white population of America," and they feared that their country would be subject to all manner of impositions from the hordes and bands of rambling trappers and bee hunters that infested the country west of Missouri.[14]

It was maintained by Colonel Gardner that the unfavorable report of the Indians was inspired by mercenary white men in Ohio who hoped to profit by the continued propinquity and trade of the Indians as long as they received annuities from the government.[15]

There were numerous factions of the Wyandot tribe living in separate localities who were much divided on the subject of emigration. However, the chiefs of the band residing at Big Spring, Ohio, met Colonel Gardner at McCutcheonsville in Crawford County, January 19, 1832, and entered into a treaty[16] by which they sold to the government for $1.75 per acre 16,000 acres owned by them in Crawford, Seneca, and Hancock counties. Refusing to emigrate at once, they were to remove as soon as they were ready, either to Canada or to Michigan.

Gardner's treaties with the Seneca, Shawnee, and Wyandots in 1831 extinguished Indian title to all land claimed by them in Ohio except what was known as the "Grand Reserve" of 146,316 acres at the Upper Sandusky in Crawford County. It was considered of great importance by the people of Ohio that this reserve also should be bought, and, urged by Governor Lucas, the state legislature adopted a resolution requesting the federal government to make this purchase. Whereupon Congress appropriated $1,000 to defray the expense of a treaty council for that purpose in the summer of 1834.[17] Governor Lucas appointed commissioners, and efforts were made to hold the necessary council, although a number of the Wyandot chiefs were absent at the time, engaged in further examination of the western country to see if they could find a place that would suit them.

No treaty resulted from this council, but the pressure was continued until a small measure of success was achieved by John A. Bryan, who negotiated with the Indians the treaty of April 23, 1836,[18] by which they yielded a small part of their land, but they still held a valuable area coveted by the whites. It was a fertile tract of 109,144 acres, twelve by fourteen miles in extent, lying between Columbus and the shores of Lake Erie. The whites were settling adjacent country, and there was a strong demand to secure this Indian land and put it on the market for sale and settlement. William H. Hunter of Sandusky, a member of Congress, and N. H. Swayne of Columbus were active in efforts to secure this land from the Wyandots.

Negotiations were still pending through 1839. The Indians were skeptical of the representations of government officials, and another exploring party of six, at their own expense, went west to look at the country. Standing three for and three against removal, they could not reach a decision. When the Delawares and Shawnee in the West proposed to sell part of their land to them, the Wyandots, taking it under consideration, and reluctant to commit themselves, sent another group out to look; but they were still unable to reach an agreement.

The last of the Ottawa of the Maumee had departed in 1839, and only the Wyandots remained in Ohio, living on their tract of 109,144 acres in Crawford County. Now in the midst of a populous community of whites, the Indians were suffering from the contact, and their neighbors were unremitting in their efforts to get them out of the country. Finally, on March 26, 1840, Colonel John Johnston was appointed a commissioner to negotiate with the Wyandots. He had much influence with the Indians of this tribe and prevailed on a delegation to meet at Upper Sandusky, where on March 17, 1842, he was successful in securing a treaty with Henry Jacques and other Wyandot chiefs.[19]

No less an observer than Charles Dickens was present a few days later to record what Johnston told him of the proceedings on that occasion. Dickens was traveling by stagecoach through Columbus and Tiffin from Cincinnati to Lake Erie, on his way to Niagara Falls. "At length, between ten and eleven o'clock at night, a few feeble lights appeared in the distance, and Upper Sandusky, an Indian village where we were to stay till morning, lay before us. . . . . It is a settlement of the Wyandot Indians who inhabit this place. Among the company at breakfast was a mild old gentleman [John Johnston], who had been for many years employed by the United States Government in conducting negotiations with the Indians, and who had just concluded a treaty with these people by which they bound themselves, in consideration of a certain annual sum, to remove next year to some land provided for them, west of the Mississippi and a little way beyond St. Louis. He gave me a moving account of their strong attachment to the familiar scenes of their infancy, and in particular to the burial-places of their kindred; and of their great reluctance to leave them. He had witnessed many such removals, and always with pain, though he knew that they departed for their own good. The question whether this tribe should go or stay, had been discussed among them a day or two before, in a hut erected for the purpose, the logs of which still lay upon the ground before the inn. When the speaking was done, the ayes and noes were ranged on opposite sides, and every male adult voted in his turn. The moment the result was known, the minority (a large one) cheerfully yielded to the rest, and withdrew all kind of opposition."[20]

By this treaty the Wyandots released all their remaining 109,144 acres in Crawford County, besides other land in Michigan on the Huron River.[21] In consideration of this cession the government agreed to give them 148,000 acres of land west of the Mississippi River, the location to be determined later, and $10,000 to defray the expense of their migration thither.

The Wyandots proceeded in a business-like way to prepare for the impending change; for nearly a year they were engaged in disposing of property and making other necessary adjustments. Subagent Purdy McElvain reported on March 3, 1843, that they were preparing for an early departure;[22] the Wyandots of Huron River, having removed to Ohio and joined their tribesmen on the Upper Sandusky River, were eager to reach the new home during seasonable weather. Their blacksmiths and other mechanics were busily engaged in preparing wagons and equipment for the journey. The federal government had promised, in the recent treaty, to furnish them the necessary iron, steel, and tools for this purpose, which the agents said had not been fully supplied.

The teamsters began collecting their effects on July 9, to accompany them to Cincinnati, where the Indians were to board the steamboat. They assembled their personal property, and that which the agent decided would encumber the emigration was put up and sold at auction; the unhappy Indians were obliged to see their cherished possessions pass into the hands of white people, along with their homes and farms. It was not until July 12, 1843, McElvain reported, that, with the exception of about fifty persons detained by sickness, they began the hegira.

Their final departure, said McElvain, "was a scene of intense interest to all who witnessed it, and called forth many expressions of deep feeling on the part of the Indians who are leaving the land which has been their home for years; and although many of them have left their nearest friends and relatives slumbering with the silent dead, yet I believe there was not a single instance of obstinate and determined disposition to combat the wishes of the United States in regard to their removal. On the contrary, the most perfect resignation to, and acquiescence in, all that has been required of them by the department, has been manifested from the commencement of their preparations for leaving."[23]

The emigrants, numbering 674 according to official count—the last Indians to leave Ohio—reluctantly departed from their old homes, leaving those who were detained by sickness planning to follow the next spring.[24] Some who were seriously ill, however, were incontinently loaded in wagons and hauled off to Cincinnati.

The Indians passed through Logan, Xenia, and Urbana (according to local newspapers—the *Logan Gazette*, the *Urbana Citizen*, and the *Xenia Torch*—but it is not clear why this roundabout route was chosen) and reached Cincinnati on July 19. The *Logan Gazette* of July 15 says that the company included 125 Wyandots from Michigan and Canada. For transportation the Indians were equipped with buggies, sixty-five wagons, and three hundred horses and ponies, all owned by them, supplemented by fifty-five hired wagons.

At Urbana the chiefs left the tribe and proceeded to Columbus, where Chief Jacques addressed the governor in a formal and florid leave-taking of the people of Ohio, to which the governor replied in kind.[25]

The editor of a Cincinnati paper observed the Indians passing through the city: "A remnant of this tribe from Crawford County, Ohio, about 650 in number, passed our windows this morning in a long train of wagons and horses, about to embark for the far west. Perhaps they are indifferent, and we hope they are, but we could not help thinking the spectacle a melancholy one. Just civilized enough to have lost their savage courage, they go forth on the broad prairies of the west like sheep among wolves. From the light complexions of four-fifths of the party we judge that in ten years more, had they remained in Ohio, all traces of the Indian would have disappeared by the process of amalgamation. Among them are white women, apparently the wives of very respectable Indians." The extreme warm weather distressed the Indians greatly, and "one of the party, a squaw, was buried yesterday between this city and Lebanon."[26]

While waiting to be embarked on steamboats, they were located for the night near a boat-landing within easy access of the white man with his inevitable supply of whiskey, which apparently the authorities took no adequate measures to keep from the Indians. One Wyandot, a fine-looking fellow, became so drunk that, while boarding the boat, he fell over the rail and was drowned. The Indians—men, women, and children—loaded on two steamboats, *Republic* and *Nodaway*, began the second stage of their melancholy journey on July 20. They descended the Ohio River and passed the tomb of General William Henry Harrison situated on an eminence at North Bend, Ohio, overlooking the river. "Many of their braves had fought under the General in the last war, and several had distinguished themselves at the Battle of Fort Meigs. For the memory of the 'White Chief' as they called him, they cherished the greatest devotion. They were in number six hundred and thirty men, women and children. On nearing the hallowed spot the principal chief requested Captain Claghorn to have the 'big gun' loaded. It was done. Meantime the chiefs and braves silently gathered upon the hurricane roof and formed in line, fronting the resting place of their departed chief. The engine was stopped, and the boat was suffered to drift with the current. As they passed the tomb, they all uncovered, and gently waved their hats in silence; and after the boat had passed, and the report of the cannon had passed away, the chief stepped forward, and in an impressive manner exclaimed, 'Farewell, Ohio, and her brave.' "[27]

The emigrants disembarked at St. Louis on July 24, and boarded two Missouri River boats that landed them on July 28 and July 31 at the mouth of the Kansas River. They first camped on the Fort Leavenworth military reservation on the east bank of the Kansas River. In 1844 their agent reported about a hundred deaths within the year from the hardships, change of climate, sickness and intemperance, and the unhealthful location in which they found themselves.[28]

When the Wyandots were debarked from the boats in Kansas, the government had not yet kept its agreement to designate their new reservation; and, failing to find any other location that suited, the Delaware Indians offered to sell them part of their country, which sale was consummated, as evidenced by an interesting document executed at an open council of the Indians on December 14, 1843. This instrument recited:

"WHEREAS from a long and intimate acquaintance and an ardent friendship which has for a great many years existed between the Delawares and the Wyandotts, and from a mutual desire that the same feeling should continue, and be more strengthened by becoming near neighbors to each other, therefore the said parties, the Delawares on the one side and the Wyandotts on the other, in full council assembled, have agreed and do agree to the following stipulation, to-wit:

"ARTICLE 1. The Delaware Nation of Indians residing between the Missouri and Kansas rivers being very anxious to have their uncles the Wyandotts to settle and reside near them. . . . ."

The Delaware Indians thus conveyed to the Wyandots thirty-nine sections of land off the east end of their reservation within the present Wyandot County, Kansas.[29] For this land the Wyandots were to pay the Delawares $46,080—$6,080 in cash and $4,000 annually for ten years.[30]

This transaction was not ratified by the government for several years, and in the meantime the Wyandots waited in suspense and uncertainty. The purchase had been conceived and negotiated by shrewd members of the tribe who had the vision to discern the great commercial possibilities of the location at the fork of the Kansas and Missouri rivers. Their agent said that they bargained with the Delawares without consulting the wishes of their people, with the expectation that they would be able to sell the land to the government in a few years at a greatly advanced price. The land, he said, was "beautiful, high-rolling, and decidedly the best site for a city and port which I have seen on the Mississippi or Missouri rivers." The future Kansas City was well within the vision of these Wyandot leaders.

The situation was an unfortunate one, however. A depraved class of white people made a business of selling whiskey to the Indians, many of whom became the degraded victims of intemperance. In this they shared the fate of many other aborigines living near white people. They spent their time in riotous dissipation, and the Missouri laws offered no remedy; for under those laws, said the agent, the testimony of an Indian could not be heard in the courts of the state against that of a white man; and, no matter how flagrant the offense, the white man had little fear of conviction on the charge of selling whiskey to an Indian. However, the Reverend James Peery established a Methodist church in the tribe; and a temperance society and two schools began to exercise a wholesome influence on the 565 surviving Wyandots who composed it. They were raising crops of corn, beans, potatoes, and other vegetables on the new land just opened up by them.

NOTES

1. 7 *U.S. Stat.* 160.
2. *Doc.*, II, 87.
3. *Doc.*, III, 472.
4. *Ibid.* Presque Isle is now covered with ore docks and other structures identified with Toledo's river and lake commerce.
5. 7 *U.S. Stat.* 420.
6. "Report of I. P. Simonton," Records of the Department of the Interior, Office of Indian Affairs, "Ottaways—1835" (National Archives).
7. Letter from National Archives, April 17, 1942.
8. *Cleveland Herald*, copied in *Cincinnati Daily Gazette*, August 1, 1839, p. 2, col. 4.
9. *Niles' National Register*, September 7, 1839, p. 32; *Louisville Journal*, August 20, 1839, p. 2, col. 1.
10. *Doc.*, IV, 9. See *Report of the Commissioner of Indian Affairs, 1841*, pp. 252, 308.
11. 7 *U.S. Stat.*, 160.
12. *Doc.*, III, 640.
13. *Ibid.*, pp. 153 and 168.
14. *Ibid.*, p. 167.
15. *Ibid.*, p. 472.
16. 7 *U.S. Stat.* 364; *Doc.*, III, 530, 542 ff.
17. 4 *U.S. Stat.* 678.
18. 7 *U.S. Stat.* 502.
19. *Report, 1841*, p. 252; *Report of Secretary of War, 1842*, p. 191; Kappler (ed.), *Laws and Treaties*, II, 395; 9 *U.S. Stat.* 581.
20. Charles Dickens, *American Notes* (Chicago, 1885), p. 398. "The attachment of the Wyandots was ardent for their native country. The night they agreed to give it up, many of the chiefs shed tears," said John Johnston, who negotiated the treaty (*Recollections of John Johnston*, p. 47).
21. *House Executive Doc. 11* (27th Cong., 3d sess.), p. 191; Kappler (ed.), *op. cit.*, p. 395; 11 *U.S. Stat.* 581; *Report, 1842*, p. 191.
22. McElvain to Crawford, March 3, 1843, Records of Department of the Interior, Office of Indian Affairs, "Wyandot—1843 (M-1627)" (National Archives). The agent said that all the Wyandots were Methodists and that two of them were preachers (*Doc.*, II, 510). Methodism was said to have been introduced in the tribe by a Negro (see Johnston's *Memoirs*) named John Steward, a "free man" from Virginia (*History of American Missions*, p. 533. In 1819 the Ohio Conference sent preachers to his assistance (Horace Jewell, *History of Methodism in Arkansas*, p. 390).
23. McElvain to Crawford, July 12, 1843, Records of the Department of the Interior, Office of Indian Affairs, "Wyandot—1843 (M-1761)" (National Archives).
24. *Report, 1843*, p. 269.
25. This obviously staged function was reported by the press that presented the addresses in stilted language and spurious terms of sentiment and mutual regard. Newspaper accounts referred to herein were collected and presented in a body by *Niles' National Register*, August 26, 1843, pp. 414 and 415. There was great jubilation in Ohio over this final expulsion of the last remaining Indians from the state and the prospective placing on the market of a great area of desirable real estate.
26. *Cincinnati Daily Chronicle*, July 17, 1843.
27. *St. Louis Republican*, July 25, 1843, copied in *Cincinnati Daily Chronicle*, July 31, 1843. This account was copied by Thomas L. McKenney in his *Memoirs with Sketches of Travels among the Indians*, Part III, pp. 89, 90; also in *Niles' Register*, August 26, 1843, p. 415.
28. *Report, 1844*, p. 444.
29. Records of the Department of the Interior, Office of Indian Affairs, "Letters Received, Wyandots, 1843" (National Archives).
30. Kappler (ed.), *op. cit.*, p. 793.

CHAPTER VI

POTAWATOMI

THE Potawatomi, who ranged over Ohio, Indiana, Michigan, and Illinois, invoked more legislative and administrative concern than any other northern tribe. Prior to the enactment of the Indian Removal Bill of May 28, 1830, eighteen treaties had been made with various divisions of this tribe, generally for the purpose of securing cessions of their domain and of limiting them to reservations progressively less in area. Following the passage of Jackson's bill, Congress, on July 9, 1832, made an appropriation to finance the holding of further treaties looking to the extinction of all Indian titles in Illinois, Indiana, and Michigan Territory.[1] During the next five years seventeen more treaties were made to secure cession of the remaining Potawatomi lands in Indiana, Illinois, and Michigan Territory and the removal of the Indians west of the Mississippi.

The Reverend Isaac McCoy had conducted an exploring company of Potawatomi and Ottawa Indians that left St. Louis on August 19, 1828. They traveled west and crossed the Missouri line at the intersection with the Osage River. They went up that stream, then southwest across the Neosho to a point 127 miles west of the mouth of the Kansas River, then east along the Santa Fe Trail, and north to the Kansas River. After friendly visits with the Osage, Kansas, Pawnee, and Shawnee, and an absence of forty-nine days,[2] they returned to St. Louis on October 9. The Indians were well impressed with this country except for its bleak lack of sugar-maple trees. They were prepared to cope with hardships, but they found it difficult to face a life void of sugar camps.

Commissioners appointed by the President convened a council at Camp Tippecanoe, Indiana, with the Indians there, designated as the "Potawatomie Tribe of Indians of the Prairie and Kankakee," and on October 20, 1832, made a treaty[3] with them, by which they surrendered to the United States the land in eastern Illinois bounded on the east by the Indiana line and on the west by the Illinois and Kankakee rivers, including the southeast corner of Cook County, most of Iroquois County, and parts of Ford and Vermilion counties.

Reservations of from one to five sections of land each were made to twenty-two individuals of the tribe on Thorn Creek, at Soldier's Village, Little Rock Village, Twelve-Mile Grove, Hickory Grove, Skunk Grove, and other places. A promise of an annuity of $15,000 for the term of fifteen years was included. Provision was made for paying $28,746 to thirty-three white men to satisfy unpaid claims, and to the Indians the further sum of $45,000 in merchandise[4] immediately after signing the treaty. The sum of $30,000 was to be paid them at Chicago in the year 1833. An additional sum of $1,000 was to be paid to twenty-one Potawatomi who fought in the Black Hawk War on the side of the United States to reimburse them for horses stolen during their service. It was also provided that, in consideration of their help in the war, the Indians were to be allowed to hunt and fish on the Wabash and Sangamon rivers in the ceded land as long as it should belong to the United States.

The commissioners at Tippecanoe also, on October 26, 1832, negotiated with the Wabash and Elkhart Potawatomi for their right of soil west of the Michigan Road in Indiana; and the next day with the St. Joseph, Cold Water, Wabash, and Elkhart Potawatomi Indians[5] for their land in Indiana and Illinois and in Michigan south of Grand River, except small reservations to bands and individuals in Indiana and east of the Illinois River in Illinois. For this cession the Indians were promised an annuity of $15,000 for twelve years; $42,000 in goods; payment of debts to traders, a schedule of which was attached to the treaty, amounting to $20,721; and the sum of $2,000 for the education of Potawatomi youth. After the signing of the treaty, at the request of the Indians, $2,700 was taken from the fund set up for the purchase of merchandise and diverted to the purchase of horses.

Governor Reynolds of Illinois had charged that all the Potawatomi had joined with the Sauk in hostilities against the whites in the Black Hawk War, which some of the tribe deeply resented; and they were supported by officials of the Indian Department in their denials. They were not well treated by the whites, and in December, 1832, a band of two hundred Prairie Potawatomi in a distressed condition left Illinois, crossed into Indiana, and camped near Logansport. Their neighbors spoke highly of them and particularly of their chief, Qui-qui-to, a man of fine character. The agent reported that they were strictly pious and totally abstained from the use of intoxicating liquors. They were industrious and engaged in hunting for a living, asking of the whites only a little bread. As soon as the grass should be high enough to sustain their horses, they wished to emigrate west of the Mississippi, if the government would provide them a few horses, a little provision, a white conductor, and the agency interpreter, who was an educated full-blood and a pious person, to go with them as far as the "Big Water."

The government dealt with the Potawatomi at times somewhat as three separate tribes: those of Indiana, of Illinois, and of Michigan Territory. An important division of the tribe confederated with bands of Chippewa and Ottawa lived on the Illinois River and its tributaries. It required seven successive treaties to secure from this confederacy the various and extensive areas in Illinois and Indiana that they reluctantly gave up. The last of these was that negotiated in Chicago in 1833, in which they parted with the remaining vestiges of their lands in Illinois and such intangible claims as they had to other lands in Indiana and Michigan Territory.

Negotiations had been carried on with the Potawatomi of Indiana to arrange for a meeting at Logansport, in the summer of 1833, when a faction of the Indians in that state agreed to organize and be removed to the West, to join the Kickapoo Prophet and his people. However, when the time came, the Indians could not command the resolution to embark on such a radical change in their lives, and most of them returned to their homes.[6] As an alternative, it was agreed to send an exploring delegation to examine the western country, under direction of United States officials. They proceeded almost to St. Louis, when reports of cholera in that city so alarmed the Indians that they refused to go farther.

An interminable amount of official correspondence resulted from the failure of the anticipated emigration, by which numerous responsible officials sought to explain the results and exculpate themselves in the face of tremendous pressure by the white people of Indiana, who were trying to get the Indians out of their state. However, the officials did succeed in organizing a small party of Potawatomi for removal. There were supposed to be 140 ready to start, but, by the time the removal agent was prepared to begin the journey, the number had dwindled to 68. The others had mounted their horses and said that they were going by way of Pickamink, their former residence, to recover some property they had cached there. The remainder of the party, in charge of Lewis H. Sands, left Logansport on July 27, reaching Danville, Illinois, four days later. Continuing by way of Charleston, they reached Vandalia on August 9 and eventually arrived in Alton on August 14, where they boarded the steamboat *Otto*, which landed them at Fort Leavenworth on August 26.[7]

After the abortive exploring adventure, when the delegation was turned back by the cholera near St. Louis, Colonel A. C. Pepper, special agent for Potawatomi removal, went to Chicago in August to attempt reorganization of the movement for their emigration. In the meantime, during the summer, messages and invitations had been sent out from the Chicago agency soliciting the Indians in that region to participate in another council, entailing, of course, presents and an abundance of the kind of food and drink that the government lavished on the red men when trying to secure their consent to land cessions. As a result, Pepper witnessed large numbers of men, women, and children gathered at the rough little village of Chicago, come to eat the food dispensed by the agent and hear what the officers present had to say to them.

For weeks the place was crowded with Indians who gave themselves up to feasting, dancing, and festivity. Companies of old warriors could be seen, sitting under every bush, smoking, arguing, palavering and powwowing with great earnestness. There seemed no possibility of getting them to convene in a regular council to consider the business for which the white men had come.

Meanwhile, the village and its occupants presented a motley scene. Fort Dearborn contained within its palisades a little knot of officers attached to the slender garrison. The quarters of the fort were too limited to afford residence for the Indian commissioners, for whom, together with their retinue, a temporary set of huts were erected on the north side of the river.

Besides the chiefs and warriors, there were thousands of other Indians present. As food was to be furnished by the government, the women and children were there to share in the bounty. Attracted by the funds that would be put into circulation, all kinds of parasites collected. Horse-traders and horse thieves; rogues of every description—white, black, brown, and red; sharpers of every degree; peddlers and grog-sellers; Indian agents and commissioners; and contractors to supply the Indians with food were all there. The settlement was in a tumult from early morning until far into the night, for during the hours of darkness, when the housed portion of the population of Chicago strove to obtain rest in the crowded makeshift buildings of the village, the Indians howled, sang, wept, yelled, and whooped in their various encampments.

A visitor to Chicago on this occasion found the settlement so crowded that it was with great difficulty he secured a place to sleep.

"The Pottawattomies were encamped on all sides—on the wide, level prairie beyond the scattered village, beneath the shelter of the low woods which chequered them, on the side of the small river, or to the leeward on the sand hills near the beach of the lake. They consisted of three principal tribes, with certain adjuncts from smaller tribes. The main divisions were the Pottawatomi of the prairie and those of the forest, and these were again subdivided into villages under their several chiefs. A preliminary council had been held with the chiefs which had been opened by the commissioner, stating that as their great father in Washington had heard that they wished to sell their land, he had sent a commissioner to treat with them." The Indians promptly answered that "their great father in Washington must have seen a bad bird which had told him a lie, for that, far from wishing to sell their land, they wished to keep it."[8] Nevertheless, the commissioner told them to consider the subject, and the meeting adjourned.

On September 21 the Indians agreed to enter into conference with the commissioners. The council fire was lighted under a spacious open shed on the green meadow on the opposite side from that on which the fort stood. Here the negotiations continued day after day.

An early resident of Chicago was Judge John Dean Caton, who witnessed this scene and described it in an address to the Chicago Historical Society on December 13, 1870, which was later published and is now a collector's item. Judge Caton said that he was a daily attendant upon the deliberations of the council. "At the close of each important deliberation, especially if much progress seemed to have been made, a keg of twisted plug tobacco was rolled into the council house, the staves cut in the middle with an ax, and the chiefs told to help themselves. This was accompanied with a box of white clay pipes. They helped themselves with great decorum, and even some ceremony."[9]

Finally, on September 26, the treaty was formally entered into between the commissioners—G. B. Porter, T. J. V. Owen, and William Weatherford—and seventy-nine Indians of the "United Nation of Chippewa, Ottawa and Potawatamie Indians," by which they ceded to the United States their last holding in Illinois.

The cession included all their land along the western shore of Lake Michigan, between the lake and the lands ceded to the United States by the Winnebago Nation at the treaty of Fort Armstrong, made on September 15, 1832, bounded on the north by the country lately ceded by the Menominee, and on the south by the country ceded by the Potawatomi in the treaty of Prairie du Chien, made on July 29, 1829, supposed to contain five million acres in Illinois and adjoining Wisconsin. The cession embraced all of Lake, McHenry, and Boone counties, the eastern fraction of Winnebago County, and northern portion of Ogle, DeKalb, Kane, and Cook counties.

This land, near the future Chicago, was now becoming valuable, and for their cession the government agreed to pay individual Potawatomi, Ottawa, and Chippewa Indians $100,000 in lieu of reservations; $175,000 to satisfy claims against them of traders and other persons; $150,000 for the erection of mills, houses, agricultural implements, and other conveniences in their new home; $100,000 in goods and provisions; $280,000 in annuities of $14,000 a year for twenty years; and $70,000 for education in their new home, besides other and smaller cash allotments.

This treaty with the "United Nation of Chippewa, Ottowa and Potawatami Indians" provided for assigning them a tract of five million acres on the northeastern side of the Missouri River which, when adapted to the subsequent survey of Iowa, became a band of country approximately one hundred miles wide, extending from the northern to the southern boundary of that state. This land had been acquired from the Sauk and Fox Indians by the treaty of July 15, 1830.

These Potawatomi agreed in the treaty to remove to their new reservation within three years, as soon as they could get ready, and the government would prepare to remove them. But still they could not bring themselves to abandon their cherished home. Permitted by the treaty to remain and hunt on the ceded land for three years, they availed themselves of all the privileges it permitted. Those of Michigan continued to hunt and, in season, to set up sugar camps and enjoy the succulent maple sugar which they grieved to know could not be had in their western home.[10]

Efforts were unremitting to remove the Indians of the Potawatomi, Ottawa, and Chippewa confederacy. A few small parties went in 1834 and located first near Fort Leavenworth on the reservation of their friends the Kickapoo, lately removed from Missouri and Illinois. Congress, on March 3, 1835, appropriated $9,453 for expenses of sending another exploring party of fifty Potawatomi to the proposed country west of the Mississippi River, pursuant to the Chicago treaty.[11] The party was conducted by Captain William Gordon through the country beyond and north of the northwestern corner of Missouri, to view the five-million-acre tract proposed for their new home.[12]

Plans were made in March, 1835, and orders given for Agent T. I. V. Owen and Captain J. B. F. Russell as disbursing officer to conduct to their western home as many Potawatomi as could be induced to depart that year.

To observe the occasion properly, receive their annuity, and make their final farewell to their old home, about five thousand Indians assembled in Chicago in the summer, and "a great war dance was performed by about eight hundred of the braves who could be mustered from among the five thousand persons." This dance, says Judge Caton, who witnessed it, "was the last ever performed on the ground where Chicago now stands, and took place about the last of August, 1835. The Indians appreciated it as the last on their native soil, that it was a sort of funeral ceremony of old associations and memories, and nothing was omitted to lend to it all the grandeur and solemnity possible."

They assembled at the Council House on the north side of the river, and Judge Caton describes the savage customs and the decorations they bestowed upon their persons. "These eight hundred men danced as they went, to the din of hideous noises produced by beating on hollow vessels and striking sticks and clubs together. They proceeded west, up and along the bank of the river on the north side, stopping in front of every house they passed to perform some of their grotesque movements. They finally crossed the north branch of the river and proceeded along the west side of the south branch to the vicinity of the present Lake Street, where they performed in front of the Sauganash Hotel, which site became the ground later occupied by the Wigwam, where Lincoln was nominated, at the corner of Lake and Market streets."

Instead of the thousand emigrants it was hoped would begin the march, only 712 were ready to depart in charge of Owen and Russell. When, on December 2, they reached the Little Platte River in the present western Missouri, they stopped and joined their brethren who had gone out the year before and refused to continue to their reservation at Council Bluffs. Here they remained on government rations until President Van Buren's proclamation in 1837 made the area part of Missouri.[13]

A party of these Indians spent the winter of 1835–36 on Skunk River near the Mississippi. After they resumed their journey through Missouri, white horse thieves raided their camp; in an effort to recover the stolen horses, whites and Indians were killed.[14]

In the spring of 1836 removal of the Potawatomi was resumed under the direction of Agent Gholson Kurcheval, with Captain J. B. F. Russell as disbursing agent, but only a few hundred could be induced to depart from Illinois. The next year efforts were renewed, and Indians recruited from Niles, Michigan, and the Kankakee River rendezvoused at the Des Plaines River west of Chicago. From here these Indians took their departure under the superintendency of Lewis H. Sands, with Captain Robert A. McCabe as conductor of the party. In order to get the emigrating Indians away from the influence of Chicago traders and whiskey sellers, they were marched about sixty miles southwest to Shabenay's Grove before their treaty money and supplies were issued to them. Here a roll was prepared that showed their number to be 497. Six families, numbering fifty people, traveled independently. Lieutenant John T. Sprague of the regular army joined the party as special disbursing agent, and in his official reports he severely criticized Sands's management and the extravagance of the operation, which included more than a dozen employees on the pay roll.

They went by way of Knoxville, Illinois, to Quincy, where they began crossing the Mississippi on September 24. Their journey through Missouri was attended by much hardship and hazard. Excessive rains had raised to unprecedented heights the intervening streams, which they were able to cross only on extemporized bridges, occasional little boats, and rafts. One time, said Sands, they waded for a mile through water waist deep. Through Missouri they went by way of Huntsville, Nichnabotnay River, Krytnesville, Carrolton, and Richmond, reaching Liberty on November 18. They started with two hundred ponies and twelve wagons loaded to capacity with the Indians' personal belongings, which Sands had not the heart to deny them. From excessive toil and inadequate forage many of the riding horses gave out in Missouri, and 160 of the emigrants left the main party, taking the short route to the Osage River to join some of their brothers who had recently gone from Indiana. Here they were received by Indian Agent Anthony L. Davis. A number of Indians had died on the march, and the remaining 287 were conducted to the Council Bluffs agency.[15]

On the march through Missouri the Indians worked themselves into a rebellious mood and, from resentment at their treatment and fear of attacks at night by wild Indians, began talking about mutiny and escape. "But a strange piece of good fortune intervened; on the horizon appeared a cloud of dust and an attendant rode ahead to investigate . . . . hoping something might develop to divert the Indians and save the lives of the white men in charge of the emigrants. He found a team of schooner wagons conveying a circus company to a town on the Mississippi River. There were the clowns, male and female trapeze performers, a snake performer, wild animals of which the monkeys seemed most fascinating. The company was induced to pitch their tents and give a performance and exhibition for the red men, who were so fascinated that they forgot their grievances. One feature that particularly delighted the Indians was the singing by the clown of the song 'The Long Tailed Blue.' "[16]

It may have been the same circus company farther along the route, which, while traveling through Kansas during extremely dry weather, chanced to cross a stream of inviting water, when the elephants, nearly ecstatic with joy, plunged in, frolicking and tumbling in the water, deaf to all commands to come out and continue the journey, until the owners nearly despaired.

In the summer of the next year another small number were organized for removal. They were assembled on the Des Plaines River west of Chicago, pending the start on July 15. A. C. Pepper of Logansport, Indiana, was appointed to superintend the removal of this party, and Lieutenant J. T. Sprague attended as disbursing officer.[17] Instead of the large number expected, however, only 151 were reported as removed this year, leaving about two thousand still to be taken west, as conjectured by Commissioner of Indian Affairs Crawford, who was not clear at this stage as to the further steps of his department, inasmuch as the treaty provided for removal only "so fast as they may be prepared for emigration." The Indians maintained that it remained with them to say when they would start. But Crawford thought that, having been allowed four years in which to remove, and the government having been ready all that time, there was no justification for indulging the Indians further.[18]

Crawford's perplexity was increased by the vacillating policy of the government. These Indians had scarcely begun to occupy their reservation in Iowa when the government approached them on the subject of giving it up in view of impending erection of Iowa Territory, which eventuated on June 12, 1838. The government had made treaties in 1836 with certain Potawatomi chiefs in Indiana, and another in Washington, by which they ceded the remainder of their lands in that state in consideration of a reservation on the Osage River in the present Kansas, to which point efforts were under way to remove the remainder of the Potawatomi tribe just settled in Iowa.

The subagent for the Potawatomi, from his station at Council Bluffs, reported in 1837 the arrival of a detachment of his Indians who came up to their reservation in Iowa by the Missouri River steamboat *Howard*. When they landed, they encamped with a former party just debarked from the steamboat *Kansas* in a grove adjacent to a fine tract of prairie. Here they were joined in a few days by the main body of the nation from Chicago that had been twenty-three days with General Atkinson on the march by land from the Black Snake Hills on the Platte Purchase.[19]

The Commissioner of Indian Affairs reported in November, 1838, that movement of the Potawatomi, Ottawa, and Chippewa living near Chicago was under way, leaving nearly fifteen hundred yet to be removed.[20] But the Potawatomi of Indiana obstinately refused to leave their old homes, despite the fact that they had conveyed their land to the United States. White men had settled on the ceded land while the Indians remained there, and collisions arose that threatened the peace of the country and possibly the spilling of blood. Surrounded by whites, the Indians were in a deplorable condition, and subsistence from government was to cease at the end of the year.

By their treaty of 1836 these Indians had retained the right to remain on the ceded land for two years. This period had expired on August 5, 1838, but the Indians refused to yield possession to the whites, hoping that a new law would be negotiated that would save them from immediate removal. When August 5 arrived, the day the Indians were to leave, the whites demanded possession and the Indians obstinately refused. Collisions ensued, violence developed, and the whites burned ten or twelve Indian cabins, thus further aggravating the situation.

Chief Menominee[21] and other leaders were under the influence of lawyers, who advised them to retain possession, in the interest of traders, to whom the Indians were in debt, and who hoped to continue profitable relations with their debtors by keeping them in the country.

The whites, determined to temporize no longer, demanded that the agent take steps to begin the removal and that the governor raise the necessary force of men to carry it out and put them in possession of the Indian land. Agent Pepper accordingly called on the governor of Indiana, David Wallace, father of General Lew Wallace, for a detail of troops.

Governor Wallace authorized General John Tipton to raise a force of one hundred men, who quickly and gladly responded and assembled in the vicinity of Menominee near Twin Lakes, Marshall County, Indiana, where they organized to drive the Indians out of the country. Pepper sent out word to the Indians to meet him at a pretended council on August 28. Not knowing that they were being decoyed, the Indians came, and when between three and four hundred had assembled, Tipton's little army surrounded the village and made them all prisoners. Tipton then proceeded to the church, where other Indians were engaged in worship, and made his presence known by firing guns, surrounding the church, and making prisoners of the people within.[22]

Various accounts have been written of this tragic enterprise. A writer in the *Indiana Magazine* says that the Indians "pled for mercy and to be let alone, but all to no effect. . . . . When evening came and they did not return home, others were sent out in search of them and they too were made prisoners. All of them were held under guard while troops were scouring the reservation for others and destroying their houses. They also rounded up about four hundred ponies that were to be used in their journey.

"Many tragic scenes were enacted in this round-up. Some fought like demons till they were overpowered and roped; some went in hiding, others sought shelter in Michigan. In one case where they had surrounded the hut and called on the Indian to surrender, he sprang for his tomahawk and rifle and when he saw the cross, which the priest wore, he threw down his weapons, crossed his arms and held them out to be tied. This work was kept up until they had gathered near fifteen hundred and had placed 859 names on the roll. Their priest, Father Petit, was permitted to assemble them for a final service. He says:

" 'At the moment of my departure I assembled all my children to speak to them for the last time. I wept and they sobbed aloud. It was a sorrowful sight and over this, our dying mission, we prayed for the success of those missions that they would establish in their new home to which they were being driven.'

"On the Sunday before their departure, they were visited by many whites who came to bid them farewell. No doubt there were some in that assemblage whose consciences were not at rest. On the last day they were permitted, under guard, to visit the graves of their departed friends, and held an impressive service; heart-rending scenes that were indescribable were witnessed. General Tipton went prepared with wagons and hired teams of horses and oxen. In the meantime these were being loaded with their goods such as would be needed, the old, sick of which there were over one hundred, the women and children.

"On September 4, 1838, they were lined up, some afoot, some on ponies, followed by the wagons, and all heavily guarded with guards at the rear with bayonets, which were often used to keep the weak ones in the procession. Before starting the torch was applied to their village, so that they might see their homes destroyed and they would not want to return. When all was in readiness, this grewsome procession, nearly three miles long, like a funeral procession, which in reality it was, started on its final journey. It was a very sickly season. The sun was hot and the road was dusty. They drove down the Michigan road to Chippewa on the Tippecanoe [River] where they camped the night of the fourth. Here their cup of sorrow was made to overflow. They wished to take their dead with them, and when this was denied, they had to leave them at the roadside or camping ground; hence every camping ground was a burial ground.

"In making preparations for this expedition it was thought a picnic by the volunteer guards, many of whom were turned away, but at the end of the first day, twenty of the troops, heat-sick, stole twenty of the Indians' ponies and deserted the command."[23]

The official journal of this unhappy enterprise was kept by William Polke, the conductor of the party. With 296 horses and 26 wagons the Indians began their march on September 4, says Polke. By the time they were ready to start, a number were found to be too ill to travel and were left behind near the ashes of their old homes, to catch up when they could. The first day of travel was distressing. The weather was exceedingly hot and sultry, and the roads were choked with dust. After proceeding twenty-one miles they camped; but in the morning fifty-one were unable to travel, and, as there were not wagons enough to haul the sick people, they were left behind with a number to wait on them. The scarcity of water added to their discomfort; a child died in the evening and was buried in the morning. An infant was born that night.

As they continued their unhappy journey, an infant died on the seventh and another the next day. Several scores of persons who had been left behind caught up with the main party, but on the ninth a doctor who was called in reported three hundred cases of sickness, for which he prescribed. "A kind of medical hospital," the conductor reported, had been erected for the care of the sick. Another child died this day. "A priest formerly attached to this tribe (Father Petit) obtained leave to say mass among the Indians, which he did, to the comfort of the Potawatomi." Two children died this day.

Notwithstanding the sickness, the party started off again at ten o'clock on the tenth, leaving behind twenty-one sick with attendants. They camped on the banks of the Wabash, where a man and a child died. There were no deaths on the eleventh, and on the twelfth they crossed the Tippecanoe battleground and camped. This day a woman more than a hundred years old, mother of We-wis-sa, one of the chiefs, died. Here $5,469.81 worth of blankets, calicoes, cloaks, etc., were distributed to the Indians.

On the thirteenth, two physicians who were called in reported 160 cases of sickness of malarial fever. On the fourteenth the conductor reported that "persons through weariness and fatigue take sick along the route. This occupies much of our time. We place them in the wagons which are every day becoming more crowded. Reached our camp ground near Williamsport at 4 P.M. As we advance farther into the country of the prairies, water becomes more scarce—the streams are literally dried up." Two persons died in the evening. Nearly all the deaths occurred after the end of the day's march and while the Indians were in camp. However, the next day two small children died along the road.

On Sunday, the sixteenth, they started at eight o'clock, after leaving seven persons ill in camp, among the number a woman who was about to be confined. This day, during a march of fifteen miles, at Williamsport they crossed the line into Illinois and camped on the Big Vermilion River west of Danville, about three o'clock. "The heat," reported the conductor, "along with the dust is daily rendering our marches more distressing. The horses are jaded, the Indians sickly," and many of the government employees engaged in the emigration more or less ailing. It was a sickly season and a sickly country; the whole land through which these unfortunate people had to travel was afflicted, the conductor reported; every town, village, and hamlet had its invalids. In the little town of Danville near which they camped, four persons died the day before their arrival. Father Petit, whose ministrations comforted the Indians, rejoined them here.

While in camp at Danville, an observer wrote for the *Terre Haute Courier* an account copied in the *Washington Globe* of October 23,

1838: "No man can look upon these poor creatures without lamenting the inevitable necessity which drives them from the homes of their fathers. They are certainly forced away from them at this time, and yet I question if their more judicious and sincere friends will not rejoice at it. If they had lingered much longer, more would have fallen a prey to the hand of violence than can now, by any possibility, die in the attempt to go West at so inauspicious a season of the year. Some affecting scenes have taken place in the camp since and before the Indians were got under way. One chieftain had a mother upwards of a hundred years old, over whom a consultation was held whether or not it would be better to put her to death before she started [one suspects that the reporter was romancing or his credulity was imposed on] as no hopes of her long surviving could reasonably be entertained. Fortunately humane counsels prevailed, and the poor creature died and was buried after a journey of four days.

"Two children were born on Friday night last, and are doing well, notwithstanding they were the next day (as is the Indian custom) strapped on a board and carried behind their mothers on an Indian pony. Others have been compelled to leave a wife after them in one place, and a child in another, in consequence of sickness; and some have had to bury, far removed from their native hunting grounds or from the promised land of their adoption in the West, their nearest and dearest kindred.

"These things of course must excite our sympathies; but how can they be avoided considering all things? They are treated with all possible kindness by the amiable conductor [Judge Polke] and those under him; but yet to see eight hundred poor, half clothed, hatless, breechless creatures in a single file, choked with dust and suffocated with heat, mounted on poor, half-starved Indian ponies, is a sight no man of sensibility can look upon unmoved or with composure."

On Monday, September 17, they left Danville at nine o'clock and traveled six miles to Sandusky Point, where they camped early on account of the distress of the people.[24] An interpreter for a party of sick people who were left behind arrived in camp with his company which had been increased by the birth of an infant. Here a young child died in camp. The Potawatomi in the company now numbered 859, who were still accompanied by "volunteers" or militiamen of a flexible number, at one time as many as 97, to guard the Indians and prevent escape.

They remained in camp here for three days, to facilitate the treatment of the sick, of whom there were sixty-seven, according to the report of the physician who arrived to assume medical charge—"forty-seven cases of intermittent fever, thirteen of continued, three of diarrhoea and two of scrofula." Eight of them were dangerously ill. A woman and child died on the eighteenth, and on the evening of the next day a six-year-old child and a man died.

Early in the morning of the twentieth, an elderly woman died; but they resumed their journey at nine o'clock. While on the march a child died, on horseback in the arms of its mother, and another death occurred after they arrived in camp. The next day they camped at Sidney, southeast of Urbana. The farther they got into the prairie, they said, the scarcer became the water. The physician reported fifty persons still sick, and three had died, including Muk-kose, "a chief remarkable for his honesty and integrity," the conductor said, who died after a few days' illness.

The twenty-second was remarkable for the fact that not a death occurred during the day. The next day, Sunday, the start was delayed so as to allow Father Petit to perform divine services for his Indians. They traveled across another portion of the Grand Prairie, where they saw no timber for fifteen miles, and camped at Pyatt's Point. The physician reported the deaths of two children, but the number of sick was reduced to forty. Their route now lay along the Sangamon River on which they made several camps.

Proceeding down the Sangamon fifteen miles, they camped at "Sangamon Crossing." The physician reported two more deaths, and the condition of several as much worse. There were not wagons enough to haul all the afflicted, and twenty-seven were left behind with persons to care for them. Another child died this evening in camp, where they remained on the twenty-fifth to allow the invalids left at Pyatt's Point to join them. This day a woman and a child died, and the remainder were little, if any, improved. The farther they advanced into Illinois, the more sickly the country seemed to the conductor. While in this camp, most of the men were permitted to go on a hunting excursion, and they brought in considerable game.

They left the "Crossing" at eight o'clock on the twenty-sixth; the weather was delightful, but the dust very bad. The country was becoming more thickly settled, and they camped near Decatur. Another child died after dark. The next day they traveled fourteen miles, until two o'clock, and camped at Long Point. During the past three days the men had been hunting along the route through the prairies and had brought in so much game that the conductor found it unnecessary to issue regular rations. The camp was full of venison. Their stop on the twenty-eighth was near Springfield, and the conductor, wishing to make a good appearance as they passed through the village, suggested it to I-o-weh, one of the principal chiefs, who was pleased with the idea. Two children died during the night.

On the twenty-eighth more than five thousand dollars' worth of dry goods, consisting of blankets, calicoes, cloths, etc., due the Indians under recent treaty agreements, were issued to them. On Saturday, the twenty-ninth, they approached Springfield early, having arisen before daylight so as to pass through the village as early as possible. The conductor reported: "The Indians amongst whom a degree of pride was excited, arranged themselves into line, and with an unusual display of finery and gaudy trumpery marched through the streets of Springfield. The wayfares were covered with anxious spectators, so much so, indeed, as to threaten for a time to impede the progress of the emigration. We passed clearly through however, and that too without the detention of a single Indian. At 3 we reached our present encampment, McCoy's Mills, distant from last night's camp seventeen miles." The scarcity of water the next day made it necessary to limit their journey to six miles, and after they went into camp at Island Grove another child died. The Indians continued to bring in large quantites of game, sufficient for their sustenance, which they preferred to government rations.

Leaving Island Grove early on October 1, they traveled seventeen miles and reached Jacksonville at three o'clock. Nothing of note occurred during this day's march, said the conductor, except that a child was fatally injured by falling from a wagon and being crushed by the wheels. During the evening they were much confused by the curiosity of visitors from Jacksonville, who came to the camp to view the unfamiliar sight of a body of emigrating Indians. At night the Jacksonville band did a gracious thing by coming to the camp and regaling the Indians with a concert—a rare and welcome treat to them.

In the morning the conductor was solicited by some of the citizens of Jacksonville to halt the Indians in town as they passed through, so the consuming curiosity of the people could be gratified by a close view of the visitors. Accordingly they marched into the square, where they remained for fifteen or twenty minutes. Presents of tobacco and pipes in abundance were made by the citizens of Jacksonville, to the great delight of the Indians, who were much touched by this evidence of sympathy and compassion for their unfortunate condition.

With the band leading and playing its best, they marched around the square and then continued on their journey for sixteen miles through heat and dust which, with the lack of water, brought great distress to the Indians. They camped at Exeter, and left there before eight o'clock in the morning for a nine-mile march to the Illinois River, which they reached just before noon. Keel- and flatboats were available for ferrying, and they spent the day in crossing the river, which they completed by nine o'clock that night. A child died directly after their arrival at the river.

They went into camp on the west side of the river opposite Naples, where they remained the next day to enable the Indians to repair old moccasins and make new ones, wash their blankets and clothes, and do many other things necessary to their comfort and cleanliness during the remainder of their journey, which the waters of the Illinois made possible. A child died the next evening.

They left Naples in the morning of the fifth and traveled twelve miles to McKee's Creek. They had been obliged to detour considerably from their route in the search for water. All they could find was in stagnant ponds. There was not much game, and they were again eating government rations of beef, flour, and potatoes. The march of twelve miles the next day brought them to Mill Creek, within six miles of Quincy. Another child died after their arrival in camp. On the seventh they camped near Quincy, and a child died shortly after they made camp.

An early start on the morning of the eighth was made, so as to begin the crossing of the Mississippi as quickly as possible. A steam ferryboat was in service, and by night all the Indians, horses, and some of the wagons had been ferried across the river. But in the midst of these activities, three children died in the morning. The next day the remainder of the wagons were taken across, and by night the undertaking was completed. During the two days that they were camped on the banks of the Mississippi, the wagoners were busily engaged in having repairs made to their wagons, so that they were able to depart on October 11 for their destination near Independence, Missouri, 213 miles away.

After their departure from the Mississippi, the company marched through the village of Palmyra on October 12. Two days later, being Sunday, they remained in camp all day and attended divine service, in which the Indians took a deep interest. The next day they traveled twelve miles and camped near Paris. On the sixteenth they traveled eighteen miles; and, while the weather turned very cold, the health of the company was improving. The next two days were made miserable by snow which turned into rain and rendered the roads difficult to travel. The succeeding Sunday was again spent in camp at the request of the Indians who desired an opportunity for worship and rest. On October 22 they ferried the Grand River and found themselves in the Missouri River bottom where travel was difficult over the flat, wet lands. The weather was now exceedingly cold, and some indigent Indians who had been traveling barefooted were given shoes to relieve them from further distress. On the twenty-fourth they reached Carrollton, where they encountered much excitement over rumored Mormon difficulties. The people of Carrollton were under arms, guarding the village. Next day the citizens of Richmond solicited Judge Polke to permit his Indians to aid them in resisting an anticipated Mormon attack that night, which, of course, the conductor declined. On the twenty-sixth they began ferrying the Missouri River at Lexington but encountered some difficulty from the fact that the ferry was much in demand by women and children fleeing from their homes from the imaginary Mormon raid. Great excitement prevailed, wrote Judge Polke. Rumors were rife of bloodshed and house-burning throughout the country, and "the people seemed completely crazed."

The journey was continued without particular interest, except that on October 29 Captain Hull overtook the party with twenty-three belated Potawatomi who had been left at Logansport and Tippecanoe. On October 31 the Indians marched through Independence and camped two miles south of the village. The next day they marched sixteen miles and camped on Blue River. On November 3 the settlement of the Wea Indians on Bull Creek was reached. Judge Polke now found his Indians exceedingly anxious to press forward and meet their friends. The next day being Sunday, they tarried only two hours for devotional services and at two o'clock crossed the Osage River, where they were met and welcomed by many of their tribesmen from Indiana, who accompanied them a few miles farther to Potawatomi Creek, the end of their journey. Most of the Indians were excited and cheered by the warm greeting of their friends and by the appearance of the country, though this sentiment was not shared by all the persons in the party, some of whom were depressed by their surroundings and resentful of their treatment by the government. On November 5 an old man of the party died, and the next day two more.

When Iowa Territory was established in 1838,[25] part of the tribe were located on their five-million-acre cession of land in Iowa. They were perplexed and disheartened by efforts of the government to remove them south of the Missouri River; but they declined to remove again until they could be joined by their 768 brethren remaining in Indiana, who were reported in a deplorable condition. Surrounded by whites, on ceded land to which they no longer had title, they were on subsistence at the hands of the government, which would soon cease.

In 1839 there were about 1,500 Potawatomi on the Osage reservation. Drunkenness prevailed to an alarming extent among the immigrant tribes, but especially among the Potawatomi. This was due to the greed and depravity of the predatory whites along the Missouri line who were engaged in introducing and selling whiskey to the Indians.[26] In a heroic effort to wean the Indians from this traffic and improve their condition, three missions were conducted by the Baptists, Methodists, and Catholics. In addition, the Baptists conducted a school attended by a dozen Potawatomi children.

Several hundred Potawatomi in Michigan who were attached to the Catholic church at L'Arbre Croche remained in their old home under the influence of their priest. In September, 1840, efforts were made to drive them west to join the remainder of the tribe. General Brady and about two hundred regulars and a hundred horsemen were quartered at Marshall (eighteen miles distant) "from whence they have been making various excursions through our forests in pursuit of the poor fellows.

"The Indians say that the treaty which our government professed to be acting under, and which exchanged their land for lands west of the Mississippi, was made by a few unauthorized Chiefs who were cheated by the she-mokimans [whites] while they [the chiefs] were squabby [drunk]. The Indians keep out of the reach of the troops as long as they are able, but when surprised, they submit to be taken without resistance. The war is a bloodless one, and doubtless will end as such. About 500 warriors, squaws, and papooses are assembled on the Nottaway prairie about 16 miles west of us, who are to take up their line of march for their new home this day. The contract for removing them has been taken by the Messrs. Godfrey, who are two French traders among them. I understand they receive $55. a head for transporting them. They are employing lumber wagons, with two horses and a driver, for which they pay $2.50 per day and expenses, and allow them to travel 15 miles a day going out, and 30 miles returning. Many of the Indians will travel on their ponies, a large number of which are owned among them. They are furnished with blankets, tobacco, &c. at the expense of the United States. I think the resort to coercive measures for their removal is unjustifiable and unfair. They are as peaceful and good-natured as any class of citizens among us. Their lands are now sold, and they have become quite reconciled to that, but are extremely unwilling to leave the State.

"A part of the summer and winter are spent in hunting, in the spring in making maple sugar. They furnish us with great quantities of berries of almost every kind, deer skins, furs, &c. in exchange for clothing.

"They are of more advantage than damage to us, and much more under the influence of civilization and Christianity here than they will be at the far West. If the department would let the poor creatures alone, they would save the country a large amount of money, and please those who are most interested much more than by forcing them to bid farewell to their native land. The old chief, Pam-tie-pee, is very obstinate, he has escaped from the officers twice, and is now on the wing and I hope will not be retaken."[27]

By 1842 the Catholic school was the only one remaining among the Potawatomi on the Osage River. The Reverend J. P. L. Verreydt reported that the Indians were improving; they had made 300,000 rails and were cultivating the soil. Looms had been received, and as soon as the Indians could raise cotton, flax, and sheep the young women would be taught to weave.[28]

By 1846 there were at the Osage River Agency 1,941 Potawatomi, made up as follows: Potawatomi of the Prairie, 496; Potawatomi of the Wabash, 735, and Potawatomi of the St. Joseph, 710. In addition there were 284 Ottawa and 27 Chippewa.[29] The Potawatomi Indians were thus found located on two reservations—one in Iowa Territory and one in the future Kansas.

As the number of Potawatomi in Iowa increased with occasional accretions from the East, the complaints of the whites grew more vociferous, and finally, on April 2, 1844, Representative James M. Hughes of Missouri, of the House Committee on Indian Affairs, conveyed to the Commissioner of Indian Affairs resolutions of the council and house of representatives of Iowa Territory on the subject of the removal of the Potawatomi from that territory. The Commissioner in reply attributed the failure to secure a treaty providing for the removal of these Indians to an interesting situation: It seemed that in 1840, on the eve of the removal of the faction that went from Indiana to the Osage River, traders had filed claims against them amounting to $248,459.81. The Secretary of War thereupon directed General Willliam B. Mitchell of Indiana to investigate these claims and recommend such as should be paid. In view of this experience and the obvious attempts thus revealed to defraud the Indians of large sums of money, the United States Senate adopted a resolution declaring that it would never ratify an Indian treaty which contained a stipulation for the payment to traders of debts claimed by them out of moneys payable to the Indians. In view of this attitude by the Senate and of pending claims against the Indians by traders whose influence and meddling with the Indians would likely invite unfavorable action by the Senate, the Indian Department had hesitated to attempt a treaty with them.

A large delegation of Potawatomi was taken to Washington in 1845, negotiations were resumed in the West the next year, and another important treaty was made with them on their respective reservations on June 5, 1846, at Council Bluffs, and on June 17 on the Osage River,[30] by which the several bands of Potawatomi previously known as the "Chippewas, Ottawas and Pottowautomies, the Pottowautomies of the Prairie, the Pottowautomies of the Wabash, and the Pottowautomies of Indiana," who had theretofore negotiated with the government in separate bodies, united to become one people, to occupy a common country and abolish all distinctions of bands, and thereafter to be known as the "Pottowautomie Nation."

By this treaty the Indians divested themselves of all claim to land in territorial Iowa and lands on the Osage River. In lieu of these reservations, they were given a tract thirty miles square in the future Kansas, containing 576,000 acres lying on both sides of the Kansas River, being the eastern part of the land ceded by the Kansas Indians on January 14, 1846. This area included contiguous parts of the present Pottawatomie, Jackson, Wabaunsee, and Shawnee counties, and conformed approximately to the area bounded by lines running from Westmoreland, Holton, and Alma to Topeka, Kansas.

Article 7 of this treaty recites a consideration of $850,000 to set up a trust for the Indians, on which interest at the rate of 5 per cent was to be paid them annually for thirty years, "until the nation shall be reduced below one thousand souls." The cold-blooded assumption as a federal policy that the Indians were going to die off was based, of course, on experience and on the probable hope that their death rate would continue high. In fact, the agent at Council Bluffs reported in September, 1846, that 10 per cent of the tribe on that reservation of several hundred had died during the preceding year. The almost un-hampered introduction of whiskey among these Indians was respon-sible for most of the deaths. The well-founded belief that several thousand members of this tribe would die before thirty years had passed was further expressed in the remainder of the article: "If after the expiration of thirty years, or any period thereafter, it shall be ascer-tained that the nation is reduced below that number, the said annuity shall thenceforth be paid *pro rata* so long as they shall exist as a sep-arate and distinct nation, in proportion as the present number shall bear to the number then in existence."

The Indians were permitted two years within which to remove from Iowa; but in 1847 several large parties had crossed the Missouri River on the way, intending to travel leisurely and hunt as they went. It was not until 1848, however, that the Indian Department was able to an-nounce the union of the factions on their new reservation on the Kan-sas River. They elicited much favorable comment by the orderly manner in which, without any assistance from the government, they had conducted their emigration to the new home. Iowa was now re-lieved of all Indian population so far as they had a legal right to the soil; already white emigration was sweeping over the country. The Potawatomi were thus subject to the capricious policy of the govern-ment that rendered it impossible for the Indians to take root anywhere and make progress. Within less than ten years they had been removed twice at least, and the Indian Department fatuously imagined it was engaged in teaching the Indians to become farmers.

On their new reservation the Potawatomi were reported by their agent at Fort Leavenworth as numbering 3,235. The Catholic father claimed a congregation for his church on the Osage River of 1,300 persons. Now, on the removal, their schools and churches were broken up and much of the labors of missionaries and teachers lost.[31]

By 1849, however, the Catholics and Baptists had their missions in operation again; but the Indians were greatly disturbed by the Cali-fornia emigrants passing through their country and by the cholera epidemic.[32] In 1851 the Potawatomi were formally consolidated with the Prophet's band of Kickapoo Indians, with whom they were inter-married.[33]

NOTES

1. 4 *U.S. Stat.* 564.

2. *House Report 87* (20th Cong., 2d sess.).

3. 7 *U.S. Stat.* 378; *Senate Doc. 512* (23d Cong., 1st sess.), IV, 135, 136.

4. At the Tippecanoe River treaty grounds more than thirty traders and merchants delivered merchandise to the Indians in compliance with the terms of their treaties. The bills rendered by these merchants, paid by the agents and subsequently audited in Washington, show an infinite variety of supplies provided to meet the necessities of the Indians and to indulge their fancy for personal adornment. Their practical needs were met by rifles, shotguns, ducking guns; beaver, otter, and muskrat traps; awls and gimlets; camp kettles; powder and lead; bridles and saddles, including "plush" saddles; shoes, sewing silk, ticking, combs; "silver-mounted spurs"; and gunflints and gunworms. They received also vermilion, chintz, taffeta, shirting, indigo-blue cloth, thimbles, linsey, stripes, prints, cloaks, satinet; tablespoons and shears; blankets and hose; "superfine cloth of various hues," crepe, calico, ginghams; fancy morocco trunk; snuffboxes; and scores of jew's-harps. Four dozen cock feathers and six dozen foxtails were needed to adorn some of the Indians. Of shawls, there was an endless list: "Indian shawls, chintz shawls, scarlet cassimere shawls, crêpe shawls, turkey-red shawls, Prussia shawls, Valencia shawls, French shawls, Thibet shawls, Palmyra shawls"; hunting coats, men's "camlet cloaks," Spanish "camlet cloaks," "Circassian and silk camlet cloaks"; and thousands of yards of piece goods of an endless variety of materials and colors (*Doc.*, V, 332 ff.). This volume of "Abstracts of Expenditures by Disbursing Agents" contains 490 pages made up principally of statements rendered by traders for merchandise sold to the Indians at treaty councils from November, 1831, to December, 1833. The tens of thousands of items included cover an incredible variety—every conceivable article useful and otherwise, whether for personal adornment or for utility, calculated to appeal to the Indian and thus put him in a compliant mood. One hundred and fifty of these pages of presents relate to the Potawatomi.

5. 7 *U.S. Stat.* 399.

6. *Doc.*, I, 893.

7. *Ibid.*, pp. 777, 780, 896-903.

8. Charles Joseph Latrobe, who wrote a graphic account of the scenes witnessed at this gathering of Indians, in *The Rambler in North America* (New York, 1835), II, 149 ff. The reader is referred to this work, and to that of John Dean Caton (see n. 9 below), for many interesting details too extensive to be included in this book. The Reverend John Schermerhorn, who was instrumental in negotiating the fraudulent treaty with the Cherokee two years later, attended the treaty council at Chicago and used his influence to bring about the acquiescence of the Potawatomi in the treaty negotiated there. He afterward claimed credit for personal influence with Chiefs Caldwell, Robinson, and Laframbois and in drawing up their final answer to the government. Agent Owen told Schermerhorn that if it had not been for his attendance and influence, the Indians would not have agreed (Owen to Schermerhorn, January 21, 1834; and Schermerhorn to Herring, January 28, 1834, Office of Indian Affairs [National Archives], Tray 259).

9. *The Last of the Illinois and a Sketch of the Pottawatomies: Address by John Dean Caton before the Chicago Historical Society, December 13, 1870* (Chicago: Rand, McNally & Co., 1870).

10. Rather than move to the West some of them loaded their personal property in canoes and paddled to the islands in Lake Huron to live; 137 of them went in 1838 (*Report of Commissioner of Indian Affairs, 1838*, p. 456).

11. 4 *U.S. Stat.* 791.

12. The journal kept by William Gordon, conductor of the exploring party, is to be seen in the National Archives, Tray 287, "Pottawatomies (Emigrations)." It begins on July 30, 1835, and ends on September 12, 1835. See also numerous Potawatomi papers in Trays 259, 260, 288, 555, and 710.

13. 5 *U.S. Stat.* 34; Richardson, *Messages of the Presidents*, III, 321.

14. *Army and Navy Chronicle*, VII (July 7, 1838), 125.

15. Records of the Department of the Interior, Office of Indian Affairs, "Council Bluffs Files" (National Archives). See also "Pottawatomi Emigration" (National Archives), Trays 259, 260, 288; "muster rolls," Trays 63, 213, 259.

Captain Robert A. McCabe, the conductor, subsequently wrote of the celebrated chief in this party named Shabonee, who was one of the signers of the treaty executed in Chicago in 1833. This Indian was a grandnephew of Pontiac, born on the Maumee River, Illinois, in 1775. His father was an Ottawa who fought under Pontiac. In the Winnebago and Black Hawk wars he performed invaluable services for the white pioneers, time and again saving the settlements from destruction by timely warnings. At a council of the allied tribes in February, 1832, Shabonee espoused the cause of the whites and endeavored to convince Black Hawk that his proposed uprising would only bring disaster to the Indians. Unsuccessful in his endeavor, he and his son mounted their ponies at midnight and, starting from a point near the present Princeton, Illinois, warned the settlers both east and west of the intended outbreak, Shabonee finally reaching Chicago in time to put the inhabitants on their guard. The Sauk and Foxes in revenge, attempted many times to murder him and did, in fact, kill his son and his nephew.

The point of McCabe's letter was, he related, how during the journey of the Indians in 1836, one evening, sitting at the camp fire, Shabonee related to him his recollections of the killing of Tecumseh of which he was a witness. He was taken to Washington in 1836, in connection with negotiations of his tribe, and there saw and met Colonel Richard M. Johnson, whom he recognized immediately as the slayer of Tecumseh (*Army and Navy Chronicle*, VI [May 31, 1838], 349).

`In recognition of his services to the whites, the government, in the treaties of 1829 and 1832, gave Shabonee two sections of land "near the Pawpaw Grove" in DeKalb County, Illinois. Soon after the Indians arrived at their new home near Fort Leavenworth, Shabonee returned to his old home in Illinois, where he lived for a few years. Later, at the solicitation of his tribe, he rejoined them in Kansas, but, pining for civilization, in 1855 again returned to Illinois only to find that speculators at public sale had bought his two sections of land which had been put up for sale on the spurious ground that he had abandoned them. The citizens of Ottawa, Illinois, then bought him a small farm on the south bank of Illinois River two miles above Seneca, Grundy County, on which he passed his remaining years. He died in Morris, Grundy County, July 17, 1859, and a monument consisting of a large granite boulder was erected near by in Evergreen Cemetery (an extended and interesting account of this celebrated chief is to be seen in *Handbook of American Indians*, II, 517). In the *Handbook* his name appears as Shabonee; contemporaneously he is Shab-eh-nay.

16. Mabel Hill, "Paul Hill, Removal of the Pottawatomie," *Nebraska History Magazine*, September, 1917.

17. *Army and Navy Chronicle*, VII (July 5, 1838), 75. A contract to provision 400-500 Indians on the journey was made with Joseph Lindsay Ward at the rate of fifteen cents each. When the Indians failed them, the Wards appealed to Congress for relief on account of their loss for rations furnished and other expenses they were obliged to incur (*House Report 529* [28th Cong., 1st sess.]).

18. Crawford to Secretary of War, February 6, 1839 (National Archives).

19. 5 *U.S. Stat.* 34, 802. When this area was annexed to the state of Missouri as the Platte Purchase, it included the present counties of Platte, Buchanan, Holt, Nodaway, and Atchison. While they remained there, Father P. J. De Smet, S.J., in April, 1838, visited these Indians, whom he found drinking themselves to death. A boat had just brought up a cargo of whiskey, and "already fourteen among them cut to pieces in the most barbarous manner, and are dead." They had no provisions and were reduced to eating acorns and roots. However, in an effort to ameliorate their condition, Father De Smet visited "in their wigwams, either as a missionary, if they are disposed to listen to me, or as a physician to see their sick. When I find a little child in great danger, and I perceive that the parents have no desire to hear the word of God, I spread out my vials; I recommend my medicine strongly. I first bathe the child with a little camphor; then, taking some baptismal water, I baptize it without their suspecting it—and thus I

have opened the gate of heaven to a great number, notwithstanding the wiles of hell to hinder them from entering" (Rev. P. J. De Smet, *Western Missions and Missionaries*, p. 322).

20. *Report, 1838*, p. 7 (with *Report of Secretary of War*, pp. 109, 413).

21. Menominee was an interesting Indian who had acquired and practiced a sort of religion that promoted the welfare of his Indians. The Reverend Isaac McCoy first heard of him in 1821, when his band of Indians were living on the Illinois River. McCoy invited the Indian to visit him at his mission at Fort Wayne. The next year the missionary visited the Indians, who were then living near Twin Lakes in what is now Marshall County, Indiana. Menominee and his people gave McCoy a cordial welcome. As the Indian huts were small, the party went out of doors. "The yard was immediately swept and mats spread for me to sit or lie upon. We were presently regaled with a bowl of boiled turtle's eggs; next came a kettle of sweetened water for us to drink. I was then shown a large turtle which had been taken in a pond, and asked if I were fond of it. Fearing that with their cooking I should not be able to eat it, I replied that I was very fond of corn and beans. This I knew was already over the fire. It was placed before us in one large wooden bowl, and we ate it with wooden ladles. Menominee had two wives, each of whom presented me with a large box of maple sugar containing about thirty pounds each." Menominee exerted much influence with his people and was largely responsible for delaying their removal to the West. The white people of Indiana erected a monument to the chief near his home at the site of the village of Menominee.

22. "Journal of an Emigrating Party of Pottawatomie Indians," *Indiana Magazine of History*, XXI (December, 1925), 315; B. P. Stuart, "The Deportation of the Pottawatomies" *Indiana Magazine of History*, XVIII (September, 1922), 255. The letters of Father Benjamin Marie Petit have been edited and annotated by Irving McKee and by the Indiana Historical Society, published in a little book entitled *The Trail of Death*. This book contains Father Petit's version of some of the incidents of this sad enterprise. The encampment within which the Indians were concentrated occupied a space of a hundred yards square on the banks of Twin Lakes. This area was almost completely filled with Indian tents, ponies, pigs, officers, dogs, cats, sentinels, wagons, etc. (*Washington Globe*, October 8, 1838; see also *Annals of Iowa*, XI, No. 6 [3d ser., July, 1841], 407).

23. According to Father Petit, the order of march was as follows: "The United States flag, carried by a dragoon; then one of the principal officers, next the staff baggage carts, then the carriage, which during the whole trip was kept for the use of the Indian chiefs; then one or two chiefs on horseback led a line of 250 or 300 horses ridden by men, women and children in single file, after the manner of savages. On the flanks of the line at equal distance from each other were the dragoons and volunteers, hastening the stragglers, often with severe gestures and bitter words. After this cavalry came a file of forty baggage wagons filled with luggage and Indians. The sick were lying in them, rudely jolted, under a canvas which, far from protecting them from the dust and heat, only deprived them of air, for they were as if buried under this burning canopy—several died thus" (*Trail of Death*, p. 99; *Indiana Magazine of History*, XXI, 315).

24. At this point General Tipton wrote a long letter to the governor of Indiana describing the journey thus far. This very interesting account is to be seen at pp. 437-40 of the *Report of the Commissioner of Indian Affairs, 1838*, appearing in the *Annual Report of the Secretary of War* for that year. At this place also General Tipton delivered the custody of the Indian emigrants to Polke, who was in charge thence to their destination. Most of the dragoons were ill and had been dropping out along the way. At Sandusky all but fourteen of those remaining were discharged.

25. 5 *U.S. Stat.* 235.

26. *Report, 1839*. The condition of these immigrant Indians was described in *Farnham's Travels* ("Thwaite's Western Travels," Vol. XXVIII), pp. 19 ff.

27. Correspondence of the *Journal of Commerce* (Union City, Mich.), September 19, 1840; *National Intelligencer* (Washington), October 31, 1840, p. 1, col. 2.

28. *Report, 1842*, p. 487. The Catholic missionary, J. F. L. Verreydt, reported in 1842 that the Potawatomi Indians in Kansas included nearly half of the St. Joseph band (of Michigan), and the whole of the Wabash band, distinguished from other bands of

the tribe by their industry, sobriety, and morality, which the good father ascribed largely to the influence of the Catholic church. These people, he said, were industrious in the cultivation of the soil; "to do this with more facility they have formed themselves into clans. They have made about 300,000 rails." All the land inclosed by them was in good condition and bid fair to raise corn enough for their consumption. They had little knowledge of the raising of vegetables but were beginning to realize the benefits to be derived by cultivating them. They stood much in need of oxen with which to break the soil, for want of which they were limited to the use of a hoe made of the shoulder blade of a deer and similar expedients. They endeavored to imitate the habits of the whites, and, he thought, deserved encouragement of the federal government. The number of Potawatomi in the settlement reached more than twelve hundred, and, since they were all Catholics, he thought that they bid fair to take a high place among civilized people (*Report, 1842*, p. 487).

29. *Report, 1846*, p. 305. With consent of the Indians, in 1846 more than four thousand Mormons halted and raised crops on their land near Council Bluffs (*ibid.*, p. 287).
30. 9 *U.S. Stat.* 853.
31. *Report, 1848*, p. 447.
32. *Report, 1849*, p. 1091.
33. *Report, 1851*, p. 323.

CHAPTER VII

MIAMI IN INDIANA

PURSUANT to the Indian removal policy, on July 15, 1833, the Secretary of War notified Governor George B. Porter of Michigan Territory that the President had appointed him a commissioner to negotiate with the Miami Indians for the cession of their lands in Indiana and their removal west of the Mississippi.[1] These Miami lands were estimated to comprise about 800,000 acres. An equal amount west of the Mississippi was to be conveyed to the tribe. Emigration was to be started within three years, or, if the Indians insisted on further time, at the latest within five years. The Andrew Jackson method of bribery was to be employed by making grants of Indian land to forty leading influential men of the tribes, besides annuities to the chiefs. William Marshall was to be associated with Porter in the negotiations. But it developed that so many individual Indians and "presents," reservations, and grants of goods were involved in the negotiations that the terms of the treaty were not actually agreed to until October 23, 1834. This was not the end, as the terms did not win departmental approval in Washington, and further negotiations and concessions were necessary, so that the treaty was not concluded until November 10, 1837.[2] The completed treaty contained no stipulations touching the removal of the Indians from Indiana, which was left for future negotiations.

Another treaty was negotiated by Commissioner Abel C. Pepper with these Indians on November 6, 1838,[3] in which they made further cessions of 177,000 acres of land to the United States in consideration of $325,680 to be paid the tribe, with special sums for Chief Jean B. Richardville and others. The United States later was to "possess" the Indians of, and guarantee forever to them, a tract of land west of the Mississippi, large enough to accommodate them, contiguous to the other Indians who had emigrated from Indiana and Ohio, to which they were to remove whenever they should be ready.

These inconclusive measures left the Miami in an unsettled and precarious situation. Living on some of the best land in Indiana along the Wabash River, surrounded by white settlers, and recipients of large annuities, they were being debauched by the introduction of whiskey. Their agent, Samuel Milroy, reported in 1839 that in eighteen years four hundred and fifty men and thirty-six women had perished by the knife in drunken affrays, and from a strong and populous tribe they were reduced to about seven hundred.[4]

A tract was set apart for the Miami on the Osage River in Kansas, comprising the western two-thirds of Linn County and a southeastern fraction of Miami County. The Miami were still owners of 511,000 acres of land in Indiana currently known as the "Residue of the Big Reserve," which they ceded in a treaty of November 28, 1840.[5] Other large sums were promised the Indians, who agreed to remove within five years to the reservation in Kansas bounded on the north by the country of the Wea and Kaskaskia, on the west by the Potawatomi, on the south by the New York Indians, and on the east by the state of Missouri.

With such large sums paid them as annuities, the Indians would not work, and they spent their time in idleness and debauchery. By 1842, said their agent, Allen Hamilton, their population was reduced to 661.[6] Some of the leading chiefs were temperate and intelligent, cultivated their lands, and lived in some degree of comfort. Among these was La Fontaine, who thus far had proved himself useful to his people and capable of managing their affairs. A large part of the Indians depended solely upon their annuities for subsistence. The accumulation of debts contracted by this tribe drew together at the payments, said Hamilton, "a large number of citizens who have credited them, for the purpose of collecting their debts, many of whom are intelligent, having some standing in society, who I regret to say, take every pains to force this tribe to pay unjust debts, by threatening lawsuits, frequently suing individual Indians, without the shadow of a hope for success at law if they are investigated."[7]

The white people were becoming clamorous for the Indians to remove; and in 1843 the agent, for once, reported no murders during the year and the annual birth rate increased to thirty—the first time an increase had been noted for eighteen years. As the five-year limit for their removal approached, the Indians became restless under the aggression of the whites and insisted on sending an exploring party to the West to examine their new reservation. The next year their condition had changed little. They were still drinking, though they had tribal laws to prohibit the sale of liquor; but under the state laws of Indiana, said the agent, an Indian was not permitted to testify in a state court, and therefore it was impossible to convict violators of laws, state or federal.

Finally, as their time was about to expire, they begged and secured an extension from November, the limit, until the following April. Still reluctant to leave their homes, they again begged permission to remain until August. White traders in their country were influential in detaining them, in order that they might profit by the funds in the hands of the Indians.

It was finally decided that the Indians could not be removed except by force; and Adjutant General Roger Jones directed Captain William R. Jouett of the First Infantry to report with a force of sixty-two men at Peru, Indiana, to aid the removal agent in collecting the Indians and starting them on their way. This force arrived at Peru on September 26, 1846.

The removal of the Miami was involved in disgraceful intrigue between the creditors of the Indians and the contractors for their removal. Engagements had been entered into by the federal authorities with individuals who treated these contracts as articles of barter;[8] and the correspondence and nomenclature relating to the subject found in the official files in the National Archives and the collections in the Indiana State Library are replete with references to "silent partners," "active partners," and coarse epithets employed in describing rival creditors and would-be contractors and relating experiences in the performance of contracts.

At last, on October 5, 1846, more than three hundred Miami Indians, all that could be taken by officers, creditors, and soldiers, were captured. Those who resisted and struggled were securely bound and loaded on five canal boats at Peru.[9] A few made their escape, closely pursued by Ezekiel French, one of the creditors, and a posse acting for the others. The loaded boats left October 6, navigated through Fort Wayne, and passed Dayton on the tenth. Their canal journey was without recorded incident, except that, while passing under a low bridge, two Indians sleeping on piles of baggage on deck were struck by the bridge and painfully but not critically injured.[10]

On their arrival at Cincinnati the Indians, on October 12, were placed on board the steamboat *Colorado* for the next stage of their journey. Information touching the experiences of the Indians is extremely meager; but the *Cincinnati Enquirer* lifts the curtain somewhat on the sordid enterprise in which the whites were engaged and exposes the heartless indifference with which the Miami were treated. Their history up to this time was marked by constant deterioration from the unrestrained use of whiskey introduced by the whites, who welcomed the mortality that worked in favor of their supremacy in the land of these red people.

The *Enquirer* observed that many of these Indians were "aged, and infirm through age. An old squaw died on Tuesday, who was one hundred and twelve years old. An old warrior was pointed out to us, said by the agent to be one hundred and twenty-six. Another, quite venerable, attracted our notice; his hair, collected at the top of his head, and confined by a singular knot, his ears perforated, his person peculiarly marked, and his stalwart frame and cunning face the very personification of a brave, whose prowess had caused many a death groan and bloody scalp and burning roof to his early enemies."

While the Indians waited on the dock to board the steamboat, white men were permitted to peddle whiskey to all who could buy until drunken Indians covered the wharf and the deck of the steamboat. From the latter one young buck, helplessly drunk, fell into the river and was drowned. Another also fell into the stream but was rescued just in time to save his life.

The *Enquirer* noted that among the captives few were full-bloods; there were white men married to Indian women, and Indian men with white wives. "Two or three young girls, whose forms the fashions of our white belles had shaped into civilized proportions—that is, corsets had contracted the waist, and dress had fitted the shape—did not suffer in a contrast with many of fairer skin, who had collected around them to gaze and wonder. One whose face bore an intelligent expression, but whose shades of countenance betrayed the canker of a secret grief and melancholy reflections, was pointed out to us as the daughter of a chief; she had left a lover—a white—to follow the fortunes of her tribe, but under the delusive hope and treacherous promise that he who had stolen her young heart would soon join her in the 'Pathless woods.' "[11]

The Ohio River was so low that navigation below Louisville was difficult. Joseph Sinclear, agent for the Miami on board the *Colorado*, reported from near Evansville, Indiana, October 14, 1846: "Too busy collecting Miamies to make an annual report until now. They have been in a state of confusion the past year, and very little attention paid by them to farming or hunting. By the treaty of 1840 they agreed to remove within five years from the lands they sold in Indiana, to the country assigned them in the west. This time expired last November but at their request it was extended to April last, when I assembled the chiefs and called upon them to comply with their treaty stipulations. They gave me no answer, and at a subsequent council in May again begged a postponement until August, promising then to 'take us by the hand' and remove to their new homes without further delay or trouble. Thinking I could rely on this, I later learned they were acting in bad faith, and by scheming with white men trying to ask for further delay. White men claiming great influence in Washington induced the Indians to raise a large sum of money to enable them to appear before the department to secure a further postponement. Under this influence the Indians failed to keep their engagements, and I suggested that a force of troops be sent here to enforce the removal. They are now with me here, proceeding to their new country contented and cheerful. The trouble was caused by white men. It is certain the Indians will be beggared if the cormorants who have been living on their means are longer permitted to prey upon them. Since the treaty of 1840, the government had paid [to creditors] $350,000 claimed to be due from the Indians, and assumed further payments."[12]

The *Colorado* reached St. Louis on October 20, and debarked the Indian emigrants on Bloody Island to await measures for their further movements.[13] After some difficulty the contractors engaged the steamer *Clermont No. 2* to convey the travelers to the Kansas River for $1,800. On the twenty-second they were taken aboard and their journey resumed the next day.[14] As the Missouri River was very low, the *Clermont No. 2* did not reach its destination until November 1.[15]

The last stage of the journey was without further incident except that four more children died, bringing the total of deaths to seven, partially offset by two births on the whole trip.[16] When they were debarked on November 1, these unhappy, ragged people went into an inhospitable and cheerless camp.

Two days after the Indians boarded the canal boat at Peru, their ponies, nearly a hundred in number, were started overland in charge of twelve men, who delivered ninety of them and several wagonloads of personal effects of the Indians at the mouth of the Kansas River the day the Indians arrived at the same place. It was a hard journey for the ponies, seven of which, old and poor when they started, gave out. Four died, one was sold for a dollar, one for two, and another for five dollars.

United here with their personal property, the Indians departed on November 2 for the Osage River subagency, arriving there a week later. Their conductor delivered to Alfred J. Vaughan, Indian subagent, 323 Miami Indians, including 42 heads of families—181 females and 142 males; of the total, 104 were children under eighteen. The Indians located temporarily near the Osage River Indian agency one mile west of the Military Road on Little Sugar Creek, thirteen miles north of the American Fur Company's fort at the ford of the Osage River.[17] The compliant contractor for removal permitted two alleged creditors of the Indians to accompany them all the way, so that they might be on hand, when their annuity was delivered, to see that none escaped from the company or evaded payment to the creditors present for themselves and for others in Indiana represented by them.

As soon as they could, the immigrants assembled in council and related a long list of grievances against the manner in which they had been treated on their emigration: they first expressed regret at their recalcitrance at the beginning of the unhappy enterprise; but they charged Sinclear with gross mismanagement. Some of their number died from neglect and indifference to their illness. Sick people were kept out on deck of the boats instead of being comfortably housed in the cabin, where their families desired them to be cared for. Their doctor, they said, was too drunk to attend the patients. They paid tribute to their agent, Alexis Coquilland, who did everything in his power to make them comfortable.

They protested bitterly against the appointment of Sinclear as their agent—a position he had hastened East to secure; in so doing, he had refused to attend the council of the Indians and listen to their complaints. Sinclear said that at the beginning of their journey he advised the Miami on their arrival in Kansas to unite with the Wea. He declared that they were "in fact the same people; they separated some years since on account of some supposed partiality in a treaty made with the Wea by Genl. John Tipton."[18]

Thirty Wea were in Indiana, all that remained of that tribe, and plans to remove them in connection with the Miami were considered but not carried into effect. Because four Potawatomi were married to Miami Indians, they were held to be Miami also, and compelled to emigrate with them.[19] Three hundred and two Miami eluded capture by the soldiers and mercenaries and remained in Indiana to be objects of administrative concern for many years.[20] In 1847 seventy more were emigrated. From the fugitive existence of these Indians and the unrestrained introduction of whiskey among them, many died and their number was rapidly reduced. By 1854, said their agent, there were only 275, representing a loss of nearly half during the five years since they came to Kansas; three years later there were but 193; in 1868 only 91 remained alive in Kansas.[21]

NOTES

1. *Doc.*, III, 733.
2. 7 *U.S. Stat.* 463.
3. *Ibid.*, p. 569.
4. *Report of the Commissioner of Indian Affairs, 1839.*
5. 7 *U.S. Stat.* 582.
6. Report of Allen Hamilton, agent, October 22, 1842, at Forks of the Wabash, Indiana, with *Report of the Commissioner of Indian Affairs, 1842 (House Executive Doc. 2* [27th Cong., 3d sess.]), p. 464.
7. Jones to Colonel J. Ewing, Washington, September 11, 1846, Records of the Department of the Interior, Office of Indian Affairs (National Archives), "Letters Received, 1846."

The almost incredible extent to which these Indians were exploited by traders was described by the Secretary of War, who told of the extravagant bills rendered by them following the making of the treaty of 1840, wherein every advantage was taken of Indian folly and inexperience. The Secretary itemized "extravagant guard chains in one instance, charged at $93.00." "Enormous quantity of ribbons, as in one case $300 worth sold to one squaw." Fourteen "coats" and "cloaks" delivered to one person within about a year. One trader presented a voucher showing the sale to a squaw in one day of $3,500 worth of goods. "A dissipated and vagrant individual whose family consisted of three persons beside himself, between November 28, 1840, and January 19, 1841, purchased goods" charged at more than $7,000. "A female whose annuity money was drawn by the head of the family to which she belonged, and who had no one to provide for but herself, is charged with nearly $6,000 for store goods within a period of less than two months." Others were charged with sums from $1,000 to $7,000 for goods delivered in a single day.

As these individuals could not possibly pay such amounts, the traders filed claims for them against the tribe as a whole, and it appears that something like $300,000 was collected in this manner (*Washington Daily Union*, September 22, 1846, p. 2, cols. 3 and 4).

8. The Miami contract in June had been assigned by W. G. and E. W. Ewing to Samuel Edwall for $341.33. A part of the contract was claimed by Robert Peebles and his son, John H. Peebles, as assignees of Thomas Dowling; Dr. Graham N. Fitch was to have accompanied Dowling (Sinclear to Medill, April 23, 1846 [National Archives], Tray 6822). Other files relating to this subject are to be seen in National Archives, Trays 681 and 682; and in great detail in the Indiana State Library.

9. Joseph Sinclear to Commissioner of Indian Affairs, Peru, October 5 and 7, 1846, Records of the Department of the Interior, Office of Indian Affairs (National Archives), "Letters Received, 1846."

10. *Ibid.*, Cincinnati, October 12, 1846. They were preceded by their chief, La Fontaine, his wife and children, and other leading members of the tribe with their families. La Fontaine was a man of considerable wealth, and he and his friends and their families were domiciled at the Mansion House while waiting for departure of the whole company (*Cincinnati Gazette*, October 12, 1846, p. 6, col. 4). After seeing his people to their new home, on his return East the next spring, La Fontaine died at Lafayette, Indiana, May 13, 1847 (*Niles' Register*, June 12, 1847, p. 226, col. 1).

11. This account in the *Cincinnati Enquirer* was copied in the *Army and Navy Chronicle* for August 17, 1843, p. 207.

12. Sinclear to Commissioner of Indian Affairs, October 14, 1846 (National Archives).

13. *St. Louis Union*, October 27, 1846, p. 3, col. 2.

14. Thomas H. Harvey to Medill, "Miami (Emigration)," File H, 2452 (National Archives), Tray 682.

15. Joseph Sinclear, superintendent of the Miami emigration, to William Medill, November 1, 1846, Office of Indian Affairs, "Miami (Emigration) Kansas File" (National Archives).

16. *Ibid.*

17. Vaughan to Medill, Commissioner of Indian Affairs, December 3, 1846, "Osage River Sub-Agency" (National Archives), Tray 682; "Clark Papers" (Kansas Historical Society), Letter Book No. 8, p. 293. This agency was about four miles north of the site of Pleasanton, Linn County, Kansas.

18. Sinclair to Medill, October 7, 1846; *ibid.*, June 5, 1846; Ewing to Crawford, January 2, 1848 (Indiana State Library). Lieutenant J. P. Simonton, in 1833, was sent to Logansport to interview the Wea Indians on the subject of emigrating to the West. In December of that year Simonton reported his failure to the Secretary of War. He said that "the tenacity with which they hold on to their present possessions will serve to show with how much reluctance the Weas leave their ancient hunting grounds. The two tribes [Wea and Miami] have long been connected by blood and policy—speak the same tongue, and possess every trait of character which would mark them as one people. The Weas therefore, readily find a residence with the Miamies, and boast that as long as the latter own a foot of land, they have a home. The few Weas remaining in Indiana are without a chief of their own and with few exceptions have attached themselves to different bands of the Miamies. The few who have not ranged themselves under some minor chiefs are to be found wandering about the country like Gipsies, plundering the corn fields and killing hogs in the neighborhood of the white settlements" (*Doc.*, I, 906).

19. *Ibid.*

20. *Senate Report 798* (51st Cong., 1st sess.).

21. *Report, 1868*, p. 268; *Handbook*, II, 854.

CHAPTER VIII

SAUK AND FOXES

THE earlier chapters of this book covered the period of unauthorized, voluntary, but haphazard emigration of some of the Indians from Ohio, Indiana, and Illinois before President Jackson established Indian removal as a federal policy. Later we accounted for the organized emigration from those states authorized by Jackson's Removal Bill. The Kickapoo had long since left Illinois before Jackson's bill. Under that authority the Potawatomi were removed from Illinois and Indiana. Only the Sauk and Foxes of Illinois are still unaccounted for.

The experiences of the Sauk and Foxes as related by their agents are more nearly typical of the whole field of Indian emigration than those of any other tribe. Since the descriptions and comments of the agents relating to this tribe are more revealing of Indian character and their problems than are those to be found elsewhere in the field, the emigration of this tribe has been selected for treatment in greater detail than that of any other.

The Sauk Indians who formerly resided near Detroit were compelled by a war with the Huron, who were assisted by the French, to abandon about 1712 their native country and to remove to Winnebago Lake, where they took refuge among the Foxes. The latter, for their hospitality, found themselves engaged in war with the enemies of the Sauk; and at length these two tribes, finding it difficult to resist the attacks to which they were continually exposed, left their villages and removed to the Wisconsin River, on the left bank of which they settled. Here they were again besieged by the French and northern Indians, who overcame them, killed a great many, and completely routed them. Those who escaped fled and erected a fort at the branches of the Rock and Fox rivers. Here they "soon afterwards were again so closely besieged by the French and Indians (among which were the Illinois) that they were reduced by famine to the last extremities; all hopes of escape failing them, and seeing no other way to extricate themselves, two of their principal chiefs, La Biche (the Lap Dog) and La Peau Blanche (the White Skin), caused their arms to be tied, took a white stick in their hands, and singing their death songs presented themselves with the utmost humility to their assailants and earnestly begged for life and peace, which were indeed granted them by the French commanding officer, but upon hard conditions which were imposed with the consent of all the Indian chiefs who composed the council that was held for that purpose. The peace thus concluded put a final end to the war and all controversies between the French and northern Indians of the one part, and the Sauk and Foxes of the other part; but it eventuated in these latter tribes entering into the alliance that was formed to destroy the Illinois Indians who, as has been already mentioned, found the combination against them too powerful to be resisted. The Sauk and Foxes, finding these Indians compelled to leave their country and in no situation to prosecute the war, left their village on the Wisconsin, gradually descended the Mississippi, and in 1764 settled on Rock River, twenty-one years after the Potawatomi and their allies had settled on the Illinois River.

"The Foxes, or rather a band of them, also removed, in the same time, to a place called the Spanish Mines (Dubuque's), and no other tribe having opposed them, they for a long time continued in the uninterrupted possession of that tract of country which is bounded on the east by the Mississippi River; on the south by the country of the Illinois Nation; on the west by the dividing ridge that separates the waters of the Missouri and Mississippi rivers, and on the north by the country of the Sioux."[1]

However, the Sauk and Fox Indians thereafter jointly claimed the country along the Mississippi River from Portage des Sioux north to the Wisconsin River. A band known as the Missouri River Sauk were induced to come to St. Louis where, as previously related herein, on November 3, 1804, General William Henry Harrison as United States commissioner persuaded them to enter into a treaty of cession in the name of the "United tribes of Sac and Fox Indians." In this treaty the Indians undertook to cede to the United States a vast area of country bounded on the west by the Mississippi, on the east and south by the Illinois and Fox rivers, and on the north by the Wisconsin, extending from the southern end of Calhoun County, Illinois, north into Wisconsin. It is generally believed that these Indians had little conception of what they were doing, but they were to learn in later years that their action was to bring them disaster. The knowledge of what the Missouri band had done so incensed the rest of the people that afterward the Missouri band withdrew to themselves. The Foxes became so angry with the Sauk for letting one of the bands act for all the people that they began to draw away from them, and in the course of a generation they had moved over into their hunting grounds in Iowa.

The Sauk and Foxes were a warlike people, and when hostilities broke out between the United States and Great Britain in what was called the War of 1812, Black Hawk's faction of Sauk and Foxes, in June, 1813, visited General Benjamin Howard, then commanding the Western Department, and volunteered to serve with the American forces against the British. When their offer was declined, determined to get in the war on one side or the other, they joined with the British and fought against the United States.[2]

Subsequently, at Portage des Sioux, where the erring Indian tribes hostile to the United States repented and made treaties of peace with the United States under the terms of the Treaty of Ghent, the Sauk and Foxes participated; and on September 13, 1815, the Missouri River Sauk made a treaty of peace[3] in which they said that they had been compelled, since the beginning of the War of 1812, to separate themselves from the warlike faction of the tribe (known as the Black Hawk or British faction) and remove to the Missouri River, to join the Missouri River faction. In this treaty they ratified the treaty of 1804 by the Missouri faction, ceding the Illinois land. They engaged also, in Section 2 of the treaty, to make permanent their separation from Black Hawk's faction, "the Sacs of Rock River, giving them no aid or assistance whatever, until peace shall also be concluded between the United States and the said Sacs of Rock River."

In consideration, the United States promised to allow the Sauk of Missouri River all privileges secured to them by the treaty of 1804, "and as soon as practicable to furnish them with a just proportion of the annuities" promised them in that treaty. The next day a treaty of peace was made with the "Fox tribe or Nation" in which the Indians ratified the cession made in 1804 in the treaty with William H. Harrison and agreed to deliver up all captives held by them.[4]

But it was not until May 13, 1816, that Black Hawk's warlike Sauk of Rock River would consent to meet the United States commissioners at St. Louis and enter into a treaty of peace[5] in which they also ratified the cession of 1804. The United States stipulated to place them on the same footing they occupied before the war, provided they returned by July 1 all the property which they had stolen from the citizens of the United States, in default of which they would forfeit all the annuities promised them in that treaty. Among the Sauk signers of the treaty was the celebrated Mucketamachekaka ("Black Sparrow Hawk").

From this time the Sauk and Foxes lived principally within the limits of the present Iowa. Many tribes having been induced to cede most of their lands to the United States, they began to crowd each other in restricted areas, where the game was being depleted, and much friction and disorder resulted. The Sauk and Foxes and the Iowa had been involved in hostilities with the Sioux for a number of years. In order, therefore, to promote peace, redefine and establish the boundaries between the various tribes in their new relation, agree on a common hunting ground in the West, and thus remove incitement to future conflict so far as possible, the government invited the Chippewa, Sauk and Foxes, Menominee, Iowa, Sioux, Winnebago, and portion of the Potawatomi, Ottawa, and Chippewa living on the Illinois River to send representatives to a general council at Prairie du Chien in Michigan Territory (now Wisconsin). Here General William Clark and Lewis Cass negotiated with them a treaty on August 19, 1825,[6] in which peace was declared, and boundary lines and a general distribution of territory agreed upon. The treaty bore the signatures (by mark, of course) of 134 Indians representing the nine tribes.

In this treaty a boundary line between the Sauk and Foxes and the Sioux was established, beginning approximately at the northeastern corner of the present Iowa and running generally southwest to the Missouri River. The interest of the Iowa Indians in the lands assigned to the Sauk and Foxes was acknowledged, subject to a later definition, pending which the Iowa were to be permitted to live and hunt in this area. An undefined interest of the Oto in the same territory was also acknowledged.

In this treaty the usual turgid language with which the white man sometimes obscured the sense of Indian treaties was replaced by picturesque description that was perfectly comprehensible to the Indians, if not susceptible of translation by a surveyor. Where the boundary between the Sioux and Chippewa was defined, for instance, a certain line ran from "the standing cedar, about a day's paddle in a canoe" above a certain lake; thence between two lakes called by the Chippewa "Green Lakes" and by the Sioux "the lakes they bury the Eagles in"; crossing Rum River at the mouth of a small creek called Choaking Creek, "a long day's march from the Mississippi"; thence to a point of woods that projects into the prairie, "half a day's march from the Mississippi," etc. Other lines were located with reference to certain Indian villages, portages, streams, falls, high cliffs, etc.

Boundary lines affecting the Winnebago, Menominee, Ottawa, and

Potawatomi also were agreed upon. By this and previous treaties the Sauk and Foxes specifically disclaimed any interest in lands east of the Mississippi, and thus their holdings were limited to the present area of Iowa.[7]

The treaty, however, did not entirely establish peace. A party of Sauk and Foxes, in 1829, were on the way to Prairie du Chien on invitation of United States officials, when they were attacked by Sioux and their beloved chief, Piemansky, killed. This infuriated the Sauk and Foxes, who for a long time could think of nothing but revenge. Nearly every tribe, in fact, had a grievance against another for injuries that had to be atoned for in kind, and thus hostilities were provoked and continued. Of all the Indians, the Sauk and Foxes were the most implacable and persistent. Their war parties ranged far to the west seeking their enemies, and early in 1830 the government dispatched its agents throughout the country soliciting delegations of Iowa, Oto, and other tribes to meet again at Prairie du Chien on July 4 for the purpose of making peace and entering into another treaty, immediately after the enactment of President Jackson's famous Indian Removal Bill.

A war party of Sauk had lately killed and "scalped twelve Yankton Sioux Squaws, besides one scalped alive." While Indian Agent John Dougherty at Fort Leavenworth was reporting these facts, three Iowa Indians from their village on the Platte came to the fort to report that a large war party of Sauk had passed their village "on their way up the Missouri in search of Oto, Omaha and Yankton Sioux."[8] Two chiefs of the Iowa and Oto tribes at the fort, on hearing this alarming report, immediately set out for their villages to warn the people and prepare for defense.

Efforts of Indian agents to secure delegations of Missouri River tribes to attend the treaty council at Prairie du Chien were seriously hampered by fear of the Indians that the Sauk would waylay and massacre them on the road. One agent, however, J. L. Bean, left Fort Leavenworth with fourteen Omaha Indians and, after nineteen days of travel, arrived at the council grounds at Prairie du Chien.[9]

The Sauk and Foxes obstinately refused to go to Prairie du Chien to counsel with their enemies; they would meet them and representatives of the government nowhere, they said, but in their village at the mouth of Rock River on the Mississippi, around their own council fire, where it had burned for time immemorial. Keokuk and other chiefs of the Sauk and Foxes were induced to paddle down the Mississippi River to St. Louis, where they counseled with General Clark on June 16, 1830. Though they refused there to recede from their position, later, through the influence of General Clark and other leading men, they did attend the council at Prairie du Chien, where, on July 15, 1830, a treaty was entered into by deputations of the "Confederated Tribes of Sac and Foxes," Omaha, Iowa, Oto and Missouri, and four bands of Sioux.[10]

The tribes united in ceding to the United States an area included in the Missouri River watershed in western Iowa, comprising almost the western third of the present state of Iowa and contiguous lands in Minnesota and Missouri. By a separate section the Sauk and Foxes conveyed also to the United States part of their reservation, roughly described as a strip of land twenty miles in width, including the site of Fort Dodge and extending therefrom northeast to the Mississippi River. The Oto, having been recognized as the owners of an immense tract of land west of the Missouri River, Article 10 of the treaty set apart this area for the joint use of certain half-breeds of the Oto, Omaha, Iowa, and two bands of Sioux Indians. This area, which lay in present northeastern Nebraska between the Platte and Missouri rivers, when surveyed in 1837–38 by the Reverend Isaac McCoy, was found to contain 143,647 acres.

This treaty made certain adjustments desired by the whites; but the cession of the Sauk and Fox land west of the Mississippi River incurred the bitter resentment of Black Hawk and his faction, who were told that they must not again cross to the east side of the Mississippi. However, in the early spring, after seeking in vain the relaxing of this order, the Black Hawk faction in a body recrossed the Mississippi at Rock River to their old corn field and in a menacing manner took possession; for by the terms of their treaty the Indians were not obliged to leave their lands as long as they were not sold by the United States.

For many years the more enterprising Sauk and Foxes had produced a large amount of lead from both sides of the Mississippi River and had operated extensively what were known as "the fox or Dubuque's mines," their ownership of which was generally recognized. However, while the Indians were involved with the government, the whites from Illinois, taking advantage of their difficulties, attempted to seize the mines, and it was necessary for the government to send troops to remove them.

Settlers in Illinois, usually squatters, besides irritating reprisals, cried out against the encroachments of the Indians, which brought military intervention by the governor and by General E. P. Gaines. Gaines, who arrived in June at Rock Island, had ordered six companies of regular troops to proceed there from Jefferson Barracks. Here he was joined on June 25 by militia ordered out by Governor John Reynolds of Illinois. In the face of such odds, Black Hawk, on June 30, 1831, signed what was called a treaty, but it was never ratified as such by the Senate. Under the terms of this document the Indians withdrew to the west side of the Mississippi.

But the treaty was soon violated by both sides. A large number of Menominee Indians who were sincerely attached to the United States had been called to Prairie du Chien for a treaty conference with their agent. On the morning of July 31, 1831, two or three hours before daylight, a party of from eighty to a hundred Sauk and Foxes in their canoes paddled up the river and surprised the Menominee asleep in their lodges near the village of Prairie du Chien, and within a mile or two of Fort Crawford. It was said that most of the Menominee were drunk, and all but one man unarmed. Of the Menominee in the lodges, eight men, six women, and eleven children were killed.[11]

Black Hawk's band remained on the west side of the Mississippi until April, 1832, when they crossed over again. Much excitement on the frontier resulted; people left their homes and the militia were called. From all this, in combination with the general unrest of the tribes of this region, arose the so-called "Black Hawk War" of 1832. The Potawatomi and Winnebago had urged the Sauk to fight the whites and had promised to aid them. The Potawatomi were the most persistent in this; they had prophets in the camp of the Sauk, preaching restoration of the old hunting grounds, the return of the game, and the sudden miraculous destruction of the whites, much after the manner of the ghost dances in early Oklahoma; but, when hostilities began, the Potawatomi chief, Shabonee (Shab-eh-nay), was the first to warn the whites against the Sauk.

Among the Sauk at this time was the able leader, Black Sparrow Hawk. He was not a chief but had a good record for bravery and leadership in war. He had fought under Tecumseh and had become imbued with some of the ideas of this great Shawnee. About this man rallied the hostile Sauk. He tried to hold them in check until he could count on the combined help of the Kickapoo and Foxes, but the fighting got under way before he was ready. The Sauk were thoroughly beaten and sought refuge among the Foxes in Iowa. This conflict broke the power of the Sauk and Foxes, who united in Iowa to avenge themselves against the Sioux, Omaha, and Menominee, whom they chastised so thoroughly that the latter removed from Iowa and left the field to the Sauk and Foxes.[12]

In the Black Hawk War it was inevitable that the Indians should suffer final defeat and that Black Hawk should find himself a prisoner in the hands of the whites after many of his followers were killed.[13] General Winfield Scott arrived at Fort Armstrong, Rock Island, too late to participate in the campaign, but he and Governor Reynolds, on September 15 and 21, 1832, did negotiate treaties of considerable importance with the Winnebago and Sauk and Fox Indians.

As a penalty for their hostilities in Illinois, at the treaty made with them September 21, 1832, at Rock Island, the confederated tribes of Sauk and Foxes were required to yield to the United States a large area of land within the present Iowa, bounded on the east for more than two hundred miles by the Mississippi River, and to remove therefrom on or before June 1, 1833. In consideration, the government secured to them out of their cession a reservation of four hundred square miles on both sides of the Iowa River, near the Mississippi, so as to inclose Keokuk's principal village.

A few years later the chiefs of the Sauk and Foxes of the Missouri and the Iowa then living west of the Missouri were called into council at Fort Leavenworth, where, on September 17, 1836, they entered into a treaty in which they relinquished to the United States all interest and claim to the lands lying between the Missouri River and the state of Missouri,[14] which later became a part of what was called the "Platte Purchase." They also agreed to accept a small piece of land south of the Missouri for a permanent home. General Clark, for the United States, assigned to them a strip of land of about four hundred sections on the south side of the Missouri, between the Kickapoo northern boundary line and the Great Nemaha River, to be divided between them, the lower half for the Sauk and Foxes and the upper half for the Iowa, now in the present Brown and Doniphan counties, Kansas. By the terms of this treaty the Indians agreed to remove to the new reservation as soon as they could select sites for villages and places for their fields; and houses, livestock, and other facilities were promised them.

Afterward, on September 27, 1836, "on the west bank of the Mississippi River opposite Rock Island," Henry Dodge called into conference "chiefs, braves and principal men" purporting to represent the whole Sauk and Fox tribe, who in the name of the tribe, entered into a "convention in which they ceded and quitclaimed to the United States all right and interest in and to the lands lying between the state of Missouri and the Missouri River, and exonerated the United States from any guarantee, condition or limitation, expressed or implied, under the treaty of Prairie du Chien, of July 15, 1830," concerning said lands.[15]

On the following day, September 28, representatives of the confederated tribes of Sauk and Fox Indians were again called into council "at the treaty ground on the right bank of the Mississippi River, in the county of Dubuque and Territory of Wisconsin [Iowa]" (opposite Rock Island), where a treaty was entered into with Henry Dodge as United States commissioner, wherein the Indians ceded to the United States their remaining reservation of four hundred sections of land in eastern Iowa confirmed to them four years before. In consideration, the United States was to pay them in June of the following year $30,000 and an annuity thereafter and make payments to certain individuals and to the heirs of others who had been killed. The government further agreed to give them two hundred horses. Finally, the Indians of the confederated Sauk and Fox tribes agreed to remove from the lands thus abandoned by them by the first day of November, 1836, with the understanding that they never again should be permitted to hunt or fish on this land, their old hunting grounds. Provision was also made in the treaty for investigating the validity of a claim made by the Iowa Indians in the four hundred sections ceded by the Sauk and Foxes and to deduct the amount from the consideration promised the latter.

However, on October 21 of the next year two other treaties[16] were made at Washington in which the Sauk and Foxes purported to cede to the United States all rights and claims, including the right to live or hunt on any land within the present Iowa, secured to them by previous treaties. At this time, reported their agent, Joseph M. Street, the confederated tribe included 2,500 Indians living on the Des Moines River, 380 on the Skunk River, and 1,666 on the Iowa. Of the total of 4,546, the Sauk numbered 2,100 and 2,446 were Foxes. They were being rapidly debauched by white men who sold them whiskey, and frequently gave it to them, in order to filch their annuities and issues of blankets and other merchandise.[17]

The Indians agreed to remove from the ceded land within eight months from the ratification of the first treaty,[18] with the exception of

Keokuk's Village, possession of which was to be retained by them for two years. On the same date another treaty was made with the Sauk and Foxes of the Missouri, with similar grants and covenants, in order to cancel all their claims and rights to live or to hunt within the future Iowa.

A final treaty of cession was made on October 11, 1842, at the Sauk and Fox agency by John Chambers, commissioner and governor of the newly organized Iowa Territory, on the one part, and the Confederated Tribes of Sauk and Foxes, without noting any distinction between those of the Missouri and those of the Mississippi.

In this treaty the Indians ceded to the United States all lands west of the Missisippi River to which they had any title or claim, with the reservation, however, that they were to be permitted to occupy certain lands approximating the southeastern third of the western half of Iowa for three years from the date of the treaty. By the end of that time they were to remove to lands on the Missouri River to be indicated by the President. If they did not prepare to be removed at the expense of the government within the three years, they would be obliged to remove thereafter at their own expense. Article 8 of this treaty is interesting in that it provided for the burial of the remains of their late distinguished chief, Wa-pel-lo, "near the grave of their late friend and agent, General Joseph M. Street, and they put into the hands of their agent the sum of $100 to procure a tombstone to be erected over his grave, similar to that which has been erected over the grave of General Street." They wished the grave of their friend and agent to remain in possession of the family of General Street, "to whom they were indebted in his lifetime for many acts of kindness." They gave to General Street's widow, Mrs. Eliza M. Street, "a section of land to include the graves and the agency house and enclosures around and near it."

There was every reason for removing the Sauk and Foxes from their location in Iowa. The agent, John Beach, reported in 1842 that when he first knew them in 1832, he never saw a confirmed drunkard among them, "while at this time, except when far distant on their hunting ground, the whole nation, without distinction of rank, age or sex, exhibits a continual scene of the most revolting intoxication. Laws, of a truth, exist; but of what avail, without the means of enforcing them?" Notwithstanding the annuities paid them, they were becoming destitute; the well-known hospitality of the Indian was in part responsible. They were on terms of "strict friendship with most of the contiguous tribes, having with some of them, perhaps, lived too amicably for their own benefit. Large parties of the Pottawatomies and Iowas (the latter especially appearing exceedingly destitute) have visited them at their villages, having prolonged their stay through a great portion of the spring and summer, to the no small detriment of the scanty supply of subsistence then remaining to the Sacs and Foxes."[19] Their population now, said the agent, was reduced to 2,300. The Indians were removing up the Des Moines River to a tributary called Raccoon Creek.

Of the recent treaty with the Sauk and Foxes, the Commissioner of Indian Affairs said: "By it we have acquired about ten million acres of as fine land probably as the world can produce." The treaty required the Indians to remove west of a certain line about the center of Iowa. The Indians "had without a murmur, or a whine about the change, gone west of the line agreed on, in fulfillment of their covenant. This is a spectacle worthy of contemplation. A race of wild and uneducated (in the broadest sense of the word) Indians, mindful of their engagements, its letter, and more—leaving the grounds on which they had hunted and roamed, to the occupancy of our citizens, and voluntarily and quietly, without any agency of ours, turning their backs, in a body of about 2,300 souls, on the scenes of their former joys and sorrows! These men are without the slightest education, except the teaching of observation; utterly opposed to schools and to the labors of the missionary; but they came from the hands of their Creator and ours, a noble, manly race. What might not be made of such material, if they could be persuaded to abandon idleness and intemperance, and to know their ignorance. But of this there is little hope, and a diminution of their number within a few years makes a philanthropic heart grieve that such high qualities should be stifled by savagism, under which they will probably be extinguished." However, on their removal to western Iowa, said their agent, "the unprincipled white population, who make a business of supplying them with whisky, still continue to follow them," and the federal government did nothing to prevent the debauching of these noble savages.[20]

Most of the Sauk and Foxes were now living on or near Raccoon Creek close to the site of Des Moines, where it was extremely unhealthful. Much of their time was taken up by dances and other religious ceremonials, councils with their agent and with one another concerning their new location on the Missouri, and plans for their removal, which they were reluctant to talk about, so great was their aversion to leaving their home in Iowa. The Sauk, under the influence of Chief Keokuk, took a sensible view of their situation and prepared to meet the inevitable. The Foxes, however, continued recusant and had to be threatened by their agent that if they were not prepared to remove by the time fixed in their treaty, not only would their annuities be withheld but the military might be employed to remove them. They objected to the country where it was proposed to send them; Indans who had been there had told them that they could not find a pole or a piece of bark with which to build a wigwam to protect them against the cold; and they thought a location on the Kansas River much preferable. They objected to moving in wagons, as their effects would be much injured and destroyed by that mode of conveyance. Such as had no horses to ride would prefer to paddle down the Des Moines and the Mississippi rivers and up the Missouri. White men were at work on the Indians, endeavoring to detain them as long as there was a prospect of selling them whiskey and filching their annuities.

Keokuk's people told Agent Beach, in March, 1845, that their horses would be too poor during that spring to stand the journey to their new home, and therefore they wished to wait until the first of September, as by then their horses would be in better condition, their corn would be harvested, and the hot days would be over. They desired their annuity paid them in June if possible, in order that they might make necessary purchases, and they would then make ready to leave. As Beach could not secure the necessary co-operation from Washington, the Indians in August again urged that necessary steps be taken so they could get away before the frosts, and perhaps snows, would kill the grass on which their horses must depend. They proposed to take along corn from their own fields to sustain them on the way. But still the Foxes withheld any sign of co-operation, refusing even to discuss a subject that was so repugnant to them.

Keokuk submitted an estimate of the supplies needed by the Sauk on arrival at their destination, promised by the government, consisting of 150 barrels of flour, 75 barrels of pork, and 1,500 bushels of corn to last them until spring. And the Foxes would need even more. These people still hoped to winter on the Kansas River before going to their own reservation. An exploring party of both factions returned in August with a favorable report, but there continued many endless objections and questions that the agent was obliged to discuss with the Indians in order to reconcile them to an early departure, though there was a strong disposition on the part of the Foxes to evade and postpone even a serious consideration of the unwelcome subject. But as to Keokuk, said Agent Beach, "he cooperates with me in everything." The first of September came, and the government still delayed the payment of their annuity, without which the Indians could not complete their plans for removal. But for other reasons the Foxes still held back. By way of contrast, said the agent, "a word of praise of Keokuck. It is a pleasure to transact business with him because of his aptness to understand motives and arguments, and to appreciate the condition of his people, while his readiness to cooperate, and forward every measure suggested by me, merits the approbation of the department."

Even the Foxes, he thought, were becoming reconciled to the plan to extract a living from the soil in their new home. But, "as to assuming any of the habits and customs of civilization, these Indians are as averse as ever, even to the idea of its probability. In regard to some of their ancient manners, and especially of their superstitions—perhaps, too, in respect to their vindictiveness, cruelty, and other unamiable traits of early character, the last fifty years of intercourse with our countrymen may be supposed, of necessity, to have modified some habits and to have softened some asperities of their original nature, yet in general, they are as much savages, and as anxious to continue such, as they were a half century ago. . . . . To one accustomed to reside among them, and knowing the abandoned character of the great portion of those with whom they are much in contact—men whose licentious dispositions, love of gain, and propensities for the most sensual indulgences, unchecked either by any respect for their own character or the opinions of the more virtuous, will ever draw them to our frontiers as long as a hope of success in their shameless course may exist—it is not a subject of astonishment that the education, the civilization and religion of the white man are held by them in so little estimation. Our education appears to consist in knowing how most effectually to cheat them; our civilization in knowing how to pander to the worst propensities of nature, and then beholding the criminal and inhuman results with a cold indifference—a worse than heathen apathy; while our religion is readily summed up in the consideration of dollars and cents."[21]

It was most important for them to leave as soon as possible their unhealthful camps on Raccoon River. During the preceding year seventy-nine Indians had died, including Pashepah, a chief of some note. The tribe was now reduced to 2,200. Finally, on September 17, Keokuk and his band began their march. Hardfish and his band followed a day or two later; while Powsheik and his Foxes postponed their unhappy departure for two or three weeks longer. The month of September was well along before they all had finished gathering their corn; they then crossed to the south side of the Raccoon and made final preparations to depart in small bodies. The agent gave several who were too ill to travel permission to remain, with some of their relatives to care for them. Finally, on October 5, the Foxes began their movement and were soon reported scattered along in parties for a distance of twenty miles. Their slow movement, the agent said, was accounted for by the great amount of sickness among them. Several had died since they crossed the Des Moines River, "mostly children, as many as five died the same night." But few took advantage of the permission granted to the sick to remain.[22]

The movement of the Indians was irregular and not well organized. They traveled in separate bodies over different routes, made protracted camps, were delayed by sickness, stopped to fish or hunt and for other reasons, and winter was upon some of them before they completed their journey. One band of 473 Foxes passed through Lexington, Missouri, on November 24. This body included five chiefs, among whom were two sons of Black Hawk. Downey, Longhorn, and Black Neck were other chiefs of the party. The *Lexington Advertiser* commented: "The appearance of the whole company is quite comfortable; and their deportment is very good. This is the first town of any size they have passed through since they left Iowa, and they manifested their pleasure by forming a procession and singing one of their peculiar songs. The braves were mounted and armed, and made a very fine appearance. The pack-horses and ponies were principally under the charge of the squaws."

A few days later these Indians passed through Independence on the western boundary of Missouri. According to the *Western Expositor* of January 6: "They traveled on cheerfully notwithstanding the mercury in the thermometer stood five degrees below zero. It was reported that they had the bodies of two or three children with them who had been frozen to death, which they were taking to their new location."[23]

Early in 1846, detached companies began arriving in the vicinity of their reservation. The entire body of Sauk and about one-fifth of the Foxes reached the Kansas River, where they awaited the arrival of the rest in order to determine which of the two locations offered them they would accept. The Foxes, who were yet behind, in passing through the country of the Potawatomi, were induced by these friends and former allies who spoke an almost identical language to halt with them for a while, said their agent, John Beach.

There was considerable confusion, owing to the difference of opinion about their location and the fact that a large element of the tribe was determined to make temporary arrangements with the Shawnee, and other tribes if possible, for emergency use of their land to put in a crop to fortify themselves against hunger. Agent Beach stated their situation on September 1, 1846, in his report to the superintendent of Indian affairs at St. Louis, in language that exhibits his understanding of the Indians and the responsibilities of the government:

"The Sacs and Foxes have been subjected to a great change; to this change with greater or less readiness they must now accommodate themselves; and besides that during the process of such accommodation our feelings and sympathies would most naturally be called into action, it does not appear that a more fitting period could offer in which, if rightly used, that could prove more eminently useful. Hitherto, and for so long a term of years that even their own history is based at best upon an uncertain tradition, they have owned and occupied the region whose last remaining portion they have finally yielded up; and, deserting forever the hunting grounds of their ancestors, leaving behind them their early neighbors and early friendships as well as enmities, they are transferred to a strange climate, and to a land, the home, even within the recollection of the present race, of their deadliest foes, there to seek new friendships and alliances, and perhaps entail upon their posterity new enmities. Reared upon prairies once rich in game, even its rapid disappearance in recent years would not constitute a necessity sufficient to overcome their fondness for a life endeared by habit and early partiality. But now brought to a country comparatively without game, aware of their situation, their thoughts seem to be settling upon some other plan of subsistence. It is these and similar considerations which lead me to view their changes as bringing up subjects of interest, not to themselves alone, but likewise to those whose aim is to advance the causes of civilization, of moral and religious culture.

"Again, these people have come out from a country endeared by tenderest recollections; their cradle, the home of their youth, the sepulcher of their ancestors, and of many dearest friends; thus left to the uncertain guardianship of strangers to be too often sacrilegiously betrayed. We are prone to attribute to the red man a stolid indifference to such subjects; but I know with what reason, or rather, with what want of it. We understand the influence of such sentiments upon more cultivated natures; and may it not be that upon those confined to a more limited range of thought, and strangers to many of the reflections that bring comfort to us, these feelings may be more keenly impressed? Not only have they thus removed, but with a promptitude and a fidelity, if not without parallel, certainly not surpassed, and most fully corroborating the high character which I have been ever proud to give them. Adhering with an unabated pertinacity to their primitive wildness, studious of no change, their nature has stamped upon it many of the noblest traits; a fidelity, a regard to truth, a sense of honesty and honor, a pride of person and nation which, even when compared with their more civilized Indian neighbors, gives them, in the eye of the multitude, a higher ground."[24]

The exalted opinion of these Indians held by their agent derived in no small degree from the character of the chief, Keokuk, who had given Beach the greatest measure of co-operation and fidelity, as indeed he had given the government generally in the effort to remove the Indians from the area in which they were being debauched by the whites to what, it was fondly hoped, would be a safe retreat beyond the border.

There was constant contention and friction between the Iowa and Sauk of the Missouri who lived within the Great Nemaha agency. The latter claimed that the Iowa stole their hogs, and, to avert further trouble, half of them removed and joined the Sauk and Foxes of the Mississippi, who were within the Osage River agency, attracted, their agent said, by the large annuity the newcomers enjoyed.

The Osage River agency included the Sauk and Foxes ("the confederated tribes of Sauk and Foxes, now recognized as one and the same"), the Kansas, Chippewa, Ottawa, Piankashaw, Peoria, Wea, and Miami (all receiving annuities but the Peoria). The agency was located in the Sauk and Fox Nation on the south side of the Marais des Cygnes (the north fork of the Osage River), about sixty-five miles southwest of Westport (Kansas City), Jackson County, Missouri.

The Sauk and Foxes in 1847 were reported by their agent as comfortably located in the present Kansas on the headwaters of the Osage River, "beyond the reach of the unhappy influences . . . . of the white population," as he fatuously believed.[25] They had built several large villages of bark huts, the Sauk occupying some exclusively and the

Foxes the others. Fields of corn evidenced commendable industry. They still devoted much time to hunting and in August, 1847, returned from a successful buffalo hunt. The buffalo were found so near that they had much more buffalo meat and robes than their horses were able to carry home.[26] But, said their agent, John Beach of the Osage River agency, they "pertinaciously reject every overture for the admission of schools or missionaries among them."

Concerning the Sauk and Foxes of the Missouri River, their agent, W. E. Rucker, of the Great Nemaha agency, who was also agent for the Iowa, had a somewhat different story to tell. They attended the mission school in satisfactory numbers. "But for the corrupt influence of the whisky traders, who live so near, I am satisfied that the school would soon have as many scholars as the building is calculated to accommodate. During the winter months they have a fine school, but when the spring returns it is difficult to prevent many of the children from returning to their old dress and habit, the blanket and the bow and arrow."[27]

The history of the Sauk and Foxes continued in much the same pattern. In 1850 a devastating drought brought much suffering from lack of food, and the next year more than three hundred of the tribe died of smallpox in spite of the fact that many yielded to vaccination. Pneumonia also took its heavy toll. By now the Chippewa were living on the Sauk and Fox reservation with the Ottawa; their languages, the agent said, were almost identical.

The population of the Sauk and Foxes continued to recede at a consistently high rate, which the agent attributed principally to the consumption of whiskey. The women were usually sent for it to the Missouri line fifty miles away. On their return they concealed it by burying it in the earth some distance from their lodges, whence, to escape detection, it was taken out in small quantities for consumption.

A delegation of four from the Sauk and Foxes of the Missouri was induced to go to Washington, where, on May 17, 1854, they entered into a treaty[28] with George W. Manypenny, commissioner on the part of the United States, wherein they ceded their reservation of four hundred square miles set apart to them on September 17, 1836, on the Missouri River area, to be divided between them and the 427 Iowa Indians, reserving to the former fifty sections if they could find it in one body—to be selected by them within six months. In consideration also, the Missouri and the Sauk and Foxes were to be paid $48,000.

The President was to have the land surveyed when the Indians had made their selection.

The immigrant Indians engaged in regular hunting expeditions for buffalo, which provided them food and raiment. They thus incurred the enmity of the resident Indians, who claimed all the game in the country and on occasions undertook to convince the newcomers of the danger of intruding. While the Potawatomi were on their summer hunt in 1853, they were attacked by a band of western Indians, whom, after a hard-fought battle lasting more than half a day, the Potawatomi put to flight, leaving twenty or thirty of their dead on the battlefield.[29] The western Indians had organized for the express purpose of driving the immigrants from the hunting grounds. They first came in contact with the Pawnee, who, said the agent, "but for the timely aid of the Pottawatomies (who happened to be but a few miles away) would have killed the last one, as they had them surrounded and had killed some ten or fifteen before the Pottawatomies reached the scene of action. All parties gave the Pottawatomies great credit for their gallant conduct on that occasion. They lost in killed and wounded some four or five. We anticipate a renewal of hostilities next summer if they should meet on the plains."[30]

Sure enough, the vanquished Indians, who had nourished their humiliation through the succeeding year, organized for revenge in the summer of 1854. At the agency near Fort Atkinson, the Kiowa, Comanche, Apache, Cheyenne, and Arapaho Indians came to receive their annuity goods. Said their agent, John W. Whitefield: "They were encamped on Pawnee Fork at the crossing of the Santa Fe road, where they were collected in larger numbers than have ever been known to assemble on the Arkansas river before. Old traders estimate the number at twelve to fifteen hundred lodges, and the horses and mules at from forty to fifty thousand head." They had met for the purpose of forming their war party in order, as they said, to wipe out all the immigrant Indians they could find on the plains. Augmented by a few well-armed Osage bucks come to share in the adventure, they departed two days before the arrival of their agent with their annuity goods. The agent sent couriers to the Indians ordering them to return, but they refused immediate compliance, saying that, with their overwhelming force, they would quickly clean up the intruding Indians, after which they would return.

About one hundred miles west of Fort Riley, in the vicinity of Smoky Hill, they met a party of Sauk and Foxes—mainly Foxes—and a few

Potawatomi, the whole not exceeding a hundred in number. The aggressors, believing, to use the words of one of their chiefs, that they "would eat so small a force in a few minutes," made a general charge. The immigrants strategically retired to the protection of a near-by ravine and allowed the attackers to approach within a hundred yards, when they opened up a well-directed fire on them, which, being unexpected, momentarily appalled the assailants. Three times these charges with bow and arrow were repeated, and at each sortie a like fatal result followed. After a siege of three hours, the attackers retired, crestfallen and dispirited, after suffering twenty-six killed and more than a hundred wounded. On their return to Fort Atkinson their appearance and deportment were quite changed, testifying to the terrible lesson they had learned from the well-armed immigrants. They seemed humble and dejected, said their agent, and quietly and submissively received their annuity goods and departed for their homes to nurse their wounded and hide their humiliation. The loss of the Sauk and Foxes, less than a half-dozen, was attributed to the rifle-armed Osage.

Later a Sauk whose brother was among those killed left the reservation alone and rode within four hundred yards of an Osage encampment. Here he met two Osage men, shot and scalped one and could have killed the other but wished him to live to carry to the Osage camp the news of what he had done. He waited until the Osage had done so, heard the cries and lamentations of those in camp for their dead kinsman, and then mounted his horse and returned to within a mile of the agency, where his friends engaged in dancing with joy and triumph over the trophy brought back from this warlike achievement.[31]

The next year Beach located his agency at the home of Baptiste Peoria, the interpreter, a remarkable Indian. Said the agent: "The character of this man for honesty, truth, and the great influence he wields over the Indians, together with his expanded knowledge of their affairs, seemed to make it necessary that I should have him near me. Much of the credit for sobriety and industry, and the consequent advancement in the paths of civilization, which the Indians seem to be entitled to, is due to Battiest Peoria. . . . . I do think, that if he was taken from amongst the Indians here by death or otherwise, they would be like bees without their legitimate head; they would scatter and decline, so that there would soon be no more of them. They look to him as children to an affectionate father. He is now warning them daily of the great changes which are soon to take place with them, and the nature of the elements with which they are soon to be surrounded, and the consequent necessity of industry and sobriety to counteract the dangerous influences to which they will be exposed."[32] His influence was needed more than ever now, as their missionary, the Reverend Jothan Meeker, to whom they were so much indebted, died in January, 1855.

The Indians continued to oppose schools; they could not comprehend the purpose or benefits of education. If, at times, children were induced to attend, the parents, resentful at their being put to work or chastised, encouraged them to desert and return home.

The agent reported the number of Sauk and Foxes in 1857 as 1,367— a loss of 381 in three years. With but three or four exceptions, "they live in bark houses, shave their heads, dress with the blanket and leggins, and universally paint; white contact has done them but little good. Women do all the work. I have never seen a man work; they go twice a year on their hunts—spring and fall." Measles among the children was very fatal.

Shortly before the Civil War the government inaugurated the allotment policy, and the agent, Perry Fuller, as one of his first official acts, on October 1, 1859, convened at the Sauk and Fox agency Keokuk and eight other chiefs and delegates of the Sauk and Foxes of the Mississippi. These he induced to enter into another treaty,[33] in which they were made to say that, "having more lands than are necessary for their occupancy and use, and being desirous of promoting settled habits of industry and enterprise amongst themselves, by abolishing the tenure in common in which they now hold their lands, and by assigning limited quantities thereof, in severalty, to the individual members of the tribe," they agreed to have 150,000 acres of their reservation set apart for allotment in severalty in tracts of 80 acres to each member of the tribe, for which certificates of title were to be issued; these allotments could not be sold to anyone but the government. The remainder of the reservation, amounting to 290,000 acres, was to be thrown on the market and sold by the government in tracts of 160 acres for the benefit of white settlers. From the proceeds of the sale the debts of the Indians were to be paid to greedy creditors. Illustrating the hypocrisy of the recitals in the treaty and pointing to the influences that brought it about, it was provided that mixed-bloods and Indian women who had intermarried with white men were to have 320 acres each, four times the amount of allotments to other Indians.[34] Indians who were separated from the tribe and did not return within one year were not to share in the proceeds of the sale.

It was notorious that this treaty was manipulated by white men for the purpose of speculation in the lands of the Indians.[35] It was managed at a time the Foxes were away from home on a buffalo hunt. When they returned and heard about it, they were indignant and refused to ratify the treaty, as a result of which the agent deposed the chief of the Foxes; but his followers refused to sanction the act. On the contrary, the Fox chief and most of the Foxes left the reservation and returned to Iowa.

Their slaughter of the Comanche four years before and the fear of punishment were partly responsible for their stealing-off to Iowa. There, with their own money, they purchased a small tract of land near Tama City on the Iowa River, on which they settled. With their unaided efforts, and cut off from annuities payable to the tribe in Kansas, they purchased more land from time to time with the proceeds of their farming efforts, until in a few years they owned more than three thousand acres, on which they lived quite independent of the remainder of the tribe.[36]

Beach, the agent for the Sauk and Foxes, was an intelligent observer, who submitted an interesting analysis of Indian character and suggested remedies for their retarded development. He observed that the first object of the government "should be to remove prejudices against labor, which are deeply fixed upon their minds while in childhood, by the recitals in the wigwam of the traditions, tales, and fabulous accounts of the chiefs and braves of heroic conflicts with the enemies of their tribe, and of their stratagems and maneuverings while on the war path in encompassing their foes; and also of their great exploits in hunting the buffalo and bear. The mind of the male child is filled with visions of their future success in attaining thus a high rank in their tribe. It is the goal of their ambition; and it is not without its influence upon the young female, who encourages with her smiles and admiration the successful warrior and hunter."

"Among the numerous elements now operating against the Red Man," he continued, "and hastening the period of his extinction, none has been more effectual to this end than the everlasting grasping of the white man for Indian lands. Scarcely has a tribe alienated the greater portion of its lands, and begun settlement upon a smaller portion retained for a new and more permanent home, when the Indians are again urged to 'sell out,' and assailed with all the appliances which those speculators who are unscrupulous enough to know so well how to use, and who have already absorbed so much of the wild land of the country as to make it, in some sections, difficult for the industrious poor man to procure a home without paying exhorbitant tribute to these land misers for this, and making their remaining vast domains more valuable.

"The question is almost daily asked 'When will the Iowas sell out? When will the Sacs and Foxes sell their reservation and remove?' This interferes with the efforts of government to teach the Indians habits of industry and economy, and makes them heedless of the future."

In 1860 a disastrous drought and crop failure prevailed throughout Kansas, and the Indians suffered for food; some left their reservations and located with other Indians farther from white people, where it was hoped to find more game to feed their families. Agent Fuller, in his report for 1860,[37] was less interested in the suffering of the Indians than he was in felicitating his superior officer, the Indian commissioner, on the wisdom of his policy represented in a recent treaty. He pretended to believe that the Indians were adapting themselves to the changes implied in the treaty and were becoming in some degree "alive to the knowledge of the additional benefits which would accrue to them as individuals and as a nation, in abandoning their Indian habits and customs, and adopting the dress and comforts of civilized life. It will doubtless be almost an impossibility to effect a change in these respects among the older members of the nation, as from the force of long habit and their deep-rooted belief in the traditions and legends peculiar to the North American aboriginal, they will feel loth to relinquish the paraphernalias and trappings of Indian costumes, in order to adopt dress and habits so widely different from their own. .... They have been much annoyed and injured by unprincipled whites who have stolen their ponies and horses[38] and committed depredations of various kinds upon their property. Yet they have borne it all with calmness, nor have they at any time manifested a disposition to retaliate upon the offenders, trusting entirely to the government to make good and indemnify them for losses sustained by them in this way. In this connection, I would state that the appropriation of a sum of money to defray such expenses, would be an act of justice towards them, which they both expect and deserve.

"Under the provisions of the treaty of October 2, 1859, a reservation was allotted to them 12 miles by 20 in extent, and containing 153,600 acres from which each individual is to be apportioned 80 acres, and given a certificate of title thereto, subject to the control and under the direction of the secretary of the interior. After such an allotment has been made, there will remain 51,200 acres yet vacant. All the members of the nation with whom I have conversed express themselves well pleased with the late treaty, and are solicitous to have the provisions and stipulations carried out during the coming fall and winter, if possible. Their situation during the approaching winter will, I fear, be characterized by destitution and suffering, as the crops of all kinds in this territory have this season failed completely; and without their usual supply of corn, they have nothing to depend upon for subsistence but their annuity and such game as they can kill while on their semi-annual hunt."

The reports of the agents for the Sauk and Foxes noted a constant rate of mortality among the Indians from a hundred to three times as many yearly and recorded also incessant complaints for the introduction of whiskey by white men. In the report of the agent for 1862 there was a touch of something a little more cheerful: "In the season for drying corn and pumpkin they leave their houses, so long have they led a nomadic life, and pitch their tents in the midst of the ripened crops. In shelling and drying the corn, in paring and cutting the golden pumpkins, with which poles suspended in crotched sticks and trees soon become festooned, all the females, old and young, gleefully unite. . . . . And here let me remark that I do not find the Indian the taciturn stoic I had been led to expect. His nature may have been greatly changed by intercourse for two or three generations with his white brother, but I suspect that, in this respect, and in very much that has been written concerning the red man, writers have been deceived by outward appearances, or have drawn largely upon their fancy.

"When in the presence of strangers they are reserved and grave, but by themselves as talkative and pleasant as whites, and I venture to say that there sits in the world no council of state wherein more jokes are cracked and retorts indulged in, always in the best of humor, than passes between the chiefs and braves of the Sac and Fox council. But to return. These Indians have worn more shoes, hats and other garments of civilization this season than ever before. They have got two or three wagons, owned by the Missouri Sacs, who have moved among them, and in these they have broken several pairs of ponies to work, and take great delight in driving them about."[39]

So much for the Sauk and Foxes in Kansas. Those remaining in Iowa, while distinguishing themselves for their foresight in acquiring land on which to make their living, at the same time presented by contrast some of the most primitive characteristics. In the warm summer days it was not an uncommon sight to witness an old man, with his blankets spread upon the ground, basking in the sunshine and teaching his grandchildren and the young men of the tribe the religion and traditions of his ancestors. The following is a brief extract from a long account written by their agent in 1898:

"Matauequa, the last war chief of the Sac and Fox Indians of Iowa who knew what it meant to meet the enemy in open battles or take him from ambush in the pioneer days of the State, died in camp along the Iowa river, about four miles west of Tama at sunrise on the morning of October 4, at the advanced age of 87 years. He was born at Dubuque, Iowa, in 1810, and had the place and date tatooed on his right arm. In physique, habits, customs, and mental endowments he was a typical Indian of the warrior days. His burial on the afternoon of October 5 was attended with considerable interest and many of the business men from Montour, Tama, and Toledo paid their respects to his memory. The district judge adjourned his court at Toledo to attend the funeral in company with other representative white men. The body had been carefully preserved according to Indian methods and customs, and was dressed in the regalia of a war chief. It was wrapped in a blanket and laid on a framework of poles, over which was spread a new piece of matting woven by Indian women from rushes in beautiful designs of various colors.

"Before his death the old chief had selected Patoka to have charge of his burial and had given minute directions as to all the appointments, and all his directions were closely followed. He was buried in a rough coffin, in a sitting posture, the painted feather in his hair coming just to the edge of the ground, his face to the west, and his face and breast laid bare. Otherwise he was clad in moccasins, leggings, and blanket, and adorned with beads and paint, much as he had appeared on many important occasions. In the coffin were placed a bottle of water, a small vessel containing food, and an Indian hand bag containing many little articles that would be useful on the journey to the happy hunting grounds and his two walking sticks. Then a lid was placed over the lower part of the coffin, covering the limbs of the body, leaving the chest exposed, and over the lid of the coffin were spread several blankets. All the blankets and clothing used by the deceased during his sickness were placed in the grave.

"After the body had been arranged in the coffin, Wapelluka, an old man who had fought in more than one historic battle side by side with Matauequa, delivered an address in the Indian language at the grave, and, according to the Indian custom, was the first to sprinkle tobacco into the grave. In this ceremony he was followed by all the other Indians present, who passed around the grave as they sprinkled the holy tobacco into the coffin, and one of their number sat by the grave for several minutes and in a low monotone performed the sad rites. The tobacco used in their burial exercises is raised by a few of the priests of the tribe on a small patch of ground set apart for that purpose, and is used only in connection with their religious ceremonies."[40]

NOTES

1. A. Chouteau, "Notes" (1804), Records of the Department of the Interior, Office of Indian Affairs, "Ancient and Miscellaneous Surveys" (National Archives). The last-described area lay within the present boundaries of Iowa.

2. *House Report 51* (19th Cong., 2d sess.).

3. 7 *U.S. Stat.* 134.

4. *Ibid.* p. 135.

5. *Ibid.*, p.141; see also "Treaties with Twenty-one Tribes," *American State Papers,* "Indian Affairs," II, 1.

6. 7 *U.S. Stat.* 272.

7. Among the thirteen Sauk signers was Chief Keokuk (or "the Watchful Fox").

8. Dougherty to Bean, May 14, 1830 (*Doc.*, II, 97).

9. Bean to Clark, July 12, 1830 (*ibid.*).

10. 7 *U.S. Stat.* 328.

11. *Doc.*, II, 516 *passim* to 554.

12. *Handbook*, II, 470.

13. Grant Foreman, *Illinois and Her Indians* ("Papers in Illinois History" [1939]).

14. 7 *U.S. Stat.* 511.

15. *Ibid.*, p. 516. See also *Report of the Commissioner of Indian Affairs, 1838*, p. 462.

16. 7 *U.S. Stat.* 540 and 543.

17. *Report, 1842.*

18. *Report, 1843.* On August 8, 1840, Congress granted to the state of Iowa 332,000 acres of former Sauk and Fox land along the Des Moines River from the mouth up to Raccoon Creek for the improvement of navigation (*Report, 1861*, p. 31).

19. The preceding and succeeding accounts by their agent, Beach, are from the archives of the Oklahoma Historical Society, Sauk and Fox Letter Books, Archives Division.

20. *Ibid.*

21. *Ibid.*

22. *Ibid.*

23. *Cherokee Advocate*, December 25, 1845, p. 3, col. 4; *ibid.*, January 8, 1846, p. 3, col. 6.

24. Oklahoma Historical Society, Sauk and Fox Letter Books, Archives Division.

25. On March 3 of this year Congress passed an act strengthening the legislation against the introduction of intoxicating liquors into the Indian country and revising somewhat the laws governing administration of Indian affairs.

26. *Report, 1847*, p. 845.

27. *Ibid.*, p. 875.

28. Kappler (ed.), *Laws and Treaties*, II, 469; 10 *U.S. Stat.* 1074.

29. *Report, 1854*, pp. 77, 90. The agent at Council Bluffs agency related that a

party of Indian hunters, having engaged in a very successful hunt and being on their return home, learned that a band of their Sioux and Ponca enemies was likely shortly to attack them. The hunters, thus forewarned, erected a barricade with the great quantity of buffalo meat and robes with which their ponies were loaded, and in the ensuing battle repulsed their enemies. "After the loss of four or five men," said the agent, "together with some forty horses, they drove the enemy back, and became victors of the field. The Sioux and Poncas, it is supposed, had eight or nine men killed and some ten or twelve wounded." Except for being forewarned and in fortunate possession of materials for a barricade, said the agent, the hunting party would have been annihilated by the superior numbers of the enemy (*Report, 1849*, p. 1077).

30. *Report, 1853*, p. 82.

31. *Report, 1854*, p. 90.

32. *Report, 1855*, p. 110.

33. 15 *U.S. Stat.* 467.

34. A schedule of forty-eight persons thus favored and identified by the ubiquitous Perry Fuller is attached to the treaty of February 18, 1867 (15 *U.S. Stat.* 499). Among them, the names of "Whistler," "Thorpe," and "Connolly" appear frequently.

35. *Handbook*, II, 477.

36. On July 13, 1857, the Foxes purchased the first eighty acres from Colonel Phil Butler of Montour, Iowa, for $1,000, which they paid with ponies. The deed was made in trust to James W. Grimes, governor of Iowa. From time to time they added to their holdings by purchasing adjoining tracts, until in 1899 they owned 1,452 acres (*Report, 1889*, p. 213). By 1896 sixteen tracts of land had been purchased and conveyed to the governor in trust for the Indians and other tracts to the agent and other trustees. On January 16, 1896, the Iowa legislature transferred to the United States jurisdiction over the "Sac and Fox Indians of Tama County, Iowa" and their lands (*Report, 1898*, p. 81).

37. *Report, 1860*, p. 334.

38. *Ibid.*

39. *Report, 1862*, p. 106. In the treaty they were induced to make on March 6, 1861 (12 *U.S. Stat.* 1174), they and the Iowa Indians gave up more of their land. Section 10 of the treaty provided for expending $3,500 of their money to construct a toll bridge for their alleged benefit. As they had no need for a toll bridge, they later petitioned that, instead of building a bridge (obviously for the convenience of white settlers), the money be used to buy them wagons, oxen, and plows (*House Executive Doc. 153* [40th Cong., 2d sess.]).

40. *Report, 1898*, p. 165.

PART II

CHAPTER IX

EMIGRANTS AND IMMIGRANTS

THE subject of migration of the Indians to their final home in Oklahoma automatically divides into tribal groups, periods, and phases. Broadly speaking, removal of the Indians from the east to the west side of the Mississippi River was substantially completed between 1830 and 1845. At the present stage of this book it may be said that the first phase of removal of the eastern Indians has been about achieved. It is now planned to consider the subject in its second aspect—the brief residence of these Indians in Kansas before they were again uprooted, compelled to move, and forced to yield a substantial part of their new reservation in compliance with the demands of the white man. This paralleled the diminished need for land as their number was reduced by death and conformed to certain political changes and divestiture of rights guaranteed to them by former legislation.

But, first, consideration should be given to the earlier arrivals in the West described in previous chapters who did not settle on reservations in Kansas set apart for them by the government but drifted down into Texas or into southern Oklahoma apart from their tribes, which subsequently were located in Kansas. The Shawnee had become widely dispersed under varying influences. When the issue of the War of 1812 turned against the Indians fighting on the side of Great Britain, some of the Shawnee left the Lakes country for a home far removed from the scenes of their misfortunes and located with some Delawares on Red River within what is now McCurtain County, Oklahoma.

White squatters in this area, then called Miller County, Arkansas, imagined they had paramount rights there, and on March 28, 1828, complained to Governor Izard of the presence of the Indians. In a memorial signed by forty-four of their number, they demanded the removal of these Shawnee and Delawares.[1]

The petitioners said that the alleged intruders were there under a permission in writing executed on March 20, 1827, at Nacogdoches by

"His Excellency Don Jose Antonio Saucedo of the Department of Texas," by the terms of which the Indians were granted the right to remain in the vicinity of Pecan Point until it should be determined whether the disputed territory belonged to Texas or to the United States, when the Indians would be confirmed in their title if the decision favored Texas. Regardless of this color of title, Izard, on April 7, 1828, ordered Wharton Rector, "adjutant general" of Arkansas Territory, to recruit a command with which he was to drive the Indians out of Miller County.[2] On May 8, 1828, Rector reported to Izard that he visited the Indians concerned; the Delewares agreed to remove at once, but the Shawnee defied him. Rector then recruited sixty-three armed militia, and, when he advanced to the neighborhood of the Indian settlement, the Shawnee sued for peace and said that they would remove from the Territory as soon as their hunters could return "from the woods." To effect this, he gave them twenty days' time.[3]

Some of these fugitive Shawnee were seen by George S. Gaines and his exploring party of Choctaw Indians in 1831, when the latter unintentionally penetrated their retreat: "A half-breed woman looking at me," wrote Gaines, "said 'you are a white man—I hoped never to see the face of another white man.' I inquired the reason for such a hope. She answered, her husband and several members of her family had been killed by the whites. 'The remnants of my relations,' said she, 'were compelled to leave their homes and we traveled to this country where we hoped to live in peace.'" However, the Shawnee gladly accepted the offer of the Choctaw chief Nitaketchi permitting them to remain and live in his nation if they would conform to the laws of the tribe.[4]

Other bands of Shawnee removed to Texas and settled on the headwaters of the Sabine River[5] with the Cherokee, where they were joined by bands separated from the remainder of the Shawnee, who subsequently were emigrated to Kansas.

The white people who began settling in Texas coveted the fine lands occupied by these Shawnee, Delawares, Kickapoo, and Cherokee, and, in spite of the favor with which the Indians were regarded by President Sam Houston, took steps to drive them out of the country. At The Bowle's Village, on February 25, 1836, a treaty was entered into between Houston and another commissioner representing Texas, and the Cherokee and associate bands then residing in that republic— the Shawnee, Delawares, Kickapoo, and a number of others. This treaty gave the Indians for their home the tract of land embracing the present counties of Cherokee, Smith, and parts of others, conditioned upon their moving upon it and forming themselves into a community.

Houston strongly urged ratification of this treaty, but the Texas senate in 1837 refused. While studying the subject, a committee appointed for the purpose reported to the president of Texas on the Indians in that republic. Among others they mentioned Kickapoo, Shawnee, Delawares, Potawatomi, and Menominee Indians living in the county of Nacogdoches, having been residents of Texas since about 1829. With few exceptions, the committee reported, the Delawares and Shawnee all were well armed and excellent hunters and marksmen and that about five hundred of them roamed the prairies in perfect confidence.[6]

After the Texas senate refused to ratify Houston's treaty, believing that the Cherokee and their associates were conspiring with the Mexican government to war on the Texas Republic, a commission was appointed by General Mirabeau B. Lamar, Houston's successor as president, supported by regiments of troops, and sent to the Cherokee people to demand their immediate removal across the border. On their refusal, they were attacked, July 15 and 16, 1839, and defeated in two engagements, The Bowle and his associate chief, Hard Mush, being among the large number of Indians killed.[7]

The Indians fled across Red River and took refuge along the Washita and Blue rivers in the Choctaw and Chickasaw nations. The latter, just getting settled in their new home, resented the presence of the newcomers, and hostilities threatened. Among the intruders was a band of Kickapoo living on the Washita River on lands of the Chickasaw. While Chickasaw agent Kingsbury spoke well of them, he sent word to the Kickapoo chief to come to Boggy Depot and explain their intrusion. The chief showed Kingsbury credentials issued to them by General Thomas J. Rusk of Texas. Some were passports through Texas, and all of a friendly nature, vouching for the good character of the Indians. However, it developed that Rusk was merely trying to get them out of Texas and had told them to cross into the Chickasaw country to the Washita River, where they would find plenty of game. He said that the Chickasaw were hospitable Indians in that country who would give the Kickapoo land on which to live. The latter relied on Rusk's information and moved over among the Chickasaw, where the chief said that they wanted to raise a little corn to keep their people from starving.[8]

The intruders, however, were charged with stealing the horses and cattle of the Chickasaw, and, by their menaces and threats, of imposing a reign of terror on the resident Indians, who appealed to General Matthew Arbuckle at Fort Gibson for help. It was not until May, 1841, that Arbuckle dispatched Captain B. D. Moore with a detachment to remove the intruding Indians, except those who had corn growing. These were to be permitted to remain long enough to harvest their crops and obtain grain to keep them from starving. Moore was directed also to find a site for an army post from which to police the country along Red River. Later, General Zachary Taylor approved his selection and ordered the establishment of a post which was subsequently named Fort Washita.[9] About 200 Kickapoo defied the whites in 1838 and returned to Texas.[10] In 1843, on Tawakoni Creek, they participated in an important Indian council presided over by Pierce M. Butler, in which representatives of the Delaware, Caddo, Shawnee, and Texas tribes took part.

Lacking a welcome from any other source, most of the fugitive Indians accepted the invitation of the Creek chiefs to settle in their country on the north side of the Canadian River. Here they proceeded to build homes and engage in farming and stock-raising.

The extent to which this part of Oklahoma was then occupied by intrusive Indians from the East was indicated by a report made by Colonel Ethan Allen Hitchcock from information derived by him while on an inspection tour of the Indian Territory in 1841 and 1842. Colonel Hitchcock traveled through the Creek Nation and made one of his stops at Edwards' Trading House, where he saw many of the Indians and took evidence concerning their presence. He reported that there were seven hundred Shawnee living on both sides of the Canadian River. Some of them, he said, had never lived in the country allotted to them in Kansas but had wandered to the Southwest after the death of Tecumseh and the defeat of the coalition formed by him. There were some seven hundred Delawares living sixty miles above the mouth of Little River who, with the Shawnee, carried on extensive intercourse with the wild Indians to the west of them. Through these Indians the Comanche had received ammunition and other supplies in the way of trade which aided them in prosecuting their predatory excursions among the white settlements in Texas.[11]

About fifteen miles up the Canadian above the mouth of Little River, fifteen hundred Kickapoo lived in a body, with the Shawnee above and below them (near their future home in the present Lincoln

County, Oklahoma). The Shawnee, Delawares, and Kickapoo all cultivated the land to some extent, particularly the Kickapoo. The Creeks permitted them to live in their country as a measure of policy to protect them against the wild Indians to the west. Besides this, Hitchcock said, there were five or six hundred Piankashaw domesticated among the Creeks, living about fifteen miles above the mouth of Little River. These were allowed, in 1841, by the Creek chiefs, $120 of their annuity, and they were recorded as part of the Creek Nation, their chiefs participating in the Creek general councils.

There was also a village of two hundred and fifty Quapaw living on the Canadian River in the Creek Nation, about eight miles from Little River. Hitchcock said that both Quapaw and Piankashaw cultivated the soil and were peaceful people, having no desire to be involved in any of the wars of the Indians.

Hitchcock's report was evoked by information that the Mexicans were trying to involve the Indians of the Territory on their side in the war against Texas, in which it appeared that the Indians who had recently been driven out of that country were anxious to take up arms against the Texans.[12]

By permission of the Creeks, these Indians were still living on the north bank of the Canadian River in 1845, when their presence was reported by the Creek agent. For the protection of the frontier a military post above Little River had been proposed, but the Indian superintendent, in 1846, reported that it was " a measure clearly unnecessary, as sufficient protection will always be afforded to the frontier settlements by the various hunting parties of Shawnees, Delawares, Kickapoos, Miamies, Quapaws and Caddoes.

"These parties, residing chiefly on the waters of the Canadian, but scattered over the whole region lying west of its mouth and between the Arkansas and Red rivers, are attached to no agency, have no connexion with the government, and but little intercourse with the tribes to which they properly belong. As they differ in many respects from the other Indians in the superintendency, and exercise a peculiar influence upon border affairs, a brief notice of them may not be amiss.

"The Delawares and Shawnees are mainly of what is called the Cape Girardeau band of which the greater part emigrated many years since, after the treaty of Castor Hill, from southwestern Mo. to the country assigned their respective tribes on the Kansas river. The remainder went to Texas—were driven back by the Texans to the Choctaw territory on Washita and Blue rivers, whence they were again removed by the United States troops at the request of the Choctaw authorities. They finally settled, by permission of the Creeks, on the north bank of the Canadian, where the greater part of them now live. They are in a semi-barbarous state, and entirely uneducated, but show great shrewdness and intelligence in their intercourse with the whites. As hunters and warriors they have a higher reputation than any other Indians on the frontier. They bring in large quantities of peltries, but are not entirely dependent upon the chase. They raise an abundance of corn, and raise large herds of cattle. Some of them carry on a regular trade with the Comanches and the Spanish settlements; getting mules from the former and specie from the latter, in exchange for various articles of traffic, chiefly domestics and calicoes. For this purpose and in pursuit of game, they traverse the prairies in every direction in small parties, their character for superior courage and sagacity being so well established that the wild tribes seldom venture to attack them."[13]

The Indian agents in the future Kansas, Iowa, and adjacent jurisdictions reported to the superintendent at St. Louis, and he, in turn, to the Commissioner of Indian Affairs in Washington. Through these reports it is possible to learn much about the progress of the Indians in their new reservation, or, if no progress, then of the deterioration suffered by them from contact with the whites in the West.

Regulations for the administration of Indian affairs were prescribed by the Secretary of War.[14] Four superintendencies under the commissioner were designated, conformable somewhat to ethnic groupings and the geographical distribution of Indian tribes. The superintendency of the Western Territory which embraced the future Oklahoma has been mentioned.

Agencies under these superintendents were as follows: the agency of Fort Leavenworth, to include the Delawares, Kansas, Shawnee, and Kickapoo; the agency of Council Bluffs, to include the Oto and Missouri, Omaha and Pawnee; the subagency of Council Bluffs, including the United Nation of Ottawa, Chippewa, and Potawatomi north of the Missouri; and the subagency of the Osage River in Kansas, including the Potawatomi, Ottawa, Peoria and Kaskaskia, Piankashaw, Wea, Sauk and Foxes, and others not involved herein. Of these agencies most important to this study was the subagency of the Osage River. This was probably more involved with the immigrating Indians discussed here than any other agency, and it was destined to continue in existence longer, from the fact that its Indians were the last to remove from Kansas to the Indian Territory.

The Commissioner of Indian Affairs reported, in 1848, that the immigrant Indians living west of the Mississippi had been divided into two colonies: one in the north, occupying approximately the present area of Minnesota, intended to embrace the Chippewa of Lake Superior and the Upper Mississippi; and the Winnebago, the Menominee, and all other northern Indians, including the Sioux, who were yet to be removed. The southern boundary of this colony was to be the "Watab River, which is the southern limit of the country of the Winnebagoes who have removed there from Iowa within the last year." The Kansas River was to be the northern boundary of the southern colony, which was to include all the immigrant Indians dealt with in this book, as well as the Omaha, Oto, and Missouri, "who are a very interesting people, being mild and tractable in disposition and much attached to the whites," who might be "easily civilized and be made the instruments of imparting civilization to others. Their proper position would be with the Osages of Kansas, as they speak nearly, if not quite, the same language, and are probably of the same primary stock."[15]

While John Bell was Secretary of War in the late 1830's, he proposed the establishment of an Indian Territory in northern Iowa Territory, now Minnesota, and steps were taken to secure cessions of land from the Sioux for this purpose. Indian administration for a limited time proceeded within that concept.[16]

In undertaking to describe the Indians after their removal to Kansas, there is no obvious order to follow; but the groupings made by the government agents of the tribes in various agencies suggest a partial plan. The sequence marking the arrival of the Indians would seem to possess features recommending it but would be realized only to a limited extent, however, owing to haphazard federal policy and necessary lack of a pattern of general or continuous application.

It will be recalled that in the early phases of the subject wandering bands of Illinois and Indiana Indians drifted across the Mississippi River long before the passage of Jackson's Indian Removal Bill. After that bill was enacted, they were removed across the line into what was to become Kansas. As Indian removal was organized according to the terms of the bill, the first and only one of the tribes to be transferred directly from Ohio to the present Oklahoma were bands of Seneca and Shawnee, who were removed in 1831 to what is now the northeastern

corner of Oklahoma and located on Cowskin River on the east side of
the Neosho. Here these Indians united as a confederated band of
Seneca and Shawnee, though they were also identified as the "Senecas
of Sandusky" and as the "Senecas of Cowskin River." The Reverend
Isaac McCoy, in 1833, described these Indians in one of his early com-
munications after their arrival. He said that there was a total of 461
of them, made up of 200 Seneca, 211 confederated Seneca and Shawnee, and 50 Mohawk; most of these people spoke English and cultivated the soil, raising enough food to support themselves and their
livestock. They inclosed their fields with rail fences. They had a tailor
and a cooper, and many of them could use edged tools. Their dwell-
ings were neat, hewn log cabins, within which were bedsteads,
chairs, and tables of their manufacture. Thirty-six of them could read
in the Mohawk language the Book of Common Prayer and the Gospel
of St. Mark, translated into Mohawk by Captain Joseph Brant in 1787,
which contained 505 octavo pages.[17] They maintained an Episcopal
church of fifty members. Notwithstanding these evidences of progress, they had neither church nor school buildings.

These Indians were at first supervised by a separate agency called
"Seneca Agency West of Mo." But, after the arrival of the Quapaw,
they were subject to the supervision of the agent of the Quapaw
agency. The Quapaw Indians, of whom a more detailed account appears elsewhere in this volume, were located here by virtue of a treaty
made with them on May 13, 1833.[18]

The confederated Seneca and Shawnee were getting along fairly
well until the agent noticed a sudden interruption of their progress.
The fields were neglected and given up to weeds. The fences were
falling down, and they presented evidences of an abandoned people.
The cause of this change in their character was a curious one: before
the removal from the East these Indians, already well advanced in
agriculture, were promised in their treaty, as an inspiration to further
progress, a grist mill and a sawmill. The mills were built,[19] but unfortunately there were no others in that part of the country. Conse-
sequently, the white settlers from the adjoining counties in Missouri
and Arkansas flocked in with grain to be ground and logs to be sawed,
and the mills soon yielded the Indians a handsome revenue; the tolls
of the grist mill alone in a good season amounted to two quarts of meal
per day to each individual of the tribe—double the ordinary flour ration then allowed to privates in the army. By this flow of easy income
into the tribe, many of the industrious and well-disposed Indians had

been induced first to give up labor and next to sell the surplus meal for whiskey. Two distilleries were established across the line in Missouri, ready to absorb these current tolls. It was said that one of them was supported and maintained entirely by meal bought from and whiskey sold to the Indians. Every Monday, said their agent, John B. Luce, the day on which the tolls were distributed, three-fourths of the Seneca might be seen about the mill drunk. A drought and curtailed water power at one time remedied this evil. Luce had better reports about the mixed Seneca and Shawnee, of whom there were 225, and hardly a drunkard among them. They were industrious farmers and lived comfortably.

In 1843 their agent reported that the Seneca, and confederated Seneca and Shawnee, were living in a beautiful and fertile country on the east side of Neosho River and doing fairly well as farmers.[20] One Indian that year had raised a thousand bushels of corn. George Curleyeyes and Small Cloud Spicer had exerted themselves effectively for a time to prevent the excessive use of whiskey in the Seneca tribe. Many Seneca died during 1845 and 1846; and by 1848 they were reduced to 144—55 men, 39 women, and 50 children.[21] The consolidated Seneca and Shawnee numbered 253—64 men, 86 women, and 103 children. Their land lay north of the Seneca, covering an area of six miles north and south, and from eight to ten miles east and west. They were said to be more progressive than either the Seneca or their neighbors, the Quapaw. They were much less addicted to drink, and after their crops were laid by and harvesting was completed, they went west on their fall hunt and brought back peltries, which they sold to traders. In 1849 the agent reported them still addicted to the use of liquor, but, under the influence of some of their leading men, they had formed a temperance society.

In 1852 the agent reported that the Seneca were increased to 177 in number—61 men, 44 women, and 72 children.[22] While they raised good crops, there was not much change in their condition, owing to the fact that across the line at Enterprise, Missouri, a white man named Houghton conducted a distillery, from which much whiskey was introduced among the Indians. At the same time their neighbors, the Seneca and Shawnee, totaled only 320 in number—68 men, 94 women, and 158 children. They were opposed to schools and still adhered to their ancient customs, taking on as few of the habits and manners of the white people as possible. They had their festivals and various kinds of dances, attended by nearly all the members of the tribes. Their dog dance was held the first full moon in each year and continued for a week. At this dance they sacrified a white dog, gaudily dressed with different-colored ribbons, and hung by the neck to a gallows erected for that purpose. He remained hanging in that situation for three days, when he was taken down and burned, and his ashes scattered to the four winds. Imagining that he went to the spirit country, the Indians commissioned him to bear such news as they wished to communicate to their departed friends and relatives. The ceremony was conducted with great solemnity, and the Indians seemed to be deeply impressed with its reality.

In spite of this and other evidence of backwardness, the agent said, in 1853, that the Indians were advancing.[23] The Seneca had broken up and fenced and cultivated much additional land; their farms were improving in appearance and promised an abundance of wheat, corn, and oats to carry them through the coming winter. They had plenty of vegetables for their own use and some for sale. Most of them had a number of cattle on their farms; several had comfortable residences and good outbuildings.

The mixed band of Seneca and Shawnee was much in the lead. They were more inclined to imitate the white people, though they still had no schools among them. Many of them were industrious, said their agent, and their farms would compare well with those in New York and Ohio. Some of them had good teams of horses and oxen, with which they earned considerable income by hauling goods for merchants in Missouri and traders in the Indian country. Their houses were mostly built of logs, with good, sound timbers, though there were a number of frame houses among them.

Between April 30, 1834, and November 12, 1835, twelve hundred and fifty Shawnee Indians had emigrated from Ohio and located on their reservation of 1,600,000 acres on the south side of the Kansas River.[24] In 1838 the tribe numbered 975 individuals, besides the small number previously described, on the Neosho River in the present Oklahoma. Their settlements in the future Kansas were confined chiefly to the fifteen square miles in the northeastern corner of the country ceded them by the treaty of 1825. They did not live in tents or villages, each family settling wherever it found a satisfactory site for a farm. Many of them had good houses, of hewn logs, and stables. They cultivated their land as the whites did. They raised corn, potatoes, cabbage, beans, pumpkins and melons, some wheat and oats, and cut hay on the prairies. They usually raised a surplus of corn and potatoes, which they sold to white citizens. Under treaty stipulations they were furnished blacksmiths, who were constantly employed in making and repairing their farming utensils—plows, hoes, axes, iron wedges, log chains, etc. As they had given up the chase, they wasted little time in the repairing of guns, and none at all in the farming season. Very few pretended to hunt, even in the immediate neighborhood. They were in a prosperous condition, raising many hogs, cattle, and horses, and were at peace with all other Indians.

They were served by Baptist, Methodist, and Quaker missions, where children obtained the rudiments of an education, and some of the girls learned to sew and weave. The condition of the Shawnee Indians in Kansas through the years continued to justify the faith and confidence of the federal government.

In 1842 the agent reported that the Shawnee were an agricultural people whose buildings and farms were similar to those of the whites in a newly settled country. All their farms were inclosed with good rail fences sufficiently high to secure their crops, many of them "staked and ridered"; every family had a farm of at least five acres, with some of them exceeding a hundred acres. Their schools were well attended. A Quaker school commenced in 1810 at Wapakoneta, Ohio, among the Shawnee was resumed in the West in the spring of 1837 and was still supported by the joint labors of three branches of the church in Baltimore, Ohio, and Indiana.[25] The schools had done so well that they attracted the interest of other tribes, who furnished some students. In the Quaker schools girls had been taught to weave carpets and spin wool.

The Shawnee, who had a small annuity—too small to attract traders —had to work hard for a living, and they became a provident, thrifty people—by far the most progressive of all the immigrant tribes in Kansas.[26]

About 1844 the question of slavery began to agitate the Indians in Kansas, and the Methodist Episcopal church was divided. Most of the Ohio Shawnee—those who came west under the treaty of 1831— sided with the southern faction of the church, some of them being slaveholders or proslavery in sentiment. The larger portion of the Missouri Shawnee—Black Bob's Band—adhered to the old church; not that any considerable number of either faction belonged to the church, but most of the latter leaned in sentiment to those who did go to church. An effort was made by the proslavery missionaries of the church to enlist all the Indians to their views. These efforts developed such violence that the Reverend Gurley, an antislavery missionary among the Wyandots, was taken from his bed at midnight by "the minions of slavery," carried across the Kansas River, and warned never to return. Other similar outrages became numerous. To escape these distractions, a large part of the Shawnee left Kansas and joined the faction on the Canadian River in the present Hughes and Pittsburg counties, Oklahoma.[27]

The Shawnee, mentioned by Hitchcock and others, who settled along the Canadian River, were seen in 1849 by Captain R. B. Marcy.[28] Marcy and his party, on the way from Fort Smith to Santa Fe, were crossing Coal Creek near the present McAlester on a northwest course, and traveled for some distance on what was called the Shawnee Trace. In what is now the northwestern part of Pittsburg County, and near the Canadian River, they entered a Shawnee village. He described what he saw as follows:

"A large peach orchard whose trees were loaded with fruit first met our view. Houses surrounded by gardens, orchards and fields of grain were scattered along the banks of a clear rivulet. Upon reaching the road we found the advance party of the survey; they were waiting for the wagon train, and refreshing themselves with melons at a comfortable-looking farm house. The Indian men were robust and intelligent; and the women dressed in neat calico frocks with silver earrings and brooches of Shawnee manufacture, were by far the best looking of their race that we had ever seen. Some of the girls were almost white, with regular and pretty features. . . . . Approaching some hills, there appeared a new road. The guide told us that it had been built by the Shawnees, and not only avoided the hills, but was very direct. It proved to be about two miles long, passing various Indian farm houses. It was cut through a dense forest, was nearly straight and level, with the gullies bridged over. We had not supposed that these Indians possessed the energy, skill and peaceable spirit necessary to construct so good a work."

For the next ten miles they continued to travel through the Shawnee settlements, which, Marcy said, were "more thickly settled and better cultivated than any we had seen since leaving the Choctaw agency. A few miles from camp we left on our right the road leading to Little River, and soon afterward were in a labyrinth of trails. We inquired of an Indian for the right road. He intimated we might as well follow him. He was mounted upon a spirited horse, and our poor mules were somewhat jaded, but we managed to continue and proceeded for about a mile, and then arrived at an opening in the forest where were cultivated fields and houses. Upon inquiring of our host the direction to Shawneetown, he seemed non-plussed. After a while, however, he made us understand that we might consider ourselves within its precincts. The numerous paths are, as it were, streets, uniting the various houses of this extensive if not populous place. From one house to another, the distance varied from a few hundred yards to half a mile. Taking the direction indicated, we passed through the town, with its numerous cultivated fields and gardens, to a small rivulet, some miles beyond, where we found the train incamped."

This Shawnee settlement was just across the river from Edwards' Trading House near the mouth of Little River, where the Shawnee were able to market livestock and produce with the traveling expedition and it necessary to stop at this important trading post for supplies.

Shawnee in Kansas, dissatisfied by recent arrivals at 1851 endeavored in vain to have them removed; io Shawnee, with the connivance of some of the souri faction, overthrew the separate tribal organization council claiming to represent both factions. They to negotiations purporting to bind the united tribe, Bob's Missouri faction claimed to be a violation of their is, and which the Ohio Shawnee so strongly resented that more of them left to join the absentee faction on the Canadian River.

The Ohio Shawnee remained on the Canadian River, and four years after Marcy visited the place, Lieutenant A. W. Whipple, in 1853, passed through these same Shawnee settlements on his exploring expedition in search of a route for a railroad to the Pacific Coast. When his party camped in the neighborhood, his journalist wrote: "Scarcely was the arrival of the white party made known, than friendly Indians came trooping on horseback and on foot into our camp, bringing with them large quantities of maize, sweet melons, most refreshing watermelons, and juicy peaches for sale. Such visitors were of course exceedingly welcome, more especially as the deportment of both men and women was remarkably orderly and modest, and they moved about in their cleanly European costumes with as much care and decorum as if they had worn it from birth. The regularly featured faces of the men were moreover adorned by a handsome moustache, of which, as of an ornament very rare for an American Indian, they were not a little proud. The women were all what might be called handsome, and the roses visible on their cheeks, despite the dark color of their skins, spoke of health and cheerfulness. In pleasant quarters does the weary wanderer find himself, when, resting before the cottage of one of these hospitable Indians in the shade of the roughly made protecting corridor, refreshing himself with new milk and fresh bread or gathering juicy peaches in their cottage gardens, or finding out the watermelons hidden away in their cool, shady bowers. The few families settled in this district appear far more happy and contented than the larger portion of their tribe who have proceeded northward to Kansas and Missouri, and have seen many of their number succumb to their cruel foes, smallpox and brandy."[29]

The next year, 1854, was enacted the Manypenny treaty with the Shawnee, which the Missouri faction claimed was a violation of their rights. It provided in Section 2 for allotting the reservation in Kansas to the Shawnee at the rate of two hundred acres per head. Black Bob and one or two other members of his faction took allotments, but very few others of his band did so, determined to stand on their rights as communal owners of their reserve. Nearly all the Ohio faction, who were the most progressive and farsighted of the Indians, claimed their allotments. Conditional provision was made in this treaty for the Indians living in the Indian Territory and elsewhere, who thereby and thereafter were officially identified as "Absentee Shawnee."

Though specifically exempted from taxation by the laws of 1854 under which Kansas Territory was organized, the lawmaking branch of that territory in 1860 declared all Indians citizens and subjected their lands to taxation. This gave rise to the celebrated case of *Charles Bluejacket* v. *County Commissioners of Johnson County*,[30] in which the United States Supreme Court, at the December, 1866, term, in an opinion rich in Indian history, reversed the Supreme Court of Kansas and held the lands of the Shawnee Indians nontaxable.

The Shawnee reservation in Kansas was located near Kansas City and was valuable not only on account of its fertile soil but because of its proximity to a growing town. White people, in defiance of law and with the acquiescence of local authority, moved in upon this fine land, dispossessing the Indian owners, to whom they paid no rent. These intruders cultivated the land, cut the timber, and in other ways profited by their illegal possession and aggression. White people also stole the horses and mules belonging to the Indians, who were thereby incapacitated to cultivate their land. Being thus deprived of their property, and having received the last of their small annuities, they were compelled to resort to the chase, as they formerly did, in order to secure food for their families.[31]

When the Civil War broke out, the Shawnee felt the direct impact of the conflict raging about them. Their reservations were raided by guerrillas from Missouri, their homes were burned, and their livestock and other personal property were stolen; and these dispersed and impoverished Indians were forced to flee in all directions seeking shelter and food.

In 1862 or 1863 the bandit Quantrell made a raid into Black Bob's reserve in Johnson County, Kansas; killed one of his men, a Union soldier; robbed others; and drove all from their homes. These outrages were said to have been committed in reprisal for the fact that Black Bob and his followers sympathized with the Union cause and provided more than a hundred soldiers for the Union Army. Black Bob's people were driven from their homes, which were destroyed; their herds were stolen; and the Indians were compelled to scatter over the country and throw themselves on the charity of other Indians. When, after an absence of two years, they attempted to return to their reserve, they found their rich lands and improvements occupied by white people, who drove them off with menaces and threats; and they were forced again to seek refuge elsewhere. During their wanderings, Black Bob and nearly a third of his people died from hardship and privation.[32]

After the Civil War the fugitive Shawnee wandered back to the site of their old home, seeking some familiar landmark. Living next to the Missouri border, they had suffered much during the war from the raids of guerrilla bands and the uninterrupted flow of whiskey from that state. At the end of the war there were 860 members of the tribe living in Kansas, 125 of whom had served in the Union army; besides these, the remaining eighty able-bodied men had organized themselves into a militia company that helped repel General Sterling Price's raiders in October, 1864.[33] Those driven from their homes by the whites were afraid to return.

In the distracted condition in which these Indians found themselves during the war, pursued and harassed by predatory white men and corporations, members of the tribe were inveigled into entering into negotiations for cessions of their tribal land. The enterprises of these white men were promoted by squatters coming into the country, settling on Indian reservations, and dispossessing the Indian owners.

They were not only unrestrained but, with the active or passive acquiescence of responsible officials, encouraged to defy the laws and treaties under which the lands were secured to the Indians.

Treaties were thus made in 1862–63 with the Osage, Shawnee, Kickapoo, Sauk and Foxes, and New York Indians. These treaties all provided for the removal of the Indian owners to the Indian Territory for the benefit of white men and railroad companies; it was claimed that in some instances agents of these companies drafted the treaties in the interest of their principals.[34]

The supposition that these treaties would go directly to Washington and, in the ordinary routine, be ratified by the Senate, and thereby in a short time become the law of the land, naturally led the Indians to believe that their removal from Kansas would occur shortly and that it would be useless to plant crops which would soon have to be abandoned. However, contrary to the usual procedure, these treaties were not ratified immediately or at any other time; but the policies implied in them were embodied in other treaties made several years later after the end of the war.

In the meantime, during the succeeding years of uncertainty, the Indians led a life of oppression, unrest, and vagrant detachment from the soil, becoming more and more impoverished and farther and farther removed from the state of improvement and independence which it was the announced policy of the government to promote.

The problems of these Indians were characterized by the Commissioner of Indian Affairs, who said that the greatest obstacle to the realization of the Indian's hopes "is to be found mainly in his almost constant contact with the vicious, unscrupulous whites, who not only teach him their base ways, but defraud and rob him, and often without cause, with as little compunction as they would experience in killing a dog, even taking his life. Another cause or hindrance is the fact that the Indian has no certainty as to the permanent possession of the land he occupies and which he is urged to improve, for he knows not how long he may be permitted to enjoy it. Should it be in a region of remarkable fertility, or in a country abounding in rich mineral ores, it may be wanted for white man's occupancy or use. The plea of 'manifest destiny' is paramount and the Indian must give way, though it be at the sacrifice of what may be as dear as life. If the incentives to build up for himself and family a pleasant home are not provided by his condition and prospects, he becomes discouraged or indifferent as to his future welfare, and if he does not really retrograde, makes no advance."[35]

From this point of departure the Commissioner adopted the popular theory that it was best for the Indian to move on into a country as yet unwanted by the whites.

Under the conditions that existed, the Shawnee realized that they could never be happy again in Kansas, and it required little persuasion to induce a delegation of this tribe to leave their reservation on November 27, 1866, for Washington, with the view to seeking ratification of their treaty of 1862, or the making of a new one, by which they would exchange their lands in Kansas for a home in the Indian Territory. They were among the large number of tribes represented there, called by the government to negotiate for radical changes in their lives.

The Shawnee delegation arrived in Washington on December 5, but the Commissioner of Indian Affairs persuaded them to return home again and await future orders from the Indian Department when they should again return, "believing that after the convening of Congress they would be the better enabled to accomplish their purpose."

The United States government, by the terms of the treaties of 1866, had acquired title to the western half of the domain of the Cherokee, Creek, and Seminole nations, and Shawnee Agent H. L. Taylor and one other were appointed commissioners to explore what is now the western half of Oklahoma and report to the Indian office their opinion of the country and its adaptability to the wants and habits of the red man.[36]

On July 20, 1867, Congress provided for the appointment of a peace commission[37] with directions to make treaties with the Indians and tribes previously hostile to the United States. The commissioners also were directed to "examine and select a district of country having sufficient area to receive all the Indian tribes now occupying territory east of the Rocky Mountains, not now peaceably residing on permanent reservations under treaty stipulations to which the government has the right of occupation, or to which said commissioners can obtain the right of occupation," the district selected to be the permanent home of the tribes. This commission proceeded with the making of the treaty of Medicine Lodge Creek and other important treaties and with the location of Cheyenne, Arapaho, Apache, and other recently hostile Indians in the western part of Oklahoma.[38]

After a delay of more than a year the Shawnee treaty of February 23, 1867, was ratified and proclaimed on October 14, 1868. The Shawnee thereupon negotiated with their friends the Cherokee, with whom they entered into a written agreement on June 9, 1869,[39] similar to that between the Cherokee and Delawares two years before. By this agreement, to the 722 Shawnee of Kansas and the Absentee Shawnee living in the Indian Territory was extended the privilege of membership in the Cherokee Nation and occupancy of tribal domain, provided they would remove into the Cherokee Nation within two years from the date of the instrument and comply with other terms. In consideration, fifty thousand dollars was to be paid to the Cherokee as soon as it should be received from the sale of the Absentee Shawnee lands, in accordance with a resolution of Congress approved April 7, 1869, entitled "A Resolution for the Relief of Settlers upon the Absentee Shawnee Lands in Kansas."[40]

Though many of the eastern Shawnee removed to the Cherokee Nation in 1870, more than five hundred of Black Bob's Band were detained while endeavoring to sell their allotments and improvements in Kansas, their efforts obstructed and thwarted, said their agent, by prolonged and unjust legislation. The government had "permitted white men to go upon and occupy the Shawnee Lands to the discomfort and pinching poverty of her suffering wards, some of whom have been driven from their humble but loved homes, and compelled, if permitted a resting place on soil of their own, to occupy such portion thereof as the coveting and unwelcome intruder did not desire for himself. These lawless occupants of the soil of others have for years from the proceeds thereof, retained counsel at the seat of government for the security of these lands to themselves, in cooperation with their members of congress, and in a recent bill, in reference thereto, provision is made for their retaining said lands on the payment of $2.50 per acre when, if they were removed therefrom, or compelled to pay the outraged owners a price which a fair compensation would secure to them, as justice should secure it, the value would at once be raised to from $10 to $30 per acre. Then these Indians would at once remove to the Cherokee country with means sufficient to enable them to open and improve homes, and to surround themselves with the necessary comforts of life, and for lack of which many of these poor Shawnees have gone to premature graves. This lingering injustice has continued the Shawnee agency two years longer than its natural life, at an unnecessary expense to the Government; and it is proper to remark here that while this class of intruders are enjoying their ill-gotten incomes, the Black Bob Shawnees are appealing to their guardian, the Government, for aid to keep them from actual starvation, and some five hundred dollars has been expended for that purpose the past year."[41]

During the period from 1867 to 1871 the Shawnee drifted south to their new home in the Indian Territory, where they became merged with the Cherokee. One band of this unfortunate tribe, belonging to the Absentee Shawnee, associated with refugee Caddo and Delaware, located on the Arkansas River in Kansas during the war, left their temporary home at the present Wichita on August 3, 1867, for a new home in the Leased District near Camp Wichita (now Fort Sill). Others were living near the Quapaw agency.[42]

As the Shawnee emigrants left Kansas, the appearance of one of the detachments was described by an observer: "A caravan of about fourteen wagons marched into town Saturday forenoon and halted in the center of Main Street . . . . it was . . . . the remnant of the once warlike *Shawnees* . . . . who were on their way from Shawnee county, near Topeka . . . . to the Indian Territory. A more motley group rarely presents itself to the eye of even the traveler of the Plains. The long association with civilization had, however, taught the Indians to provide for the future; so, in front was an ox team, with a full wagon load of corn for the stock; wagons with household furniture, baby coach, farming implements, and everything denoting civilized life; and a happy family of chickens, ducks, and young pigs in one coop, tied to the end of a wagon. A prominent feature of the procession was an old squaw, with a long pipe held familiarly between the lips, which she continued to puff with the most perfect Indian nonchalance; that she had once been an Indian maid of much beauty, no one who looked upon her pure Caucasian outline of features could doubt; . . . . and those wagons contained all that was left of the once numerous and powerful tribe."[43]

The Shawnee agent in Kansas in 1871 made a feeling report on the condition of his wards, remarking that forty years had elapsed since they were "forced to relinquish their home at Wapakoneta, Ohio, and suffer the privations of a new and untried home on the southern banks of the Kansas river. Here they passed through many hardships, their number materially diminishing from various causes, and with reluctance they now again leave the graves of their fathers and friends, and some of them well cultivated farms, with comfortable and attractive residences, to undergo the fatigue and hardships of a new country."

About five hundred of the most solvent of them, immigrants in the Cherokee Nation, had made much progress in erection of improvements and were beginning to send their children to a school constructed on the Wyandot reserve for the children of the Wyandots, Seneca, and Shawnee. A number of old people had succumbed to the hardships of removal and a strange climate.

Black Bob's Band, however, dispossessed of their fine land near Kansas City, discouraged and destitute, had become wanderers and were scattered among other tribes in the Indian Territory, until finally they settled with the Absentee Shawnee on the Canadian River.

The Shawnee who were absorbed into the Cherokee tribe were thus cared for, but the Absentee Shawnee living on the so-called thirty-mile-square tract set apart to the Potawatomi by the treaty of 1867 were as yet unprovided for.

The last report from the Sauk and Fox agency in Kansas was made on August 10, 1869. The Indians of this tribe were removed to their new home in the Indian Territory in November, 1869, and the agency re-established there. The agent, making his first report on August 18, 1870, said that there were 567 Absentee Shawnee living south of the North Fork of the Canadian about thirty miles southwest of the Sauk and Fox agency and the same distance west of the Seminole agency. They accordingly fell within the jurisdiction of the new Sauk and Fox agency.[44]

The "Citizen Potawatomi" having removed from Kansas and located within the same area (the thirty-mile square), Congress provided for allotting the land to the members of both tribes.[45] The act limited the right, however, to Absentee Shawnee who were of pure or mixed blood, and this caused much opposition to allotment, for among them were Indians of numerous other tribes who were thereby excluded. This alien element contained some of the best talent, men whose influence was used in causing dissatisfaction and cultivating the old Indian ways among the Shawnee, who desired to keep them in the tribe and share with them all their rights and privileges.

Because federal policy opposed this attitude, the Absentee Shawnee were in a continued state of dissatisfaction and unrest, many of them refusing to take their allotments. Finally, in order to continue the integrity of their organization with the friends they had adopted, in the spring of 1876, under the leadership of Sam Warrior, half of them left the reservation for a new location a few miles northwest and settled on the Mexican Kickapoo reservation on Deep Fork.[46] Here they built comfortable log houses, cultivated the soil, raised large herds of cattle, and made a reputation for themselves as honorable, industrious, self-supporting people.

However, as they were intruders on the Kickapoo reservation, they were ordered to return to their own. This they were reluctant to do, and, as the government did nothing about it at once, they continued to enjoy Kickapoo hospitality. Finally, the government ordered the Indian agent to remove them and employ force if necessary. In the spring of 1883 the movement was planned to take place, but, as the Indians had planted crops, action was postponed until autumn.

In October the agent wrote the Commissioner that he was ready to proceed, but, as force would be required, he asked for a detail of troops. A detachment of fifty soldiers from Fort Reno arrived at the agency on November 8, 1886. These Shawnee, now known as Big Jim's band,[47] had been living in comfortable log houses for more than ten years and could not comprehend that the government really meant to inflict such hardship on them as that threatened. Accordingly, they had made no preparation for this change in their lives; but, when they were faced with soldiers and the drastic action thus implied, they appealed for 1,600 yards of ducking to make tents in which to live while new houses were being built.

The removal took place in November, 1886, and sixty Shawnee families, numbering between three and four hundred people, were removed at a very considerable financial loss to the Indians, as well as with much suffering. The Indians had a large number of cattle which were also rounded up and removed.

The losses thus sustained by the Indians, obvious to the agent and other observers, were reported to the department in Washington and eventually to Congress; but it was not until August 19, 1890, that $17,215 was appropriated to compensate the Indians, or the heirs of many who had died in the meantime, for their losses. But payment was not made until 1891, five years after the damage had been sustained.

The Cherokee commission, on June 26, 1890, entered into an agreement with the Potawatomi and Absentee Shawnee for the cession of their lands in Indian Territory held under the treaty of February 27, 1867, and the act of Congress of May 23, 1872. The land of four tribes—Sauk and Foxes, Iowa, Citizen Band of Potawatomi, and Absentee Shawnee—having been divided into counties by the Secretary of the Interior, as required by law, the President, on September 18, 1891,[48] issued his proclamation opening them to settlement at noon four days later. In the midst of a mad scramble and turmoil, the land was practically all occupied the first day by twenty thousand people, anxious to pay the required $1.25 per acre for the fewer than seven thousand 160-acre tracts available. There was also lively rivalry for lots in the town sites of Chandler and Tecumseh, which had been reserved by the government.

NOTES

1. Office of Indian Affairs, "Delaware" (National Archives).
2. Grant Foreman, *Indian Removal: The Emigration of the Five Civilized Tribes,* p. 36; "Papers Relating to Expedition against Certain Shawnees," Office of Indian Affairs; "1828 Delawares and Shawnees (in Arkansas), George Izard, Peter Bean and Others" (National Archives).
3. *Ibid.*
4. Foreman, *op. cit.*, pp. 36, 66.
5. Thomas Wildcat Alford, as told to Florence Drake, *Civilization,* p. 11.
6. *Advancing the Frontier,* p. 152.
7. *Ibid.,* p. 165.
8. *Ibid.,* p. 95.
9. *Ibid.,* p. 100.
10. *Ibid.,* p. 154.
11. *Ibid.,* p. 97.
12. *Ibid.,* p. 154; Foreman, *A Traveler in Indian Territory: The Journal of Ethan Allen Hitchcock,* p. 256.
13. *Arkansas Intelligencer,* February 7, 1846, p. 1, col. 4.
14. *Ibid.; Report of the Commissioner of Indian Affairs, 1837,* p. 658.
15. *Report, 1848,* pp. 388–89.
16. *Report, 1841,* p. 253.
17. Among the Seneca resided a Mohawk Indian missionary named Daniel Adams. His house was " a neat little cabin, better than many in the States, and pretty well furnished. He speaks the Seneca and some other languages very fluently. His wife is a Stockbridge Indian, well educated in common English literature, and upon the whole one of the most intelligent ladies I have seen for many days. I spent the night with Bro. Adams and was most hospitably entertained. He is very comfortably situated in a little cabin, had twenty acres of good wheat and seven of corn with everything else necessary. His wigwam is furnished with two beds, a table, trunks, plenty of queensware, and the best library I have seen on the district, save one (Horace Jewell, *History of Methodism in Arkansas,* p. 389).
18. 7 *U.S. Stat.* 424.
19. Built by Thomas J. McCausland of Pennsylvania; begun January 31, 1834, and finished June 1, 1835 ("Seneca West Sub Agency" [National Archives], Tray 293).
20. *Report, 1843,* p. 428.
21. *Report, 1848,* p. 534.
22. *Report, 1852,* p. 393.
23. *Report, 1853,* p. 136.
24. *Report, 1835,* p. 296.
25. *Report, 1842,* p. 484.
26. *Report, 1851,* p. 341.
27. *Handbook,* II, 356.
28. Grant Foreman, *Marcy and the Gold Seekers,* p. 135.
29. Grant Foreman, *A Pathfinder in the Southwest,* p. 47.
30. "The Kansas Indians," 5 *U.S. Supreme Court Reports* (Wallace) 737-57.
31. In recognition of the sufferings and losses of these helpless people at the hands of the whites, Congress, on May 9, 1860, appropriated $36,711, to be paid to the Shaw-

nee "for depredations committed upon their property by citizens or inhabitants of the United States"; but added the following interesting and revealing qualification: "It shall not be incumbent upon the parties claimant *from the peculiar condition of affairs in the Territory of Kansas at the time the spoliations were committed* to show that the offenders were apprehended and brought to trial" (12 *U.S. Stat.* 15).

32. *Report, 1864.* A hundred and sixty Shawnee who had been living on the Creek domain on the Canadian River fled to Kansas when driven out by the Southern forces and sought protection of the United States Indian agent (*Report, 1865*, p. 501).

After the Civil War there were more than six hundred Shawnee Indians living in the present Oklahoma between the Red and Washita rivers. Because this region had been set apart for the wild Indians in the treaty with the Choctaw and Chickasaw, creating what was known as the "Leased District," the Shawnee found it impossible to raise any crops there; they therefore removed east and located on the lands recently vacated by the Seminole Indians near the old Seminole agency, where they proceeded to plant an adequate corn crop that received the approbation of the agent (Henry Shanklin, Indian agent, to Commissioner of Indian Affairs, June 6, 1868, "Kiowa Agent's Reports" [Oklahoma Historical Society]).

33. *Report, 1865*, p. 498.

34. *Report, 1866*, p. 245; *Report, 1867*, p. 1.

35. *Report, 1867*, p. 294.

36. The Taylor Commission was engaged for three months in the spring of 1866 in exploring western Indian Territory, but their labors were reported of little value.

37. 15 *U.S. Stat.* 17.

38. The Peace Commission officially designated the Indian Territory as one of the two great territories (the other was the Dakota Territory) upon which to concentrate a large number of Indian tribes living in other areas (*Report, 1872*, p. 33).

39. *Constitution and Laws of the Cherokee Nation of 1875*, p. 281.

40. 21 *U.S. Stat.* 53. It will be observed that Congress very frankly designated this resolution as being for the relief, not of the Indians, the owners of the soil, but of the white squatters on their lands.

41. *Report, 1870*, p. 356.

42. *Report, 1871*, p. 500.

43. *Ottawa* (Kan.) *Journal*, Thursday, April 14, 1870, p. 2, col. 4.

44. They occupied this and other land up and down the Canadian River until hostilities of the Civil War obliged them to flee to Kansas.

45. Act of May 23, 1872.

46. Near the present Harrah, Oklahoma.

47. Big Jim was the popular name of a noted full-blood Shawnee leader, known among his people as Wapameepto ("Gives Light as He Walks"). His English name was originally "Dick Jim," corrupted into "Big Jim." He was born on the Sabine reservation, Texas, in 1834, and in 1872 became chief of the Kispicotha band, commonly known as Big Jim's band of Absentee Shawnee. Big Jim was of illustrious lineage, his grandfather being Tecumseh and his father one of the signers of the "Sam Houston treaty" between the Cherokee and affiliated tribes and the republic of Texas, February 23, 1836. He was probably the most conservative member of his tribe. In the full aboriginal belief that the earth was his mother and that she must not be wounded by tilling the soil, he refused until the last to receive the allotments of land that had been forced upon his band in Oklahoma and used every means to overcome the encroachments of civilization. For the purpose of finding a place where his people would be free from molestation, he went to Mexico in 1900; while there, he was stricken with smallpox in August and died. He was succeeded by his only son, Tonomo, who, in 1905, was said to be about thirty years of age (*Handbook*, I, 146).

48. In 1935 the records of the Sauk and Fox agency accounted for 2,711 Potawatomi (677 families) of all degrees of blood on the rolls; 613 Absentee Shawnee, 831 Sauk and Foxes, 258 Mexican Kickapoo, and 108 Iowa.

CHAPTER X

IMMIGRANT INDIANS IN KANSAS

DELAWARES

IN SPITE of Delaware Chief Anderson's overtures to the indigenous Pawnee Indians, in 1831, after his death, resentment against the newcomers manifested itself in sporadic exhibitions of hostilities. On one occasion, in revenge for an attack on them by the Pawnee while the Delawares were out on a hunt, the latter burned a Pawnee town. Finally, the Stokes Commission undertook to compose the jealousy between the tribes suddenly thrown together in an unaccustomed relationship and called a conference at Fort Leavenworth, which, under the pacific influence of Henry L. Ellsworth; General Bennet Riley, commandant of the post; John Dougherty, the Pawnee agent; P. L. Chouteau; Baptiste Peoria, and others, on November 12, 1833, resulted in a treaty of peace. This treaty was signed by representatives of the Delaware, Shawnee, Kickapoo, Potawatomi, Ottawa, Peoria and Kaskaskia, Wea, Oto, Omaha, Grand Pawnee, Tappago Pawnee, Republican Pawnee, Pawnee Loups, Kansas, Iowa, Sauk, and Piankashaw tribes.[1]

The Delaware Indians living on the reservation set apart to them by the treaty executed at Cape Girardeau, were served by Baptist and Methodist missionaries who endeavored to combat the evils introduced by white people along the line in Clay and Jackson counties, Missouri. The Chouteaus and other Frenchmen at the mouth of the Kansas River were among those who persisted in selling whiskey to the Indians.[2] During 1834 and 1835, eight hundred and twenty-six more Delawares were emigrated to their reservation of 2,808,000 acres lying southwest of the Kickapoo reservation.[3] They were included with the Kansas, Shawnee, and Kickapoo in the Fort Leavenworth agency.[4]

Roving bands of several hundred Delawares on both sides of Red River engaged in hunting expeditions for a livelihood. While they were described by some as a vagabond class of people, they were renowned as brave fighters who often demonstrated their prowess when they met hostile wild Indians. Besides these, in 1838 there were 1,050 Delawares living on their reservation on the Kansas and Missouri rivers.[5] They cultivated about fifteen hundred acres of land, on which they raised corn, beans, peas, pumpkins, Irish potatoes, melons, and a small amount of oats and wheat. They raised many hogs, cattle, and horses, which, with the crops produced on their land, were their main reliance for food. Recognized as an enterprising people, parties of from ten to twenty-five frequently made excursions west as far as the Rocky Mountains in search of beaver and often returned with a wealth of peltries, one man bringing home on one occasion as much as a thousand dollars' worth. But the proceeds of these trapping expeditions did them little good, as they usually were spent on liquor, which did much to demoralize the Indians.

By 1839 the population of the Delawares on their reservation was reduced to 970. They were doing well with their crops, though not quite so well as their more temperate neighbors, the Shawnee. They were still devoting too much time to the chase, particularly in pursuit of beaver and otter furs.

During the Gold Rush and for some years thereafter the Delawares and other immigrant tribes were greatly annoyed by the passage of white people through their land, who stole their horses and in other ways made their life difficult. Several hundred Delaware, Shawnee, and Kickapoo warriors, enticed by government officials, the offer of money, and the prospect of adventure, enlisted in the United States service in Florida, where the government, in 1837, was trying to drive the Seminole Indians from their southern home[6] and force their removal to the Indian Territory. For this service these soldiers in 1851, after waiting more than ten years for their pay, received from the government $15,000.[7] This ill-advised government policy naturally interrupted the peaceful activities of the Indians, to their great harm.

Their agent reported, in 1852, that the Delawares were still annoyed by the white emigrants passing through their country; and the whites continued to rob them of their horses, which they sold to passing emigrants. The Indians were still prospering in their farming, though they loved to hunt, and on these expeditions they were sometimes obliged to fight the Sioux. They were not much interested in education, though their children who attended the mission schools were doing good work.[8]

According to Thomas Moseley, Indian agent for the Kansas agency, which included the Delawares, their hunting trips were attended by much peril. On one such excursion two sons of Captain Kitchum, the principal chief, were killed by a war party of Sioux on the Platte

River, between Forts Kearney and Laramie. "All their furs, horses, traps and blankets fell into the hands of the Sioux. Another Delaware Indian was shot through the leg with an arrow, but made his escape. The Delawares are brave, chivalrous, enterprising Indians. They hunt and roam through the length and breadth of the great western plains, some as far as California. It appears that quite a number of this tribe, engaged in the chase and trade of the plains, are annually killed by wild tribes, or die from great exposure." That the peril of the Delawares was not alone from the wild Indians is indicated by another story told by the agent:

"A small party of Delawares consisting of a man, his squaw, and a lad of about eighteen years, and which was recently returning from the mountains with the avails and profits of a successful hunt and traffic, after they had commenced their journey homewards, the second day the man sickened and died. Before he died he directed his squaw and the young man to hasten home with their horses and mules— thirteen in number—the money—$445.00—besides many other articles of value. After a few days travel, near some of the forts of Arkansas [River], they were overtaken by four white men—deserters from the United States army, three on foot and one riding a mule. The squaw and young man loaned each of the men on foot a horse or mule to ride, and furnished them with provisions.

"They all traveled on friendly together for some six or seven days until they arrived on Cottonwood Creek, thirty-five or forty miles west of Council Grove. One evening while resting for a noon snack the young man was killed by these men, and the squaw was also supposed by these wretches to be dead, having had her throat cut badly and her head severely fractured. The two were then dragged off in the grass, supposed to be dead. The men then gathered the mules, horses, money, guns, blankets, &c, that they supposed of value, and then made for Jackson County, Missouri, where they disposed of the stock the best they could, and some of the last at auction in Independence; and three of them took the first steamer to St. Louis. The squaw, on the day after receiving her wounds, resuscitated and soon discovering that her companion had been killed, and everything they possessed had disappeared, she, in her feeble and dangerous condition, took the road to Council Grove; and the fifth day out she says she was overtaken by a Kaw Indian and brought into Council Grove, where the traders at that place had every attention paid her, and sent a runner to the Delaware traders and myself, and we soon succeeded in capturing one of the men at Liberty, Clay County, Missouri, when he voluntarily confessed the whole tragedy—the murder, robbing, &c. The three others had by this time left for St. Louis. A telegraphic dispatch to St. Louis, however, had the desired effect; and the three men were taken and brought back to Liberty, where, upon a trial before two justices of the peace, they were all committed for trial in the District Court of the United States for the State of Missouri. As feeble as the squaw was, I was under the necessity of having her taken to Liberty as a witness on the trial. She readily recognized and pointed out in a large crowd of persons three of the prisoners.

"I have caused four of the recovered mules and horses to be turned over to the unfortunate squaw. With the assistance of the Delaware traders I expect to recover two or three more. The balance, I am of the opinion will never be obtained. Some of the effects of this unfortunate squaw and young man were burned, some thrown in the water— so says one of the party, who turned state's evidence at the examining trial."[9]

By treaty of May 6, 1854, one of the numerous Manypenny treaties, the Delaware Indians ceded to the United States all their land in Kansas save a small tract or "diminished reserve" and four sections which were reserved for the Christian or Munsee Indians.[10] By a later treaty of May 30, 1860,[11] the Delawares were made to say that they wished their "diminished reserve" allotted to them in severalty in the proportion of eighty acres to each allottee. Certificates were to be issued, but the land was not to be alienable except to the United States or to a member of the Delaware tribe. In this treaty they were also recorded as saying that, believing the value of their lands would be enhanced by a railroad in their country, and that the Leavenworth, Pawnee and Western Railroad Company, just incorporated by the legislative assembly of Kansas, possessed advantages of travel and general transportation over every other company proposed to be formed, they wished this company to have preference in the purchase of their surplus lands, after allotments were made, for the sum of $1.25 per acre. The indulgent government agreed that the wishes of the Indians in this respect should be gratified. By the terms of the treaty the Indians conferred upon this company a perpetual right-of-way over their allotted lands. It was also stipulated that the company could sell the surplus lands of the reservation within seven years.

Taking notice of the depredations committed on the Delawares by the white people since the treaty of 1854, the government, in **Article VI** of the Delaware treaty, agreed to pay them $9,500 for ponies stolen from them and $30,000 as indemnity for timber cut and removed from their land by the intruders. It was also agreed in the treaty that eighty acres should be allotted to each of the two hundred Delawares living in Indian Territory when they should return to claim the land.

In 1864 the Delawares were induced to make another treaty for the benefit of the Union Pacific Railroad Company, which wished to build through their reservation; their lands were to be sold to this company on condition that it would build a road from the mouth of the Kaw River to Fort Leavenworth. But ratification of the treaty was delayed in the Senate for various reasons, and in the meantime another company built the road.[12]

As a result of the failure to ratify this treaty, another was entered into on July 4, 1866,[13] in which the Indians were made to say that they desired to remove from their reservation to the Indian Territory. The United States agreed to secure and pay them for the lands sold to the Missouri River Railroad Company and to sell to this company all the remaining land of the reservation and all other lands of the tribe in Kansas, amounting to about 100,000 acres, at not less than $2.50 per acre. The Indians were to elect whether to continue as members of the tribe or to become citizens of the United States whose lands should be withheld from sale to the railroad company. The United States was to sell the Delawares a tract of land in the Indian Territory recently acquired from the Five Civilized Tribes, or which might be ceded by the Cherokee, to be selected by the Delawares in a compact form, sufficient to provide each member of the Delaware tribe 160 acres, to be paid for out of the proceeds of the sale of Delaware lands in Kansas.

The government not having paid the Delawares the sum of $39,500 promised them in the treaty of 1860 for depredations committed upon them by the white people in Kansas, a new obligation was assumed and a new engagement made in Article 14 of the treaty of July 4, 1866, to pay them in lieu of the first promise the reduced sum of $30,000 in full of all claims against the government for timber stolen by the whites, not actually to be paid, but to be "credited to the Delawares in the purchase of their new reservation in the Indian country."

At this time other radical changes were entered into by the Delawares. Of the 201 able-bodied young men of the tribe, 170 had been serving in the Union Army. On their return home they were thoroughly demoralized. Undisciplined, unrestrained, made reckless by the whiskey brought to them by the whites, they were guilty of disorders, assaults, and homicides. During the postwar campaign against hostile plains Indians, however, a number of Delaware young men continued in the service of the army as guides and scouts, in which capacity they achieved a high reputation.

In the hope of establishing order and restraint in the tribe, the chiefs and councilors met on July 21, 1866, and adopted a code of laws. This excellent measure was made up of ten articles, each with from one to fourteen sections, to cover the many wholesome provisions designed to establish law and order in the tribe. Besides criminal statutes, there were appropriate civil laws—laws providing for the payment of debts and the distribution of property of decedents, and laws regulating marriage and divorce, domestic relations, contracts, and other measures of a civilized society.[14]

The construction of the Union Pacific Railroad, Eastern Division, was a source of grievous trouble and damage to the Delawares. A trespassing company which called itself the Delaware Lumber Company caused much loss to the Indians by its unlawful cutting of timber on their land. By direction of the Indian Department, special agents investigated and assessed the damage caused by these unlawful activities.[15] At this phase, soon to terminate with the removal of the Delawares to the Indian Territory, the agent reported 1,065 members of the tribe in Kansas, besides 114 connected with the Wichita agency in Western Indian Territory but temporarily, as a result of the war, residing in Butler County, Kansas.

Representatives of many Indian tribes of Kansas were taken to Washington in the winter of 1866–67 by the Indian Department and, while there, induced to execute treaties with the government providing for the sale of their reservations in Kansas and their removal to lands ceded by the Cherokee and Creek Indians in their treaties of 1866. Treaties were thus made with the following tribes: Delawares, Kansas, Sauk and Foxes of the Mississippi, Sauk and Foxes of the Missouri, Seneca, Shawnee, Confederated Seneca and Shawnee, Quapaw, Kaskaskia, Peoria, Miami, Ottawa, Wyandots, Kickapoo, Potawatomi, Wea, and Piankashaw. For some undisclosed reason, and to the perplexity and embarrassment of the Indian Department, these treaties were not acted upon promptly by the Senate, though hopes were entertained that they would be in due time; but it was more than a year before they were ratified.

During the ensuing period of uncertainty the Delawares waited in suspense, making no effort to construct improvements or to plant or till the soil, in the belief that they would be removed before crops could be harvested. In the meantime white squatters moved upon and appropriated the Indians' lands, going so far, without a vestige of law or right, as to parcel out individual selections and inaugurate what they called "squatter laws" to protect them.

This intolerable condition was allowed to continue not only without redress but with the approval and encouragement of the authorities, the newspapers sometimes expressing the belief that this course would break down the resistance of the Indians and force their removal, in which opinion they were justified by events. After the Delawares had endured this form of oppression for a time, a delegation approached the Cherokee, with whom, on April 8, 1867, they entered into a contract[16] by which the latter conveyed to them a "quantity of land east of the ninety-sixth degree of west longitude, in the aggregate equal to 160 acres of land for each individual of the Delaware tribe, who has been enrolled upon a certain register made February 18, 1867, by the Delaware agent, and on file in the office of Indian affairs, being the list of the Delawares who elect to remove to the 'Indian country,' to which list may be added, only with the consent of the Delaware Council, the names of such other Delawares as may, within one month after the signing of this agreement, desire to be added thereto." The Delawares, in turn, agreed to pay to the Cherokee tribe part of the Delaware tribal funds held or thereafter received for them by the United States, equal to one dollar per acre for the "whole amount of 160 acres of land, for every individual Delaware who had already been registered upon the aforesaid list, ... with the additions thereto, theretofore made." When this contract was executed, a roll was compiled showing 985 Delawares thus admitted into the Cherokee tribe.[17]

In September, 1867, a delegation of Delawares of Kansas went to the Cherokee country and, pursuant to their contract, selected a tract of land lying on the Verdigris and Cana rivers. Well pleased with their choice, they returned home in November to report to their people.[18]

During the following winter some of the more solvent members of the tribe were able to move to their new home and begin farming.

Many others, however, were very poor and had no means to defray the expense of removal and building new homes. This situation was aggravated by the fact that the money due from the government and railroads was delayed in the manner that characterized government performances of obligations to the Indians. They managed, nevertheless, to move southward in detachments at different times from December, 1867, through the following spring and summer. Many of these destitute people depended for food upon the game of the country. Naturally, they were not in a position at once to develop or operate farms and begin the cultivation of the soil, but all these shortcomings were more than compensated for by the distance they put between themselves and the white people of Kansas.[19]

The Delawares continued unsettled, however, desperately poor, and in need of the money owing them, now long overdue. In 1869 they were still waiting for the railroad money to enable them to build improvements and to pay the Cherokee the consideration agreed upon for admission into that tribe, so as to enjoy the privileges of membership and ownership of tribal domain.

They had been working hard to improve the land and had made farms, only to discover that through an error in the survey some of them were expending their labor on lands sold to the Osage or already claimed by other Cherokee settlers. Because of the friction growing out of this and other difficulties with the Cherokee, about three hundred Delawares removed to the east side of the Neosho River on the lands of the Peoria, on the invitation of the latter, where they opened up small farms. However, after a year or two, they returned to the Cana River, much poorer from their experience and toil in building improvements and the delay in getting their farms started.

Under their contract 985 Delawares were now merged with the Cherokee, to whom they paid $279,424.28 for tribal membership and for their proportionate share of tribal lands, amounting to 157,600 acres.

By 1875 this once powerful tribe, now numbering a thousand members, belonging to the Cherokee Nation, said the agent, showed in their habits of dissipation and lack of thrift the debasing influence of frequent removals of which they had been the unhappy victims for more than two generations.[20] Thirty members of the tribe were living on the Kiowa and Comanche reservations as wild Indians, employing neither the white man's dress nor his habitations, and obtaining their sustenance partly from hunting and partly from agriculture. Sixty-one Delawares at the Wichita agency had merged with the Caddo under their chief and with their Caddo tribal name. By 1890 the number of Delawares living at this western agency had increased to 95. Next to the Caddo they were regarded as the most progressive Indians in that agency.

The white people of Kansas having stolen much of the livestock belonging to the Delawares, hope of partial restitution was held out to the Indians when their treaty of July 4, 1866, was made with the government. Article 14 of the act provided that the Secretary of the Interior should cause to be ascertained the value of the stock so stolen since the treaty of 1854, to be reported to Congress with recommendation for an appropriation to pay it.

Subsequently, believing that Congress meant to pay the Indians the amount of their losses, an investigation was held and evidence was submitted by the Indians, from which the Secretary ascertained that they had suffered losses of at least $26,284, and on January 31, 1870, the Secretary of the Interior asked Congress to make an appropriation of that amount, as stipulated in the treaty. No favorable action having been taken by Congress, the department again, on February 28, 1872, repeated its request, urging that, as the proceedings complied with treaty stipulations and as the Indians were in desperate need of whatever was owing to them, the amount should be appropriated without delay. To this request Congress paid no heed up to the time the Commissioner of Indian Affairs made his report in the autumn of 1872,[21] nor at any other time so far as available records disclose.

The Delawares thus passed out of existence as a tribe, and the survivors were merged into the Cherokee tribe. Subsequently, when the Dawes Commission made up the rolls of the Cherokee tribe, what were classified as Delaware-Cherokee comprised about a thousand of the total.

OTTAWA

The Kansas home of the Ottawa Indians of Blanchard's Fork and Roche de Boeuf was in Franklin County, where they were at first subject to the corrupting influence of whiskey peddlers along the Missouri border; but in time, through the efforts of the Reverend Jothan Meeker, they learned to appreciate the practical benefits of temperance. In fact, Mr. Meeker was given credit by Indian officials for much of the progress soon achieved by these Indians. They were a sensible people and adopted a simple code of laws to regulate their tribal affairs. Their agent conceived the idea of confederating the Ottawa and Chippewa and locating them on the Ottawa land:

"The language of the Ottawas and Chippewas and their per capita annuity are about the same," said Mr. Meeker, "and I feel confident that the confederating of these tribes would have a beneficial influence on the ultimate prospects of both of them. The Ottawas present a spectacle more gratifying than any other tribe in this agency; they have cast aside the Indian costume, abandoned the chase, shaken off that cloud of Indian superstition and prejudice which formerly prevented them from seeing and appreciating the advantages resulting from a civilized life, devoted now to agricultural pursuits, and being generally industrious, the eye of the traveler who passes through their country is cheered with the sight of comfortable houses and respectable and well-cultivated farms."[22]

From the excessive use of whiskey the Ottawa tribe had diminished to about 205 in 1847. "They themselves estimate that in 1825 they numbered 1,500. About 300 emigrated into this country from Ohio in 1837–38. In February 1848, they, in general council, without the immediate suggestion of any white person, no one but Ottawas being present, formed and wrote a law in their own language, the following being a literal translation, viz.: 'Whiskey on the Ottawa land cannot come. If any person shall send for it, or bring it into the Ottawa country, he who sends or he who brings shall pay five dollars, and the whiskey shall be destroyed. Any one sending or bringing the second time, shall forfeit all of his annuity money. For the third offense, he shall be delivered over to the United States officers, to try the severity of the white men's laws.'

"The penalties contained in the above, together with those in all of their printed laws, twenty-five in number, are most rigidly enforced by the proper officers; so that since February 1848 there has been but one violation of the whiskey law; consequently we see a gradual improvement in their houses, on their farms, in their habits, health and numbers, their last payment having advanced, as you are aware, to near 230."

In 1849 the Ottawa Indians organized an "anti-running-into-debt society," to the great benefit of all.

When Kansas was torn by dissensions between the slavery and antislavery elements, the Ottawa tribe convened in formal council on August 21, 1856, declared its neutrality between the opposing forces, and decreed that any member who should violate the law thus established should be expelled from the tribe. But ten days later the reservation was invaded by a mob of forty men who fired the home of one of the tribe, robbing him of six hundred dollars and destroying the house and all its contents.[23]

The Ottawa were induced to send a delegation to Washington, where, on June 24, 1862, they made a treaty with Commissioner of Indian Affairs William P. Dole, providing, among other things, that at the end of five years their tribal organization should be dissolved and the members of the tribe become United States citizens.[24]

Their treaty provided also for setting aside 20,000 acres of their land in Kansas to endow a school ostensibly for the tribe, to be called Ottawa University, and administered by two whites and three Ottawa. The remaining land of the tribe was to be allotted to the members; heads of families were to have 160 acres, and others 80 acres each.

In 1865 thirty members of this tribe died from smallpox, introduced by refugee Seneca and Quapaw Indians whom they permitted to live among them during the war; but the deficit in the population of two hundred was restored by Ottawa immigrants from Michigan. The treaty of February 23, 1867, extended for more than two years the period when they were to become United States citizens, and provided that in the meantime they could be made citizens by the United States Court. They were thus qualified to sell their allotments. This treaty provided also for the sale to the Ottawa of part of the Shawnee reservation in the Indian Territory.

White settlers soon began buying the Ottawa land, but long before it was all sold a thriving village named Ottawa grew up on the reservation, adjoining the section on which the school was to be located. Of the 20,000 acres set aside for the school, 5,000 were soon sold for $6,250, and the school building was started.[25]

Construction of the Ottawa school was badly managed, and in 1866, for lack of funds, work came to a standstill, though 7,000 acres of their land had been sold to produce funds for building it. These Indians were subject to the same pressure that removed other tribes from Kansas to the Indian Territory; and soon after the end of the five-year probationary period, July 25, 1867, when their lands became alienable, they sold their individual allotments and, in 1868–69, removed to the Indian Territory and located adjoining the Peoria confederacy. Here, said their superintendent, they were endeavoring to establish themselves permanently but were suffering from lack of funds owing them by the people of Kansas, who had taken their land to promote the building of Ottawa University. They had waited several years since the sale was made, and still, said the superintendent, "they had to struggle in poverty and suspense, unable in their new settlement to receive when most needed, the benefits of the money owing them. And now, while the white people of Kansas were educating their youth at the expense of the Indians, the latter were unable to build needed improvements for their new homes, and a schoolhouse in which to educate their children."[26] In 1870 the Ottawa Indians numbered 150, against 400 thirty years before.

The Ottawa proved a good example to his neighbor, the Indian of the Peoria confederacy, who had built a schoolhouse and had begun to make some progress, impossible while living in Kansas. Afterward, wanderers from the Shawnee of Kansas also became identified with these Indians.

Now at last these small tribes, or what was left of them, were located in their permanent home; previous assurances had proved unreliable, so that it would not have been surprising if they had entertained misgivings about their permanence within the jurisdiction of the Quapaw agency.

WYANDOTS

After the Wyandots recovered in a measure from the shock of removal from Ohio and resultant demoralization, and in spite of the great mortality in the tribe, they began the erection of permanent and comfortable houses, though they were still embarrassed by the want of money owing them from the sale of their improvements in Ohio by the federal government. They also were handicapped by the introduction of whiskey by white men from across the line in Missouri. Prosecution of this criminal element, said the agent, was hampered by the fact that an absurd law of Missouri made an Indian incompetent to testify in the courts of that state; and therefore no effective prosecution could be conducted against the introducers of whiskey.[27]

The Wyandot Indians were largely intermarried with the whites, and it was only natural that some of them should become interested in educating their youth. Their agent reported that, with the money provided by the government for that purpose, "several families have sent their daughters and sons to select schools abroad [to Missouri], some of whom have recently returned with education and accomplishments

rarely met with amongst their more highly favored white neighbors."
Among these were the daughters of William Walker, a leading Wyandot citizen in whom white blood predominated. One of the daughters accompanied the agent to St. Louis and purchased a piano which she soon learned to play well—one of the first in Kansas. "Strange sounds these in an Indian country!" exclaimed the agent.[28]

Schools were well attended, and the Methodist church, presided over by the Reverend James Peery, flourished. A commodious brick church building erected by private subscription was used by 240 members, with two native preachers and four exhorters. Realizing the baneful effects of intemperance, the Wyandots lately reorganized a temperance society, and at the first meeting forty names were affixed to the "cold-water pledge."[29]

The Wyandots held their national election for chiefs on August 15, 1848. On this occasion the agent announced to them the passage through both branches of Congress of the joint resolution confirming their purchase from the Delawares of the territory on which they were residing.[30] As these Indians had waited in suspense and uncertainty for this action since the purchase was negotiated five years before, "their manifestation of joy," as related by the agent, was quite comprehensible.[31] Now that they knew they were living on their own land, they began making better-class improvements which they had not felt safe in constructing theretofore.

The Wyandots were rapidly improving their condition. Good houses were being built, the women were good housekeepers, and the children presented a clean and neat appearance. The Gold Rush and cholera spread through the Wyandot country in 1849, though the latter did not afflict this tribe as much as it did others. But these people demonstrated their advancement and enterprise when fifteen of their young men organized a stock company and, with all necessary equipment, set out for the gold region of California in 1849. Nine more went the next spring, and twenty-four were reported at work "in the diggings."

About this time a very perceptible decline in the condition of these people developed. In addition to the influence of the predatory whites in the adjoining Missouri who were bringing them into debauchery and ruin, Henry Jacques and other leading men who had exercised a wholesome influence died, and the tribe lost their much-needed assistance. The tribal government declined in strength and failed to function effectively; many of the Indians lost confidence in themselves and their capacity as a tribe to exist.

Pupils were doing well in their two schools and the manual labor school in the Shawnee Nation; some attended the school kept by the Quakers, and others went to academies and seminaries in Missouri. The Methodist church, with its 240 members, two preachers, and four exhorters, was in a flourishing condition when the question of slavery intruded to divide the people. There were some slaveholders among the Wyandots; and, when the Methodist church was divided on that subject, the Conference placed this tribe in the division known as the Methodist Episcopal Church South.

Conditions were satisfactory until, in 1848, some of the wicked abolitionists began to use their influence to locate a preacher from the northern branch of the church in the Wyandot Nation. This infamous conspiracy was soon detected and a remedy prepared. The agent announced his intention of running out of the country any such preacher who might appear. During the unhappy days of bloody civil contention in Kansas, the Wyandots endeavored to maintain a state of neutrality between the zealots of North and South, and thus they escaped somewhat the depredations that blighted other sections of the state.

Of all the Indians in Kansas, the Wyandots and Ottawa were the only ones who had adopted a prescribed form of government with a few simple laws. None of the others made any pretensions to such advancement. The Wyandots owned and lived upon their valuable tract of land in the forks of the Missouri and Kansas rivers, adjoining Kansas City on the west, which they had purchased from the Delawares in 1843. The land was too valuable for the whites to permit the Wyandots to keep it. Accordingly, steps were taken to remedy the situation. Influences were brought to bear that resulted in the taking of a delegation of Wyandots to Washington, where, on January 31, 1855, they made a remarkable treaty with the United States. Finding that these Indians were sufficiently civilized or desired to become so, they were declared citizens of the United States with the immunities and privileges (implying principally the right to sell their land) of white people, subject to the laws of Kansas Territory. Their lands were ceded to the government, surveyed into sections, half- and quarter-sections, and then distributed to the Indians. The treaty contained the futile and, to responsible officials, stultifying provision that any Indian realizing his incompetency might apply to the Indian Department to be restored to the protection of the government for a limited time.

Within two years the Wyandot land was all allotted in severalty to the individuals.[32] At first they began improving their holdings. An unprecedented tide of white emigration was now pouring into Kansas, and all the Indians suffered by the cupidity of the speculator and the disregard of their rights by settlers. They were trespassed upon everywhere. Sawmills were set up on their lands, and thieves boldly cut their fine timber and sawed it up into lumber. Threatened with personal violence, and unable to cope with the superior race that everywhere surrounded and menaced them, the Indians became disheartened. Many abandoned their reserves and asked for patents so that they could sell and get out of the country. Most of the Wyandots speedily lost their lands. Much was taken for taxes. Guardians appointed by the courts for Wyandot children squandered the estates of their wards.[33]

Many of the Wyandots who had accepted the status of citizens of Kansas under the treaty of 1855, became disorganized and dismayed by their condition and desired to return to a tribal organization, outside the encroachments of the white settlers. They complained that, however much they tried to live like the whites, the people about them, in many cases, appeared to think that Indians had no rights which white men were bound to respect and that they were constantly robbed of their stock and other property and were not able to obtain the same redress as white persons. They said that the semicompulsory manner in which they were made citizens, and the temptation held out by giving patents for the lands, induced many to accept the provisions of the treaty who were utterly unfit to assume the responsibilities of citizenship; and, having sold their allotments, they became vagabonds. They said that there were many incompetents whose property had been placed in the hands of guardians and squandered; that the property of others had been taken from them illegally under process from courts of probate; that their lands had been sold for taxes which they did not understand and were not able to pay. Many who had comfortable homes had squandered their all by dissipation and had become homeless and destitute. This situation was not peculiar to Kansas. With necessary variations, it is part of the history of many states that included an Indian population.

Thus despoiled of their lands in Kansas, the Wyandots found themselves destitute and homeless. In this situation, in 1857, at the invitation of the Seneca, two hundred Wyandots drifted down to the Seneca reservation.[34] Many years before, the Wyandots had befriended the

Seneca Indians in a substantial manner which had never been forgotten. In 1817 they gave them thirty thousand acres of land on the Sandusky River in Ohio and the next year added ten thousand more adjoining the first. The grateful Seneca told their benefactors that if at any time in the future misfortune should overtake them, they would take them in as brothers and give them a home. And now, as the Wyandots were indeed overwhelmed by misfortune, they turned to the Seneca, who proceeded to make their forty-year-old promise good.

Accordingly, on November 22, 1859, Little Tom Spicer, head chief, and four councilmen of the Seneca tribe, entered into a writing with Matthew Mudeater, principal chief, and the councilmen of the Wyandots, by which the former conveyed to the Wyandots a tract of 33,000 acres, being a strip of land across the north end of the Seneca reservation four miles from north to south, and extending from the Missouri line west to the Grand or Neosho River. And the contracting parties joined in a request to the United States to validate the conveyance. Many of the Wyandots, dispossessed, homeless, and destitute in Kansas, left there and wandered south to the Indian Territory, where they were given refuge by their faithful old friends, the Seneca.

In 1867 there was a general readjustment and revision of the Indian reservations in northeastern Indian Territory. Included in this undertaking was confirmation of the sale by the Seneca of 21,000 acres of land off the north side of their reservation to the Wyandots, for the sum of one dollar per acre. On this the government authorized the location of all those Wyandots who desired to be known as Indians and such other members of the tribe as the agent should find were, through poverty or incompetency, unfit to exercise the responsibilities of citizenship of the United States and likely to become public charges.

When the Civil War came, the Wyandots furnished more than their quota to the Union Army, but they suffered much from the depredations of bandit bushwhackers who robbed them of all their best horses. Many of the Wyandot soldiers rendered good accounts of themselves on more than one battlefield by their heroism and daring. In 1863 they numbered 435, according to their agent, who said that a majority of them had deteriorated greatly since they were made citizens of the United States and permitted to sell their land.

These people had been decimated and despoiled by their contact with the white man, and it was not until 1871 that the survivors reorganized themselves into a tribe, on their lands in the Indian Territory, and solicited the fostering hand of the government. Those who had elected to remain as citizens of Kansas rejoined their brothers in the Indian Territory, and by 1875 they numbered 247. They were under the Quapaw agency, which had supervision over the Ottawa, Miami, Seneca, Modoc, and Peoria. Because of their anomalous career, the Wyandots had no claim for annuities from the government and were thrown entirely upon their own resources. The result, the agent reported, was a great improvement in their condition. In a few years they became a self-reliant people, energetic and enterprising, owners of good farms and surrounded by the conveniences of civilized life.

The Wyandots were the most progressive of the small tribes, but even they still clung to their old practices. Said the agent in 1882: "The custom of celebrating August 15 was observed by them in a most appropriate manner. This practice dates back farther than the memory of the oldest living members of the tribe, but the manner of celebrating has changed from year to year as they have advanced in civilization, and this year witnessed a good, old-fashioned basket picnic." Speeches were made, the newborn children were named, a full-fledged brass band, composed of Indians entirely, discoursed sweet music, all joined in the singing, and a general reunion was held in the woods. There was to be seen the "great iron kettle" in which they annually cooked their beef and corn for that time-honored feast. All the culinary operations were conducted by the women. All the tribes of the agency joined with them, and perfect order prevailed. "Had it not been for the red faces, one would have thought they were mingling with the whites of our western progressive sister states. No one thing that has transpired during the year goes farther to show the real progress these people are making. Instead of the old-fashioned pow-wows and hootings, the green corn and dog-dances, these people have stepped from superstition to our own degree of civilization."[35]

These Indians suffered at times for funds owing them, and for which they waited the belated action of government. In the "Omnibus Treaty" of February 23, 1867, the Wyandots were promised that they would be reimbursed for taxes illegally collected by the Kansas authorities on their tax-exempt land in that territory. It was not until May 29, 1872, that Congress appropriated $11,703.56 for this purpose. The payment was exceedingly timely for the Wyandots who were just getting settled on their new reservation. Congress provided also, on May 3, 1881, for payment to the Wyandots of $28,109.51 for horses stolen from them in Kansas by the whites, twenty or twenty-five years before. This had been promised them in the Omnibus Treaty of 1867, but Congress did not get around to making good the promise for many years. The Wyandots maintained their tribal organization, with first and second chiefs and three counselors. They held annual elections and business meetings monthly for the adjustment of tribal differences.

Congress authorized the allotment of their lands in severalty among the Wyandots, but it was opposed by many, as they would receive less than eighty acres each, and most of the soil was rocky and poor. However, their resistance was eventually overcome in 1888, to the extent that a hundred and fifty Wyandots consented to receive their allotments. Another five years witnessed the population of the tribe increased to more than three hundred and the land all allotted; steps were then taken to care for the more than three hundred "Absentee Wyandots" wandering through the Choctaw and Chickasaw country.

In the treaty with the Choctaw and Chickasaw Indians of April 28, 1866, in Articles 30, 31, and 37, provision was made for locating on the lands of those tribes not to exceed ten thousand civilized Indians living in Kansas.[36] By virtue of this agreement, and by subsequent acts of Congress,[37] $15,686.80 was made available for the purchase from the Choctaw and Chickasaw nations of land for a home for Absentee Wyandots. But the Choctaw and Chickasaw Indians then informed the government that they had no room for the wandering Wyandots. Congress, on June 7, 1897, directed that the money appropriated for that purpose be used by the Secretary of the Interior to locate these Indians on any available lands elsewhere.[38]

NOTES

1. These were nearly all immigrant tribes from the East (see Foreman, *Indians and Pioneers*). This treaty, with names of contracting parties, appears in *Doc.*, IV, 727 ff. A readable account of this most interesting treaty conference was written by Washington Irving's nephew, John T. Irving, who accompanied Ellsworth (John T. Irving, Jr., *Indian Sketches, Taken during an Expedition to the Pawnee and Other Tribes of American Indians*).

2. *Report of the Commissioner of Indian Affairs, 1834*, pp. 170, 193.

3. *Report, 1835*, p. 297.

4. *Report, 1837*, p. 662.

5. *Report, 1838*, p. 447.

6. Foreman, *Indian Removal*, pp. 161, 348.

7. *Report, 1851*, p. 342; 9 *U.S. Stat.* 559. The Secretary of War, on July 22, 1837, directed the several Indian agents to secure 400 Shawnee, 200 Delaware, 100 Kickapoo, 200 Choctaw, and 100 Sauk and Fox warrior recruits who were promised $270 each for six months' service in Florida; after recruiting began it was discovered that under the law then in force it would be impossible to pay them more than $70 each. In the meantime 91 Shawnee had been mustered and sent to Florida. General Thomas S. Jesup,

commanding general, directed that information of the mistake be withheld from the Indians from fear that it might have an unfavorable influence on the campaign in Florida. It required several acts of Congress during the next thirteen years to redeem the promise made by the government to the Indian warriors, and payment was thus belated during these many years (*House Report 541* [28th Cong., 1st sess.], and contemporary acts of Congress).

8. *Report, 1852*, pp. 365–67, 369, 371–72.

9. *Ibid.*, p. 365.

10. 10 *U.S. Stat.* 1048.

11. 12 *U.S. Stat.* 1129. Ratified July 27, 1860. The Delawares had vainly petitioned the government to finance a party that desired to explore in Colorado in search of a home in the country seen by their hunters on their expeditions.

12. *Report, 1866*, p. 8.

13. 14 *U.S. Stat.* 793.

14. *Report, 1866*, pp. 247–48.

15. At the sum of $28,000 (*Report, 1866*, p. 245).

16. *Constitution and Laws of the Cherokee Nation of 1875*, p. 277.

17. *Ibid.* For some years Delaware funds were disbursed to them separately from the Cherokee; thus, in August, 1876, Union Indian Agent Marston disbursed $27 per capita to 786 Delawares who were living in their settlements about forty miles apart in the Cherokee Nation. A posse of soldiers accompanied him to keep whiskey peddlers away from the Indians who came to the payment.

18. *Report, 1868*, p. 255.

19. *Ibid.*, p. 263.

20. *Report, 1875*, pp. 61–62. The government owed the Delawares $900,000 for the land they gave up in Kansas. It was not until December, 1891, that the first instalment of $425,000 of this amount was disbursed to 836 surviving members of the tribe living with the Cherokee, by Leo E. Bennett of Muskogee, Indian agent. The payment was made at Lightning Creek near the home of their old chief, Journeycake.

21. *Report, 1872*, p. 104.

22. *Report, 1851*, p. 330.

23. *Report, 1856*, p. 127.

24. 12 *U.S. Stat.* 1237.

25. *Report, 1864*, p. 393.

26. *Report, 1870*, p. 257. A disgraceful scandal resulted, entailing interminable investigations from Washington.

27. *Report, 1846*, p. 302. Congress endeavored to improve that situation, and in the act of March 3, 1847, amending the act of 1834 relating to trade and intercourse with the Indians, it was enacted that in prosecutions in a United States court for the introduction of intoxicating liquor into the Indian country Indians should be competent witnesses (9 *U.S. Stat.* 203). In a subsequent act of February 13, 1862, enlarging the powers of Indian officials touching the same subject matter, it was again provided that in all cases arising under the recent act, Indians should be competent witnesses (12 *U.S. Stat.* 339).

28. *Report, 1847*, p. 872.

29. *Ibid.*, p. 874.

30. 9 *U.S. Stat.* 337.

31. *Report, 1848*, p. 488.

32. By 1860, allotments had been made to 557 Wyandots (*Report, 1860*, p. 238).

33. *Report, 1866*, p. 245.

34. *Report, 1857*, p. 493.

35. *Report, 1882*, p. 82.

36. 14 *U.S. Stat.* 769.

37. Of August 15, 1894, and March 2, 1895 (28 *U.S. Stat.* 301, 908), and the act of June 10, 1896 (29 *U.S. Stat.* 344).

38. 30 *U.S. Stat.* 62. There is evidence that since the disorganization of the Wyandot tribe some of the members went to Ohio and some to Canada, where they settled on the Detroit River (Dale and Litton, *Cherokee Cavaliers*, p. 94).

CHAPTER XI

MIAMI, ILLINOIS, AND KICKAPOO INDIANS IN KANSAS

MIAMI

AMONG the last of the emigrant Indians to reach Kansas were the Miami, who arrived at their reservation in the early part of November, 1846.[1] Soon thereafter twenty-five substantial log houses were erected for them and paid for out of their annuity.

Their agent caused to be broken, fenced, and planted 227 acres of prairie land in detached locations selected by the Indians. They authorized the agent to retain fifteen hundred dollars from the annuity of 1847 and apply it to the erection and maintenance of a manual labor school, which they wished to be operated by the Catholics, under whose influence they had been in Indiana. These Indians enjoyed a large annuity derived from the valuable lands they yielded in Indiana, which would have secured to them many advantages, such as blacksmiths, millers, and agricultural assistants; but they acquired none of these, for, under the influence of the whites, they were still the victims of a pernicious indulgence in whiskey. Their agent reported that improvement was almost hopeless until the state of Missouri would adopt laws to "suppress the whiskey groggeries along the lines."[2]

However, through the enterprise and zeal of the Catholic priests, their school was opened in the autumn of 1848. These Indians were located on the Marais des Cygnes River and its tributaries, where they enjoyed the best land to be found in Kansas, and where, after two years' residence, there was but a single field tilled during the year, though they were almost starving for bread. A majority of them were living within fifteen miles of the Missouri state line, all along which were placed the so-called "groceries," which were nothing more than grogshops whose proprietors contrived to evade the law so as to furnish the Indians great quantities of whiskey, and receive from them, when their money was gone, blankets, horses, and clothing of all descriptions. They were a miserable race of beings, said the agent, "and, in consequence of their dissipated habits," were fast dying off. They not only were destroying themselves by liquor but were continually murdering one another. There was less intelligence among them than among any others in that agency. "Indeed, there is scarcely a successful man among them. Their present wretched condition I conceive to be the result of excessive indulgence in drink. During that year the mission was abandoned and the mission property vacated."[3]

In 1850, however, the agent observed some improvement among the Indians, about thirty of whom signed a pledge to abstain from the use of intoxicating liquors for a year. Their farming operations were improved, and "many of the Indians were to be seen following the plough and wielding the maul. They are now preparing to sow wheat. They have now fully completed a very superior mill which has been recently put into operation. I think they will now build themselves good houses and open more farms. These people are now in a better condition than ever before; they have raised an abundance of corn and have a mill to grind it; and, what is still better, all those little hordes which have heretofore been hanging about the state line and the groceries along the line, have mostly broken up and moved near to the mission buildings. For their improved condition much credit is due to Amos H. Goodin, their farmer." They were much concerned about the fate of their abandoned mission and asked the government to place it in the hands of the Baptist church, and they promised to aid in building up a flourishing school.[4]

While the Commissioner of Indian Affairs in 1851 reported the condition of the Miami as favorable, he was contradicted in the same volume of his own reports by the agent for the Sauk and Fox agency which included the Miami, who said that all the Indians within his jurisdiction were making some advancement in civilization except the Miami, who were cursed by the receipt of a large annuity with which they purchased all manner of indulgences and dissipations. These annuities, he said, instead of being applied to any beneficial object calculated to elevate them, encouraged them to live an idle life and to indulge in frivolous extravagances and in the free use of intoxicating liquors.[5]

The same story was reported year after year by the agent, who found that the large annuities arrested all industry and thrift and brought only idleness and dissipation. The agent in 1852, reporting on the Wea, Piankashaw, Peoria, and Miami tribes included within his (Osage River) agency, had much to say in praise of the first three tribes, who, he said, in habits of sobriety would "compare favorably with the same amount of white population promiscuously selected from any part of the country. They have not only unanimously taken the pledge of total abstinence from all intoxicating drinks, but by solemn ordinance of their councils they have resolved to prevent its introduction among them, and have appointed persons whose duty it is to destroy it wherever found—an ordinance which I have reason to believe is strictly and rigidly enforced.

"A recent visit to their cabins and inspection of their fields afforded me the highest gratification, in the evidence of increasing comfort and improvement, both physical and moral. Justice to my interpreter, Baptiste Peoria, requires that I should say, that to his exertions and influence is mainly attributable the fortunate change in the habits of these people. Himself a reformed inebriate, possessed of much good sense and benevolence, his untiring efforts are directed to the reformation of his people."[6]

The condition of the Miami, said the agent, "presents a very different picture. Although living in close proximity, speaking the same language, and in habits of constant social intercourse with their brothers, the Piankeshaw, Peoria and Wea, yet in disposition and habits they are greatly dissimilar"; and the agent refers in strong terms to the indulgence and dissipation of the Miami and to their patronage of the grogshops on the Missouri border. Unfortunately, their chiefs, with one honorable exception, said their agent, "are all drunkards, and by their evil example encourage habits and dissipations which are resulting disastrously to their tribe. Since their emigration to this country—a period of only six years—their number has diminished more than one half; and sickness, disease and murder—the result of dissipation—are constantly thinning their ranks. Recently one of their women committed fratricide by plunging a knife into the breast of her brother. The members of this tribe labor less, have fewer of the comforts of life, but more of vice and wretchedness, than either of the others."[7]

The Miami of Kansas were jealous of those remaining in Indiana from a belief that the number of the latter was greatly overestimated and that therefore they received more than their share of the tribal annuities. The dissipation and general worthlessness of the Miami Indians seemed to justify the efforts of the federal government to reduce the size of their reservation, and the agent reported in 1853 that these Indians were ready to yield to the government's demands for a treaty giving up a substantial part of their reservation.

In order to liquidate the property of the Miami in Kansas, promote their removal, and advance the interests of the whites who were squatted on their lands, Congress, on March 3, 1873, enacted appropriate legislation.[8] It provided for the appraisement of lands occupied by white squatters, who were to be permitted to purchase the same at the appraised value. Any surplus land not occupied by squatters was to be advertised and sold to the highest bidder. The act provided also for making citizens of those members of the tribe who satisfied the court of their competency when they should cease to be members of an Indian tribe. The Secretary of the Interior was authorized to approve the contract made on January 15, 1872, between the Miami and the Confederated Wea, Peoria, Kaskaskia, and Piankashaw Indians.

The Secretary thereupon, on November 4, 1873, advertised 2,493 acres of land for sale. So much of this land was in possession of whites, thus discouraging bidders to venture offers for it, that only 165 acres were sold. It brought the sum of $1,823.56, from which was deducted the cost of advertising. By a curious coincidence the cost of advertising amounted to precisely the same sum—the land sold for $1,823.56 and the advertising bills were $1,823.56.

In 1846 the number of Miami who had emigrated from Indiana was 500, which in 1873 had been reduced to 106.[9]

ILLINOIS INDIANS

The confederacy known as the Illinois Indians, now reduced to a weak remnant of former powerful tribes, was composed of the Kaskaskia, Peoria, Michigamea, Cahokia, and Tamaroa Indians. They had been living in western Missouri and eastern Kansas, where they had a village on the Osage River. To settle misunderstandings with these Indians and to insure their complete removal to the west of Missouri, the government made a treaty with them at Castor Hill on October 27, 1832. Two days later at the same place a treaty was made with the Wea and Piankashaw.[10] By these treaties, for certain considerations the Indians ceded to the United States all claim to land in Illinois and Missouri, and the government gave them 250 sections of land, bounded on the east by the western line of Missouri for fifteen miles and on the north by the Shawnee reservation. The western 150 sections, which contained their town on the Osage River, was designated as the home of the Kaskaskia and Peoria; and the remainder reserved for the Piankashaw and Wea, contained their two villages. There were now (1832) 400 members of these small tribes and 350 Wea in the West.

The Illinois Indians, for official convenience known collectively as the "Peoria and Kaskaskia," were located within the Osage River agency and in 1840 entered the decade with a population of 200. In the same agency were the Piankashaw with 100 and the Wea numbering 200. The Indians of this agency were cursed by a predatory class of white men on the Missouri side of the line, who shamelessly persisted in clandestinely bringing whiskey into the country to filch from them their little annuity and other property. Fortunately the annuity of the Peoria and Kaskaskia had expired, and, as they had little or no money to exchange for whiskey, the whites left them alone. The result was that, under the influence of a Catholic mission, they were becoming good farmers. According to the superintendent of the mission, most of them had become models of temperance and industry and good examples to the neighboring drunken Potawatomi.

Their agent reported in 1850 that they and the Wea and Piankashaw were living on adjoining land in mutual friendship and content; in fact, he said, the four tribes were so nearly one in all respects that they desired to merge in one tribe, which, with the encouragement of the government, they later did. They owned a total of 356,000 acres of land on Osage River which they wished to sell and locate elsewhere, away from their white neighbors. They had lately taken the pledge to abstain from drinking—a movement promoted by the enlightened Indian, Baptiste Peoria, who was often mentioned by the Indian agents as a man responsible for much of the progress made by these Indians.

But, in spite of these favorable omens, they declined in progress and population. A few applied themselves to tilling the soil, though they retained their interest in hunting expeditions. Because of their kinship, the Piankashaw, Wea, Peoria, and Kaskaskia were grouped together in one reservation which they shared with the Indiana Potawatomi and the Ottawa of the Maumee. The Piankashaw were much given to wandering far on their hunting expeditions and at times made protracted stays with the Creek Indians. Their agent considered and treated the four as a single tribe. "By frequent intermarriage and adoptions their distinctive characteristics, if any ever existed, have disappeared," said their agent in 1851. "They reside upon the same territory, speak the same language, are in constant social intercourse, have similar habits, and in all respects are so completely identified as not to admit of any practical discrimination."[11] Speaking of the Kaskaskia as a tribe, the agents said that they had "a nominal existence only; there remain but a few of them, and those few, by intermixture with the others, have lost their tribal existence."[12]

The records show that in 1854, at a joint council, to increase their strength, these fragments of tribes agreed to unite into a single tribe or confederacy and asked the government thereafter to recognize them as such. They were urged to this course in order to facilitate the Manypenny treaty entered into on May 30, 1854, by which the confederacy ceded their land to the United States in exchange for allotments to be made to the individuals.[13]

The Indians were smart enough to take as their allotments some of the most desirable part of the reservation in northern Linn County, containing nearly all the best timberland. Because they did so, they provoked the resentment and ill will of white people living on adjoining land, who coveted and had been stealing the timber belonging to the Indians. Hardly had they made their selections than the agent recommended that they be permitted to sell a portion on the theory that they had no use for more than forty acres each. The agent thought that this would placate their white neighbors and would encourage the settlement of the country by them.[14]

Under the influence of this sort of governmental protection the Indians continued their downward course. They held their lands in Kansas by the treaties of October 27 and 29, 1832. Permission having been given by the treaty of May 3, 1854, to alienate their lands, many of them sold their allotments and moved into more compact settlements in the vain hope of resisting trespasses by their rapidly increasing white neighbors. Their lands, allotted under the treaties of 1854, were taxed and sold by the state authorities in violation of the law; and, when the government undertook the general reorganization of the small tribes after the war, they looked hopefully for relief. The treaty of February 23, 1867, provided for the purchase for their use of the north half of the Seneca and Shawnee reservation and part of the Quapaw reservation, both in the Indian Territory east of the Neosho River. Restrictions on the sale of allotted lands in Kansas were removed so they could sell their allotments, and they agreed to take up their new abode within two years.

They soon began removing to their beautiful home in the Indian Territory, where they received much help and encouragement in opening up their little farms from Baptiste Peoria, their intelligent and progressive chief, and a leading man in the confederacy.

KICKAPOO

The Kickapoo Indians in 1838, to the number of 724, lived on their reservation four miles north of Fort Leavenworth. Many of them were under the influence of the Catholic priest, as they had been in Illinois. Others were followers of Kenekuk, the Prophet. They were good farmers and sold corn to the garrison. There was a large element of the tribe, however, which preferred hunting to farming; and in 1837 several hundred of this faction went to Red River on a hunting trip and never returned. There they joined with a faction of the tribe which had settled in Texas before the Republic. The Texans, fearing that they would side with Mexico in their dispute, drove them, with the Cherokee and others, out of the country across Red River into the Choctaw Nation, whence they were again driven out by the soldiers from Fort Gibson.

When Captain Marcy was engaged in his tour of exploration from Fort Smith in 1849, he met a band of these Kickapoo Indians on the Canadian River who were friends of his Delaware guide, Black Beaver. They numbered a hundred warriors—fine-looking, dashing young fellows, all well mounted and armed with good rifles, upon some of which Marcy saw the familiar names of Derringer and Tryon of Philadelphia, armament manufacturers. They had their families with them and were going to pass the winter hunting upon the Colorado River in Texas, where game was abundant. They had a large number of horses and mules to transport their provisions and baggage and were in every respect well fitted for their expedition. These Indians, said Marcy, were brave warriors, good shots, and prepared to meet any of the prairie tribes, either in business or in war. They carried out articles to exchange with the wild tribes for mules that they drove back to the settlements in the spring; thus they formed a commercial and communicating medium between the white traders and the wild tribes and carried on a profitable business while they indulged in the chase, their favorite occupation.

Three years later, while on his exploration of Red River, Captain Marcy entertained another company of these Indians a short distance west of Fort Arbuckle. Some Kickapoo hunters, said Marcy, "came into camp this evening, and we could not but remark the striking contrast between them and the Wichitas. They were fine-looking, well dressed young men with open, frank and intelligent countenances and seemed to scorn the idea of begging." The officers of Fort Smith were also impressed by the superior character and appearance of these roving Kickapoo. When writing to the commanding officer at Fort Arbuckle about permitting these Indians to remain in the Chickasaw Nation, the adjutant, speaking for the commandant at Fort Smith, said: "The Kickapoo band is well known to the major commanding the department; many of them are well educated, and speak and write the English language fluently."[15]

The Creeks encouraged these and other immigrant Indians to make their settlements in the western part of the Creek Nation and along the Canadian River. These Kickapoo were renowned as brave and fierce warriors and for some years afforded the newly arrived Creek Indians a considerable measure of protection against the wild Indians farther west.

At one period of their occupation of the Indian Territory, a band of these Indians selected as a village site an eligible location near Wild Horse Creek west of the present Davis, Oklahoma. Under the influence of the famous Seminole Indian, Wild Cat, these Kickapoo removed from there with him and his followers to a point across the Rio Grande in Mexico and thus became identified with that country. The site from which they removed was occupied by Captain Marcy in 1851, and on it was located the army post named Fort Arbuckle.

The Kickapoo, with parties of Miami whom the Creek agent, Logan, identified with the Piankashaw and Peoria, left their homes on the Missouri River about 1858 under the Kickapoo Prophet and took up their residence in the Creek Nation. They were quite as daring as the Shawnee and Delawares and as successful in hunting, to which they devoted themselves exclusively, said Logan; but in other respects they were inferior. They were much less intelligent and had not the same ability of acquiring and taking care of property, and they were much more savage in appearance and mode of life.

Delegates of the Kickapoo tribe in Kansas were induced to go to Washington in 1854, where they entered into a treaty purporting to cede to the United States all their land in the present Kansas set apart to them in the treaty of Castor Hill on October 25, 1832, reserving only a tract of 150,000 acres on the western part of their reservation or in such other location as they could agree upon.

A treaty was made June 28, 1862, with the Kickapoo living in Kansas.[16] "Believing that it will contribute to the civilization of their people to dispose of 150,000 acres of their present reservation in Kansas," and to allot land in severalty to those who desired to have separate tracts of land and had adopted the customs of the whites, and to set the remainder apart to those who prefer to hold in common, engagements to these ends were accordingly entered into. Dissolution of tribal holdings was thus promoted, but the main purpose of the treaty appeared in Article 5, wherein it was stated that the Indians were greatly concerned in having a railroad constructed through their reservation to enhance the value of their lands. And entertaining the opinion that the Atchison and Pike's Peak Railroad Company, recently organized under the laws of Kansas, possessed advantages over all other companies, it was provided that this company should be permitted to buy the surplus part of the reservation set apart for the portion of the tribe who wished to hold their lands in common for $1.25 an acre.

Taking notice of the Kickapoo who had gone to Texas, the Indian Territory, and Mexico, Article 10 excluded them from any benefits arising from membership in the Kansas tribe unless they should return within one year from the ratification of the treaty.

When the Civil War broke out, the Kickapoo on the Canadian River were solicited by both North and South to enlist. The Shawnee, who were their neighbors on the Canadian, were loyal to the United States. They removed to Walnut, Kansas, and the able-bodied members enlisted in the Union Army. The Kickapoo's other neighbors, the Seminole, were owners of slaves and to a considerable extent sympathized with the South. The Kickapoo, confused by opposing influences, had no conviction on the subject other than the wish to avoid being involved on either side. With this motive, and incensed by the treaty of 1862 opening up their country to a railroad, about 250 of them, early in the fall of 1862, broke camp and started for the Little Concho River[17] in Tom Greene County, Texas, where they arrived in December, stopping near the town of Knickerbocker. They took with them a large herd of horses which the Confederates later attempted to capture.

The Indians defended their property, and in the ensuing battle sixteen Confederate cavalrymen were killed and a number injured. The Kickapoo again broke camp and started for Mexico, where they took refuge in the state of Coahuila.[18] They were surrounded by the fierce and murderous Lipan, Apache, and Comanche, who had driven the Mexican population out of the northern part of the state. The Mexican authorities welcomed the Kickapoo, whose reputation as bold hunters and warriors recommended them as potential protectors against the wild Indians from the North. The Kickapoo did, in fact, render valuable service to Mexican civilians and army in driving the Comanche and Lipan beyond the borders of their country.

Dissatisfied with their condition and prospects, more than one-half, in the spring of 1866, started to return home; but their ponies gave out, and all but forty went back. Only No-ko-what, with fourteen others, succeeded in reaching the Kickapoo agency in Kansas in May, 1870.[19]

For several years after the Civil War the Kickapoo in Mexico raided the country above the Rio Grande, stealing large herds of horses and cattle from Texas, which were driven across the river, where they were secure against recovery. A considerable renegade element of Mexicans operated with and encouraged them in this, and they were a constant source of annoyance and danger to the border settlements of Texas. The Superintendent of Indian Affairs estimated their number in 1866 at eight hundred. The cavalry at Forts Brackett and Stockton were constantly engaged in the pursuit of these Indians, whom they could follow no farther than the international boundary on the Rio Grande.

On July 15, 1870, Congress appropriated $25,000 to be expended by the Secretary of the Interior in collecting the Kickapoo and other roving bands on the Mexican border and locating them in the Indian Territory.[20] Under this and a later act of Congress steps were taken in the spring of 1871 to effect that object.[21] Indian Agent John D. Miles, with a delegation of Kickapoo from Kansas, proceeded to Santa Rosa in Mexico, where he met the Mexican Kickapoo Indians and communicated to them the wishes of the United States government.[22] The mission, however, was unsuccessful, as the Indians were influenced against the proposed measure by misrepresentations of Mexican officers and citizens as to what would be their condition in the United States and by the Mexicans' deceiving them with assurances that their government would take care of them and liberally supply their wants. "As it is important to the welfare and peace of the citizens of Texas residing near the frontier, who have suffered severely by the depredations and outrages of these Kickapoos in the past, further efforts to effect what is so desirable, it is thought, should be made early next year," said the Commissioner.[23]

This situation led to the sensational raid of 1873 by Colonel Ranald Slidell Mackenzie of Fort Brackett, who took his cavalry to the river and then, without legal authority and in disregard of international law, crossed into Mexico and followed the Indians a hundred and fifty miles in the interior, through a rugged and mountainous country, to the Kickapoo reservation where he shot down and murdered resisting Indians, capturing women and children, and returned with them to the American side. Some of the Kickapoo men were absent on a hunt at the time, and, when they discovered the loss of wives and children, they crossed over into Texas and united with their families temporarily held as prisoners at San Antonio. The Mexican war department records account for 76 Kickapoo who escaped capture and remained in the country.[24]

About the time of Mackenzie's raid, a commission authorized by the Department of Indian Affairs was on the way to Mexico with directions to bring back to Kansas, if possible, the several hundred Kickapoo and Potawatomi Indians remaining there.

This commission, composed of Henry M. Atkinson and Thomas G. Williams, made an interesting report on October 8, 1873, on their return to Washington.[25] They encountered much opposition by the Mexicans, who still relied on the visiting Indians for protection against the Lipan and other wild Indians along the border.

However, after many conferences, the exercise of much patience, and in spite of threats of violence, the commissioners induced about four hundred Indians, including warriors, women, and children, consisting of all the Potawatomi and a large part of the Kickapoo, to return to the United States. One band of Kickapoo numbering about two hundred and eighty remained in Coahuila. Three of the warriors accompanied the commissioners on their return by railroad from Texas. One they left at Fort Gibson with the captives, who had been taken by Mackenzie to San Antonio. [26]

The returning Kickapoo proceeded by way of Fort Sill and in the autumn arrived at the Washita River,[27] where they camped during the winter and were fed by the agent for the Wichita agency. Early in the spring Andrew C. Williams, detailed by the Indian superintendent in Kansas, assumed charge of the party and conducted their further removal. In April, 1874, he located them west of the Sauk and Fox agency on the Deep Fork, where they had lived before the Civil War.

There were now 317 Kickapoo on their reservation, and on June 22, 1874, Congress appropriated $65,000 to complete the removal within the Indian Territory of the remaining Kickapoo and other tribes who up to now had refused to leave their homes in Mexico.[28] José Galliendo, a Kickapoo chief of Chihuahua, was at San Antonio with fifty-five of his tribe, waiting permission to go to the Kickapoo reservation in the Indian Territory.[29] In October, 1874, Che-qua-me-ko-ho-ko, a Potawatomi chief, and a Kickapoo councilor from the Deep Fork reservation, were detailed to return to Mexico with Commissioner Atkinson, to bring up the remainder of the tribe.[30]

Early in November, 1874, another detachment of Kickapoo, including women and children, arrived at the Sauk and Fox agency and all were cheered by food and five thousand dollars' worth of presents, blankets, etc. For some time previous to this issue, their agent reported, the Kickapoo on the Deep Fork, between the present Meeker and Harrah, had subsisted almost entirely on water-lily roots, about twenty-eight acres of inferior corn, a few vegetables, and a little wild game. They were not a begging people and seldom asked for food from their neighbors. They solicited farming implements so they could begin tilling the soil. These Indians were in a destitute and starving condition and were trading off their blankets, calicoes, and other dry goods for food. Before leaving Mexico, as an inducement to them to return to the United States, they had been promised by the federal agent that they would be subsisted in their new home, but this promise went unredeemed for many months. On their return the Mexican Kickapoo were settled on land adjoining the Sauk and Foxes. Here, said the agent, the Indians "were very industrious in their hunting and trapping, and have perhaps the most elegant and substantially built little village of bark houses in the Indian Territory."

Their agent reported in 1875 that the Mexican Kickapoo had built two hewn-log houses. "To them it would seem too much like civilization for many of their number to live in houses. They shelter themselves from the storm by a kind of hut, about sixteen feet long, twelve feet wide and ten feet high, built artistically of poles and the bark of trees. These huts, over thirty in number, are grouped together in some order and present the appearance of an old-time Indian village."[31] But they knew little of sanitation and remedies for illness, so that ten had died since the recent "sickly season" had set in.

Another party of 115 that left Mexico in March, 1875, in charge of Che-qua-me-ko-ho-ko, arrived at the Kickapoo village on July 29. The Sauk and Fox agent went to see them to ascertain their condition. When he reached the camp, he said, he "found them holding a feast which was to continue all day, for the purpose, as the chief said, 'of thanking their creator for their safe arrival.' Not a single member of the party who had left Mexico died on the road. One child born on the road has since died. As they seemed much devoted to their religious exercises, I did not attempt to enroll them or disturb them in any way."[32]

However, most of the recent immigrants in the Indian Territory continued dissatisfied and restless because of neglect by the government; but they were reassured in a measure by the news that their brothers who yet remained in Mexico were going to join them. That year also the chief of the Kansas Kickapoo visited them with the view to bringing down, and uniting with them, the members of the tribe remaining in that state. He returned to the reservation in Kansas in August, 1875, with the report that he had selected the Kickapoo location on Deep Fork as a home for the remainder of the tribe in Kansas. Three years later forty members of the Kansas Kickapoo joined the Mexican faction in the Indian Territory.[33]

Che-qua-me-ko-ho-ko's recent arrivals were in a destitute condition; their horses were broken down and the Indians nearly famished for food, so they gave themselves up to drawing their rations and eating. They lived mostly in their bark town, said their agent, "twenty-eight miles southwest of the Sauk and Fox agency. They rejected the offer of a school, saying that they were alarmed by efforts to talk so much about school and crowd them so fast into white ways. If it were not for the good influence of their neighbors, the Sacs and Foxes and Absentee Shawnees, I should have hope of accomplishing but little with these Kickapoos."[34]

The faction remaining in Kansas was subject to a peculiar influence that profoundly affected their lives. About 1820, while they were living in the state of Illinois, one of their men named Kenekuk, a prophet and leader who opposed innovations, devised a religion for his people. Soon afterward a large band of Potawatomi Indians previously mentioned in this book, attracted by the forms and formula of Kenekuk's religion, came to live with the Kickapoo Indians that they might be near their prophet and worship with them.

The Reverend Isaac McCoy, during his early ministrations among the Indiana and Illinois Indians, having heard of Kenekuk, visited the Kickapoo on the Illinois River that he might observe the Prophet and his influence on the Indians. McCoy described him and the ceremonies in the following language:

"Kenekuk, the Prophet, claimed the honor of being the founder of his own sect, which he had been enabled to do by divine inspiration. His adherents were about four hundred souls, about half of whom were Potawatomies. He professed to receive all that he taught immediately from the Great Spirit, by a supernatural agency. He taught abstinence from the use of ardent spirits, the observance of the Sabbath, and some other good morals, though, in point of practice, the morals of the party were scarcely, if any, better than those of their dissolute kindred.

"The religious opinions of Indians who have received no impressions from other people are remarkably uniform, excluding the absurdity of idol worship, and embracing the fundamental truths of the existence of God and his overruling providence, man's accountability, the immortality of the soul, future rewards and punishments, a consciousness of guilt for offences against God, &c. Their external ceremonies embrace sacrifices for the purpose of propitiating the Deity, and festivals, accompanied with music, dancing, speeches, unmeaning noises, &c.

"The formula of the Prophet had evidently not been framed from ideas purely *Indian*, and they more nearly resembled those of the Catholics than any other sect. Congregational worship was performed among them, and the exercises lasted from one to three hours. They heard speeches from the Prophet, and all united in articulating a kind of prayer, expressed in broken sentences often repeated, in a monotonous sing-song tone, equalling in length about two measures of a common psalm tune. All in unison engaged in this; and, in order to preserve harmony in words, each held in his or her hand a small board, about an inch and a half broad and about ten inches long, upon which was engraved arbitrary characters, which they followed up with their finger until the last character admonished them that they had completed the prayer. These characters were 5 in number. The first represented the heart; the second, the heart, affections, and flesh; the third, the life; the fourth, names; the fifth, kindred. During the service these characters were gone over several times; the first time, the person spoke as if he supposed himself on earth; the second, as if he were approaching the door of the house of God; then at the door, &c. Putting their finger to the lowest character, they would say, 'O, our Father, think of our hearts as thou dost think about the door of thy house, &c. O, our Father, bless our heart and its clothing, (the body,) make it like thine, as strong as thine, &c. Make it like thy house, like the door of thy house, like the ground about thy house, like thy staff, &c. O, our Father, put our name with thy name, think of it as thou dost of thy house, the door, the ground about thy house, thy staff.' The repetitions were exceedingly frequent, almost the same words of a short sentence being repeated many times, and all apparently unmeaning. Certain persons were appointed to use the rod, for the purpose of maintaining order in religious worship. The application of the rod to offenders, by these whippers, was used as a kind of discipline in all cases of offences. The offender, whose crime might be known only to himself, was taught that it was his duty to apply to one of the four or five whippers, and state that he had committed an offence, for the punishment of which he desired that so many stripes might be inflicted upon his bare back. Having received the flagellation, which often brought blood, the penitent would shake hands with the executioner, and others near, returning thanks for the favour done him, and declaring that he felt relieved of a heavy burden.

"The Prophet had two or three wives; and other vices, such as gambling, &c., were not punishable. The party became connected in some way, not distinctly understood, with the Methodists, and nearly four hundred of them received baptism (by sprinkling) from the Methodist missionaries, in the course of two or three days, and the Prophet was licensed to preach. But while little, if any, improvement has been made in the morals of the party, excepting in the respects already noticed, the Prophet's influence has made them more industrious than they formerly were. They are now improving in comfort, and consequently are getting into circumstances more favorable for receiving religious instructions."

The Prophet exercised such influence on the lives of his people that it accounted for the permanent division of the tribe, for the Kansas faction took their allotment of land in that state and to this day are residents there. When the Prophet died of smallpox about 1854, "thirty or forty of his infatuated followers died also who, remaining with his body after death, were desirous of witnessing his last prophecy, that 'in three days he would rise again.' "[35]

On August 15, 1883, President Chester A. Arthur by executive order[36] established for the Mexican Kickapoo Indians a permanent reservation of nearly 200,000 acres where they were then living on the north side of Deep Fork of the Canadian River, adjoining on the west the Sauk and Fox reservation in the present Lincoln County, Oklahoma. At the time the Mexican Kickapoo were described by their agent as a rather sarcastic, haughty, and yet peaceable people, numbering about 420, distinct from those in Mexico and Kansas. From this time these Mexican or Absentee Kickapoo maintained more or less communication with their relatives in Mexico, and they all continued to speak the Spanish language, while none of them could speak English.[37]

The Kickapoo tribe was about equally divided between those in Kansas and the Mexican Kickapoo living in the Indian Territory. The relative number was fairly constant, the principal variation having been made in 1878, when 40 Kickapoo came down from Kansas and joined those on the Indian Territory reservation. The latter faction of the tribe differed from the other in several respects. One of these was noted in 1901. The 247 Kickapoo then in the Indian Territory were governed by two chiefs, the one a man and the other a woman, whose name was Wahpahhoko, under whom, however, the jealousies within the tribe were reconciled. The agent said of her: "While she is doubtless the only woman chief in America, yet she rules her people with an iron hand, and is a woman of great determination; her wish and will are absolutely irrevocable, though her actions are usually founded after mature deliberation."[38]

At the time President Arthur established the reservation in Indian Territory, then occupied by the Mexican Kickapoo, the remainder of the tribe, numbering 234 Kickapoo, were residing on their diminished reservation of 20,273 acres in Brown County, Kansas. The agent reported that they were living in comfortable houses in possession of several fine-bearing apple and peach orchards. They frequently visited the Mexican Kickapoo in the Indian Territory and in fact spent considerable time there.[39] The Kansas Kickapoo "were surrounded by finely cultivated farms, and by churches and schools . . . . owned by 243 Kickapoo Indians who speak the English language, wear the American dress, and while they are not much given to industry, are well qualified to look after their pecuniary interests and to determine what is best for them in view of all the surrounding circumstances." Thus wrote the House Committee on Indian Affairs in support of a pending bill providing for the sale of their Kansas reservation.[40]

While the Kickapoo in Kansas were making satisfactory progress, those in the Indian Territory did not respond readily to the overtures of the agent. They refused to take any interest in education. "Last spring," said the agent in 1888, "the Society of Friends requested permission to locate a lady instructor among them, which was granted by this office. She coaxed, petted, and fed them for six months without securing a pupil, and left in disgust, minus a gold watch."[41] He said that many among them were petty thieves and proverbial liars.

They were unalterably opposed to the allotment of their lands. They reasoned that to take allotments they would sacrifice some of their cherished rights; that to become definitely located would be to destroy their visiting, feasts, and dancing. And so they rejected the efforts of the Cherokee Commission to make a treaty looking to the allotment of their reservation and sale of the surplus to the government. It was not until March 3, 1893, that Congress enacted legislation, based on an agreement with the Indians providing for the allotment of 22,529 acres to the then 283 members of the tribe, and sale of the remaining 125,000 acres to white settlers.[42] The President then, on May 18, 1895, issued a proclamation opening this land to white settlement five days later.

NOTES

1. In twenty-two years they were reduced in number from 500 to 92 (*Report of the Commissioner of Indian Affairs, 1875*, p. 69).
2. *Report, 1847*, pp. 866–67.
3. *Report, 1849*, p. 1094.
4. *Report, 1850*, p. 57.
5. *Report, 1851*, p. 327.
6. *Report, 1852*, p. 387.
7. *Ibid.*
8. 17 *U.S. Stat.* 631.
9. *House Report 188* (45th Cong., 3d sess.), p. 20.
10. 6 *U.S. Stat.* 403, 410.
11. *Report, 1851*, p. 269.
12. *Report, 1852*, p. 387.
13. *Kappler* (ed.), *Laws and Treaties*, II, 474.
14. *Report, 1857*, p. 477.
15. Grant Foreman, *Adventure on Red River*, pp. 131, 173.
16. See treaty of February 28, 1867 (40th Cong., 1st sess. [*Ex. F.* ("Confidential")]).
17. *Report, 1879*, pp. 79–80 (Mexican Kickapoo).
18. *Report, 1869*, p. 451; *Report, 1868*, p. 87; *Report, 1867*, p. 291. These Kickapoo joined other members of their tribe who went there twenty years before.
19. *Report, 1866*, p. 87.
20. 16 *U.S. Stat.* 359.
21. 16 *U.S. Stat.* 569.
22. *Report, 1871*, p. 192.
23. *Ibid.*
24. *Report, 1873*, p. 169.
25. *Ibid.*
26. *Ibid.*, p. 17.
27. *Report, 1874*, p. 237.
28. 18 *U.S. Stat.* 157.
29. *Senate Miscellaneous Doc. 23* (45th Cong., 2 sess.).
30. Sauk and Fox, Agent's Report (Oklahoma Historical Society).
31. *Report, 1875*, p. 285.
32. Pickering to Hoag, July 27, 1875, Sauk and Fox Letterpress Book (Oklahoma Historical Society).
33. *Report, 1878*, p. 69.
34. *Report, 1875*, pp. 64, 263.
35. Isaac McCoy, *History of Baptist Indian Missions*, p. 456.
36. *Report, 1886*, p. 330.
37. *Report, 1878*, p. 69.
38. *Report, 1901*, p. 338.
39. *House Doc. 765* (48th Cong., 1st sess.).
40. *Ibid.*
41. *Report, 1888*, p. 111.
42. 27 *U.S. Stat.* 558.

CHAPTER XII

INDIANS AGAINST RAILROADS

POTAWATOMI

THE Potawatomi in Kansas were not included in the Manypenny treaties of 1854. But they were later, on November 15, 1861, induced to enter into a treaty in which they were made to say that they believed it would contribute to the civilization of their people to sell 576,000 acres of their reservation (acquired by them on July 23, 1846) and to allot the remainder to individual Indians in the proportion of 80 acres to each, "such allotment to be exempt from levy, taxation or sale."[1]

The remainder of this interesting treaty contains other provisions incorporated for the benefit of the state of Kansas and a proposed railroad which, it would appear from article 5, the railroad philanthropists were building for the sole benefit of the Indians. The signers of the treaty were made to say that construction of the Leavenworth, Pawnee and Western Railroad through their reservation was a consummation devoutly to be wished, and they therefore conceded a right of way over their land for that purpose. But subsequent history showed that they were not to be permitted to enjoy the illusory benefits, if any, accruing from the road, for in a short time they were removed to the present Oklahoma.

Article 3 provided that "when the President of the United States shall have become satisfied that any males and heads of families who may be allottees under the provisions of the foregoing article, are sufficiently intelligent and prudent to control their affairs and interests, he may at the request of such persons cause the lands severally held by them to be conveyed to them by patent in fee simple, with power of alienation; and may, at the same time cause to be paid to them in cash or in the bonds of the United States, their proportion of the cash value of the credits of the tribe, principal and interest, etc., and on such patents being issued and such payments ordered to be made by the President, such competent persons shall cease to be members of said tribe, and shall become citizens of the United States."

Through the Civil War and afterward these Indians were in a state of suspense and dissension. Forty went to the Cherokee Nation to hunt and look over the country for a new home. Another contingent went to Iowa and Wisconsin for protracted visits. Some of them said that they left Kansas because they were afraid of the white people; but all were discouraged by droughts and crop failures. The agent reported in 1864 their population as 1,874,[2] a decrease of 404 from the previous year, part of which was attributable to the departure of a large band to join the Kickapoo on Red River, where they intended to hunt in order to secure food for their families to compensate for recent crop failures. They went for the further reason that incursions by warring Indians from the plains had made it necessary for federal troops to occupy the buffalo country, and the peaceful Potawatomi feared to venture where they might be mistaken for hostile Indians. A thousand of the tribe, having received their allotments, had opened up farms and gone to work. Seventy-one young men of the tribe, under the influence of their chiefs and head men, had enlisted in the Union Army; many of them had died on the battlefield or were in hospitals or in southern prisons. The small number of survivors were mustered out and sent home.

Some of those who had gone south to hunt with the Kickapoo returned to Kansas to report a fruitless quest for food, so that there was little inducement for them to come home. Others went to Mexico. Whiskey was sold to the Indians on all sides of the reservation. The whites were also stealing their timber in vast quantities, and offenders escaped conviction by the device of having timber thieves placed on the juries that tried them. The whites declined to recognize the Indians as citizens with the rights thus implied, in spite of their admission to citizenship by the courts. This was the picture of the Potawatomi immediately following the close of the Civil War.

The Potawatomi tribe at this time numbered about two thousand individuals who differed widely in their mental capacity. Some were blanket Indians who still followed the chase and visited and hunted with their friends, the Kickapoo, in the Indian Territory. About two hundred of the more enlightened faction, authorized by the act of Congress of 1861, had appeared in a Kansas court in 1864 with evidence of competency, upon which the court issued citizenship papers to them.[3] By 1868 six hundred Potawatomi had thus received their citizenship papers and patents to their lands, which were quickly sold to the white people and the proceeds squandered. Four hundred of the prairie band, or "blanket Indians," refused to apply for citizenship papers and continued to hold their 87,680 acres of land in common. Some of the Indians were progressing satisfactorily, and the agent attributed their happier condition largely to the Catholic mission, where the teachers rejoiced over the progress made by pupils in their studies and their proficiency in handicraft. The population in 1865 was 1,817; in 1866, 1,992; in 1867, 2,180. In 1868 the agent reported 2,025, and suggested the removal to the Indian Territory of all blanket Indians who did not wish to become citizens of the United States.

Citizens of Wisconsin memorialized the governor to aid in securing the removal from that state of stray bands of vagrant Potawatomi and Winnebago Indians intermarried with them who were "depredating" in the northwestern part of the state. The governor and legislature thereupon appealed to the Commissioner of Indian Affairs to secure their removal to the Indian Territory. The Secretary of the Interior in turn asked Congress for an appropriation of $67,000 for the removal of these Indians. Congress, on July 15, 1870, made an appropriation of $21,000 for the removal of 500 Potawatomi Indians from Wisconsin to the Indian Territory.[4] A special agent reported their number as 720 and said that many of the whites hoped that they would be allowed to remain in Wisconsin, as they were valuable to them in furnishing maple sugar, berries, and needed labor.[5] As the Indians themselves were opposed to leaving, they were not disturbed.

A treaty was entered into with the Potawatomi of Kansas on February 27, 1867, wherein it was proposed to send an exploring party to the Indian Territory to select a site for their future home.[6] They, and representatives of other Kansas tribes, were to accompany a United States commission that was to visit the Territory as soon as possible after the ratification of treaties looking to their removal.

The Potawatomi who had started with the commission changed their minds and returned home without making a selection, and the commission, under instructions from the department, made an arbitrary selection for them of a tract of country lying immediately west of and adjoining that selected for the Sauk and Foxes. The Potawatomi strongly protested this selection and on a subsequent visit made some amendments to the location which were approved by the Secretary of the Interior on November 9, 1870. Lying in the present Pottawatomie County, Oklahoma, the reservation, on which were located also the Absentee Shawnee, contained an area of 575,870.42 acres, of which 222,736.82 acres were embraced in the Creek cession, and 353,133.60 in the Seminole cession. By the terms of their late treaty this reservation was to be paid for by the proceeds of the sale of their surplus 340,180 acres in Kansas to the Santa Fe Railroad Company. This was the treaty in which the Potawatomi were made to say that they wished the railroad built through their land in order to carry their surplus products to market. Yet as soon as they were able to sell their land, more than three-fourths of those who had sold left Kansas in 1870 and 1871 and were removed to the Indian Territory, more than a hundred miles beyond the reach of any railroad.

Nearly half of the tribe had established to the satisfaction of the Kansas court their capacity to receive and manage their allotments of land and distributive share of tribal funds and concomitantly therewith the capacity to sell their allotments; a few justified this view and prospered, while others squandered their money in drinking and gambling and became destitute. These, then, the "citizen" Indians, the landless and destitute, were legitimate objects of immediate removal to the Indian Territory reservation between the Canadian and North Fork rivers.

However, according to official hair-splitting, the "citizen" Potawatomi were no longer Indians, and therefore could not legally occupy or possess the land on which they were located; but, as by 1872 there were 1,800 Potawatomi living on the reservation, and only 400 remaining in Kansas, congressional consideration was invoked which resulted in the act of May 23, 1872,[7] authorizing the allotment of the "thirty-mile-square tract" in the proportion of eighty acres each to the heads of families and other individuals of the 2,263 Potawatomi and Absentee Shawnee Indians living on the reservation,[8] and directing that certificates of allotment be issued them therefor.[9]

In a few years vagrant white men began to intrude in this area, which soon became such a notorious hideout for horse thieves and other outlaws that a detail of the Twenty-second Infantry tried in vain to drive them out of the country. Major A. S. Hough reported on August 7, 1879, that the Potawatomi on the reservation were mostly white men of a low class who had married into the tribe.[10]

Generally speaking, these Indians were doing well, in spite of the fact that many of them refused to wear the clothes of the white man or conform to his customs. The Absentee Shawnee cherished a prophetic tradition generally known as the "grandmother story" as told by a Shawnee woman, having reference to certain present and eternal judgments that would be visited upon the unfortunate head of any Indian who laid aside the blanket to adopt the white man's dress and ways. This tradition carried great weight with the Indians and was overcome only by patient efforts on the part of the agents.

The Potawatomi and Absentee Shawnee obtained a comfortable living from their allotments, though in a few years they were much annoyed by intrusive white men settling on their reservation, killing what little game was left, and in other ways making life difficult for them. This situation continued until a treaty was negotiated with these Indians in June, 1890, by the Jerome Commission, under which 215,679.42 acres were allotted to 1,498 Potawatomi, and 70,791.47 acres to 563 Absentee Shawnee; and the sale of the remainder, amounting to 275,000 acres, by the Indians to the United States for white settlement. This thirty-mile-square tract of land soon became embraced approximately within the present Pottawatomie County, Oklahoma.[11]

SAUK AND FOXES

Another treaty was made with the Sauk and Foxes on March 6, 1861, this time with the band known as the Sauk and Foxes of the Missouri, by which they ceded to the United States a large part of their reservation on the Great Nemaha River, with provision for its sale to the public at not less than $1.25 per acre, the proceeds to be applied to various uses. The Iowa Indians, who were parties to the same treaty, thereby relinquished to the Sauk and Foxes part of their reservation also lying on the Nemaha River.

The Sauk and Foxes living in Kansas at the end of the Civil War numbered about eight hundred, occupying their "diminshed reserve" of 240 sections. A few of them were so progressive that they wished to wear white man's garb but, remembering Keokuk's admonition, feared that if they did they would lose some of their influence with the tribe.

Under the stress of the Civil War, the trespasses of the white people on their reservation, and the determination to get the Indians out of the country, another treaty was made with the Sauk and Foxes of the Mississippi similar to that with the faction of the Missouri of two years before. It was never ratified by the President and Senate. While waiting for its ratification, and reluctant to spend time and labor putting in crops which they would not be able to harvest before the removal implied in the treaty would take them out of the country, the Indians waited in suspense, bewilderment, and unrest.

The clamor to secure possession of this land continued, and on February 23, 1865, the senators and representatives from Kansas united in an appeal to the Commissioner of Indian Affairs to sell the lands of these Indians, ostensibly to pay their greedy creditors whose demands had not been satisfied by the previous sale authorized by the treaty of October 1, 1859.[12]

Nothing came of the movement immediately, but in the following winter Keokuk and four other leading men of the tribe were taken to Washington, where, on February 18, 1867, the Commissioner of Indian Affairs induced them to agree to a new treaty,[13] providing for the sale of their old "diminished reserve" of 86,400 acres in Franklin County, Kansas, for one dollar an acre, in which it was provided also that the Indians of this tribe should remove to a reservation of 750 square miles in the present Lincoln County, Oklahoma, part of the tract recently acquired from the Creeks in their treaty of 1866.[14]

These Indians were diminishing in number year after year and were suffering greatly from the diminution of the buffalo. Most of the tribe was greatly disturbed about the recent treaty, and many of them repudiated it, charging that it was fraudulent and that Chief Keokuk had been made drunk to secure his signature. Ratification by the Senate was withheld for months, and finally another Indian delegation was rounded up in the summer of 1867 at an expense of two thousand dollars—charged against the tribe. In company with the agent and William Whistler, an Indian trader, they went to Washington, where they renewed their objections in the face of efforts to secure ratification of the treaty. After certain objections raised by the Indians were overcome by amendment, it was ratified by the Senate on July 25, 1868, and proclaimed the following October 14.

The Indians, however, continued reluctant to leave their old home, and it was necessary to call them into a council in the summer of 1869 to urge upon them the necessity for removing to the Indian Territory in accordance with the treaty recently made. This council was described by observers as a pathetic occasion. Keokuk and Mokohoko addressed the Indians and whites present and with impressive pathos expressed the grief of all the Indians at the prospect of leaving their home. One-half of the audience seemed to be crying, said the observer, when Keokuk finished his address warning them there was no alternative but to leave.

Mokohoko, however, was defiant and said he would never give up his old home and the graves of his dead. A delegation selected on this occasion went to inspect their new land and returned with unfavorable reports. However, as the whites were crowding them out of their property in Kansas, there seemed to be no alternative but to remove at once. By this time several hundreds of them had been made citizens with the priceless privileges of voting, suing, being sued, paying taxes, and selling their land.

After the purchase of necessary equipment for the removal and planting in their new home, the Sauk and Foxes (except 240 under their chief, Mokohoko, who refused to go south), in charge of their agent, departed from their Kansas home on November 25, 1869.[15] Favored by good weather, they completed the journey in nineteen days. The emigrants traveled with seventeen wagons that afforded accommodation for the aged, infirm, and children, while the larger portion of the more able had gone to the plains on their usual hunt "to join us on the new reserve, on their return in the spring, thus saving the Department the expense of their removal." The agent added: "Twenty-three additional wagons, laden with Indian baggage, farm implements, provisions, etc., had preceded us, and were on the ground on our arrival. It was now mid-winter; we had no shelter except linen tents, yet owing to the mildness of the weather, the Indians experienced no suffering.

"During the winter," said the agent, "we were engaged in plowing, making rails, and fencing lots for the Indians, they assisting us. In preparing for removal, we had purchased nine yoke of oxen, wagons, plows, chains, etc. This enabled us to do the necessary farm work preparatory to planting in the spring. We plowed and planted 150 acres. Our corn made a good crop, and the Indians are now drying it for winter food.

"I think these Indians have done well under the circumstances, and they appear to be quite satisfied and contented in their new home. I have visited the chief [Mokohoko], who with his people refused to remove from the old reservation several times, and the superintendent has visited him. We have urged that it would be far better for him to join his people in their new home than to remain detached therefrom, exposed to annoyances from unfriendly white people, but our appeals have been unheeded. About forty of this chief's band, however, have in small companies left him and united with us, as they cannot receive their share of tribal annuities off the new reservation.

"On the 31st of last month [May] the Sac and Fox Indians upon the new reservation were enrolled for the purpose of receiving the semi-annual payment, and the following is the result, viz: adult males, 147; adult females, 132; children, 108; total on new reservation, 387. The others not being here and refusing to be counted, their number cannot be given with any degree of certainty.[16]

"There appears a desire with some of the tribe to build log-houses, instead of rude bark lodges in which they have heretofore generally lived, and with their assistance and cooperation we have helped and encouraged them to make this desirable change. Situated as they are, near more civilized tribes, living in houses and wearing citizen's dress, I think they will be influenced and encouraged to adopt the better habits of civilization. Most of them, however, still wear the blankets and dress otherwise in accordance with their tribal customs.

"We had a small but very good school in operation from the date of last annual report up to the time of our removal south, with an attendance of eight to ten children, and as it was deemed not best to take the children from comfortable quarters to be exposed in tents through the winter season, the school was continued at the mission buildings on the old reservation until spring, under the charge of John Craig, superintendent, and Henrietta Woodmas, teacher. Last spring I removed the children down here, but we have not been able yet to have a school put in operation, which, however, we hope soon to be able to do."

By June, 1870, only 387 Sauk and Foxes had located on their new home. Scarcely had the Indians got settled and begun the building of improvements and the cultivation of the ground when it was discovered, to their consternaton, that through stupid blundering and mismanagement the survey of the boundary line between the Creek Nation and the Sauk and Fox reserve had been incorrectly located seven or eight miles too far east. The newcomers, after expending their energies on their best improvements on lands of the Creeks, were obliged to abandon and start over again a few miles farther west.[17]

Said the agent: "Some had made nice improvements, built good log-houses, and fenced good farms. It rendered them very unhappy for a time; but they concluded to look for new locations. They selected lands, commenced immediately to make fields, and some of them to build houses; and quite a number of them have now built log-houses. Three have put up frame houses, and there have been houses built (according to treaty stipulations) for two of the chiefs. A dwelling house, designed for a physician, is nearly finished, and is now being used for the accommodation of the mission or boarding school—a house for that purpose not having been erected yet for want of funds."[18] As they were still wearing blankets according to tribal custom, the agent hoped they would adopt the dress of their Creek and white neighbors.

A factor that always weighed heavily with the Indians in their reluctance to leave old homes was the dread that the graves of their dead would not receive from the whites the reverence and care that they bestowed on them. How well founded was this fear was illustrated in the case of the Sauk and Foxes. On August 24, 1875, Edward McCoonse of Ottawa, Franklin County, Kansas, wrote Indian Agent J. H. Pickering that the graves of two distinguished Sauk and Fox Indians had been violated and their bones thrown out on the ground by ghouls, who carried away medals that had been buried with the owners. Over one of the graves was a marble slab bearing the inscription: "Sacred to the Memory of Keo O Kuck, a distinguished chief born at Rock Island in 1788. Died in April, 1848." A similar slab on the other grave was likewise inscribed: "Sacred to the Memory of Hard Fish, a Sac chief born at Shock-o-ton in 1800. Died in 1851."

McCoonse later secured the medals, which he restored to the graves, together with the bones of the dead Indians, and replaced the inscribed slabs. He told Pickering that if the government would acquire a plot for the reinterment of the Indian bones, he would make it his business to help protect them from future violation.[19]

At first there was much sickness among the Indians in their new home, and the agent reported in 1872 that one out of ten in the tribe had died, leaving but 433 in the autumn of 1872, indicating a loss of nearly 2,000 since they had removed to Kansas twenty-six years before. In their strange surroundings the Indians displayed a somewhat rebellious spirit; they rejected the innovations of civilization and even refused the construction of a church desired by the more enlightened members of the tribe. Mokohoko's band came down in 1875 but, pining for their old home, soon returned to Kansas, where they endeavored to live near the graves of their dead. Here their old homeland was in possession of the whites, with whom they were in frequent trouble, and they were reduced to a vagabond and destitute life. Finally, in November, 1886, with the aid of a force of cavalry, these poor people, then numbering 113, were removed to the Indian Territory to join the remainder of the tribe. But in the following February a delegation of seven of Mokohoko's unhappy band visited Washington to make a last vain appeal to the Secretary of the Interior for permission to return to Kansas.

The Sauk and Foxes enjoyed a large annuity which was sufficient to maintain them and complete their ruin, as the payments made it unnecessary for them to work, though, as their agent said: "This seeming unwillingness to work is not from habits of indolence; it is solely because they regard themselves to the manor born, and having a large annuity they consider themselves rich enough without laboring."[20]

Gradually, however, the agents overcame this reluctance to work, and the Indians began to take some interest in field and garden crops and their herds. As late as 1881 the agent reported: "Very few of the tribe have adopted citizens' dress but most of them prefer the breechcloth and blanket, some of them having beautiful and expensive Indian costumes." They still went out on their winter hunts, but, as the buffalo by now were practically destroyed and the Indians began to realize that they could no longer depend on the chase, there was a corresponding increase in industry and cultivation of the soil. They were now beginning to plant garden seed extensively.

The most deadening influence of Indian administration derived from the frequent political changes of agents and lack of co-operation among them. Agent Isaac A. Taylor, on August 11, 1884, made his first report, which was filled with criticism of his predecessors, in contradiction of whom he said there was not yet 10 per cent of the reservation in cultivation. He described the Indians as of good native intellect but wedded to traditions and extremely cautious and suspicious. But he noted an innovation in that they began putting in small gardens and raising sweet and Irish potatoes, beans, and onions.

The population of the tribe had now become fairly constant, remaining at about 450 through several years. Through the influence of the agent the principal men of the tribe met in convention at the Sauk and Fox agency, where, on March 26, 1885, they established and adopted a "constitution of the Sac and Fox Nation." There was a preamble conforming to the usual verbiage of such documents, and three branches of government were set up: legislative, executive, and judicial.[21]

Their courts, thus established, commanded the respect of the Indians, who gave their approval of decisions in a number of minor cases. However, in spite of these evidences of progress, by 1890 a majority of the tribe were still wearing blankets and were living in tepees and bark houses. Their recently adopted code was expanded to include other wholesome laws requiring a marriage ceremony, prohibiting polygamy, and imposing other social restrictions. By now the tribe was actually increasing slightly in population, for which it was indebted to the fact that the Indians had escaped deadly contacts with whiskey dealers. But they were suddenly menaced by the intrusion of land-boomers. A number of white people had established themselves on the reservation, where they farmed the land of the Indians on shares. But there were also hundreds of the most undesirable vagabond white migrants, wandering and squatting throughout the reservation, and no adequate effort was made by the government to eject them.

This situation soon led to the agreement between the Indians and the so-called Cherokee Commission for the allotment of their lands to the 526 members of the tribe and a sale of the surplus to the government. Allotment began on March 23, 1891, and was completed on the following July 14. Because of subsequent births, the number of allottees reached 549.

At the beginning there was considerable difficulty with the "Kansas Sacs," so called from their recent protracted residence in Kansas. Living in their village near the Cimarron River in the northern part of the reservation, they refused to have anything to do with the allotting agent and protested against the allotment. They said that they had no voice in the treaty with the Cherokee Commission and were not bound by it. However, they were finally persuaded from this recalcitrant position and agreed to take allotments in the vicinity of their village on Uetchie Village Creek. Most of the Sauk and Fox allotments were made along this stream and the North Fork of the Canadian and Cimarron rivers. The allotments covered 87,040 acres, leaving 385,000 acres for white settlement.

NOTES

1. 12 *U.S. Stat.* 1191; Kappler (ed.), *Laws and Treaties*, II, 628.
2. *Report of the Commissioner of Indian Affairs, 1864*, p. 370.
3. Unless the mores of the Kansas people were vastly different from those of Oklahoma during the days the Indian lands were being conveyed to the whites—and there is nothing to indicate that they were—the probabilities are that, when the Indian came into the Kansas court to have his competency established, he was accompanied and aided by a white man who brought the proof, and had in his pocket a deed from the Indian, to which was attached the decree of the court validating it, by which the white man acquired the Indian's land.
4. 16 *U.S. Stat.* 359.
5. *Report, 1870*, p. 60.
6. 15 *U.S. Stat.* 531; Kappler (ed.), *op. cit.*, p. 748.
7. *Senate Executive Doc.* 78 (51st Cong., 1st sess.).
8. 17 *U.S. Stat.* 159.
9. In 1873 Superintendent Hoag reported a total of 2,180 Potawatomi, of whom 1,400 were made citizens by the courts. The Prairie band, numbering 780, continued to hold their lands in common. A number of the Prairie band remained in Wisconsin and later joined the tribe in the Indian Territory (*Report, 1873*, p. 199). A portion of

the tribe fled to Mexico, whence they raided in Texas, carrying their booty back to traffic with the Mexicans (*Report, 1875*, p. 80).

10. 17 *U.S. Stat.* 159 (not ratified and proclaimed until October 14, 1868). About 350 members of the Potawatomi tribe, headed by their chief Pokagon, declined to participate in the treaty of September 26, 1833. They were Catholics and preferred to remain in Michigan under the influence of the priest at L'Arbre Croche, where they were in possession of 164 sections of land. Later, however, they were required to surrender this land and join the remainder of the tribe in the West (*Senate Report 129* [51st Cong., 1st sess.]).

11. By 1899 the agent reported that 58,298.51 acres had been allotted to 587 Potawatomi Indians (Grant Foreman, *History of Oklahoma*, p. 245).

12. *Report, 1865*, p. 382.

13. 15 *U.S. Stat.* 495.

14. Attached to this treaty are two schedules of names of favored individuals—mixed-bloods and women married to white men—nominated by the treaty of 1859 to be recipients each of several times the shares of other Indians. One schedule of thirty-seven names was compiled and presented by one Perry Fuller, a local trader of unsavory repute, and the other, of eleven names, by another. On these schedules the names "Whistler," "Thorpe," and "Connolly" appear frequently.

15. *Report, 1870*, p. 269.

16. *Ibid.*

17. *Report, 1871*, p. 493; *Report, 1872*, p. 244.

18. *Report, 1872*, p. 244.

19. Sauk and Fox Letter Book (Oklahoma Historical Society Archives).

20. *Report, 1885*, p. 98.

21. *Ibid.*

CHAPTER XIII

GOVERNMENT AND LEGISLATION

UP TO this point we have dealt solely with Indians who emigrated from east of the Mississippi River. The subject of a common government for all the Indians in this western country, designated in the act of Congress of 1834 as "The Indian Country," was much agitated by federal officials, to the great perplexity and anxiety of the Indians, who favored a simple and informal government of their own planning rather than one prescribed and executed by the "White Father."

Before the Indians had all been removed from the East, bills were introduced in Congress looking to the setting-up of a government for the western territory. The Reverend Isaac McCoy was directed, in April, 1837, to submit one of these pending bills to the Indians, and subsequently he assembled in full council representatives of eleven tribes—the Delawares, Shawnee, Kickapoo, Potawatomi, Sauk, Iowa, Wea, Piankashaw, Peoria, Kaskaskia, and Ottawa—who were reported by him as approving the plan.[1] The Five Civilized Tribes, however, refused to have anything to do with it.

This problem occasioned many meetings and conferences of the tribes, one of which took place in the autumn of 1848 and was described by Richard Hewitt, subagent for the Wyandots. On his return from St. Louis with the annuity money, he learned that a sort of international council was in session on the Wyandot reservation and that this tribe had left an urgent request for him to attend. As soon as he could deposit the annuity money in a safe place, he hastened to the Indian council. "For grandeur of Indian costume displayed on this occasion," he reported, "the social and friendly feeling exhibited amongst the people there congregated, the enjoyment of the dances, and the great number engaged in them, the sober and staid countenances of the older chiefs, the amiable deportment and the musical voices of the females present was, all together, such a scene as I had never witnessed and one that pen cannot describe."[2]

Upon their invitation, the agent addressed the council and endeavored to impress upon them the necessity of adopting measures to promote peace among all the tribes and the proper respect for the rights of one another. From some misapprehensions and unfounded suspicions the Sauk suddenly left without explanation and before the purpose of the council had been explained to them. Next day the Kansas chief announced the intention of his people of withdrawing, but he was dissuaded by the advice of the agent, and they remained to become parties to the compact adopted.

This proposed league of the immigrant Indians was entered into by the Wyandots, Delawares, Potawatomi, Shawnee, Ottawa, Kickapoo, Miami, Kansas, Peoria, Wea, Piankashaw, and Foxes. "This colorful ceremony of union and allegiance took place on Sunday, October 17; each chief handing in his wampum as his sign manual or autograph. Hereupon, the council adjourned in due form, with an understanding that they would meet again during the next season, when it is expected to secure the attendance of many other tribes not represented at this."

After witnessing the ceremony and observing the friendly spirit of the Indians on similar occasions, the agent expected much good to result, especially if the Indian Department would encourage the red men and would secure an appropriation for feeding them during similar councils. This council obtained some notoriety for a few years;

and, while it did not assume a place of great importance, it undoubtedly contributed to the welfare of the Indians and to the friendly relations among them and with the federal government.

It was not long, however, until the immigrant Indians in Kansas came to realize how precarious was their possession, how ephemeral the guaranties of title by the government, and how soon they were to be driven from what, by solemn covenant and for a valuable consideration, had been conveyed to them as their permanent home.

Kansas and Nebraska were discovered to be on the great route to California and in much demand by the restless, aggressive white people swarming into the country. The latter began agitating the subject of making possible the acquisition of the lands of the Indians which, for their protection, had been made inalienable. Under pressure of these persons, Congress, on March 3, 1853, authorized the President to negotiate with the Indian tribes west of the states of Iowa and Missouri to secure their assent to the settlement of white people on their lands and for the purpose of extinguishing their title to these lands; $50,000 was appropriated to carry the plans into effect.[3]

Accordingly, under the direction of President Pierce, Commissioner of Indian Affairs George W. Manypenny, in September and October, 1853, visited and discussed the subject with the Omaha, Oto and Missouri, Iowa, two bands of Sauk and Foxes, Kickapoo, Delawares, Shawnee, Wyandots, Potawatomi, Wea, Piankashaw, Peoria, and Miami.

"I found some of the people discussing with considerable warmth in the press and otherwise," the Commissioner reported, "the question whether that country was not then open to occupation and settlement by the citizens of the United States; and in some instances those who held to the right to settle in the Indian country had gone over to explore with the intention to locate in it. This discussion and these explorations had a very unfavorable influence on the Indian mind. The Indians were alarmed. Reports reached them that large bodies of white men were coming into their country to take possession of and drive them from it. Many of them were contemplating the necessity of defending themselves; and the proposition was abroad among some of the Indians for a grand council, at which they should (as one said to me) light up their fires after the old Indian fashion and confederate for defense."

From the time the original title to the country was extinguished, said Manypenny, under the authority of the act of May 28, 1830

(Jackson's Indian Removal Bill), and the Indians transplanted from the states and territories east of the Mississippi and located in it, until after the adjournment of the last Congress, it had always been considered that no person other than an Indian could reside there except by permission of the government, and then only for a special purpose. The suggestion, therefore, that the country might be opened for settlement was alarming to the point, in some instances, of demoralizing the Indians.[4]

No treaties were made that year, but with the $50,000 provided by Congress, the desired results were soon achieved; in 1854 the Omaha, Oto, Missouri, Sauk and Foxes of Missouri, Iowa, Kickapoo, Delawares, Shawnee, Kaskaskia, Peoria, Wea, Piankashaw, and Miami Indians living in the future Kansas and Nebraska were induced to "send" deputations to Washington, where, during May, the so-called "Manypenny treaties" with the government were entered into, which were the more urgent from the enactment of the bill organizing the territories of Kansas and Nebraska.

Of the dozen treaties negotiated by Manypenny, six of them were with immigrant tribes living in the country previously set apart exclusively for Indians. In these treaties the Indians ceded to the government most of the lands conveyed to them twenty years before. All but one of these treaties were made preceding the signing of the bill by President Pierce on May 30, 1854, setting up the territories of Kansas and Nebraska. In return for the cessions the United States agreed to survey the boundaries of the remaining tracts held by the Indians— so-called "diminished reserves"—pay small annuities, and do other things purporting to be considerations for the relinquishment by the Indians. By these cessions the Indians parted with title to nearly 18,000,000 acres, leaving them only 1,342,000 acres.

The troubles of these Indians were presently about to begin in earnest. They had been located in what is now Kansas under most solemn assurances and guaranties that the country assigned should belong to them and their descendants as a permanent home. The treaties of 1854, retroceding most of this land, did not purport to relax any of these guaranties. As a prescribed condition for admission to the Union, the organic act of the Territory of Kansas declared that nothing in the act should "be construed to impair the rights of persons or property now pertaining to the Indians of said Territory, as long as such right shall remain unextinguished by treaty between the United States and such Indians." In spite of these obligations and assurances, the whites began trespassing on the Indians by cutting their fine timber, making improvements on their land, committing waste, and ignoring the warnings of the agents. In increasing numbers they sold whiskey to the Indians and held in contempt the laws.

In 1856, two and a half years after the execution of the first of these treaties, Manypenny wrote: "The rage for speculation and the wonderful desire to obtain choice land cause those who go into our new Territories to lose sight of and entirely overlook the rights of the aboriginal inhabitants. The most dishonorable expedients have, in many cases, been made use of to dispossess the Indian; demoralizing means employed to obtain his property. . . . . In Kansas particularly, trespasses and depredations of every conceivable kind have been committed on the Indians. They have been personally maltreated, their property stolen, their timber destroyed, their possessions encroached upon, and divers other wrongs and injuries done them."

The troubles of the Indians had become greatly aggravated in spite of their determined efforts to remain neutral during the civil war of the fifties in Kansas and the practical suspension of all law. Robert J. Walker, of Mississippi, the governor of Kansas Territory, reflected the sentiments and conscience of the white people in an address delivered in 1857, in which he urged that the Five Civilized Tribes be moved to the West, their lands sold, and the eastern half of the Indian Territory be made into a state. "The Indian treaties will constitute no obstacle, any more than precisely similar treaties did in Kansas." This attitude of a governor who once represented Mississippi in the United States Senate boded ill indeed for the Indians of Kansas.

The first of the Manypenny treaties was made with the Oto and Missouri on March 15, 1854;[5] the second, with the Omaha the next day. The Delaware tribe made the third treaty, after an interval of nearly two months, on May 6. By this treaty the Delawares ceded to the United States all their land in Kansas save only a small tract or "diminished reserve"; and save also four sections which were reserved for the Christian or Munsee Indians.[6]

On May 30, 1860, at Sarcoxieville, the Delawares were induced to enter into another treaty reducing the area of their reservation fixed in the Manypenny treaty of 1854, and providing for the allotment of the land retained by them, the so-called "diminished reserve," in tracts of eighty acres to each member of the tribe.[7]

Article 3 of this treaty recites that "the Delaware tribe of Indians, entertaining the belief that the value of their lands will be enhanced by having a railroad passing through their present reservation, and being of the opinion that the Leavenworth, Pawnee and Western Railroad, incorporated by an act of the legislative assembly of Kansas Territory, will have the advantage of travel and general transportation over every other company proposed to be formed, which will run through their lands, have expressed a desire that the said Leavenworth, Pawnee and Western Railroad Company shall have the preference of purchasing the remainder of their lands after the tracts in severalty and those for the special objects herein named shall have been selected and set apart, upon the payment into the United States Treasury, which payment shall be made within six months after the quantity shall have been ascertained, in gold or silver coin, of such a sum as three commissioners, to be appointed by the Secretary of the Interior, shall appraise to be the value of said land."[8] The indulgent government agreed that the whim of the Indians in this particular should be gratified.

The oft-recurring handiwork of the railroad lawyer in these Indian treaties is obvious to the reader. An investigating committee of Congress subsequently wrote:

"The phraseology of these treaties is peculiar. They all express the conviction on the part of the Indian of the benefits to be derived from railroads in advancing the value of their land, and in one case—the Pottawatomi—in carrying the surplus product of their farms to market. Two of the tribes entertained the opinion that the 'Leavenworth, Pawnee and Western' possessed advantages over all other railroad companies. The third 'entertained the opinion' that the 'Atlantic and Pikes Peak Company' possessed those advantages. All three tribes desire that the companies specified shall have the preference in buying their land, the Kickapoos and Pottawatomi at $1.25 per acre; the Delawares at an appraisement, which practically amounted to the same thing, 223,966 acres being appraised at $286,742."[9]

Now, by means of the "diminished reserves," and again diminishing the "diminished reserves," having whittled the Indians' holdings down as far as could be justified and permitted under any theory of Indian rights and administration, the next step was to remove the Indians altogether from the state. Accordingly, on March 3, 1863, Congress authorized President Lincoln to negotiate with the Indians of Kansas for the extinction of their tribal land titles and for their removal beyond the boundaries of the state.[10] There being no place for them to go, the President in the same act was authorized to negotiate with the loyal portions of the Five Civilized Tribes of Indians within the present Oklahoma, then known merely as the "Indian Country," to receive the Indians it was proposed to remove from Kansas. The exigencies of the Civil War prevented the immediate carrying into effect of the measure lately enacted by Congress, but the general movement was attempted by a treaty entered into with the Osage Indians on September 29, 1865, hereinafter described.

The termination of the Civil War furnished the opportunity to secure a location for the Indians it was desired to remove from Kansas. In the celebrated peace conference of 1866 at Fort Smith the pretense that the defection of some of the Five Civilized Tribes who had sided with the Confederacy worked a forfeiture of their lands was the occasion for declaring that forfeiture and enforcing it by compelling these Indians to surrender the western half of their landed territory— the western half of the present Oklahoma—on which to locate other Indians, meaning primarily the Indians of Kansas.[11]

Government of the Indians never ceased to be a matter of deep public concern. The Indians themselves had primitive conceptions of the subject which were evidenced in their rudimentary expressions of authority and rule in the tribes. As such regulations were wholly inadequate, and as there was no other legal machinery in existence, Congress, on May 27, 1878, authorized a force of Indian police composed of 430 privates and officers, to function under the direction of local Indian agents. Later, without legal authorization, the Commissioner of Indian Affairs established "courts of Indian offenses." Patient Indian agents from time to time induced the tribes to adopt this innovation and submit to the rulings of the courts, which later won their favor and in time met with popular approval. This makeshift became such an effective arm of government that Congress recognized it in 1888 by making an appropriation to pay the Indian judges a salary of five to ten dollars a month.

With the passing of time Indian administration became more complex and more and more invested with uncharted fields of inquiry and speculation for lack of substantive laws. A widespread interest developed among the lawmakers and all who were concerned for the welfare of the Indians, and at its annual meeting in Boston on August 26, 1891, the National Bar Association adopted the following resolution:

"*Resolved,* That it is the sense of this association that the government should provide at the earliest possible moment for courts and a system of law in and for the Indian reservations."

A committee of three was appointed and instructed on behalf of the association to take steps to "bring to the attention of the President and Congress of the United States the expediency of legislation" such as was contemplated by this resolution. According to their instructions, Messrs. Hitchcock, Thayer, and Hornblower, composing the committee, presented the matter to President Benjamin Harrison during the early part of October, 1891.[12]

Four years previous to this, in 1887, Congress enacted legislation providing for the allotment of lands of certain tribes to the individual Indians. From this time on, the subject of legislation for the government of the Indians, constantly before the lawmakers, found expression in enactments that led to the opening of reservations to white persons and the allotment of the residue of some reservations to the individual Indians and eventually to the establishment of the state of Oklahoma.[13]

NOTES

1. *Report of the Commissioner of Indian Affairs, 1837,* p. 618. McCoy recommended establishing the capital on a site of seven square miles of land on the Osage River (*Senate Executive Doc. 1* [25th Cong., 2d sess.], pp. 579–84; see also *Farnham's Travels* ["Thwaite's Western Travels," Vol. XXVIII], p. 120). An interesting debate in the United States Senate on the subject is reported in the *National Intelligencer,* April 16, 1839.

2. *Report, 1848,* p. 489.

3. 10 *U.S. Stat.* 238.

4. *Report, 1853,* pp. 9 ff.

5. Kappler (ed.), *Laws and Treaties,* II, 451. The new Indian policy of 1853–54 involved also the creation of new agencies for the Kansas, the Kickapoo, and the Delawares (10 *U.S. Stat.* 700).

6. 10 *U.S. Stat.* 457.

7. *Ibid.,* p. 610.

8. *House Report 188* (45th Cong., 3 sess.), p. 15.

9. *Ibid.,* p. 20; 12 *U.S. Stat.* 793.

10. Kappler (ed.), *op. cit.,* p. 673.

11. This was by means of treaties with the Seminole, March 21, 1866 (*ibid.,* p. 694); Choctaw and Chickasaw, April 28, 1866 (*ibid.,* p. 702); Creeks, June 14, 1866 (*ibid.,* p. 714; and Cherokee, June 19, 1866 (*ibid.,* p. 724).

12. *Report, 1892,* p. 25.

13. This legislation and the steps by which these Indians and their lands passed to the jurisdiction of the white man are discussed at length in Grant Foreman, *A History of Oklahoma.*

CHAPTER XIV

IMMIGRANTS FROM WESTERN STATES

FROM this point on we shall deal with immigrant Indians who came principally from regions west of the Mississippi River and who were generally classified with the uncivilized or "wild" Indians. Reference is here to the Pawnee of Nebraska, the Ponca of Dakota, the Oto and Missouri of Nebraska, and the Iowa temporarily sojourning on a reservation lying between Kansas and Nebraska.

PAWNEE

The Reverend Isaac McCoy, previously employed by the government, was directed on May 8, 1831, to survey the reservations upon which to locate the Delaware and other Indians being removed from the East to the present Kansas.[1] In the course of his engagements he recommended, in March, 1832, that steps be taken to extinguish the title of the Pawnee and Omaha Indians "in the northern part of what we term the Indian [Nebraska] Territory to so much country as may be requisite in the designs of the Government." He found the Pawnee Indians living in four towns in an association that the government officials called the "Pawnee Republic." According to McCoy, half of the Pawnee population had recently died from smallpox, and he shuddered at the sight of "more than 3000 human carcasses cast upon the open field in the space of a few days."[2]

Failure to extinguish the title of the Pawnee and Oto to the lands occupied by them before locating the emigrating Indians on it led to misunderstanding and bloodshed between the Pawnee and Delawares; so that in the summer of 1833, while the former were absent on their hunt, in reprisal for some grievance, the Delawares destroyed an entire Pawnee village, and 2,500 Indians were driven to the prairie without shelter. Propinquity and common danger had united the Pawnee and Oto in measures for defense, and all Indians south of the Kansas River were regarded as common enemies. The Osage, who sided with the Delawares, proceeded with a hundred warriors to attack an Oto town, but the intended destruction was averted by the intervention of troops from Fort Leavenworth.[3]

To remove the cause of war, quiet the title of the emigrants, and establish peace between the new neighbors, a treaty was negotiated

on October 9, 1833, at the Grand Pawnee village with the four confederated bands—the Grand Pawnee, Pawnee Loupe, Pawnee Republi-
cans, and Pawnee Tappaye—residing on the Platte and Loup fork,
by which they ceded to the United States all claim to lands on the
south side of the Platte River, amounting to several million acres.[4] On
the eleventh of the next month, representatives of the Pawnee, Delawares, Shawnee, Kansas, Iowa, Oto, Omaha, Kickapoo, Wea, Peoria,
Piankashaw, Kaskaskia, Ottawa, and Potawatomi were induced by
the Stokes Commission to meet at Fort Leavenworth, where they
entered into a treaty of peace among themselves.[5]

On August 6, 1848, another treaty with the Pawnee was made at
Fort Childs in Nebraska, in order to secure from them a relinquishment of more of their domain.[6] On September 24, 1857, they were
induced to make still another treaty by which they ceded more of
their land, retaining only a "diminished reserve" about fifteen by thirty
miles in extent.[7]

Because some of the land thus confirmed to the Pawnee formerly
had been hunted over and claimed by the Sioux, the latter pursued a
course of relentless destruction of the Pawnee and their property. As
the Pawnee were the weaker, they suffered greatly at the hands of
their murderous neighbors, and the government was frequently called
upon for protection. But their peril was not alone from the Sioux, for
the white man soon began to encroach upon them, and the government agents were deeply concerned for their welfare. According to
the agent, writing on September 7, 1853, annuities due under the last
treaty were delayed; but, in spite of this, he said, the Indians had
shown a remarkable degree of patience. "I cannot too strongly urge
the removal of this tribe from their present location at the earliest
practicable moment next spring. They are now almost entirely surrounded by settlers, a majority of whom, as the more worthy settlers
would testify, are less civilized than the Indians."[8]

From this time, the Pawnee were harassed by war parties of the
Sioux, Cheyenne, Brulé, and Arapaho, who were constantly marauding on the reservation as well as in the white settlements. In addition to these hardships, the agent reported in 1860 that "the country
from the Missouri to Pike's Peak and the Rocky Mountains is now and
has been during the past season infested with organized bands of
daring and desperate horse thieves who have committed their depredations indiscriminately on the white man and the Pawnee Indians."

While the Pawnee continued to resort to the chase for food, they responded in a gratifying manner to the efforts of the Indian agent to make farmers of them and to educate their children. In 1863 the agent had over seven hundred acres of their land plowed, with the result that the Indians enjoyed a bountiful crop of corn, beans, and other products. In addition, on a recent hunt they had secured the largest supply of buffalo meat they had ever enjoyed at one time. This was in marked contrast to their former destitute and starving condition. Thus they lived, said their agent, "a famine one year and surfeited with food the next." Opposed to these happy portents were the continued intrusions of the Brulé Sioux Indians, who attacked the Pawnee in the summer of that year. On the twenty-second of June, said the agent, "they returned in great force and killed and scalped several squaws who were at work within a few yards of my residence. On this occasion they were driven off by a company of the Second Nebraska Cavalry which had been stationed here upon my request, for the protection of the place." The Pawnee were in such constant fear of their enemies that at times they could not be induced to go to the fields for work, and their crops thereby suffered.[9]

The year 1864 was most unfortunate for these Indians, for there was no rain to water their crops until the last of June. With the little rainfall they were still promised a partial crop which never materialized because of a visitation of grasshoppers in August. "After their disappearance," said the agent, "not a green thing in the form of corn or vegetables was left except a few corn patches on the low lands bordering on the creek." This was not their only trouble, for when they went on their summer hunt and had overtaken large herds of buffalo, they were attacked by superior numbers of Sioux and driven from the hunting grounds. Having neither corn nor meat, the Pawnee Indians were dependent on the small annuity paid by the government. The Sioux not only drove the Pawnee in from the hunts but attacked them in the fields and spread terror among the white settlers.

The Pawnee were more fortunate in 1865, when they raised a thousand acres of excellent corn, besides a hundred acres of beans and squashes. Their summer hunt for that year was exceptionally successful, and they had meat enough to live on until the ensuing winter hunt. The government had recruited into the army a company of eighty-seven Pawnee warriors as scouts, who rendered valuable service in the recent campaign against the roving Indians of the plains.

By 1867 the population of the Pawnee had dwindled to about 2,750. They were regarded by government officials as loyal friends, having sent many of their young men into the Union Army, and in the spring of that year they furnished 200 warriors for service under General Jacob A. Augur in his campaign against the marauding Sioux.

But the valor of these Indians could not protect them against another enemy that mocked their efforts at farming. In 1868 the Indians were happy as they viewed the promising, smiling fields of corn and vegetables, when suddenly their fine prospects were blasted in a single day. On the third day of August appeared the scourge that brought terror alike to the white and Indian farmers in the West— the grasshoppers. Said the agent: "They came in a cloud so thick as to actually obscure the sun, and fell to devouring every green thing. They covered the entire surface of the land in some places two or three deep. They were upon all the vines and every blade of corn; upon the houses and upon the the trees. In three days the destruction was complete. The vines were all destroyed, every leaf of corn had disappeared, and the silks and small ends of nearly every ear of corn had been eaten off down to the cob; all the beans and potatoes nearly destroyed, and many of the trees were as destitute of foliage as in mid-winter."

Besides this visitation, the Pawnee on their summer hunt were again driven in by the Sioux, to face another meat famine in the fall. A hundred more Pawnee warriors had again enlisted in the United States service as scouts under Major Worth, engaged in protecting the construction of the Union Pacific Railroad.

An act of Congress of June 10, 1872, provided for the sale of 50,000 acres of the Pawnee reservation out of their total of 288,000, the proceeds of which were expected to improve their condition by building two additional schoolhouses and stocking their farms. At that time their population numbered 2,447, an increase of 83 during the year.

In the summer of 1873 a party of Pawnee buffalo hunters, including 250 men, 150 women, and 50 children, left the reservation for a hunt in the valley of the Republican River. The hunt, though very successful, was to have a tragic ending. On August 5 the women had dried the meat and partially cured the robes of eight hundred slain buffalo, which they had packed and were in the process of loading on three hundred horses. Happy in the possession of so much wealth, the camp became a festive scene, ringing with mirth and laughter. The town crier circulated through the tepees proclaiming the chief's orders to prepare for breaking camp; some of the women were occupied in striking their tents and suspending the lodgepoles from the sides of

their horses; others were engaged in harnessing the travois and loading them with their tents, camp equipment, and babies; others were
organizing the loaded horses to begin the journey home; reluctant
hunters lingered for a last chance to secure straggling or wounded
buffalo. While thus scattered and dispersed, and at a great disadvan-
tage, the camp was attacked by a band of 600 Sioux warriors, who
killed 20 men, 39 women, and 10 children; 11 were severely wounded
and 11 more captured. "So complete was the suprise that Sky-Chief,
in command of the Pawnees, was killed while skinning a buffalo."[10]
The survivors of this massacre made their melancholy way home to
report the loss both of life and of the fruits of their hunt.

Scourged by their enemies—the grasshoppers and the Sioux—the
Pawnee listened with approval to the plans of the government to
remove them to a more friendly environment in the Indian Territory.
In the autumn of 1873 following the massacre, a band of 30 lodges or
360 Pawnee individuals voluntarily took up their march from the
reservation, which did not end until they reached the Wichita reservation in the present western Oklahoma, where the resident Indians
made them welcome. The leader of this body, a warrior at home, was
received and recognized as a chief of the tribe and a delegate to the
great international council of the tribes in session at Okmulgee, which
extended an invitation to the Pawnee to remain there. This invitation,
in connection with reports spread among them by emissaries of the
fatness of the land—that it was flowing with ponies and "ox-bread,"
articles dear to the Indians' hearts—their crops on the reservation having been destroyed by grasshoppers, had a tendency to demoralize
and unsettle them. It was believed that a large portion of the tribe
would be willing and ready to start for the Indian Territory with a
view to making it their home if they could go at once without the delay
caused by waiting on congressional action.

The next year the prospect of a winter of destitution and suffering
consequent on the entire destruction of their crops by the grasshoppers induced many of the remainder of the tribe to follow the example
of those who had gone and to ask the government that their lands in
Nebraska be sold and the proceeds applied to the purchase of a new
reservation for their future home.

At a council held by them on July 5, 1874, they strongly urged that
they be removed, as they were threatened with starvation, and
they had been invited by their relations, the Wichitas, to join them.
To hasten their departure for the Indian Territory, they pulled down

the lodges of three of their villages and sold the lodgepoles and lumber in order to buy food.[11] The subject was constantly in their minds, and at a council presided over by the agent, on October 8, 1874, all the members present expressed their wish to go to the Indian Territory and join several hundred who had preceded them.[12] There were then remaining in Nebraska 1,788 members of the tribe.[13]

Accordingly, the agent, with a delegation of chiefs and head men, proceeded to the Indian Territory in the fall of 1874 and, after careful examination, decided on a tract of good farming, grazing, and timber land, "including a fine water power lying between the forks of the Arkansas and Cimarron rivers, and east of the 97th meridian." In the meantime nearly all the remainder of the tribe, numbering between fifteen and sixteen hundred, proceeded to join the first contingent on the Wichita reservation, where they arrived in February, 1875. Here their agent had been awaiting them since the first of the year. Soon after their arrival, he took a delegation of forty to inspect the new reservation he had selected. The others continued on the Wichita reservation until the end of June, when the main body left for their new land. Four hundred of them, however, remained with the Wichita to look after the crops of corn, melons, and pumpkins which they had been permitted to put in, on the lands of their hosts, and to gather when matured. When these crops were harvested, the four hundred more Pawnee joined their brothers on the Cimarron.

On the Pawnee reservation in Nebraska there still remained between four and five hundred old or infirm adults and children under the protection of the agency. Through the year they raised 5,500 bushels of wheat, 5,600 bushels of corn, 3,600 bushels of oats, and 1,600 bushels of vegetables, under the direction of the agency farmer. The children continued to attend the schools at the agency. Though the reservation was under a measure of protection by United States infantry, the Sioux made two more raids, killing a Pawnee each time. However, in the autumn of 1875, the last of those still in Nebraska removed to the Indian Territory.

Here the whole tribe made a satisfactory reputation for industry and sobriety. They were regarded with much favor by the white neighbors because of their peaceable disposition and inclination to adopt the industries of the white people. They even contributed funds from their annuity for the erection of a hospital for the sick at the new agency, for an industrial school building, and for a flour mill.

On April 10, 1876, Congress passed a bill directing the sale of the

Pawnee reservation in Nebraska and appropriating $300,000 to cover the expense of Pawnee removal to the Indian Territory, to defray other expenses for the benefit of the tribe, and to pay for the reservation on the Cherokee Outlet, already agreed upon and defined in the act, at not to exceed seventy cents per acre.[14]

All four bands of the Pawnee Republic were consolidated, with a population of 2,376, on the new reservation by the spring of 1876. Some of the Indians were induced to remove to separate allotments of land and thus to break up their village life and many hereditary customs. The more progressive adopted civilized clothing and habits of productive industry. Their hopes and those of the agent for carrying out a better program were seriously hampered by the failure of Congress to sell their Nebraska reservation according to promise. Their enterprising ideas, however, did not immediately supplant the love of the hunt; but their removal to the Indian Territory synchronized closely with the extirpation of the buffalo, so that their winter hunt of 1875–76 was a failure.

Notwithstanding the optimistic expressions of these Indians soon after their arrival, the agent reported in 1877 that most of them still wore the blanket and indulged in dancing and gambling. Two-thirds of them lived in "cloth lodges," and the rest in large sod lodges containing several families each, inadequately protected against the weather. There was much sickness from chills and fever and malaria, from which large numbers had died in 1876. Not more than a third of the children patronized the schools, but their attendance was well sustained. By 1876 the population of this tribe then living in Indian Territory had been reduced to 1,521.

A marked improvement in the tribe was noted by the agent in 1878. Better houses were being built, and there was more of a disposition to break away from native customs and adopt those of the whites. More than a thousand acres of land were in cultivation, and some of the Indians were raising onions, beets, tomatoes, and other garden crops. They were splitting out rails and building good fences. Some were trading their ponies for cook stoves, household furniture, and hogs.

Hoping to have one more hunt for the fast-disappearing buffalo, eight hundred Pawnee men, women, and children, escorted by a sergeant, a corporal, and six privates of the Fourth Cavalry, left the reservation on November 1, 1877, for the buffalo ground near Camp Supply, where they arrived about four weeks later. They had permission from their agent to remain away until the next spring. When they departed, they were provisioned for thirty days, but, as they found no buffalo or other game, they were soon destitute and hungry, and much suffering resulted before they returned to the reservation.

The government, as a matter of policy, favored this indulgence in part to make the Indians more contented and in part because the food and buffalo skins used for lodges and raiment thus obtained reduced the expenses of federal administrators and, in some instances, nourished their grafting enterprises.

Evidence of the progress of the Pawnee Indians in their new home as disclosed by their agents is conflicting; one would report them as improving, forsaking their mud huts for substantial log houses, and the next would leave them in their unsanitary surroundings. But they generally agreed that the Indians sent their children to the government schools on the reservation. These were often inadequate, as illustrated by the fact that, in one school, thirty-nine girls were obliged to sleep in thirteen beds. However, in one year nineteen students were sent to Carlisle. The agents were agreed also on the statistics that showed an appalling death rate over the birth rate, so that, from a population of 2,376, when the agency was first established in 1876, the number of Indians diminished every year by about 100, to register a loss of 1,300 in thirteen years, leaving in 1890 but 804. The death rate was accounted for by pulmonary disease, syphilis, and scrofula, and by the stubborn adherence of many to the Indian medicine man, who constantly fought the agency doctor not only in his scientific methods and influence but also in his efforts to reform the habits and sanitary surroundings of the Indians.[15]

At the head of the four bands of the Pawnee Republic were the Skidi (Skeedee), who were further advanced in the ways of civilization than the other bands. They had furnished many scouts to the army. In 1890 many of them lived and dressed like white people; about two-thirds of them spoke English; some had horses and buggies and seemed happy. The Chow-ee, Kit-ke-hock, and Pe-tal-i-how-e-rat were not so far advanced; only one-fifth dressed and talked like white men, and these were principally young people who had been away to school. The Pawnee improved slowly. The agent said that at an annuity payment in 1889 he saw gambling near the clerk's office and under every green tree and bush. But the next year at the payment there was neither gambling nor drinking.[16]

An influence that greatly retarded the progress of the western Indians, and particularly the Pawnee, was the Ghost dance. This was a ceremonial religious dance connected with the Messiah doctrine which originated among the Paviotso in Nevada in 1888 and spread rapidly among other tribes until it numbered among its adherents nearly all the Indians of the interior basin from the Missouri River to or beyond the Rockies. The prophet of the religion was a young Paiute Indian known among his own people as Wovoka ("Cutter") and commonly called by the whites "Jack Wilson," from having worked in the family of a ranchman named Wilson. Wovoka seems to have used his reputation as a medicine man when, about the close of 1888, he was attacked by a dangerous fever. While he was ill an eclipse spread excitement among the Indians, with the result that Wovoka became delirious and imagined that he had been taken into the spirit world and there received a direct revelation from the God of the Indians. The revelation was to the effect that a new dispensation was close at hand by which the Indians would be restored to their inheritance and reunited with their departed friends; that they must prepare for the event by practicing songs and dance ceremonies which the prophet gave them. Within a very short time the dance spread to the tribes east of the mountains, where it became known commonly as the spirit or Ghost dance. The dancers, men and women together, held hands and moved slowly around in a circle facing toward the center in time to songs that were sung without any instrumental accompaniment. Hypnotic trances were a common feature of the dance. Among the Sioux in Dakota the excitement, aggravated by local grievances, led to an outbreak in the winter of 1890–91. The principal events in this connection were the killing of Sitting Bull on December 15, 1890, and the massacre at Wounded Knee on December 29. In the Crow dance of the Cheyenne and Arapaho, a later development from the Ghost dance proper, the drum was used; and many of the ordinary tribal dances incorporated Ghost-dance features, including even hypnotic trances.

The Indians were promised by some members of the Sioux tribe who later developed into medicine men that the Great Spirit had told them that their punishment by the dominant race had been sufficient and that their number, having become decimated, would be reinforced by dead Indians, who were all returning to reinhabit the earth, which belonged to them; they were driving back with them as they returned immense herds of buffalo and beautiful wild horses to have for the catching. The Great Spirit also promised them that the white man would be unable to make gunpowder in the future, that all attempts at such would fail, and that the gunpowder on hand would be useless against them, as it would not propel a bullet with sufficient force to pass through an Indian's skin. The Great Spirit, who had deserted the Indians for a long period, had returned to side with them against the whites, and he would cover the earth with over thirty feet of additional soil, well sodded and timbered, under which the whites would all be smothered.

The excitement reached the Cheyenne Indians in Oklahoma when, in June, 1890, through the War Department, came the account of a Cheyenne medicine man called Porcupine who claimed to have left his reservation in November, 1889, and to have traveled by command and under divine guidance in search of the Messiah to the Shoshone agency, Salt Lake City, and the Fort Hall agency, and thence—with others who joined him at Fort Hall—to Walker River reservation, Nevada. There the "Christ," who was scarred on wrist and face, told them of his crucifixion, taught them a certain dance, counseled love and kindness for one another, and foretold that the Indian dead were to be resurrected, the youth of good people to be renewed, and the earth enlarged.

There was a report that Porcupine had declared himself to be the new Messiah and had a large following ready to believe in the new doctrine. Those who doubted were fearful lest their unbelief should call down upon them the curse of the "Mighty Porcupine." The order went forth that, in order to please the Great Spirit, a dance of six days and nights must be held every new moon, with the understanding that at the expiration of a certain period the Great Spirit would restore the buffalo, elk, and other game, resurrect all dead Indians, endow his believers with perpetual youth, and perform many other wonders well calculated to inflame Indian superstition. Dances, afterward known as "ghost dances," were enthusiastically attended. The Arapaho Indians of Oklahoma were so interested in the reports that they raised money to defray the expenses of sending two members of the tribe to Wyoming to investigate the matter. After an absence of two months they returned, reporting that they had been prevented by snow from completing their journey to the mountains to see the "Christ" but that they had been assured of the authenticity of the reports by Shoshone Indians.

Great excitement soon prevailed among the Oklahoma Indians; all industrial work came to a standstill; meetings were held in which hundreds of Indians would rise from the ground, circle around and sing and cry until they fell exhausted to the ground. At one time the Arapaho even contemplated leaving their reservation in a body to go and seek the "Christ."

While the Messiah excitement did not so completely possess the Indians of Oklahoma as it did those farther northwest, it was serious enough there. The vicious doctrine not only permeated the older members of the tribes but affected the children in school. In the winter of 1891–92, when the craze was at its height, children were greatly excited, and it took the closest vigilance of the school authorities to keep them in school as well as to keep them from coming under the influence of this peculiar belief, which did more to revive the old barbarous customs of the Pawnee and other tribes than any other practice of the Indians for many years.[17]

In addition to this malign influence, the Pawnee on their new reservation were not entirely free from the conditions they sought to escape in Kansas. The agent told of one of the wonders of early Oklahoma on the Pawnee reservation, a magnificent grove of one hundred acres in extent of cedar trees of great size and height, that in those early days was in the process of being destroyed by timber thieves from Kansas.

The Pawnee reservation contained 283,020 acres.[18] The Cherokee Commission reached an agreement with the Pawnee on November 23, 1892, whereby they sold their surplus, after allotment, to the United States for $1.25 per acre. Out of their reservation, which lay in the Cherokee Outlet, allotments were made to 820 members of the tribe early in 1893. Subsequently the agreement for the sale of their surplus was approved by Congress on March 3, 1893. For this transaction the Pawnee were paid $80,000. By the terms of the act the Secretary of the Interior was required to attach part of the land so purchased to Payne County, Oklahoma.

By 1892 there were forty-five Pawnee students in the Indian school at Chilocco, with thirty-two Shawnee, twenty-seven Sauk and Foxes, eighteen Caddo, fifteen Potawatomi, and small numbers from twenty other tribes.[19]

PONCA

The Ponca Indians living in South Dakota on the border of Nebraska, in 1858 by treaty[20] ceded to the United States a portion of their lands; in consideration the government promised to protect this tribe in the possession of the remainder of their domain as their permanent home and to secure them in their persons and property. By a subsequent treaty in 1865 these Indians, at the solicitation of the United States, ceded an additional 30,000 acres of their reserved land.[21] In consideration for said cession and "by way of rewarding them for their constant fidelity to the government and citizens thereof, and with a view of returning to said tribe of Ponca Indians their own burying ground, and cornfields," the government ceded to the Indians certain definitely described lands. The lands thus held by them under this guaranty from the United States constituted their reservation of 96,000 acres.

The next year a United States commission sent to negotiate with the Sioux Indians, through inexplicable and almost criminal carelessness, ceded to the Sioux the land of the Ponca. Thereafter the Sioux depredated on the Ponca living on their own land, by stealing their ponies and murdering their people. The United States made no adequate effort to correct this amazing blunder or to protect the Ponca against marauding Sioux and make good the promise of protection contained in the treaty with them, though frequently called on to do so.

This lamentable condition of affairs continued eight years without correction or redress, the government seeming to consent to the sacrifice of the rights and the peace of a tribe which had never made war upon it and had never broken faith with it rather than seek a just settlement with a powerful tribe which had defied it.

Finally, in 1876, a provision was inserted in the Indian appropriation bill authorizing the Secretary of the Interior to use the sum of $25,000 for the removal of the Ponca to the Indian Territory and to provide them a home therein. This was done without previous consultation with the Ponca, nor were they informed of what was in contemplation until January, 1877, when there appeared among them an agent of the Indian bureau, who at once inaugurated a course of intimidation of these peaceful Indians. They and their friends repeatedly and forcefully appealed to the Secretary of the Interior and the Commissioner of Indian Affairs, representing that they did not consent to be removed, but, on the contrary, were bitterly opposed to leaving their homes. Disregarding their appeals, an order was made on April 12, 1877, to force their removal, with army troops if necessary.[22]

E. A. Howard of Hillsdale, Michigan, appointed agent for these Indians, arrived on April 28, 1877, at Columbus, Nebraska, where he was expected to meet Agent Lawrence with the Ponca tribe en route to the Indian Territory; but he found Lawrence with only 170 of the Indians, the remainder having resisted removal, saying that they would rather die in defense of their homes than abandon their country and languish in the unhealthy miasmic country which they claimed had been selected for them in the Indian Territory.

On the thirtieth, E. C. Kemble, United States Indian inspector, arrived and, assuming control, arranged to conduct the 170 Indians to the Indian Territory. He ordered Howard to visit the reservation, where, after repeated councils, by his tact and kind treatment of the Indians, he persuaded them that resistance would be useless. Menaced by a detachment of twenty-five United States troops under Major Walker, they took their departure on May 16. Their removal was a ghastly and miserable experience for these unhappy people. At the beginning they had a terrible time crossing the flooded Niobrara River, the Indians rescuing some of the soldiers swept from their horses by the treacherous stream. Heavy rains fell nearly every day, and there was much sickness among them.[23] After crossing the river it was not until May 21 that they were organized and got under way, one child having died during the delay in camp. On the twenty-third, in the midst of heavy rains, another child died, and they delayed the next day to give it Christian burial. The roads were terribly bad, the agent reported, and much time was required to rebuild bridges swept away and to repair roads deep in mud through which they toiled.

They crossed Nebraska by way of Neligh, Columbus, Seward, and Beatrice. When they arrived at Columbus, Major Walker and the twenty-five soldiers under him, who had come along as guards to prevent escape, left the expedition and returned to Dakota. Every few days someone died of disease or exposure. On June 5, near the village of Milford, Prairie Flower, the daughter of Ponca Chief Standing Bear, and wife of Shines White, died of consumption. She was given a Christian burial in the little cemetery on the bank of Blue River. "In this connection," said their conductor, E. A. Howard, "I wish to make official acknowledgment and recognition of the noble action performed by the ladies of Milford in preparing and decorating the body of the deceased Indian woman for burial in a style becoming the highest civilization. In this act of Christian kindness they did more to ameliorate the grief of the husband and father than they could have done by adopting the usual course of this untutored people, and presenting to each a dozen ponies. It was here in looking upon the form of his dead daughter, thus arrayed for the tomb, that Standing Bear was led to forget the burial service of his tribe and say to those around him at the grave that he was desirous of leaving off the ways of the Indian and adopting those of the white man."[24]

Later in the day of the funeral the camp was devastated by a tornado that carried wagon boxes, camp equipage, and some of the people through the air as much as three hundred yards; several were seriously injured, and one child was killed. After they broke camp the next day and proceeded on their way, another child died; a coffin was procured and the body sent back to Milford to be interred in the grave with Prairie Flower.

They crossed the line into Kansas and on June 16 reached Marysville; their route took them by Manhattan, Council Grove, Emporia, Iola, Columbus, and Baxter Springs; deaths continued along the way, two old women dying in the camp near Council Grove. They, too, were given Christian burial, which was becoming popular with the Indians. Not far from Marysville four families, homesick and discouraged, turned their faces north and departed for their beloved home. The conductor rode back nine miles and, by the use of patience and diplomacy, succeeded in inducing them to return and rejoin the expedition.

It was not until July 9 that they passed through Baxter Springs and crossed the line into the Indian Territory on the lands of the Quapaw. After nearly two months the march ended as it had begun and continued throughout: "Just after passing Baxter Springs and between that place and the reservation, a terrible thunder storm struck us. The wind blew a heavy gale and the rain fell in torrents, so that it was impossible to see more than four or five rods distant, thoroughly drenching every person and every article in the train; making a fitting end to a journey commenced by wading a river and thereafter encountering innumerable storms. During the last few days of the journey the weather was exceedingly hot, and the teams terribly annoyed and bitten by 'greenhead' flies, which attacked them in great numbers; many of the teams were nearly exhausted, and had the distance been but little farther, they must have given out; the hot weather and flies being particularly severe on the ox-teams. The people were nearly all worn out from the fatigue of the march, and were heartily glad that the long, tedious journey was at an end, that they might take that rest so much required for the recuperation of their physical natures."[25]

The other band of Ponca that preceded those brought by Howard were all quartered in tents they brought with them, absolutely no other provision having been made by the government for their accommodation. The conductor was shocked at the lack of preparation for the comfort of the Indians, who were broken down by sickness and the hardship of the journey, discouraged, homesick, and in every way a pitiful band of expatriates. They were located on the lands of strangers, hopeless, in the middle of a hot summer, with no crops nor prospects of any.

The Ponca thus placed in the Indian Territory numbered 681 persons, embracing 197 heads of families; 36 had remained in the north with the Omaha. They had hardly been established in their tent city when the whiskey dealers of Baxter Springs, directly across the line in Kansas, began the surreptitious sale of liquor to them. There was a Kansas law against this offense; but, when the agent undertook to prosecute one of this band of whiskey-sellers before a Kansas justice of the peace, the latter promptly declared the law unconstitutional and discharged the prisoner.

The Ponca, unhappy and dissatisfied with their surroundings, asked for a more congenial home. Some of the leading men of the tribe, with an Indian inspector, made an examination of other locations and decided on one on the west bank of the Arkansas River, covering both sides of the Salt Fork. This land, of which a reservation of 101,894 acres was afterward set apart to them, was part of the country obtained from the Cherokee in the famous treaty of 1866. About May 1 a large delegation of dissatisfied Ponca left the Quapaw country for the location on Salt Fork without consulting the agent and without assistance from him. They remained at their new home without sufficient food and medical attendance, and a number of deaths occurred as a result. Preparations were made by their agent for the removal of those remaining at the Quapaw agency; the large amount of freight, consisting of personal effects, supplies, agricultural implements, and camp equipage, was loaded for the journey. There were also a large number of aged, decrepit, and sick Indians, who were carried in the wagons.

The Ponca Indians departed from the Quapaw agency on July 21, 1878, and arrived at their new home, 185 miles distant, eight days later. In spite of the great heat, which varied from 95 to 100 degrees every day, they made the journey without loss of life, though the people, oxen, horses, and mules were well-nigh exhausted with the hardship of the journey. The new agency was located in the bend of Salt Fork River about two miles above its confluence with the Arkansas.

At first the Indians lived in tents in one large village, but the agent at once began a movement to scatter them over their reservation. He soon induced the half-breed band to remove to the mouth of Chikaskie Creek, eight miles from the agency.

Having been on the move through the summers of 1877 and 1878, this was the second year the Indians had been in a distracted and unsettled condition, unable to cultivate the land and raise anything from the soil. The season was a very sickly one, and the Indians suffered greatly from chills and fever. Coming from their northern home, where such ills were little known to them, unacclimated to the new location, the malaria had been peculiarly fatal, and many had died since they reached the Indian Territory.

Their sufferings had greatly discouraged them and made them dissatisfied; many of them, homesick and broken in spirit, begged to be permitted to return to their old home on the Niobrara. Sixty-six of them under their chief, Standing Bear, whose brother, Big Snake, had been killed by the soldiers, did escape and return to the north; thirty of them stopped with the Oto Indians in Nebraska and begged for asylum with them.

The escape of Standing Bear was directly attributable to the death of his little son, whom the father refused to bury in the strange country; instead, gathering a few members of his tribe, he started for the old home on the Niobrara, intending to bury the child in the Ponca burying ground where generations of Ponca chiefs lay. A pitiful procession made its way slowly northward from the Indian Territory, bound for the prairies of Nebraska. In one party there were thirty Indians on foot and one old wagon drawn by two worn-out horses. In the wagon was the body of the Indian child.

Secretary of the Interior Carl Schurz, was notified of the movement and, wasting no sympathy on the unhappy Indians, inaugurated drastic measures. He caused a telegram to be sent to General George Crook to arrest the Indians and return them to the Indian Territory. In the meantime Iron Eyes, chief of the Omaha Indians, met the Ponca and offered them food and asylum on his reservation. But General Crook, pursuant to his orders, took the Indians into custody. The abominable treatment of the Ponca had become notorious in Nebraska, and soon the city of Omaha was seething with indignation at this latest evidence of the government's cruelty. Quickly, sympathetic residents of the community, with the approval of General Crook, employed legal talent to apply for a writ of habeas corpus in the United States court in Omaha. On the hearing of the application, the government resisted with the contention that an Indian could not invoke the remedy of habeas corpus because he was not a "person" within the intent of the Constitution. The trial aroused intense interest, and the courtroom was crowded with white sympathizers of the Indians, who were spellbound by an eloquent speech by Standing Bear in his own defense.

A newspaper reporter who was present wrote: "There was silence in the court as the chief sat down. Tears ran down the judge's face. Gen. Crook leaned forward and covered his face with his hands. Some of the ladies sobbed. All at once that audience by common impulse rose to its feet and such a shout went up as was never heard in a Nebraska court room. No one heard Judge Dundy say 'Court is adjourned.' There was a rush to Standing Bear. The first to reach him was Gen. Crook. I was second. The ladies flocked toward him and for an hour Standing Bear held a reception."

A few days later Judge Dundy filed his famous decision, a landmark in American jurisprudence, holding that an Indian is a person the same as a white man and similarly entitled to the protection of the Constitution.[26]

Standing Bear and his followers were set free, and, with his old wagon and the body of his dead child, he continued to the hunting ground of his fathers, where he buried the boy with tribal honors.

By the summer of 1879, twenty-six more persons died and sixteen births were recorded; the population of the tribe in Indian Territory now stood at only 530. Those who remained, however, were regaining their courage and fortitude. Under the direction of the agent seventy houses were constructed for their homes; the logs were cut, hewed, and laid in place by the Indians, who were paid for their labor. Cattle, horses, wagons, and harness were purchased for them, and three hundred and fifty acres of sod were broken, which they planted in corn and vegetables. But their labors were mocked by drought that burned their crops and left the Indians with disillusionment and disappointment. However, they cut and stacked about three hundred tons of prairie hay. A day school was now established and attended by fifty children. The agent reported in 1878: "The Poncas are good Indians. In mental endowment, moral character, physical strength and cleanliness of person they are superior to any tribe I have ever met.

I beg for them the prompt and generous consideration of the government, whose fast and warm friends they have ever been."

By 1880 the condition of the Ponca had improved so that the birth rate slightly exceeded the death rate. From July 1, 1877, to December 31, 1880, there had been 129 births and 117 deaths, not including those who had died in the band that had prematurely removed to the Salt Fork. During the year 1880 seventy families had moved into log and box houses, furnished with bedsteads and other furniture made by the agency carpenters.

The complaints of the Indians, and white friends in the East, of the abominable and unwarranted treatment of these people by the government had reached the proportions of a national scandal. The press of the country devoted much space to it. A committee of the United States Senate, after a very full investigation of the subject, on May 31, 1880, reported their conclusions to the Senate; both the majority and the minority of the committee agreed that "a great wrong had been done the Ponca Indians." As a further result of the agitation, President Hayes, on December 18, 1880, appointed Generals George Crook and Nelson A. Miles, William Stickney of Washington, and Walter Allen of Boston a commission to hold a conference with the Ponca and ascertain the facts relating to their enforced removal from their home to the Indian Territory and inquire into their present condition.

The committee took testimony at the Ponca agency in the Indian Territory and then went to Niobrara City, Nebraska, where they heard the testimony of witnesses representing the more than a hundred Ponca who had left the Indian Territory and succeeded in getting back to their old home. Among them was the old chief, Standing Bear, who related his unwillingness to leave his native land and his seizure by the soldiers, who carried him to Fort Randall. "When I came back the soldiers came with their guns and bayonets; they aimed their guns at us, and our people and the children were crying." He told how they were taken to Baxter Springs and how great numbers of their people died.

The commission made its report to the President on January 25, 1881, showing the incredible ineptitude, indifference, mismanagement, and neglect that had made the experience of the Indians needlessly disastrous and cruel.[27] They found that the removal of the Ponca from their reservation in Dakota was "injudicious, without sufficient cause, and without lawful authority," was most unfortunate for the Indians, resulting in great hardship and serious loss of life and prop-

erty. The report, too long to be copied here, contained many interesting findings and recommendations for the future.

As a result of the inquiry into the condition of these unfortunate
Indians, an appropriation was made by Congress on March 3, 1881, of
the sum of $165,000 to indemnify them for losses sustained in conse-
quence of their removal and for other purposes intended to ameliorate, make restitution, and promote their welfare.[28] Under the adjustments provided by this act, the 537 Ponca then in the Indian Territory
began to reconcile themselves to their new lot and settle down to the
lives of farmers. A large brick industrial boarding-school began operation on January 1, 1883, attended by sixty-five children whose parents were eager for them to receive the benefits of an education;
others, equally desirous to enrol, were prevented by lack of room. On
the Niobrara 170 Ponca under Standing Bear were living and cultivating the soil, raising corn, wheat, and potatoes. Formerly known as
the "Poncas of Dakota," they became in 1882 the "Poncas of Nebraska" when the boundary line between the states was established
on the forty-third parallel.

The Ponca in the Indian Territory were improving, but the agent
deplored their attachment to old customs, such as polygamous mar-
riages, though he said that during the year there had not been a crime
committed in the tribe—a record which he challenged the whites to
equal. "Kindness, good nature, and love for their children and for one
another is a striking characteristic of this people, and they are generous to a fault to all poor Indians of neighboring tribes," said the
agent. The tendency of numbers of them to live in idleness in collections of tepees was attacked by the agent, who refused to issue to them
the rations and seeds provided by the government until they should
move into houses on separate tracts provided for them and begin
cultivating the soil. Nearly every head of a family had a garden spot
on which he raised potatoes, watermelons, beans, and other vegetables.

While they were adapting themselves to the customs of the white
man, the newly appointed agent in 1884 found conditions not all that
they should be. His agency included the Ponca, Pawnee, and Oto
Indians. He found fault particularly with their inveterate habit of
visiting. "When the fit takes them to go off on a visit, they will drop
the plow in the furrow, leave their wheat dead ripe in the field, or the
mowing machine in the swath and go. . . . . A party of fifty or two
hundred and fifty from some distant reservation suddenly quarter

themselves on some of my tribes and stay there, feasting and dancing, till they have eaten their hosts out of house and home, and completely exhausted the patience and resources of the agent; and they leave, taking with them a drove of ponies which their entertainers for some inscrutable reason feel bound to give them, thus leaving the tribe which has been the victim of the raid sadly depleted and impoverished."[29]

The agent complained also of the carelessness of the Indians with their horses and farm implements and particularly of some of their barbarous customs, such as the sun dance, practiced only by the Ponca, once a year, although it was losing some of its most revolting features. He also deplored their selling girls in marriage as they would barter a horse or ox. An unmarried girl of more than fourteen or fifteen was rare.

During the decade following location on their reservation the Ponca showed little substantial improvement. Their agents deplored their dances and the custom of giving away on these occasions their last blanket or pony to their friends. The disposition to rob the bereaved of all their effects, in case one of the family died, figured conspicuously in the tribe in spite of the opposition of the agent. The custom of strangling ponies at the grave of an Indian also was deplored.[30]

Loose marriage relations likewise came in for criticism. The agent said that the Ponca thought lightly of changing wives should any of them become dissatisfied with the one or two they had. Divorces and exchanges of wives, of which formal announcement was made, were public occasions when they were gathered at their dances. When all were assembled, the discontented warrior would strike a drum used by the revelers, give away a pony, and then in a short, bombastic speech stigmatize his wife by giving her over to the tender mercies of another brave. On one of these occasions a young student, returned from Haskell Institute on a short vacation, met his death. His forsaken wife, Comes-at-Rain, urged on by her demon of a mother and the terror of the tribe, Traveling Sun, sprang through the window of the dance house, near which sat her husband who had just cast her off, and, before she could be restrained, stabbed him to death.

The marriage ceremony continued to be regulated by tribal custom, though some nuptial rites had been performed according to the white man's formula. However, in the case of four of these, the principals required the blinds of the houses drawn, so that they could not be observed by Indians outside. Reports had reached the agent that the more conservative members of the tribe had threatened with death any who abandoned the Indian custom of marriage. Two couples had been married at Haskell Institute according to the white man's form, and the superintendent sent the neatly framed marriage licenses to the agent to be delivered to the principals; but these licenses continued to adorn the walls of the agency for a long time, as the principals refused to take them home for fear of being punished by the leading men of the tribe.[31]

In 1891 the agent noted that the custom of the Ponca of sacrificing a horse on an Indian grave was still practiced to a limited extent, though they were careful to keep the ceremony as secret as possible. During the year, he said, so far as he had heard, no horses had been choked to death at an Indian's grave; on the contrary, services of a missionary at the grave had been invoked in some instances.

In the main the Ponca remaining on the Niobrara, now numbering a little more than two hundred, were improving at a more satisfactory rate than those in the Indian Territory. Chief Standing Bear and about sixty of his people, in 1890, went to the latter reservation with a view to uniting with his brothers; but upon mature consideration decided to return to his old home, which he did with all but about twenty-five of his companions.

President Harrison issued an order on September 6, 1890, requiring all Ponca Indians to take their individual allotments of land.[32] Three hundred Ponca in the Indian Territory were induced, in 1892, in spite of much opposition, to do so. The same year what was known as the Cherokee Commission, composed of David H. Jerome, Alfred M. Wilson, and Warren G. Sayre, negotiated in vain for three months to induce this tribe to agree to sell their surplus land. This year, too, the Indians began to be harassed by marshals operating out of the court at Guthrie, to their great exasperation and that of the Indian officials.

The Cherokee Commission came again in March, 1893, and, though they negotiated with the Ponca for twelve weeks, left again unable to induce the Indians to agree to the sale of their surplus land. By August 8, 1894, allotments had been made to 410 Ponca, and the remainder, who were known as the Standing Buffalo or anti-allotment band, were notified that, unless they made their selections by September 6, 1894, arbitrary allotments would be made to them.

Two grazing leases of the Ponca land were made in 1896, one of the East Ponca Pasture of 33,000 acres to James W. Lynch for $1,500, and another of a similar area known as the West Ponca Pasture to George W. Miller at a rental of $2,500. The next year the East Pasture was leased to Frank Witherspoon for $1,700. The individual Ponca had made 134 leases of their lands to white men.

By the time Oklahoma was admitted to the Union in 1907, more than 75,000 acres of the Ponca reservation had been allotted to 628 allottees, about half of which were arbitrary allotments. Two hundred and thirty-seven of the original allottees had died and the heirs had sold the land inherited by them. Under the act of Congress of April 21, 1894, the surplus land had been allotted the next year to 156 children and the remainder among the old and new allottees so that each now had an equal area of land.

The Indians had leased to white men a great part of their land either for grazing or for agricultural purposes; the large amount of money thus received encouraged a life of ease if not of idleness, and official reports expressed a doubt whether it had improved their condition. Births continued to exceed slightly the number of deaths, and their population did not vary much from six hundred. They adhered to their ancient custom relating to marriage, having it afterward solemnized according to the white man's laws. They sometimes buried their dead in the best coffins available and always planted a United States flag on a long pole over the grave. "Sackcloth and ashes" and the giving-away of nearly all personal property was considered the proper thing by the members of the family of the deceased. Two societies of mescal-bean eaters were organized, which the agent thought had exercised a restraining influence among the younger members of the tribe in the use of intoxicating liquor. No harmful physical results had been observed from the use of the bean.[33]

OTO AND MISSOURI

The Oto, Missouri, and Iowa were the three Siouan tribes forming the Chiwere group and speaking a similar language. At an early date they were found in what are now the states of Nebraska and Iowa. While they were parties to the treaty of peace negotiated at Fort Leavenworth by Commissioner Ellsworth in 1833, they continued a restless, vagrant life, and, inflamed by the intrusion of the whites, who were killing off the buffalo, their young men, in common with the Osage, raided the white settlements in Missouri, where they killed hogs and stole other livestock. Finally, it became necessary to send

Captain Nathan Boone and two companies of the Seventh Infantry to drive them back to their own country.[34]

In the Manypenny treaty of 1854 the Oto and Missouri ceded the principal part of their holdings in Nebraska.[35] After the Civil War, the confederated tribe numbered 434 members, of whom 50 were Missouri Indians; they were living on their "diminished reserve" of 43,000 fertile acres of land on the Big Blue River on the state line between Kansas and Nebraska. As it was said to be one of the finest tracts of agricultural land west of the Missouri River, it was inevitable that it should be coveted by white people; as usual, the latter made the lives of the Indians so wretched that they were anxious to escape to the Indian Territory, where they hoped to enjoy the hospitality of the Indians there and to have better access to the buffalo and other game. They were so oppressed by the whites that 180 of them determined not to await the action of the government, and in the summer of 1880 they left their reservation to join 30 others who left Nebraska in January, and, three months later, settled on the Deep Fork of the Canadian River near the Sauk and Fox reservation.[36]

Intrusion of white people and agitation of the subject of removal kept the Indians who remained on the reservation in a state of uncertainty and unrest. By act of Congress of March 3, 1881, provision was made, with the consent of the Indians, to survey and sell their reservation and remove them to another in the Indian Territory; this was subsequently located on the Arkansas River, south of and adjoining the Ponca, and west of and adjoining the Pawnee. Under authority of Article 16 of the Cherokee treaty of July 19, 1866, it contained 129,113.20 acres and was located within the present Noble and Pawnee counties, Oklahoma.[37]

After these steps were taken, the Indians were impatient to begin their removal, and they were in such a "ferment" to be on the way, said the agent, as to cause him considerable trouble in preventing them from leaving before a number of essential matters could be attended to, such as putting up four hundred tons of hay on the new reservation for their livestock on arrival there and the erection of at least a few necessary buildings.

Finally, however, when the preliminaries had been attended to, the agent got his Indians under way. First he tried to secure satisfactory rates from the railroad company for the movement as far as Arkansas City in six box cars of 120,000 pounds of freight; failing in this, he took his people overland. There were 234 Indians traveling with a train of 70 wagons and 200 ponies; they departed October 5, 1881, passed through Arkansas City, and eighteen days later arrived at Red Rock, the site of the agency. The herd of 224 cattle was started two weeks ahead of the train of Indians, who traveled on ponies and in the wagons that hauled their personal effects.

One of the first concerns of the immigrants was the opening of a school for their youth; this the agent promised to establish as soon as the first house on the reservation was constructed so that a tent could be released for that purpose. What the agent called "Wild Otoes," the delegation that came down in 1880, now numbering about three hundred souls, were living on the Deep Fork of the Canadian River, which they much preferred to the reservation indicated for them, and persisted in claiming that the near-by Sauk and Fox agency was theirs also. Their agent was engaged for several years in efforts to make this band remove to, and locate with, the remainder of the tribe on their reservation. Finally, in 1883, eighty of them came to their agency and enrolled with the reservation Indians; but they soon declared they were going back to the Deep Fork, where there was plenty of timber and water, which, they said, was lacking on their reservation. The agents spoke highly of the chiefs and other leading men among them. It required much time, patience, and effort to bring the factions together so that the whole tribe was located on the reservation.[38]

The agents reported on the Confederated Oto and Missouri as a unit, and about 1887 they ceased to mention the Missouri at all, so closely were they merged into one tribe, which became known only as the Oto.

A good picture of the Oto was furnished by a visitor to their reservation in 1887: "White Horse's Lodge is a famous rendezvous for Indians, and great curiosity for white people. The Indians find in it comfortable beds, ample room, substantial food and open-hearted hospitality. It is a sort of a receptacle for everything, and is used in common by many of the tribe whose tepees are not far distant. It is the stronghold, the fort, and contains treasure found in no other place. It was built by Mrs. White Horse and Mrs. Light Foot. They cut the poles, turned up the sod and matted the straw out of which it is made. It took two years to complete the spacious, comfortable dwelling, which looks like a giant prairie dog house, or an upheaval made by a huge ground mole. Mr. White Horse, who has a title, was probably having his hair tastily cut into that well-known style of his, a la Pompadour, while Mrs. White Horse was building his house for him. Such is Indian life. But the higher civilization is gradually leading the men to bear the heavy burdens and to treat their wives as human beings, and not beasts of burden. One example of improvement in this respect was manifested by old John Mincus who wanted to be placed in the guardhouse instead of his wife, who had some trouble with the superintendent in regard to their little treasure, surnamed 'Little John Mincus.'

"But Indian women are very much to blame for their present mode of life. If they would, in a measure, follow Keapohone's rule they would make more honorable and more thrifty husbands out of the old braves and the young warriors. Keapohone was assistant laundress at Chilocco. Mr. Keapohone did the greater part of the work while she drew the salary. Some said that she whipped him occasionally. We do not know how true this is, but, at any rate, he was a model Indian husband and father.

"White Horse's lodge is a monument of patience, persistent effort and ingenious skill. The day we visited it Mrs. White Horse, Mrs. Light Foot and a young married daughter were the only ones of the large family at home. Mrs. White Horse spoke with pride of her work and the length of time it took them to build it. It is a regular polygon, having ten equal sides. In each side, excepting one, and just the length of it, is a stationary bed. One of the sides is cut in the center and a door formed which leads into a hall and then into an arbor. When you enter the arbor, and through the hall, you get a glimpse of the interior of the large mud house which looks like a circus tent. In the center is a hole dug in the ground where the fire is built, the smoke curling out of an opening at the top. Mrs. Light Foot was busily engaged in browning coffee, two dogs were lying near her, and a remarkably affectionate old cat that did not seem satisfied to sleep elsewhere excepting upon the old dog's back. It was amusing to see the dog trying to get rid of it. It changed its position several times, but the cat always followed and found the old resting place.

"White Horse's lodge looks like 'Old Curiosity Shop' or a certain old lady's room that comes back to-night in all its glory, and the beauty of having everything just where you can lay your hands on it. We counted fifteen trunks, two boxes of eggs, guns, old rusty ones that had been used in the War of 1812, saddles, harness, mocisins, beaded leggins, fancy bows and arrows, a huge drum which is used on state occasions, numerous cooking utensils, black as coal, old dried skins, furs, and everything excepting money. It is truly a comfortable Indian home, and if one were benighted on this open, lonely prairie it would be a palace.

"The Otoes are feasting again. The interpreter's daughter eloped with an Indian very much her senior. Her father was absent on a business trip to Arkansas City, and she took advantage of this and sealed her fate to one who may not be worthy of her. On his return, when he found out the true state of affairs, he sent up to the agency, bought a large beef, and sent out invitations to his many friends to attend the marriage supper. All afternoon they have been passing in wagons, on ponies and some walking. There is a striking similarity between Indians and white people."[39]

IOWA

Closely related to the Oto and Missouri were the Iowa Indians, who lived at the Great Nemaha agency on a reservation of about 2,200 acres of excellent land in northeastern Kansas and southeastern Nebraska, contiguous to reservations of the Sauk and Foxes. Thirty of the Iowa having left for the Indian Territory, there were but 171 enrolled members left on their reservation in 1880, living in houses furnished with many of the comforts and conveniences of civilized life. Twelve houses had good wells near their doors and three had cellars under them. Seven families, said the agent, owned as their individual property sewing machines, which were not infrequently employed in sewing for whites as well as for themselves. Some of the families carpeted their floors with rag carpets made by themselves. Their fields were nearly all fenced, and in every aspect they were a provident and progressive people, requiring no financial assistance from the government. They were sustained by the income from their herds and fields and from the interest accruing from the stocks and bonds held for them by the government.

Those who left the reservation for the Indian Territory without permission settled near the Sauk and Fox agency on the Deep Fork of the Canadian in the present Lincoln County, Oklahoma, attracted there by the water, timber, and hunting. These wanderers had cut themselves off from their agency in Kansas and the annuities they might have shared there, and from their destitution they appealed as objects of charity to the near-by Sauk and Fox agent. Occasionally, some of them wandered back to their agency with alluring tales of the advantages of the country on the Canadian River as contrasted with the Kansas country now surrounded by white people. The leading men of the Iowa tribe became interested and solicited their agent for permission to remove the whole tribe. The authorities took advantage of this desire and told the Indians that if the others of the Great Nemaha agency, the Sauk and Foxes, were willing to go, they might all be removed. Accordingly, on August 15, 1883, an executive order was issued by President Arthur setting aside for the Iowa Indians a tract of 219,446 acres of land west of the Sauk and Fox reservation in the northwestern part of the present Lincoln County, Oklahoma. This tract lay between the Cimarron on the north, the Deep Fork–Canadian on the south, the Sauk and Fox reservation on the east, and the Indian meridian on the west. These Indians, said the agent, in 1884, "left their reservation in Nebraska and Kansas some five years ago, and have undergone many privations and hardships since that time. Not being assured as to their possessions, until the issue of the order above referred to they made very little effort to do anything in the way of agricultural producing, but since that time their efforts are commendable." They had planted fields of corn and gardens and, with the provision of agricultural implements, seemed in the way of improvement.[40]

In 1886 the Iowa on this reservation, theretofore wandering hunters, were reduced to 84 in number;[41] 90 per cent of them were still blanket Indians, having only small patches of corn, potatoes, and other vegetables. Like most of the reservation Indians, they spent much of their time roaming around hunting and visiting other tribes; therefore they lived mainly in tepees, though some had comfortable log houses with good cribs and stables. It was thought by the agent that if the civilized remnants of the tribe still living in Kansas and Nebraska could be removed and consolidated with those on the Canadian, and a blacksmith shop and school established, they would all settle down and discontinue their wandering habits. Numbers of them were sending their children to schools in the states, and it was thought that they would support a local school if it were established.[42] In 1890, 8,685 acres of this reservation were allotted to 138 Iowa Indians, while the reservation in Kansas was allotted to 159 Iowa remaining there.[43]

NOTES

1. *Doc.*, III, 230.
2. *Ibid.*, p. 239. More than four thousand Pawnee, Oto, Omaha, and Ponca had died of the disease when it was arrested among the three latter tribes by vaccination (McCoy to Secretary of War, March 23, 1832, Office of Indian Affairs, 1832, "Misc. Rev. Isaac McCoy").

3. "Report of Indian Commission at Fort Gibson, February 10, 1834," in *House Report 474* (23d Cong., 1st sess.), p. 80; the commission reported the population of the Pawnee Confederacy in 1834 as 12,000.

4. *7 U.S. Stat.* 448.

5. *House Report 474* (23d Cong., 1st sess.). For an extended account of this conference see John T. Irving, Jr., *Indian Sketches*. At the request of Commissioner Ellsworth, one hundred Pawnee who had walked all the way to Fort Leavenworth, continued their journey to Fort Gibson, to meet the Creek, Cherokee, Choctaw, and Osage at their homes, entailing a round-trip journey of nearly a thousand miles. They arrived at Fort Gibson in December and were rewarded by securing from the Osage, with whom they made a peace treaty, a Pawnee prisoner captured from that tribe (Grant Foreman, *Pioneer Days in the Early Southwest*, p. 216).

In the spring of 1841, while the Pawnee men were off on a hunt, "a company of 65 Kansas warriors attacked the defenseless Pawnee town and massacred all but eleven of the women and children of the encampment. One woman sold her life dearly. She sprang on one of the Kansas warriors like a tigress, clutched his throat and would have strangled him if her arms had not been hewn from her body" (*Niles' National Register*, April 3, 1841, p. 68, col. 1).

6. *9 U.S. Stat.* 949; Kappler (ed.), *Laws and Treaties*, p. 422.

7. *11 U.S. Stat.* 729. The Indians of this tribe agreed with the agent to the organizing and uniforming of a police force of six from each of the four bands. The agent said, in 1860, that they took great pride in keeping order in their villages and in securing and surrendering stolen horses (*Report of the Commissioner of Indian Affairs, 1860*, p. 239).

8. California emigrants in 1849 brought cholera into the country, from which 900 Pawnee women and children and 250 men died during that year (*Report, 1849*, p. 1076). From then until 1853 the tribe was reduced 50 per cent by sickness and by murders committed by the Sioux and Cheyenne (*Report, 1853*, p. 108).

9. *Report, 1863*, p. 252. The Pawnee had thirteen hundred acres of corn that promised a good yield until late in June, 1863, when in a day the grasshoppers so completely destroyed the crop that not an ear was gathered, and the Indians were threatened with starvation.

On July 5, 1874, at a council with government officials the Pawnee urged that they be permitted to remove to the Indian Territory, as the grasshoppers had destroyed their corn, pumpkins, and melons (*Report, 1874*, p. 35).

10. *Report, 1873*, p. 186.

11. So they claimed; but really it was to promote their removal to Indian Territory (*Report, 1874*, pp. 200, 207, 237).

12. *Report, 1875*, pp. 30, 77, 288, 321. Those who had joined the Wichita were principally of the Skidi band.

13. *Ibid.*

14. *19 U.S. Stat.* 28.

15. Of a population of 2,376, more than 800 died in the first two years (*Report, 1877*, p. 5). Contact with the white man, destruction of the buffalo, and other disruptions of their normal way of living brought confusion and suffering to the Indians. Thus, in 1885, their agent reported that the drought of the preceding year had so destroyed their crops that the Indians were dependent for food on parched corn and were in a chronic state of hunger.

16. *Report, 1890*, p. 197.

17. *Report, 1892*, p. 396.

18. Pursuant to prior legislation and particularly to the Cherokee treaty of 1866, separate Cherokee deeds were executed on June 14, 1883, conveying parts of the Cherokee Outlet to the United States in trust for the use and benefit, respectively, of the Pawnee tribe, the Oto and Missouri tribe, the Ponca tribe, and the Nez Percé tribe. Prior to the removal of the latter to their old home in Idaho, by their deed of May 22, 1885, they quitclaimed their land to the United States, and the Tonkawa tribe of Indians were afterward located on it (*Senate Executive Doc. 78* [51st Cong., 1st sess.]).

19. The Indian school at Chilocco, Oklahoma, was opened on January 15, 1884. It

was named for James M. Haworth, first superintendent of Indian schools. The 8,640 acres of land embraced in the school reserve were set aside for the use of the school by executive order on July 12, 1884 (*Report, 1892,* p. 670).

20. 12 *U.S. Stat.* 997.

21. 14 *U.S. Stat.* 575.

22. In order to make room for the Ponca, orders were given to H. W. Jones, Indian agent at the Quapaw agency, "formerly agency for Captive Indians," to remove the Quapaw to the Osage reservation in accordance with a so-called "agreement" with the Osage, with whom the Quapaw were expected to amalgamate. The Ponca were to have possession of the whole of the Quapaw reservation (Nicholson to Jones, March 26, 1877, and April 2, 1877, Oklahoma Historical Society, Quapaw–Ponca Indian Archives). The latter, however, refused the plans of government, and eventually they were abandoned.

23. Agent Howard kept an interesting "Journal of the March," which was published in *Report, 1877,* beginning at p. 96.

24. "Journal of the March."

25. *Ibid.*

26. *United States* ex rel. *Standing Bear* v. *Crook,* 25 Federal Cases 695 (5 Dill. 453).

27. *Report, 1881,* p. 217.

28. 21 *U.S. Stat.* 422. Much of public and official reaction was due to the efforts made by Standing Bear himself. In the winter of 1879–80, accompanied by Omaha interpreters Francis La Flesche and his sister Susette ("Bright Eyes"), he visited the cities of the East, where, by relating his story of the wrongs suffered by his people, he won attention and sympathy. Many people wrote to the President, to other government officials, and to members of Congress, protesting against unjust treatment of the Indians with the result stated in the text.

Payment was made to all who had lost property and a home was provided for Standing Bear and his followers on their old reservation. Here in September, 1908, after being instrumental in bringing about a change of governmental policy toward all Indians, the chief died at the age of seventy-nine and was buried among the hills overlooking the village site of his ancestors.

29. In 1887 the agent reported many deaths from syphilis, consumption, and scrofula. The first was communicated principally the preceding winter by a visiting band of Omaha Indians, nearly all of whom were syphilitic (*Report, 1887,* p. 87).

30. *Report, 1890,* p. 192.

31. *Report, 1891,* p. 355.

32. Under the "Allotment Act" of 1887 (24 *U.S. Stat.* 388). The Ponca continued their love for the sun dances. "They came to me in July and asked for their annual Sun Dance, and with many eloquent speeches made their claims, urging especially one reason, viz., the dry season, saying 'If we can have this dance it will rain; it is our manner of worship' etc. I reasoned with them to convince them that rain did not come in that way" (*Report, 1890,* p. xlv). In this report the agent said that their population that year was 605, of whom 292 were males and 313 females. Of this number, 177 were children between the ages of six and sixteen, who were in school at Ponca, Chilocco, and Haskell.

33. On April 21, 1904, Congress provided for the abolishment of reservation lines and the division of the Ponca, Oto and Missouri, and Kaw reservations among the three adjoining counties of Oklahoma (30 *U.S. Stat.* 217). See Earl W. Hayter, "Ponca Removal," *North Dakota Historical Quarterly,* Vol. VI, No. 4 (July, 1932).

34. *Army and Navy Chronicle,* X, No. 16 (1840), 248. Eight hundred Oto men, women, and children in the summer of 1838, spent three festive months on a buffalo hunt during which they killed twenty-five hundred buffalo, according to Isaac McCoy. They were accompanied by their missionary, the Reverend M. Merrill (*National Intelligencer,* April 16, 1839).

35. *Handbook of American Indians,* II, 164.

36. *Report, 1880,* p. xliii.

37. Kirkwood to Commissioner of Indian Affairs, June 25, 1881, Sac and Fox Letter Book (Oklahoma Historical Society).

38. Most of the preceding information is derived from the Sauk and Fox agency letter books in the archives of the Oklahoma Historical Society.

39. *Fort Smith* (Ark.) *Elevator*, May 20, 1887; see *Army and Navy Chronicle*, X, No. 16 (1840), 248; for another mention see *Report, 1888*, p. 107, and *Report, 1894*, p. 22: "Allotments have been made to 175 of the 352 Oto, and 410 of the 759 Poncas."

40. *Report, 1883*, pp. 75–78; *Report, 1884*, p. 94. Out of a total population of 293, and a male population of 78, during the Civil War, 41 Iowa Indians served in the Union Army.

41. *Report, 1886*, p. 144.

42. *Ibid.*

43. *Report, 1891*, p. 44.

CHAPTER XV

OSAGE AND KAW (KANSA)

OSAGE

PERHAPS the most picturesque and historically potent of the Kansas-Oklahoma Indians are the Osage, who were removed from Oklahoma to a reservation in Kansas after the treaty negotiated with them at Fort Gibson in 1839. They were to live there less than thirty-five years and then be forced to return to their final home in Oklahoma.

The Osage were an aggressive and enterprising people who carried on a profitable business with the Comanche Indians. From the traders they bought guns, blankets, powder, and lead, which they took on their hunting and trading expeditions to the popular rendezvous, the salt plains of northwest Oklahoma, where they traded them to the Comanche. The latter in turn carried them to Mexico and bartered them to Mexicans or Indians.

In these transactions the Osage would exchange a gun which had cost them twenty dollars to the Comanche for one or two mules worth forty to sixty dollars back home. In the spring of 1847 the Osage received from the traders $24,000 worth of goods for which they pledged their annuity for two or three years. These goods they carried to the prairies of western Oklahoma and Kansas and with them purchased from the Comanche fifteen hundred head of mules worth $60,000. But, said their agent, John M. Richardson, these expeditions did them little good; for some of the leading men who controlled them would exchange five hundred mules with the liquor dealers of Missouri for as many gallons of whiskey, at the rate of approximately forty dollars a gallon.[1]

Later in the same year the Osage departed on their fall hunt, but, as they were delayed in starting, the returns were disappointing. However, they brought home six thousand buffalo robes, with a current market value of $3.00 each; ten thousand deerskins, averaging $0.75 each; and $2,000 worth of other skins—a total of $28,000. Their agent considered them an industrious, persevering tribe of Indians. Based upon data in his possession, and an intimate knowledge of the Indian trade, he said that, during the thirty years since A. P. Chouteau, in 1817, set up his trading post at the Grand Saline, their peltries and furs averaged $80,000 to $100,000 in value a year, or a total of $1,200,000. But these peltries were exchanged with the traders for goods whose original cost did not exceed $500,000, thus accounting for the great fortunes some of these traders accumulated in their intercourse with the Indians.[2]

The Osage lived in lodges covered with mats made of the flag growing in the swamps of their prairie country. By 1853 life was becoming hard for them because of the difficulty of securing game. They went in the full moon twice a year out on the "Grand Prairie," sometimes as far as six or eight hundred miles in pursuit of buffalo, deer, and antelope and to trade with the wild Indians. They made the spring hunt in May and returned in August; went again in October and returned in the winter. The white emigration through the country had driven the game so far away that the Osage had lately returned with but few buffalo robes, tallow, and skins, formerly staple articles for sale to the whites, and with little meat to eat, which they usually dried over their camp fires and brought home with peltries for barter or consumption. Lacking credit with the traders, the Indians were destitute, hungry, and unhappy.

To aggravate their difficulties, after Fitzpatrick made his treaty with the Comanche Indians in 1853,[3] the Osage discovered that the annuity thus accruing to their former good customers made them independent of the merchandise previously brought to them in trade. This was a serious blow to the Osage, who bitterly resented the action of the federal government and the defection of their former friends. Bad feeling and hostilities between the tribes followed. The Osage decided that if the Comanche could have tribute regularly paid them by the government, they would have similar contributions, and proceeded to collect it in their own way. For several years they greatly hampered overland emigration by holding up travelers and boldly taking what they considered compensation for permitting them to pass. They had regular places along the overland trails where they halted parties too weak to resist and collected their toll. In 1854 not an emigrant or freighter's team had been permitted to pass without molestation somewhere along the route. This business continued to harass the emigrants until mounted troops broke it up.

The Osage were not included in the nine Manypenny treaties negotiated in 1854, but they were not allowed to forget the pressure of white people crowding into their country. In common with other Indians of Kansas, they suffered much from drought and want of food in 1860 and from depredations committed by whites during the Civil War.

Under the stress of these unhappy days, the government induced several tribes to enter into treaties by which the Indians were committed to yielding lands in Kansas to the white people and the railroads. A treaty was made with the Osage in 1863 which was so unpopular in the tribe and caused so much criticism that it was not ratified by the Senate. Another made with them on September 29, 1865,[4] was ratified in June, 1866. In this the familiar formula was employed reciting that the Indians had more land than they could use and that they therefore, in consideration of $300,000, ceded a large part of their reservation to the United States. Their country being already overrun by importunate white squatters, it was provided that those who had settled on the reservation of the Indians might have valid title to the lands so occupied by paying $1.25 per acre for it and conforming to certain requirements. It was provided also that the Osage tribe might unite with any other friendly tribe in the Indian Territory, and if they removed there, the "diminished reserve" in Kansas abandoned by them would be sold by the government for their benefit.

Even this measure did not satisfy the whites and railroads, under whose continued pressure the Osage were induced to send representatives to meet officials of the government at Plum Creek, fifty miles below Humboldt, where, on May 27, 1868, they entered into a treaty by which they ceded to the United States and the Leavenworth, Lawrence and Galveston Railroad all their land in Kansas (amounting to eight million acres). This was regarded as a great achievement by the whites and the railroad interests.

"The day before the arrival of the Commissioners at the council grounds, a party of 316 Osage warriors started out on the warpath, to fight the Arrapahoes, to get revenge for a young man killed in one of their towns a few days previous, by the Arrapahoes. After being out about six days, the war party returned and reported that they had taken two scalps. After the making and signing of the treaty, a young man by the name of Dunn, living on Walnut Creek, Butler County, Kansas, arrived at the camp of the Commissioners and reported that on Sunday the 17th his brother and a partner, Jas. Anderson, were killed by this war party, scalped and their heads severed from their bodies. The Commissioners immediately called the chiefs into council and peremptorily demanded the surrender of the perpetrators of this deed. The next morning they brought two young men, and after about two hours parleying, and the crying of the squaws and the utmost excitement among the warriors and chiefs, the parties were given over to the Commissioners, who brought them to Ottawa, Kansas, and turned them over to U.S. Marshal Whitney to be put on trial for the crime alleged to have been committed."[5]

Ratification of this treaty by the Senate was vigorously opposed by many friends of the Indians outside Kansas. Their position was justified by Peter Cooper and the other nineteen members of the United States Indian Commission on the ground that it was a "pretended treaty," fraudulently obtained, "an outrage on the rights of the Indians, and a disgrace to the Nation."

They reported also that, while the Osage were out on their summer hunt in 1868, more than two thousand whites invaded their reservation, occupied the cabins and improved lands of the Indians, took possession of their corn fields, cattle, and hogs, and threatened the lives of the returned Indians when they endeavored to occupy their houses and recover their property.[6]

While this treaty was not ratified by the Senate, the sale of the land described in it and the removal of the tribe to the Indian Territory were authorized by a subsequent act of Congress of June 15, 1870,[7] which also appropriated funds to atone for defaults committed by the government in carrying out engagements entered into in the treaty of 1839 providing for their removal from the Indian Territory to Kansas.

The Osage subsequently in council in September, 1870, ratified this act of Congress. As these activities implied a removal from Kansas to the Indian Territory, this council also appointed a delegation to select land for their new home in the Indian Territory. The greater part of the tribe then went to the plains on their regular fall and winter hunt.

On October 26 of that year the chiefs authorized for the purpose made a selection of country in the Indian Territory for the occupancy of the tribe. Improvements were begun, and land was cultivated, when it was discovered that the surveyors, in locating the ninety-sixth meridian, which was to be their eastern boundary, had incorrectly located it, with the result that the Osage were required to abandon the country selected by them and move farther west, to the great confusion and exasperation of the Indians.

The government officials found themselves in an embarrassing situation and, in an effort to compose the dissatisfaction of the Osage, agreed to increase the size of their new home and acquire for them a tract of 1,700,000 acres lying west of the ninety-sixth meridian, bounded on the north by the south Kansas line and on the west and south by the Arkansas River. This tract was part of the Cherokee Outlet, acquired from the Cherokee in their treaty of 1866 by the United States for the settlement of friendly Indians. The Osage were to pay for it from the proceeds of the sale of their lands in Kansas. It was also stipulated that the Osage were to assign 100,000 acres of this tract as a home for the Kaw or Kansas Indians, which was set apart in the northwestern corner of the Osage tract.[8]

The condition of the Osage Indians at that time was epitomized in the report of their agent on the eve of their removal from Kansas to the Indian Territory:

"The population of the Osages one year ago, as appears by the report of my predecessor, was 4,481. The enrollment made last spring showed their number to be 2,962, a decrease of 1,519 compared with last year. The census just completed showed the present population to be 3,150, an increase of 184 in six months. The first difference should not be understood as an actual decrease, but arises from a reduction of the enumeration to a correct standard. Physically, the Osages are strong in constitution; the men are large and erect, the women strong and healthy, the children bright and active; hence, under circumstances at all favorable to health, the tribe should show an annual increase at the latter rate.

"About 250 of the tribe are mixed bloods, who live by farming. They have comfortable cabins, and though surrounded by unfavorable influences are, as a class, industrious and temperate. The others are divided into seven bands, each having their chiefs and councillors, and living in separate villages of lodges constructed of poles and inclosed with puncheons and buffalo hides, or long webs of matting made of flags. These bands have had extensive fields near their towns,

which they planted in corn, beans, and pumpkins. These are cultivated mostly by the women and children, with a heavy hoe, for a few
weeks, when the whole go off to the plains, two or three hundred
miles distant, to procure buffalo meat, which they dry in large quantities, and bring into their homes on ponies by the time their corn is in
roasting ear. The corn is of a variety that matures early, and by the
middle of the Tenthmonth it is usually gathered, shelled, and packed
in dry hide sacks, and stored with dried pumpkins and beans in pole-
cribs, chinked and daubed with mud, and roofed with bark and skins.
They now depart on the fall and winter hunt, and remain on the plains
most of the winter. If the hunt is successful, a large amount of jerked
buffalo meat and tallow, robes, and furs are brought in. Then, in early
spring, the crop is planted, and another year of hard work and exposure is repeated. The manual labor thus performed, if properly
directed in agricultural pursuits, would soon place them in affluent
circumstances.

"The condition of the Osages upon their reservation the past year
has been simply a continuance, in a more aggravated form, of that
related by my predecessor in his monthly and annual reports to the
Indian Department. In the spring of 1867 he asks for the assistance of
the military to remove the settlers that have intruded on the Osage
diminished reserve, and otherwise enforce the laws for the protection
of the Indians. In the following Tenthmonth he states: 'Their horses
are constantly being driven off by the white men. One Osage lost 23
head in June, which were seen driven through Topeka. Another lost
20 head on the night of the 5th of September; they were seen going
through Humboldt, and that was the last I could hear of them. Immigration is still crowding on their lands. They threaten me with Crawford's militia, and say they will hang me if I interfere with them. They
seem determined to occupy the best of the Osage diminished reservation. By the time the Indians are in next spring all their camping
grounds on the Verdigris River will be occupied by whites. This
should not be allowed by the Government, and I cannot check this
settlement without a small armed force.'

"I quote from succeeding reports to Sixthmonth, 1868: 'The people
on and near these lands are made to believe, by speeches delivered by
so-called leading men and newspaper articles, that those Indians have
no rights which should be respected by white men. They have had, to
my certain knowledge, over 100 of their best horses stolen since the
1st of May last. I learn that scarcely a day passes that they do not

lose from five to twenty horses. Marshal Dickenson followed 20 of these stolen horse over one hundred and fifty miles. The Indians dare not follow their stock five miles into the white settlements; and those thieves have always managed to baffle the officers sent in pursuit, and not one of them has as yet been brought to justice, or one in a hundred of the Indians' horses returned to them.' In Thirdmonth following, he states: 'Men are taking claims, building houses and mills on the diminished reserve, which disturbs the peace of the Indians very much.' He again asks, later in the spring, for military assistance, to remove the settlers and enforce the laws, and adds: 'If this is not done there will be much trouble, and the Indians will be driven from their homes. The settlers are preparing to organize a county, entirely on Indian lands, and they have applied to the governor of the State for protection. I can do nothing in the matter without instructions from the Government, which I will await with great anxiety.' His next and last report, in Sixthmonth, 1869, says: 'More than 500 families have settled on the eastern part of the Osage diminished reserve; have built their cabins near the Indian camps, taken possession of their corn-fields, and forbidden them cutting fire-wood on their claims.'

"The 1st of Tenthmonth I assumed charge of the agency. The condition of affairs, so well presented by my predecessor, was unchanged, save that aggressions upon the Indians were more frequent and more aggravated. Increasing numbers had given boldness to the aggressors.

"Having in view the practicability of the civilization of the Osages at an early day, I was disappointed at finding their surroundings so utterly unfavorable, and was forced to the conviction that no attempts could be successful until a separation of the Osages and whites was made by the Government. To preserve the peace and prevent the effusion of blood until that could be accomplished seemed the work for the time being. The settlers were generally associated in clubs, pledged to defend each other in the occupation of claims, without regard to the improvements, possession, or rights of the Indians. Many of the latter were turned out of their homes and threatened with death if they persisted in claiming them. Others were made homeless by cunning and fraud. While absent on their winter hunt, cribs of corn, and other provisions so hardly earned by their women's toil, were robbed. Their principal village was pillaged of a large amount of puncheons, and wagon-loads of matting hauled away and used by the settlers in building and finishing houses for themselves. Even new-made graves were plundered, with the view of finding treasures, which the Indians often bury with their dead. To my surprise the Indians listened to my advice, and submitted to these wrongs, while the settlers often quarreled among themselves over claims to which they had not a shadow of right, ending their disputes frequently with loss of life. The question will suggest itself, which of these people are the savages? Since my residence among the Osages, in no case within my knowledge has one of them attempted or threatened the life of his fellow. For all the unmitigated wrong and outrage heaped upon them, the only semblance of retaliation, and but few cases of that, has been the taking of horses without legal process, in lieu of those that had been stolen of them. These cases were made pretexts for further and greater outrages. Bands of armed men would seize and carry off a much greater number of horses than they ever claimed to have lost, and generally persons innocent of all complicity with the matter were the victims. That these wild Indians would submit to such treatment as this for years, without resorting to the scalping-knife, seems incredible, but such is the fact. These aggressions and wrongs were largely committed before any steps were taken for the purchase of the Osage reservation. In evidence of this fact, I again refer to the report of my predecessor.

"I encouraged the Indians to plant, as usual, this spring. They replied that it was useless; that if I did place them in possession of their fields as I proposed, the herds of cattle and other stock of the settlers would destroy their growing crops, and as their ponies were being stolen in large numbers, they decided that to preserve the balance of their property, and peace with the Government, they would remove to the Indian Territory, permission to do so having been generously given by the Cherokees. Two small bands remained; at my urgent request planted, but their products have been mainly destroyed by the settlers' stock as predicted. My efforts thus far have been fruitless to obtain damages for them. The eastern part of the reservation is now mostly surveyed and claimed in 160-acre lots, three counties duly organized, and elections held. One county has voted $200,000 stock in a railroad; courts are held with all the ceremony of legal tribunals. The press of Kansas teems with vivid descriptions of 'town-sites,' and the fertile valleys of the Osage country. Numbers have thus been led to believe that the lands were open to settlement. Some who came with their families and stock withdrew when undeceived. Such examples, however, of respect for the laws of the United

States, and the rights of others, were lamentably few. The errors and mistakes of the past, if wisely used, may become profitable guides for the future. Had the Government, at an early stage of these violations of law and of the acknowledged rights of the Indians, which they themselves were not allowed to defend, extended the protection asked for by its officers, and that had been solemnly promised, a long list of depredations and outrages that will mantle the face of every true man with shame, would not now be on the record, and a higher standard of morality and justice would obtain certainly in all the border States. The neglect of the Government to assert the supremacy of law over a few border men, professional squatters, was regarded as a tacit approval of criminal acts by men professing to be just and honest; hence this class perpetrated the same crime, claiming the right to do what was allowed by others. The attempted purchase of these lands by a railroad company was used as a justification for intruding. Others insisted that they had purchased their claims of Indians, knowing that no Indian could give a title, or even a privilege to settle here; and again, that they were kind and generous to the Indians; that they paid yearly a stipend to some chief, &c. Yet all these do not relieve these men from the reproach of being trespassers, intruders and violators of the nation's law; and not one can show that he had a right in law or equity to occupy these lands before the treaty was approved by the Government, and a new home was provided for the Indians.

"While these efforts were being made to force the Indians from the country, their enemies in Congress were equally zealous to legalize the possession of their lands without reasonable or just compensation. This was prevented, however, by the passage of a bill on the 15th of Seventhmonth, which provided for the sale of the Osage diminished reserve at $1.25 per acre, the proceeds, after deducting the cost of survey, to be placed to the credit of the Indians at 5 per cent interest. Thus did Congress make a just disposition of this vexed question, that has for years been a disturbing and corrupting element in the political and railroad organizations of Kansas."[9]

The actual removal of the Osage from Kansas to the Indian Territory took place in 1871. Before they removed, some of the mixed-bloods of the tribe accepted the terms of the recent act of Congress and filed notice in court of their intention to become United States citizens and remain on their farms legally entered and occupied by them according to the terms of the act.

"But their claims were soon occupied by white settlers, and the series of outrages and persecutions perpetrated upon them that shames humanity. All except eight have abandoned their homes, or taken what they could get for them. Some of their houses were burnt by mobs of white men; one half-breed died from injuries received and exposure on such an occasion. These murderers were arrested, went through the forms of a trial, and were discharged. The eight still remaining will probably lose their land, as they have not the means to engage in a long contest at law; and if the past is an earnest of the future, they can hardly hope that an Indian's rights will be protected in a Kansas court.

"Last fall the military removed a number of white settlers who had intruded on the lands of the Indian Territory bordering on Kansas. Most of them returned promptly when the soldiers had left. Early this spring I asked for the removal of nearly a hundred families from the Osage lands; then applied to the officers in command at Fort Gibson, then at Fort Scott, but the necessary assistance could not be obtained. Immigration has continued to pour in even more rapidly than it would on lands that it was lawful to occupy. My unaided efforts to remove them and prevent immigration have been futile. The Osages feel that their new home is being wrested from them even before they have got possession.

"Last spring a gang of seventeen border men made an unprovoked, murderous asault upon ten unarmed Osages, killing one and severely wounding others, and robbing them of several ponies, blankets, and robes. I applied at once for assistance to arrest the guilty parties. That request was responded to a few days since. On a preliminary examination, three of the party were placed under bond of $250 to appear at some future time. This is a gratifying evidence that the life of an Indian is regarded as of *some* value."[10]

In this new home some of the more progressive of the Osage responded to the efforts of their agent, undertook to till the soil, and produce food for their sustenance. Most of them, however, continued to rely on the buffalo meat for their food and the robes for clothing and shelter.[11] During the Indian uprising in western Oklahoma in 1874, the peacefully inclined Indians were compelled to forego their buffalo hunts in the West by fear of being mistaken for hostile Indians by the United States troops then engaged in rounding up the Cheyenne, Kiowa, and other hostiles. However, a small party of Osage with their women and children started out to see if they could find some game without venturing into the country of the plains

Indians. While traveling along in southern Kansas they were the innocent victims of what became known as the Medicine Lodge Massacre, which took place near the town of Medicine Lodge in Barbour County, Kansas. Their agent, in reporting this outrage, described it in part as follows:

"Upon hearing threats and preparations made by some of the plains Indians to make war on the whites, I anticipated the order of the Department by sending runners to the plains, where the Osages had just gone with their women and children and herds of ponies. In order to find buffalo they scattered over that vast country, and it was impossible to reach all the parts of bands with the information. One party of twenty-nine persons, including ten women and children, wandered to the State line of Kansas. Asking some white men who came to their camp if they knew of any buffalo, they were directed forward into the State to a sandy and uninhabited portion of the country, where they at once proceeded and found buffalo, a number of which they killed and dried the meat. They had no thought of doing wrong, as this was their former reservation, where they reserved the privilege of hunting as long as game could be found there, and the country remained unsettled. The party was preparing to start home, when they discovered a company of people in the distance. They decided to await their arrival and learn who they were. They proved to be about forty white men, mounted and armed with breech-loading guns and revolvers. They stopped when within half a mile of the Osages. The Osages sent two of their men to speak to them; they shook hands friendly, then disarmed the Osages and detained them. Other Osages, two together, continued coming up, until eight were treated as the first and held as prisoners. As no more were seen coming, it was thought best to make sure of these, and the work of death commenced. Four were shot on the spot, and four miraculously escaped the murderous fire. The white men then charged on those who remained in the camp. They sprang on their ponies, not having time to gather up saddles, clothing, or anything else, and fled for their lives. They were pursued three or four miles under a shower of bullets, but fortunately no more of them were killed.

"At night two of the party returned to look after the dead and their property. Three bodies were found, two of them scalped and otherwise mutilated after death. Fifty-four ponies, colts, and mules, that they had left behind when escaping, had been driven off by the marauders, and all their other property either carried off or destroyed.

"They made the journey to their reservation in five days, without food, several of them on foot, and most of them nearly naked. I immediately provided them with supplies of food and clothing, and examined them separately in relation to their treatment and misfortunes, and obtained from them the facts given here. They also positively affirmed that they had but four guns (muzzle-loading) and two revolvers with them, and the white men took two of the guns and the two revolvers from those who were taken prisoners."[12]

In 1876 Agent Bede induced the Osage Indians to elect members to an informal sort of government. In time they gave the matter more mature consideration, and, under the influence of Agent Laban J. Miles, a general council was held in December, 1881, when a large committee was appointed to draft a constitution for the tribe. Taking the Cherokee code as a guide, a constitution was framed which was formally submitted and adopted at a general election of the tribe held on December 31, 1881.

Under its provisions, the Osage elected a council composed of members from five districts; a principal and second chief, four sheriffs, three judges, and other officers were appointed by the chief and approved by the council. "The council has, since its election, been recognized by the tribe as having authority to act for the tribe as far as their laws provide. There has been one session of the court. It has proven itself satisfactory in settling difficulties between members of the tribe, and some of the cases would have been considered good in an ordinary county court. One Indian was sentenced to twenty lashes for stealing, which penalty was duly executed. I believe the move a good one, and that they should be encouraged, as it will gradually but surely destroy the old chieftainship and Indian forms of government."[13]

The Osage Indians endured years of hardship and privation before their lush oil lands in Oklahoma made them the richest people in the world and before one of their youth, John Joseph Mathews, went to Oxford University to be educated, to return to his people and write a book that became a Book-of-the-Month Club selection.

KANSAS (KAW) INDIANS

The Kansas Indians, poor kin of the Osage, likewise had lived a life of contrasts when they gave to their country a United States senator, Charles E. Curtis, who became vice-president of the United States. These Indians were first known in historic times as inhabitants of the area occupied by the state of Kansas, and it was natural that their name should be given to the river and state. "Kans," "Kansas," "Kanzau," and "Konza" are only a few of the twenty-four spellings of the name ascribed to early explorers and writers.

Subsequent intrusions of other tribes detailed in this book brought many other Indian names into the region and made them also in another sense "Kansas" Indians, though not indigenous to the area. This introduction of other Indian names into the nomenclature of the area naturally led to confusion in the popular mind, which after the Civil War resulted in giving to the indigenous Kansas Indians the name of "Kaws" for reasons not at once obvious, though it is said to have been suggested by early French explorers as sounding something like the name employed by the Indians themselves.

The name of "Kaw" is not recognized by ethnologists or in congressional enactments. In 1868 it was first used in the report of Indian Agent E. S. Stover and since has been the popular though wholly unauthorized name of the tribe. For differentiation, therefore, and not from choice, the name "Kaw" will be used herein in order to avoid confusion with the "Kansas" Indians who were brought from other states and were temporarily and geographically but not ethnologically "Kansas" Indians.

In 1825 the "Kanzas" Indians ceded to the United States an extensive area on which to locate other tribes.[14] In 1846 they ceded two million acres more in Kansas save a "Diminished Reserve" assigned them at Council Grove on the Neosho River in Morris County.[15] They were ignored among the signers of the Manypenny treaties in 1855, but on October 5, 1859, they entered into a treaty prefaced by the conventional language employed in dealing with other Kansas Indians, that they had more land than they could use and that, therefore, they conveyed most of their "diminished reserve" to the United States to be sold for their benefit.[16]

The population of the Kaws in 1850 was about 1,700 but this number rapidly diminished during the succeeding years from several causes; smallpox alone carried off more than 400 members in 1852–53. Many died from other epidemics and from hardships to which they were subjected by the pressure of white settlers, the killing-off of the game, and the introduction of whiskey. The principal wealth of the Kaws consisted of their herds of thousands of ponies, on which they were dependent for their pursuit of the buffalo, the most important consideration in their lives.

The intrusion of the Civil War affected the lives of these Indians profoundly. More than eighty men of the tribe volunteered for service in the Union Army, leaving their women and children to conduct their meager farming operations. The population in 1863 was reduced to 741, and the next year to 701.[17] During the latter part of the war, the Indians were unable to go on buffalo hunts to secure meat for their families, because of the campaign against the plains Indians and the warning that the Kansas Indians might be mistaken for hostiles and killed.

After the war the agents endeavored to improve the condition of the Indians who were still dependent upon their buffalo hunts for food. Immediately after the annuity payment, in September, 1865, the Kaws ventured forth into the buffalo country, and by November few of them remained at home, to obtain a precarious support, said the agent. Those out among the buffalo lived well and were generally healthy. It was estimated that they killed three thousand buffalo and obtained nearly as many robes that fall and winter, which sold for an average of $7.00 each, yielding an income of $21,000 in addition to the meat and tallow. During the winter, they sold sufficient to buy their groceries and clothing, selling the remainder in the spring for enough to sustain them while putting in their crops. They also carried on considerable traffic with the western Indians for horses which they sold to the whites and thus supported themselves in the summer. At this time, under the influence of the agent, they were beginning to take some interest in farming. But their progress in general was seriously retarded by the introduction of whiskey, which was easily brought into their country by emigrants and traders over the Santa Fe Trail, which ran through their reservation; and there was almost no disposition on the part of local courts to enforce the laws against this illegal introduction of liquor.[18]

Nearly the whole tribe spent the next winter, 1866, in futile efforts to secure buffalo meat and robes. Owing to the severity of the weather, they procured but little meat and few robes in comparison with the number they usually obtained. They lost forty-four of their horses stolen by the Cheyenne, and many of the others died from the effects of exposure and starvation, the remainder going out in the spring in very poor condition, according to this agent.[19] Another effort in the summer of 1867 was equally unsuccessful for the same reasons. The railroads and the rush of emigrants to the plains were crowding the buffalo so far back that the distance became a serious handicap which would necessitate the entire abandonment of the hunt or a removal to a more suitable and convenient location.

The situation of these Indians became more desperate each year. In 1868, while on their annual buffalo hunt, the Kaws had a serious encounter with the Cheyenne Indians that prevented the securing of food and set in motion a feud between the tribes that was to interfere with their future progress.[20] Lawless white intruders persisted in invading the Kaw reservation, and local sentiment was hostile to enforcement of the laws enacted for the benefit of the Indians. This attitude was made a matter of record by an influential Kansas newspaper in the following language: "This is as beautiful a country as lies in the Neosho Valley, and yet it lies uncultivated, the home of a squalid, dirty, vile, idle, mischievous race of Indians. We hope the day is not far hence when the Kaws will be removed from the state. . . . . We would suggest the hint, that in violation of the orders of the Indian department settlers are locating on the Kaw trust lands. If others will go on and swell the number, it will hasten the removal of the Indians; at least it is our fervent wish and desire."[21]

A treaty had been made with the Kaws looking to their removal from Kansas, which resulted in an endless amount of speculation concerning that subject, seriously interfering with efforts to cultivate the soil and produce food to sustain them. For two or three years they led an unsettled life from the fact that they expected at any time to have to leave their old home. It was planned that they should remove to join the Osage in the Indian Territory. Commissioners Uriah Spray and Thomas H. Stanley were appointed to meet in February, 1872, with the Osage and Kaws, to work out the territorial problems involved. This meeting, postponed by the fact that the Osage were engaged in a protracted and unsuccessful hunt in the buffalo country, finally convened at the new Osage agency in the Indian Territory on the Little Verdigris (now Cana) River and reached an agreement on March 5 by which the Osage were given a much larger tract of land than that originally offered them. This extension of their domain amounted to 1,700,000 acres. In consideration, the Osage agreed to assign for use of the 627 Kaws 100,000 acres.

Finally, after several years of suspense and uncertainty, the removal of the Kaws was organized by the agent. They took their departure from the old agency at Council Grove, June 4, 1873, and seventeen days later arrived on their new reservation in the Indian Territory. They were too late to engage effectively in planting a crop, and drouth and grasshoppers nullified their efforts.

Soon after their annuity payment in November, 1873, all the able-bodied men, women, and children left their new reservation for the buffalo country, as their chief said, "to make their last general hunt." As hunters they were more successful than they were as farmers, for they secured about five thousand dollars' worth of furs, besides their subsistence and the meat they brought home. They were healthy, and had but few deaths during their absence, returning home in February, 1874, in good spirits, saying that they were ready to settle down, make farms, and go to work, as the chase would no longer support them. In this they were sound prophets, for the buffalo was very soon afterward practically exterminated.[22]

Under the influences to which the Kaws were subjected, their number continued to decline until, in 1892, there were only 125 full-bloods and 84 mixed-bloods. Said the agent that year: "The full-bloods have done but little farming the past year, preferring to frolic and dance or to visit their Indian neighbors. The latter is a pleasure they dearly love, but not more so than to entertain their Indian friends who may come to visit them. So generous are they at such times, they will often rob themselves of the necessaries of life in order that their friends may carry away kind recollections of them."[23]

The Cherokee Commission met with the Kaws in June, 1893, and endeavored to negotiate a treaty providing for the allotment of their reservation. Their efforts, however, were rejected by the nation as a whole, though the mixed-bloods favored it.

NOTES

1. *Report of the Commissioner of Indian Affairs, 1848; House Executive Doc. 1* (30th Cong., 2d sess.), p. 537.
2. *House Executive Doc. 1*, p. 544.
3. 10 *U.S. Stat.* 1013.
4. 14 *U.S. Stat.* 687. According to the Commissioner of Indian Affairs, the whole Osage tribe, with the exception of Black Dog's Band of a thousand, remained loyal to the federal government throughout the rebellion. To emphasize their fealty to the government, in June, 1863, "they captured and destroyed a party of 19 rebels who were passing through their country and who, by the instructions and papers found upon their persons, were fully proven to have been commissioned by the Rebel authorities to enroll and organize the disloyal in Arizona and Dakota. Occupying as they do, a position between the white settlements in the southern portion of Kansas and the region in possession of the Rebels (in the Indian Territory) their fidelity to the Government has been of inestimable value in protecting the frontier from the incursions of the guerillas" (*Report, 1864*, p. 318). Two hundred and forty Osage were enlisted in the Union Army but deserted on account of difficulty with their officers (*Report, 1865*, p. 40).

5. *Fort Smith Herald,* June 13, 1868, p. 1, col. 5.
6. *Report, 1869,* pp. 97 and 98.
7. 16 *U.S. Stat.* 362.
8. This was justified by the claim that the two tribes were related and spoke a common language. Congress validated this arrangement by act of June 5, 1872 (16 *U.S. Stat.* 362).
9. *Report, 1871,* pp. 483 ff.
10. *Ibid.,* p. 491.
11. *Report, 1874,* p. 226.
12. *Ibid.,* pp. 226 and 227.
13. *Report, 1882,* p. 73.
14. 7 *U.S. Stat.* 244.
15. 9 *U.S. Stat.* 842.
16. 12 *U.S. Stat.* 1111.
17. *Report, 1864,* p. 367.
18. *Report, 1866,* p. 274.
19. *Report, 1867,* p 297.
20. *Report, 1868,* p. 260.
21. *Kansas Daily Commonwealth* (Topeka), Saturday, May 14, 1870, p. 2, col. 6.
22. In 1875 the full-bloods numbered 516 (*Report, 1875,* p. 64).
23. *Report, 1892,* p. 391.

CHAPTER XVI

TEXAS EMIGRATION

THE first government emigration of Indians from Texas to the present Oklahoma took place when 258 Tawaconi, 171 Waco, 380 Comanche, 244 Caddo—including some Shawnee and Delaware intermarried with them—and 235 Anadarko, a total of 1,492 Indians, were removed from their reservation in that state. These Indians were located on a reservation in Texas by the government, but the neighboring Texans so bitterly resented their presence, made their lives so unhappy, and interposed such difficulties to federal administration that the section of western Oklahoma known as the "Leased District" was created as a home for these and other Indians indigenous to that region.[1]

Their removal under the guidance and protection of army escorts and Indian officials took place in August, 1859, and before the end of the month the Indians were located on the Washita River, near the site of the present Anadarko. These Indians were placed under the jurisdiction of the Wichita agency, first presided over by Agent S. A.

Blain. The agency was so called from the indigenous Wichita, who, with three hundred Kickapoo, Shawnee, and Delawares somewhat intermarried with them, occupied that area. The agency had been established that year to deal with these Indians and others expected to be brought from Texas.[2]

During the Civil War this agency was broken up. A band of some two hundred roving Indians came to the Wichita Agency on October 23, 1862, killed the employees of Agent Matthew Leeper, and then burned the agency building with the bodies in it. The next day they pursued and overtook several hundred Tonkawa, largely women and children, who had fled from the agency, of whom they massacred about a hundred and fifty.[3] The surviving Indians fled to Butler County, Kansas, where they were looked after by an agency established there called the Wichita agency.[4] In 1866 the agent reported nineteen hundred destitute refugee Indians within his care, most of whom were widows or orphans, having no means of support. They included Wichita, Waco, Tawaconi, Caddo, Shawnee, Delawares, and Kichai.[5]

Efforts made in 1866 to return them to their home in the Indian Territory were frustrated by floods and cholera. In order to cross part of them over the swollen Arkansas River in June, a boat was brought up a distance of a hundred miles. After an effort in which one of the Indians was drowned, the project was abandoned for the time.

The attempt was resumed the next year, but violent sickness interfered. When the agent again endeavored to get them under way, the Indians refused to go, declaring that if they neglected to gather their corn, planted in the spring, the Great Spirit would refuse them the ability ever to plant in the future. Another objection to immediate removal was that they wished to remain and conclude the ceremonies of mourning over their friends and relatives who had died in that remote land.

However, 313 Absentee Shawnee, 92 Caddo, 58 Delawares, and 8 Ioni, a large proportion of whom were women and children, were organized late in August and took their departure. Before they reached their destination, cholera broke out among them, and 50 Shawnee and 47 Caddo died.[6] By the autumn of 1867 only 471 of these Reserve Indians, consisting of Delawares, Shawnee, and Caddo, identified as the "Affiliated Tribes," had been removed. Left in Kansas were 1,200 Wichita who refused to remove until they had harvested their crops, declaring that "the Great Spirit who had given them health and strength to plant their crops, would be displeased with them if they should prove so negligent as to abandon them in the sure process of maturity."[7]

However, in 1868, the Wichita Agency was re-established at what became Anadarko; the Wichita Indians, wholly destitute of everything except scant supplies furnished by the government, then returned to their old home near the site of the destroyed Fort Cobb. They and the Kichai, Waco, and Tawakoni located their lodges on the south side of the Washita River near the mouth of Sugar Creek. Here the agent reported that they were making good progress, considering their habits, the women doing all the field labor, the men thinking it degrading to work like a squaw.[8] During the first year after their return the women constructed nearly a hundred of their remarkable grass houses that looked to wondering visitors like haystacks.

What was known as the Wichita-Shawnee Reservation continued to be the home of the Wichita and the Affiliated Tribes, including those removed from Texas in 1859. It was located on the north bank of the Washita River on the road leading from Fort Sill to the Cheyenne Agency. Belonging to this agency were about 1,200 Indians—392 Caddo, 85 Ioni, 299 Wichita, 140 Waco, 126 Kichai, and 127 Tawaconi. Their agent reported in 1871 that "the Caddos and Ionies are virtually one people, and the Wacos, Kichais and Towakonies, originally from Texas, have long been affiliated with the Wichitas."[9]

In 1873 a band of 345 Comanche known as the Penetethka Comanche left the more warlike faction of their tribe and located with the peaceful Wichita and Affiliated Tribes, bringing the total of that agency to 1,528.

In 1874 the Caddo, Iowa, and Delawares of that agency, who had been living as separate bands, met in council and agreed to amalgamate as one tribe and join the Caddo under a Caddo chief. This agreement was facilitated by the fact that they had mingled harmoniously for a number of years and desired this union in the belief that their combined strength would be of general benefit to them all. They were all known thereafter as Caddo Indians.[10]

The Wichita and Affiliated Tribes were well regarded by the authorities because of their interest in agriculture and their probable influence for good upon the wild tribes.[11] The agent said, in 1877, that the Wichita, Waco, and Tawaconi were practically one people, speaking the same language, "the names of Wacos and Towakonies being given to the descendants of two bands of Wichitas who, about 100 years ago, left the main tribe on the Neosho River in Kansas, one taking up a residence on the Arkansas River near the present town of Wichita, and the other pushing on to Texas."[12]

A departure in Indian administration was introduced in a bill before Congress in 1878 calling for the consolidation of certain agencies. Among the combinations noted at that time were the Union Agency at Muskogee and that of the Kiowa and Comanche Agency with the Wichita Agency, which took place in September, 1878. Thereafter, Indian administration in this remote country was simplified, said the agent, by the fact that these western tribes all spoke the Comanche language, which was, as it were, the court language among them.[13]

In 1880 "the 1,237 Wichita and affiliated bands belonging to the Kiowa Agency, except the Caddoes and Delawares," entered the decade with continued evidence of industry and thrift. They wore citizen's dress, lived in houses, cultivated some land, and required little help from the government. They would have been entirely self-sustaining but for the proximity of the idle Kiowa and Comanche.[14]

By 1886 the agent reported that the Wichita, Waco, Tawaconi, and Kichai, "all of whom speak the same language, have the same habits and customs, and have intermarried until they have become one and the same people, number all told about 480, nearly all of whom are farmers. They do not depend upon their squaws to do most of the work, as do the wild Indians."

The combined Caddo and Delawares numbered 521 and 41, respectively. They had been retrograding for twenty years, largely because of the settlement near them of the wild Kiowa and Apache. They were unfortunate and unsettled from the fact that Congress had never given them title to the lands occupied by them.[15]

Including 1,014 Kiowa and 1,531 Comanche, the Indians of this agency in 1892 numbered 3,870, a decrease of 386 within two years, caused by epidemics of whooping cough, measles, and pneumonia, which were particularly fatal to infants from the fact that their medicine men caused the sick and feverish children to be immersed in cold water, thereby hastening their death.

Upon inauguration of the allotment policy of the government, efforts were made to settle the Wichita and Affiliated Tribes, who had never had a reservation set apart to them. A treaty had been made on October 19, 1872, assigning them a reservation, but it had never been ratified. Following a compact with the Cheyenne and Arapaho Indians, the Cherokee Commission began negotiations with the Wichita and other Indians of their agency, with whom they came to terms on

June 4, 1891. This agreement, however, was not ratified by Congress until March 2, 1895. Under it allotments of 152,991 acres were made to the 965 Indians of the Anadarko Agency, made up of Wichita, Tawaconi, Kichai, Waco, Caddo, and Delawares, leaving 586,468 acres for future white settlement.

TONKAWA

The Tonkawa Indians lived in Texas near Fort Griffin, where some of them had often served the army as guides and scouts. They were known in an early day in Young County, Texas, where they lived with the Caddo, Ioni, and other tribes; and immediately before the Civil War, about six hundred in number, they were among the Texas Indians removed to Fort Cobb, Indian Territory.[16]

Overtures were made, about 1863, to the Tonkawa by the Comanche and Kiowa to induce them to join these hostile tribes in a raid upon the white people of Texas.

Captain J. B. Irvine of the Twenty-second Infantry, acting Indian agent, in writing to a member of Congress on January 7, 1880, about these Indians, said that "with a loyalty to the interests of the whites unparalleled in Indian history, they refused to join the war party of Kiowas and Comanches, which so exasperated the hostile Indians that they turned on the Tonkawas and massacred nearly the whole tribe. Only about 200 of them succeeded in effecting their escape from Fort Cobb into Texas, where they have remained, trusting to the hardy Texans for protection from their implacable foes. Previous to this time the band had made considerable advance in agriculture under the supervision and care of an agent; they raised their crops of wheat, corn and vegetables, and had accumulated extensive herds of horses and cattle; but in this indiscriminate slaughter of their men, women and children, their agent was killed, their stock run off or slaughtered, and many of the children carried away captive, and are now held by their old enemies, the Comanches, at Fort Sill. The chief and head men have often spoken to me of these captives; they claim that they can identify them, and ask that the Comanches be made to give them up.

"There are incorporated with the Tonkawas 17 Lipan Indians who are particularly industrious and provident and have repeatedly asked for land to cultivate and own as a permanent home; the Tonkawas have also made a similar request and I appealed to the Commissioner of Indian Affairs last July for permission to purchase them a farm adjoining their camp but I was refused, and instructed to prepare them for removal to the Indian Territory. Occupying and cultivating the soil as they do, by mere sufferance of the land owners, with a constant liability to removal, it is obvious that the few who are inclined to be industrious must necessarily be in a state of disquiet and uncertainty, discouraging and retarding them in advancement in the industries of civilization.

"These Indians have always been good friends to the white people, and have aided the citizens of Texas in all their conflicts with the hostile Comanches and other Indians; acting as guides and scouts and bravely fighting on the side of the whites in their numerous encounters with the predatory savages. The Tonkawa have never been known to kill a white person, and pride themselves on their uniform fealty to the whites from the earliest settlement of the country to the present time.

". . . . The number of the Indians now here and subsisted at this agency is 115; it is only during the past four years that they have received regular supplies from the government. When Fort Griffin was first established some of them were employed as scouts, and a few gratuitous issues of provisions were made to them by the military authorities; but no regular supplies were furnished them until 1876, when congress appropriated $2,000 for their support, and small appropriations have been made since then, providing each of them less than one-third as much food as furnished to a soldier."[17] With the decrease of game, and until the Tonkawa could become somewhat self-supporting through pastoral and agricultural activities, Irvine urged that appropriations for their support be increased and continued. He added that a delegation had been appointed to proceed to the Indian Territory to select a permanent home and was then waiting for final instructions from the Commissioner of Indian Affairs.

This delegation, consisting of the Tonkawa chief and four of the principal men, in charge of Lieutenant R. N. Getty of the Twenty-second Infantry, left the Tonkawa agency at Fort Griffin on February 9, 1880, to examine the country in the vicinity of the Nez Percé and Ponca reservations.

Unfortunately, the delegation encountered a storm from which the Indians suffered severely. While they were there, a large number of Nez Percés died from pneumonia. From their experiences and observations the Tonkawa delegation thereafter entertained a strong prejudice against that country. The subject of removal was constantly kept before them, and in two or three years negotiations were entered into with the Quapaw Indians, who consented for the Tonkawa to settle on their reservation. In the meantime, on August 15, 1883, an executive order was made by President Arthur assigning a tract of land for the settlement thereon of the Iowa Indians and such others as the Secretary of the Interior might designate. But plans were again changed, and it was decided to locate the Tonkawa on what was known as the Iowa Reserve. On October 22, 1884, in charge of Agent Isaac A. Taylor, the ninety-two Tonkawa Indians left Fort Griffin, Texas, and in due time arrived at the Iowa reservation.[18]

The Tonkawa were in a destitute condition when they reached the Indian Territory; as there was no pasturage or other food for their ponies, the latter nearly all died during the winter. The Indians had nothing in the world with which to establish themselves in a new home. They pathetically referred to the fact that, being peaceable, faithful, and loyal to the government, they had never shared the bounty with which federal officials purchased the peace of the wild depredating Indians. Believing that the emigrants were permanently located, their agent, during the winter and next spring, secured wagons and farming implements with which it was expected they would begin farming in 1885. However, there was constant objection on the part of the Iowa to sharing their reservation with the newcomers; the latter were so unhappy with the situation that the government again reversed its attitude and planned to start them on a new move. The Nez Percés, having left their reservation for their former home in Idaho in May, 1885, it was decided to locate the Tonkawa on the land thus vacated and establish them in the improvements this western tribe had constructed and abandoned.[19]

Accordingly, on June 16, 1885, after a residence of less than eight months with the Iowa, they were again uprooted and started on a new trek. Six two-horse teams were employed to go to their settlement about twenty miles west of the Sauk and Fox Agency, where their effects were loaded for removal. Heavy rains interfered with their efforts, and it was not until three days later that the Indians and their outfits were able to cover the distance of two and one-half miles to the south bank of Deep Fork River.

The next day, June 20, 1885, the removal agent reported: "With eight teams moved the Tonkawa Indians, with rations and camp outfit to the Deep Fork River; all supplies, implements &c. and Indians with their rations, effects, &c. were ferried across the river on the afternoon of the 19th and forenoon of the 20th in a boat 3 × 12 ft. having to float the eight wagons, and swim all horses across. The eight with four (4) additional wagons were loaded on the afternoon of the 20th, and moved out across a bottom almost impassable, for mud, some two miles to camp, having to double all teams across the bottom.

"June 21st.   Travelled twenty miles, rained very hard for several hours.

"June 22nd.   Reached the Cimarron river 10 o'clk A.M., river past fording; the remainder of the 22nd and the 23rd consumed in transferring across the river in a small boat 3 × 14 ft. Rained continuously the 22nd and 23rd.

"June 24th.   Rained all day very hard; the entire day was consumed in moving three miles all teams bogging down more or less the entire distance.

"June 25th and 26th.   Drove to Black Bear Creek near Pawnee Agency arriving at 10 oclk A.M. the 26th distance travelled about 32 miles. Rained the 26th. The Black Bear being unfordable the outfit was detained until 11 oclk A.M. the 27th.

"June 27 and 28.   Travelled to Salt Fork arriving at 11 AM the 28, ferried the Salt Fork arriving at Ponca Agency late in the evening of the 28th.

"June 29th.   Departed from Ponca early, drove 14 miles to Duck Creek, part of the bridge being washed away was detained to repair it; reached the Sha-kas-ka river at sun down, found it unfordable.

"Rained the 29th.

"June 30th.   Crossed the Sha-kas-ka river by placing lumber across the top of the wagon beds and loading the freight thereon, reaching Oakland Agency in time to unload freight &c; turning over all goods, supplies & 92 head of Tonkawa Indians to U.S. Ind. Agent John W. Scott taking his receipt therefor, thus closing the removal on the evening of the 30th so far as the delivery of every thing at the Oakland Agency, I. T.

". . . . The entire distance travelled being through mud almost axle deep most of the way and across unfordable water courses. All of the teams were loaded to their utmost capacity from the point of starting to Oakland."[20]

In their new home the Tonkawa and Lipan presented to their agent an unprepossessing appearance: "In every respect [they are] a marked contrast to the high-minded, alert and reliable Nez Percés whose place they will poorly fill. They nearly all speak English more or less, showing that they have at some time and place had considerable intercourse with the whites, but it was such intercourse as did them little good since, to use a well worn expression, they have acquired all the vices of the white man without any of his virtues. The Nez Percés left plenty of comfortable houses to accommodate all these people, but instead of occupying them they all huddle around the agency, and live in delapidated tents or in booths made of boughs covered with a bit of canvas. Their object in this is to be handy, so that when ration day comes around they can get their grub with the least possible exertion. They are very poor, a few ponies and some worn-out tents constituting their worldly wealth. It seems the tribe never owned wagons till they came here, and not one of them knew how to hitch up a team. A few lessons, however, have been given them in matters of this kind. They have been assisted to break some of their ponies, and seem quite interested. It is possible that patience and perseverence may do something for them yet."[21]

The combined Tonkawa and Lipan began life on their final reservation with a total population of 92. The number gradually diminished until 1887, when, under the "Dawes Act," 11,273.79 acres of their land were allotted in severalty to the reduced tribal membership of 73 Indians. Their remaining 79,276 acres were sold to the government for $30,000 and subsequently thrown open to white settlement in the famous "run" of 1893 into the Cherokee Outlet. The Tonkawa and Lipan thus were merged with the white population of Oklahoma and their identity forgotten.

WACO

The Waco (Hueco) were one of the divisions of the Tawakoni, whose village existed nearly to 1830, on the site of the present city of Waco, Texas. Later, in 1834, the Waco Indians were found in the Wichita Mountains by Leavenworth's dragoon expedition. In company with the Wichita, they were members of the important Indian council held at Fort Gibson with the representatives of the United States in 1834. In 1835 Colonel A. P. Chouteau, Indian Commissioner, found on the present Cache Creek in southwestern Oklahoma bands of Tawakoni and Waco who were returning to occupy the country from which they had been driven by the Osage some years before, and which, in view of the treaty just signed, they felt safe in reoccupying. They were agriculturalists and told Chouteau that they were preparing to plant corn. At one time they were suspected of being in the employ of the Mexican government in trying to entice the Indians of present Oklahoma to take up arms against the United States. They became residents of the Anadarko Agency, and to them were allotted their proportionate shares of the lands of that agency.[22]

ANADARKO

The Anadarko Indians were a tribe of the Caddo Confederacy whose villages were scattered along the Trinity and Brazos rivers in Texas. They became embroiled in tribal wars, and their villages were abandoned. Those who survived the havoc of war and the new diseases brought into the country by the white people were forced to seek shelter and safety with their kindred toward the northeast. In 1812 a village of two hundred and forty Indians was reported on Sabine River. They lived in villages having fixed habitations similar to those of the other tribes of the Caddo Confederacy.

The Anadarko were represented at the treaty council on May 15, 1846, at Council Springs, Texas, where they and other tribes made a treaty with Governor Pierce M. Butler that had much to do with establishing peace with the wild Indians of Oklahoma and Texas;[23] but they appeared as parties to no other treaty with the government, and their merger with what were known as the Wichita and Affiliated Tribes removed them from the field of independent negotiations. Thereafter their interests were absorbed and disposed of in treaties made by the Wichita and Affiliated Tribes.

In 1854 there were 205 Anadarko living on the reservation in Texas with the other Indians of that reservation, whom they accompanied in the summer of 1859 across Red River to their new home in the present Oklahoma, where they were settled in the Leased District under what became known as the Wichita Agency.[24] There were then 235 Anadarko in the total of 1,492 composing the Wichita and Affiliated Tribes. In 1891 the Cherokee Commission negotiated a treaty with these Indian providing for the allotment of their lands and the sale of their surplus.

LIPAN

The Lipan was an Apache tribe which, at various periods of the eighteenth and nineteenth centuries, roamed over the lower Rio Grande in New Mexico eastward through Texas to the Gulf coast. Between 1845 and 1856 they suffered severely in Texan wars, the design of which was the extermination of the Indians within the Texas border. Most of them were driven into Coahuila, Mexico, where they resided in the Santa Rosa Mountains with Kickapoo and other refugee Indians from the United States; others went to New Mexico. A few of them came into the present Oklahoma with the Tonkawa and located under the Ponca, Pawnee, and Oto Agency; and a total of thirty-five Lipan joined the Kiowa-Apache in the same territory.[25]

CADDO

According to tribal traditions, the lower Red River of Louisiana was the early home of the Caddo, from which they spread to the north, west, and south. Several of the lakes and streams connected with this river bear Caddo names, as do some of the counties, parishes, and towns which cover ancient village sites. Cabeza de Vaca and his companions in 1535–36 traversed a portion of the territory occupied by the Caddo, and De Soto's expedition encountered some of the tribes of the confederacy in 1540–41; but the people did not become known until they were met by La Salle and his followers in 1687. At that time the Caddo villages were scattered along Red River and its tributaries in what are now Louisiana and Arkansas, and also on the banks of the Sabine, Neches, Trinity, Brazos, and Colorado rivers in East Texas. The Caddo were not the only occupants of this wide territory; other confederacies belonging to the same linguistic family also resided there. There were also fragments of still older confederacies of the same family, some of which still maintained their separate existence, while others had joined the then powerful Hasinai. These various tribes and confederacies were alternately allies and enemies of the Caddo. The native population was so divided that at no time could it successfully resist the intruding white race. At an early date the Caddo obtained horses from the Spaniards through intermediate tribes; they learned to raise these animals and traded with them as far north as the Illinois River.[26]

During the eighteenth century, wars in Europe led to contention between the Spaniards and the French for the territory occupied by the Caddo. The brunt of these contentions fell upon the Indians; the trails between their villages became routes for armed forces, while the villages were transformed into garrisoned posts. The Caddo were friendly to the French and rendered valuable service, but they suffered greatly through contact with the white race. Tribal wars were fomented, villages were abandoned, new diseases spread havoc among the people, and, by the close of the century, the welcoming attitude of the Indians during its early years had been changed to one of defense and distrust. Several tribes were practically extinct, others seriously reduced in numbers, and a once thrifty and numerous people had become demoralized and were more or less wanderers in their native land. Franciscan missions had been established among some of the tribes early in the century, those designed for the Caddo, or Asinais, as they were called by the Spaniards, being Purisima Concepción de los Asinais, and for the Hasinai, San Francisco de los Tejas.[27] The segregation policy of the missionaries tended to weaken tribal relations and unfitted the people to cope with the new difficulties which confronted them. These missions were transferred to the Rio San Antonio in 1731. With the acquisition of Louisiana by the United States, immigration increased and the Caddo were pushed from their old haunts. Under their first treaty in 1835 they ceded all their land and agreed to move at their own expense beyond the boundaries of the United States, never to return and settle as a tribe.[28] The tribes living in Louisiana, being thus forced to leave their home, moved southwest toward their kindred living in Texas. At that time the people of Texas were contending for independence, and no tribe could live at peace with both opposing forces.[29] Public opinion was divided as to the treatment of the Indians; one party demanded a policy of extermination, while the other advocated conciliatory methods. In 1843 the governor of the Republic of Texas sent a commission to the tribes of its northern section to fix a line between them and the white settlers and to establish three trading posts; but, as the land laws of the republic did not recognize the Indians' right of occupancy, there was no power which could prevent a settler from taking land that had been cultivated by an Indian. This condition led to continued difficulties, and these did not diminish after the annexation of Texas to the United States, as Texas retained control and jurisdiction over all its public domain. Much suffering ensued; the fields of peaceful Indians were taken, and the natives were hunted down. The more warlike tribes made reprisals, and bitter feelings were engendered.

Immigration increased, and the inroads on the buffalo herds by the newcomers made scarce the food of the Indians. Appeals were sent to the federal government, and in 1855 a tract near Brazos River was secured, and a number of Caddo and other Indians were induced to colonize under the supervision of Agent Robert S. Neighbours. The Indians built houses, tilled fields, raised cattle, sent their children to school—lived quiet and orderly lives. The Comanche to the west continued to raid upon the settlers, some of whom turned indiscriminately upon all Indians. The Caddo were the chief sufferers, although they helped the state troops to bring the raiders to justice. In 1859 a company of white settlers fixed a date for the massacre of all the reservation Indians. The federal government was again appealed to, and, through the strenuous efforts of Neighbours, the Caddo made a forced march for fifteen days in the heat of July. Men, women, and children, with the loss of more than half of their stock and possessions, safely reached the banks of the Washita River in Oklahoma, where a reservation was set apart for them near Fort Cobb. There they were absorbed in what became known as the "Wichita and Affiliated Tribes." Neighbours, their friend and agent, was killed shortly afterward as a penalty for his unswerving friendship for the Indians.[30] During the Civil War the Caddo remained loyal to the government, taking refuge in Kansas, while some went even as far west as Colorado.

Early in 1868 most of the Caddo were living at Cherokee Town,[31] where they were fed by Smith Paul. Later they were moved up the Washita River and relocated on their reservation near Fort Cobb as part of the Wichita and Affiliated Tribes, under the supervision of the Wichita agency.[32] In 1872 the boundaries of the reservation of the Wichita and Affiliated Tribes were defined, and in 1902 every man, woman, and child received an allotment of land under the provision of the severalty act of 1887, by which they became citizens of the United States and subject to the laws of Oklahoma Territory. In 1904 they numbered 535. Missions were started by the Baptists soon after the reservation was established. Thomas C. Battey, a Quaker, performed missionary work among them in 1872. The Episcopalians opened a mission in 1881; the Roman Catholics, in 1894.

NOTES

1. A more extended account of these Indians and their removal is to be seen in Grant Foreman, *A History of Oklahoma*, pp. 94 ff., and authorities there cited; see also *Handbook*, II, 778.

2. *Report of the Commissioner of Indian Affairs, 1859*, pp. 648 ff.; *Report, 1860*, p. 378.

3. The identity of the murderers has been the subject of conflicting accounts (Foreman, *op. cit.*; W. S. Nye, *Carbine and Lance*). Captain Irvine says that, because they refused to join the Kiowa and Comanche Indians in hostilities against the whites, they were murdered by them (Irvine to Wellborn, January 7, 1880, Fort Griffin, Texas, Letter Press Book [Oklahoma Historical Society]).

4. From which the town of Wichita, Kansas, was later named.

5. *Report, 1866*, p. 332.

6. *Report, 1867,* p. 322.

7. *Ibid.,* p. 316.

8. Indian Agent Henry Shanklin to Superintendent of Indian Affairs, June 6, 1868, "Kiowa—Agents' Reports" (Oklahoma Historical Society).

9. *Report, 1872,* p. 134. The agents were confronted by many problems in their management of these Indians. Issue of trousers was found useless. The men cut off the legs to use as leggings and threw away the remainder of the garment.

10. *Report, 1874,* p. 237.

11. *Ibid.,* p. 236; *Report, 1875,* p. 289.

12. *Report, 1877,* p. 112.

13. *Report, 1879,* p. 62.

14. *Report, 1880,* p. xxxv (see *Report, 1881,* for other accounts).

15. *Report, 1886,* p. 128.

16. Foreman, *op. cit.,* p. 90.

17. Irvine to Wellborn, January 7, 1880, Letter Press Book (Oklahoma Historical Society); Nye, *op. cit.,* p. 38; Foreman, *op. cit.,* p. 114.

18. Sac and Fox Letter Press Book (Oklahoma Historical Society).

19. *Report, 1885,* p. 96.

20. "Tonkawa Indian Agents to Commissioner of Indian Affairs"—a series of reports and letters through 1883 and 1885 (Sac and Fox Letter Press Book [Oklahoma Historical Society]).

21. *Report, 1885,* p. 98.

22. Grant Foreman, *Pioneer Days in the Early Southwest,* p. 239.

23. *Ibid.,* p. 296.

24. Foreman, *A History of Oklahoma,* p. 97.

25. *Handbook,* I, 768.

26. John G. Shea, *The Catholic Church in Colonial Days,* p. 559.

27. *Handbook,* I, 179.

28. The general council of the Choctaw Nation, in October, 1844, enacted a law requiring all intruding Indians residing in that nation to leave there as soon as practicable. Excepted therefrom, however, were some Caddo who, at a previous session of the council, had received permission to live in the nation; and excepted also were three families each of the Delaware, Cherokee, and Shawnee tribes, and one family of Quapaw living on Red River above the mouth of the Washita (*Laws of the Choctaw Nation* [1869 ed.], p. 83).

29. In 1834, when the famous Dragoon expedition made its excursion from Fort Gibson to the Comanche Indians, a company of thirty Caddo recruited in the vicinity of Fort Towson joined the Dragoons at Fort Washita to act as guides and scouts for the expedition (Foreman, *Pioneer Days in the Early Southwest*). Immediately after the Civil War forty Caddo scouts were attached to Fort Arbuckle, at that time occupied by the Nineteenth Infantry (*Fort Smith Herald,* January 24, 1867, p. 3, col. 1).

30. *Report, 1859,* pp. 589 ff.; *Report, 1860,* p. 378.

31. Later called Paul's Valley.

32. The Caddo, Ioni (Hainai), and Delaware Indians belonging to the Wichita Agency, who had theretofore been living as separated bands, met in council in 1874 and decided to affiliate as one band; or, rather, it was decided that the Delawares and Ioni should be joined to the Caddo, with whom they had mingled harmoniously for several years, and that they should adopt a Caddo chief as head of the united band. They were thereafter known as Caddo Indians. Thus united, they conceived that they would be stronger and better able to maintain their rights. Chickasaw Agent A. M. M. Upshaw told Colonel E. A. Hitchcock, in 1841, that the Caddo tribe had been reduced to 250 in number, of whom 167 were living in the Choctaw Nation. Beluxi Indians also were driven over into the Choctaw Nation (*Report, 1874,* p. 237).

CHAPTER XVII

INDIGENOUS—IN A MEASURE

CHEYENNE AND ARAPAHO

AT FORT LARAMIE a treaty was entered into with the Cheyenne and Arapaho Indians on September 17, 1851, by which they were assigned certain territory on the Upper Arkansas River, reserving to the whites the right to establish roads through their country. With the discovery of gold in Colorado soon afterward, the whites overran their country, destroying their game and threatening them with hunger and destitution. The Indians were then called into another treaty council on February 18, 1861, by which they gave up all their vast holdings in exchange for a small reservation on the Arkansas River in the "short-grass" country of western Kansas and eastern Colorado.

Still these Indians continued at peace with the whites. Provoked by a minor disturbance on April 12, 1864, Colorado troops attacked the Cheyenne in May and killed twenty-six of them. The Indians were afterward directed to remove their village near Fort Lyon for their protection. About five hundred men, women, and children did so. Later a battalion of the First Colorado Cavalry commanded by Colonel John M. Chivington marched from Denver to Fort Lyon and at daybreak of November 29, 1864, surrounded the Indian camp and commenced an indiscriminate slaughter of nearly two hundred friendly unarmed Cheyennes. The particulars of this massacre are too gruesome for repetition here. Of this atrocity, General Nelson A. Miles said: "The Sand Creek massacre is perhaps the foulest and most unjustifiable crime in the annals of America."

Naturally the Indians were infuriated, and a bloody war resulted which cost the government thirty million dollars. Other measures were then attempted through a commission representing the United States, when a treaty of peace was negotiated on October 14, 1865, at the mouth of the Little Arkansas River, with the Cheyenne and Arapaho.[1] By its terms the Indians agreed to relinquish their lands on the Upper Arkansas River in exchange for a reservation that lay in southern Kansas contiguous to the Cherokee Nation in the northern Indian Territory. Three days later these Indians made another treaty by which they agreed to receive the Apache in a confederacy of the three tribes.

These measures still did not establish peace, and further violence followed. Congress then, on June 20, 1867, passed an act authorizing the appointment of the celebrated Peace Commission that met with five thousand Indians at Medicine Lodge Creek in southern Kansas. On October 21, 1867, a treaty was entered into with the Kiowa and Comanche by which they were assigned a reservation in the Leased District of the Indian Territory.

On the same day another treaty was made by which the Apache, whom the government two years before had tried to amalgamate with the Cheyenne and Arapaho, were now incorporated in a confederacy with, and granted a right to locate upon and share the reservation set apart to, the Kiowa and Comanche. A week later another treaty was made at the same place with the Cheyenne and Arapaho, by which they also entered into obligations of peace and were given as a reservation about three million acres of land now in northern Oklahoma, bounded by the south line of Kansas, the Arkansas River, and the Cimarron. This tract was later called the "Cherokee Outlet."

The principal objective of these treaties was to remove the Indians from Kansas to the country in the future Oklahoma, which became their permanent home, and to establish them in a life of peace and amity with the whites. To this end liberal provisions were made for the future welfare of the Indians to compensate them for the destruction of their game and to remove them from contact with white travelers and railroads occupying the country they were to abandon. It was proposed to move them from a country where white settlers were lawfully located to a country where whites could not legally settle, thus further confirming the lands of Oklahoma as an Indian country closed to white occupancy.

Removal of these Indians to, and permanent settlement of them in, the Indian Territory were still in the future. Soon after the treaties were made at Medicine Lodge, the red men complained that the government had not issued to them the guns and ammunition for their spring hunt of buffalo, which had been promised in their treaties; and they again became restless and troublesome. The following August the Cheyenne and Sioux engaged in bloody raids in Kansas. Many Comanche, Kiowa, Apache, and other Indians with their families, who tried to keep out of trouble, were encamped at the Salt Plains in northwestern Oklahoma. The location there also of hostile Indians and other current conditions aggravated a situation that resulted in the celebrated massacre of Cheyenne Indians known as the "Battle of the Washita."

General W. B. Hazen, late commandant at Fort Gibson, was detailed by General Sherman to attend the Peace Commission at Medicine Lodge Creek and to use his influence with the plains Indians to bring about their acquiescence in the peace proposals and removal to the country intended for them in the future Oklahoma. Hazen and General Sheridan arranged with the Kiowa, Apache, and a band of Comanche who were at Medicine Lodge to go to Fort Cobb, where rations would be issued them by General Hazen and where they would be removed from danger of involvement in further difficulties with the soldiers.

General Hazen arrived on November 8, 1868, at Fort Cobb, where he found two companies of troops under Lieutenant J. T. Lee of the Tenth Cavalry, and seven hundred Comanche, Caddo, Wichita, and affiliated bands—in all, about seventeen hundred Indians. There was no agent here, and Hazen faced the problem of feeding these Indians and others of the plains tribes who soon began arriving. It was his task to entice all the wandering Indians to the neighborhood and endeavor to locate them on their reservation. The Comanche put their own construction on their treaty at Medicine Lodge, which made them say that they would not war on the Texans any more. They said truthfully that they never had ceded Texas, that they had a perfect right to raid there and had raided there from the time of the earliest white settlements, and that they would continue to do so. Which, indeed, they did. They made the people of West Texas dread the moonlight nights, which facilitated these Indian raids.

General Sheridan accompanied General Grierson from Fort Cobb and, finding a location that suited him, on January 8, 1869, held a stake while it was being driven to denote the location of a military post for six companies of cavalry. The Seventh Cavalry, two companies of the Tenth Cavalry, and the Nineteenth Kansas Cavalry under Governor Crawford camped near. As soon as Sheridan got established, General Hazen removed his Indian agency to the place, and Colonel Albert Gallatin Boone, a grandson of Daniel Boone, arrived to act as agent for the Kiowa and Comanche. This place was called "Camp Wichita, Wichita Mountains," until July, 1869, when the name was changed to Fort Sill, in honor of General Joshua W. Sill, who was killed at Stone River on December 31, 1862.

General Sheridan remained in the neighborhood from December 20, 1869, to the end of the next March and assumed the chief direction of affairs. He entered into negotiations for peace with representatives of the Cheyenne and Arapaho, and hostilities were suspended. In February sixty lodges of Cheyenne under Little Raven came in; on April 1, one hundred more; around the end of May they all removed to Camp Supply to be joined on the way by thirty more. They were thus somewhat tentatively located on their reservation. In April seventy lodges of Cheyenne timidly came in and joined the Arapaho.

Following the publicity given to efforts to reform the Indian Service, on November 10, 1868, General Hazen, at his post at Fort Cobb, had written to the celebrated philanthropist, Peter Cooper, in New York, who was prominently connected with the movement for the amelioration of the Indians. Hazen told him that there were eight or ten thousand Comanche, Kiowa, and other wild Indians collecting around him in response to plans of the government to feed and locate them on reservations, where the evils so loudly condemned in the East could no longer exist and where they might be taught to be self-supporting from the cultivation of the soil. He asked Cooper to send a member of the United States Indian Commission to Fort Cobb, to accept his hospitality during the winter, where he could study the condition and wants of the Indians. Hazen urged that steps be taken for sending missionaries, farmers, house-builders, and cattle-raisers to these Indians, to start their education that would fit them for the new life the government wished them to adopt.

Hazen was standing now at the beginning of Indian civilization in western Oklahoma. Efforts made ten years before, with the Indians lately removed from Texas and a few others, had been nullified by the Civil War, which had scattered and introduced them to renewed scenes of carnage and bloodshed. Hazen had not only the indigenes of the soil—the Comanche, Kiowa, Wichita, and Caddo—to deal with; the comparative strangers, the Cheyenne and Arapaho, driven from their old homes far to the west, were also on his hands to locate and to implant in their minds and cultivate the revolutionary idea of extracting subsistence from the soil, habits of thrift, and the adoption of new methods of living. Baffling as his problems were, Hazen had sane ideas that no doubt contributed substantially to the civilization of our western Indians.

Upon consideration of Hazen's suggestion and other information, the Honorable Vincent Colyer, of New York, was selected to accept his invitation. Colyer came to Camp Wichita (Fort Sill), where, on March 29, he found General Hazen, lately removed from Fort Cobb. Here Major General Benjamin H. Grierson, of the Tenth Cavalry, was in command of the new post, with Hazen exercising supervision over the Indians, having been specially detailed from the army by General Sherman to locate them on their recently defined reservation.

Colyer saw thousands of Indians camped in the neighborhood— Cheyenne, Arapaho, Comanche, Kiowa, Apache—held interviews with their chiefs; told them of the messages from President Grant, and discussed with them the subject of teaching them to read and write, to plow the earth, to plant corn, and to live in houses.

Colyer and Custer went to the Wichita agency, twenty-two miles north of Camp Wichita on the Washita River, in a beautiful plain called Eureka Valley. The Wichita Indians had been agriculturists long before the white man first saw them, and Colyer marveled at their well-cultivated and well-fenced gardens and fields. Their village was an object of wonder to him: "A level plain, dotted with 'huge hay-stacks,' symmetrical and beautiful; thirty to forty feet high, and as regularly built as though they were laid out by rules of geometry. As we neared them we soon discovered that our haystacks were the houses of the Wichitas, built of straw, thatched layer upon layer, with stout bindings of willow saplings, tied together with buffalo hide, or stripped hickory."[2] Near the Wichita village and tributary to the same agency were Caddo, Waco, and Kichai, numbering in all about seven hundred.

Near Camp Supply the commissioners saw a camp of two hundred and seventy lodges of Cheyenne, all desperately poor but scrupulously clean. Their chief promised to bring in three hundred more lodges of his tribe and locate them all on the proposed reservation if the military would agree to protect them there.

The further career of these Indians was marked by their involvement in the hostilities of 1874 and the subsequent confinement at Fort Marion, Florida, of seventy-two Cheyenne, Kiowa, and Comanche warriors, some of whom later became the nucleus of the celebrated Indian school at Carlisle, Pennsylvania.

The immigrant Cheyenne and Arapaho and Apache were at last settled on their reservations in the Indian Territory, of which the government tried to invest them with exclusive possession until they were induced to enter into treaties in 1890 agreeing to the allotment of their lands and the sale to white people of the remainder.[3]

APACHE

New Mexico had been the habitat of the Apache Indians for years. A band of them had separated from the tribe and soon after the Gold Rush were found with the Kiowa and Comanche on the Arkansas and Upper Canadian River participating with them in raids on traders' caravans, on emigrant trains, and on white settlements as far south as Mexico. For this reason they were included by Thomas Fitzpatrick on July 28, 1853, in the peace treaty at Fort Atkinson with the Kiowa and Comanche Indians.

In this association they later came within the jurisdiction of the Wichita agency when it was re-established after the Civil War, under General Hazen. In 1869, at that place, he reported that, because of the restrictions on their activities imposed by the military after the war, additional lodges of Apache were leaving their old home in New Mexico to join their brothers on the Wichita reservation.[4]

These Apache were formally confederated with the Kiowa and Comanche in a treaty entered into at Medicine Lodge Creek on October 21, 1867,[5] and from that time on the three were treated as one tribe on a reservation set apart to them in that treaty. In 1872 there were 517 Apache, living with the 1,763 Comanche and 1,200 Kiowa on what was called the Kiowa agency at Fort Sill.[6]

The Apache remaining in New Mexico later gave much trouble, and in 1886 Geronimo and other Apache prisoners—men, women, and children numbering 407—were taken from their mountain home in New Mexico to Florida as prisoners of war. After a year's confinement at Forts Marion and Pickens, these Indians were transferred to Mount Vernon Barracks, Alabama. Here the band was so decimated by tuberculosis that, under authority of Congress, they were removed to the Fort Sill reservation in Oklahoma.[7] Three years later the Kiowa and Comanche generously agreed to cede to the unfortunate Apache more than 26,000 acres of their reservation for a home. Congress, on June 28, 1902, made an appropriation of funds for the erection of necessary buildings for these Apache and for the purchase of stock and household facilities.[8] By 1910 they had seven thousand head of cattle and had become good and useful citizens.

It was not until that year that Congress discovered that, of the 407 Indians placed in custody, only 17 were known to have been engaged in hostilities against the United States, and only 5 of them were then living. The survivors and their descendants were thereupon, on April 2, 1913, given permission to return to the Mescalero reservation in

New Mexico; 183 took advantage of the opportunity, and 78 elected to remain at Fort Sill, where they had received allotments preceding the "opening" of the Kiowa, Comanche, and Apache reservation on August 6, 1901.

SKIDI

The Skidi (Pani Loups, Panimaha) was one of the tribes of the Pawnee Confederacy sometimes called Wolf Pawnee, and by the French, Pawnee Loup.[9] During the two centuries prior to their removal from Nebraska to the Indian Territory in 1874, the Skidi, in common with other Pawnee tribes, tried to hold their hunting grounds against intruders, and to that end strove for the possession of herds of horses. To get this booty was the chief incentive of war parties, and the possession of ponies became the sign of wealth.

During their hunting and war expeditions the Skidi carried their activities into the present western Oklahoma, where they were known as fierce and fearless warriors. On one occasion, in 1836, they attacked the agricultural Wichita Indians and killed several of their tribe. Colonel A. P. Chouteau related how, in 1837, they even ventured to attack the Comanche in western Oklahoma, from whom they stole more than a hundred horses.[10] These Indians also became part of the Anadarko agency, where they received allotments of land in 1895.

WICHITA AND KICHAI

There were several small tribes represented in Oklahoma whose contribution to Indian history is not great, but this account would not be complete without some mention of them. Most conspicuous of these tribes were the Wichita, a confederacy of Caddoan stock, closely related linguistically to the Pawnee, ranging from about the middle Arkansas River in Kansas southward to the Brazos River of Texas, of which general region they appear to be the aborigines, antedating the Comanche, Kiowa, Mescalero, and the Siouan tribes. The existing remnants of this tribe now reside in Caddo County of western Oklahoma, within the limits of the former Wichita reservation. Of the numerous former bands of these Indians, the only divisions now existing are the Wichita proper (possibly synonymous with Tawehash), Tawakoni, and Waco. To these may be added the incorporated Kichai remnant, of cognate but different language. About 1840–45, just previous to the annexation of Texas to the United States, the Tawakoni and Waco resided chiefly on the Brazos River and were considered as belonging to Texas, while the Wichita proper resided north of Red River, in and north of the Wichita Mountains, and were considered as belonging to the United States.[11]

The Wichita as residents of the present Oklahoma were first made known by the celebrated Dragoon Expedition from Fort Gibson to their home in 1834. The next year they became parties to the first treaty made with western Indians by the United States. In the correspondence relative to this expedition, these Indians were known by the name of Tawehash. They were agriculturists and raised quantities of corn, which they exchanged with the wild Indians for furs and other merchandise. They were regarded as consistent friends of the United States since they signed the treaty of 1835, and thus they contributed measurably to efforts to prepare the present Oklahoma for the reception of the immigrant Indians. They were victims of the appalling smallpox epidemic of 1837, which almost depopulated a number of western tribes. The sickness and mortality among the Wichita were so great that in many instances there were not enough well persons to remove the dead from their lodges.[12]

The Wichita gave their name to the agency on their reservation which had supervision over remnants of a number of tribes located in their neighborhood. With the breaking-out of the Civil War, these Indians fled to Kansas, where they remained during that conflict in a settlement near their agency.[13]

Kichai, a small Caddoan tribe, were first known in Texas, whence in May, 1842, they sent delegates to attend the Indian council on the Canadian River near the present Eufaula, Oklahoma, attended also by representatives of nearly a dozen other tribes.

With several other small Texas tribes the Kichai were assigned by the United States government to a reservation on the Brazos River in 1855; but, on the dispersal of the Indians by the Texans three years later, they fled north to the Indian Territory and joined the Wichita, with whom they have since been associated, and whom they resembled in their agriculture, house-building, and general customs. In the Indian Territory the Kichai were located under the Anadarko agency which included the Wichita, Tawakoni, Waco, Caddo, and Delawares, and were part of the 965 Indians of that agency who participated in the allotment of lands there. In 1906 it was said by the Bureau of American Ethnology that about fifty Kichai still kept the tribal name and language.[14]

In 1869 the Wichita agency was expanded to include the Comanche, Kiowa, and Apache Indians, while A. G. Boone was agent, with his agency established at Camp Wichita (Fort Sill). Soon General Hazen was sent by General Sherman to assume charge of Indian administration in that area, and he also operated from Camp Wichita. The Cheyenne and Arapaho were brought within his jurisdiction, following their massacre at the Battle of the Washita.

KIOWA AND COMANCHE

The Indians of Oklahoma are divisible roughly into two classifications—those strictly native and those intrusive. The first class includes those who were first known to explorers in the earliest historical times. Near the border line were Indians whose more or less fugitive existence made them inhabitants at different times of the area that is now Oklahoma and of other sections.

Of the strictly indigenous Indians, the Kiowa, Comanche, and Wichita are still residents of Oklahoma. Even those Indians, however, lived a restless life, annually following the buffalo north and south into other areas in quest of the flesh of these animals for food and of their skins, which were used for clothing and shelter.

The Kiowa at an early period lived on the upper Arkansas and Canadian rivers in Colorado and Oklahoma, though one of their early traditions locates them at the head of Missouri River, whence they moved down from the mountains and formed an alliance with the Crows. From here they drifted southward, driven by the Cheyenne and Arapaho, with whom they finally made peace about 1840. Lewis and Clark found them in 1805 living on the North Platte. According to the Kiowa account, when they first reached the Arkansas River, they found their passage opposed by the Comanche who claimed all the country south of that stream. A war followed, but peace was finally concluded when the Kiowa crossed over to the south side of the Arkansas and formed a confederacy with the Comanche, which has continued ever since.

In connection with the Comanche they carried on constant warfare upon the frontier settlements of Mexico and Texas. Among all the prairie tribes, they were noted as the most predatory and bloodthirsty, and had probably killed more white men in proportion to their numbers than any of the others. They made their first treaty with the government in 1837[15] and were put on their present reservation jointly with the Comanche and Kiowa-Apache in 1868. Their last outbreak was in 1874–75 in connection with the Comanche, Kiowa-Apache, and

Cheyenne. While probably never very numerous, they were greatly reduced by war and disease, particularly in 1892, when measles and fever took the lives of more than three hundred members of the confederated tribes.[16]

The Kataka or Kiowa-Apache, also called "Bad Hearts," were not Apache Indians at all, though they were on friendly terms with that tribe. They came to Oklahoma with the Kiowa from the northwest plains region. They were mentioned by La Salle in 1682 and by La Harpe in 1719. La Harpe found them living with the Tawakoni and other affiliated tribes on the Cimarron River near its junction with the Arkansas. In the treaty of Medicine Lodge in 1867, they were formally reunited with the Kiowa, although a part of them continued to live with the Cheyenne and Arapaho until after the adjustment at the close of the outbreak of 1874–75. In 1905 only 155 lived on their reservation in Oklahoma.[17]

The Comanche are one of the southern tribes of the Shoshonean stock and the only one of that group living entirely on the plains. Under pressure of the Sioux and other prairie tribes they were driven south and became residents of Oklahoma. The Sioux called them Padouca, by which name they were known to early French explorers in the West.[18] At the time of the Lewis and Clark Expedition they roamed over the country about the heads of the Arkansas, Red, Trinity, and Brazos rivers in Colorado, Kansas, Oklahoma, and Texas. "For nearly two centuries they were at war with the Spaniards of Mexico, and extended their raids far down into Durango. They were friendly to the Americans generally, but became bitter enemies of the Texans by whom they were dispossessed of their best hunting grounds, and carried on a relentless war against them for nearly forty years. They were close confederates of the Kiowa since 1795."[19] In 1834 they were visited by the famous Dragoon Expedition sent out from Fort Gibson, as a result of which they made their first treaty with the United States, the next year, at a point near the present Purcell, Oklahoma. Afterward, in 1867, at the treaty of Medicine Lodge Creek, they agreed to go on the reservation assigned them between the Washita and Red rivers in southwestern Oklahoma. But it was not until after the outbreak of 1874–75 that they and their allies, the Kiowa and Apache, finally settled on it. Through great loss by war and disease, their number in 1904, when attached to the Kiowa agency of Oklahoma, had been reduced to fourteen hundred.

Most of the immigrant Indians demonstrably contributed to the population of Oklahoma. But there is another and much smaller class of immigrant Indians whose contribution to the Indian bloodstream in Oklahoma is so tenuous as to be almost on the border line; but, because there is a strong probability that their blood is represented in Oklahoma, they also are mentioned. These Indians include the Nez Percés, who lived in the Indian Territory only a short time before they were returned to their reservation in Idaho, though long enough, probably, to leave some descendants; the Catawba, Munsee, Chippewa, and the New York Indians; and a few others whose almost casual contacts with the Oklahoma Indians have been described herein.

It is a matter of some interest, and perhaps somewhat pertinent to this work, to mention other Indians whose removal to Indian Territory was attempted but never carried into effect, having been prevented by the announcement of a new federal policy. Consolidation of the Indian tribes in the Indian Territory was becoming more and more the settled policy of the government; after the eastern tribes had found their final home there, western tribes already named had been located in that area.

In November, 1873, Major J. H. Stout, agent for the Pima and Maricopa Indians of Arizona, conducted a delegation representing the forty-five hundred Indians of his agency, in order that they might examine the present Oklahoma County and surrounding area with a view to removing there.[20] The Indians changed their minds, however, and the project was abandoned.

The Sioux next became the object of removal from South Dakota to the Indian Territory. A delegation of more than ninety Indians, conducted by government agents, examined the same area in 1876, but the proposal to locate a large body of warlike Indians in the Indian Territory aroused a storm of protest from the people of the surrounding states, who believed that the removal of alien Indians to their midst had gone far enough. When Congress ratified the treaty of September 26, 1876, with the Sioux, at the instance of Representative Roger Q. Mills of Texas, it expressly forbade the removal of the tribe to the Indian Territory without the authority of Congress.[21]

The subject continued to be agitated, and in his annual report for 1878 the Commissioner of Indian Affairs recommended the removal of all the Indians in Colorado and Arizona to the Indian Territory. At the ensuing session of Congress the House Committee on Indian Affairs requested the Commissioner to draft and submit a bill providing for the removal to Indian Territory and consolidation of certain Indians living in Oregon, Colorado, Iowa, Kansas, Nebraska, Wisconsin, and Minnesota; but nothing came of it.[22]

NOTES

1. Kappler (ed.), *Laws and Treaties*, II, 679.

2. *Report of the Commissioner of Indian Affairs, 1869*, p. 83. These houses were constructed by the Wichita women; their men would not degrade themselves by engaging in manual labor (*ibid.*). By authority of an act of Congress of April 10, 1869 (16 Stat. L. 40), President Grant on May 26, 1869, named members of a special commission to aid him in the administration of Indian affairs. Vincent Colyer of New York was appointed to that commission in July, 1869.

3. A detailed account of this phase of Indian history is to be seen in Grant Foreman, *A History of Oklahoma*.

4. *Report, 1869*, p. 395.

5. Kappler (ed.), *op. cit.*, p. 759.

6. In 1879 Congress specifically forbade the removal of any more Indians from New Mexico or Arizona to the Indian Territory (20 *U.S. Stat.* 313).

7. Act of August 6, 1894 (28 *U.S. Stat.* 238).

8. 33 *U.S. Stat.* 26; see also *Senate Executive Doc. 83* (51st Cong., 1st sess.).

9. The early history of this tribe is complicated, and the reader is referred to *Handbook*, II, 590. See also George A. Dorsey and James R. Murie, *Notes on Skidi Pawnee Society*, prepared for publication by Alexander Spoehr.

10. Grant Foreman, *Pioneer Days in the Early Southwest*, pp. 234, 238.

11. *Handbook*, II, 947.

12. Foreman, *Pioneer Days in the Early Southwest*, p. 234.

13. The negotiations that led to the allotment of the Wichita reservation to the Indians there are described in Foreman, *A History of Oklahoma*, p. 248.

14. *Handbook*, I, 683.

15. 7 *U.S. Stat.* 533.

16. *Handbook*, I, 699.

17. *Ibid.*

18. Le Page du Pratz, *Histoire de la Louisiane*, III, 211.

19. *Handbook*, I, 327.

20. *Report, 1874*, p. 293.

21. 19 *U.S. Stat.* 254.

22. *Report, 1878*, p. iv.

CHAPTER XVIII

QUAPAW AND MODOC

QUAPAW

OF THE many interesting tribes of Indians forming the background of Oklahoma civilization, one of the oldest historically indigenous to the West is the Quapaw tribe. These Indians were known by Marquette and other early French explorers as residents of the country near the mouth of the Arkansas River. The name by which they were known—"Akansea"—was given to the stream, which afterward became the "Arkansas."

The Quapaw were known as a chivalrous people, and a tale has survived from long ago that, when they were at war with their neighbors, the Chickasaw, on the Mississippi River, a war party fell in with a company of that tribe who, having no powder, withdrew to avoid an encounter. When the Quapaw chief was informed of the cause of their retreat, he called his warriors about him and directed them to empty their powder horns on a blanket spread out for the purpose. When they had done so, he divided the powder into equal parts, and, keeping one for themselves, he desired the Chickasaw to come and take the other. Then a furious battle began in which the Quapaw lost one of their number but had the satisfaction of hanging up the scalps of eight of their enemies to dry in their wigwams.

After the Louisiana Purchase was consummated, the United States recognized the Quapaw Indians as the owners of all the land south of the Arkansas River, within what became known as the Arkansas Territory. This included the present Oklahoma, except the northern area of that domain claimed by the Osage. As the white people began to crowd into the homes of these Indians, efforts were made to induce them to give up their country. Finally, a treaty was entered into with them in 1818,[1] by which they were persuaded to cede to the United States all of their vast domain of nearly thirty million acres except a small tract on the south side of the Arkansas River, between Arkansas Post and Little Rock. For this territory they were paid the sum of $4,000 and promised an annuity of about $1,000 in goods. This was at the approximate rate of $1.00 for one thousand acres, or one-twelfth of one cent an acre.

The tract of land retained by them was coveted by the white people. The Quapaw were assembled at Little Rock in the summer of 1824, and, with the influence of much whiskey and $500 paid to each of four chiefs, they were induced to enter into another treaty,[2] by which they conveyed this land to the United States and agreed to leave their homes and remove to Red River, there to locate with the Caddo Indians, no other provision having been made for these Indians thus dispossessed. For this last cession they were to receive $4,000 and an annuity of $1,000 for eleven years. Accordingly, the next year the Indians were removed under the supervision of a Frenchman of Arkansas named Frederick Notrebe, whom they knew and trusted, to Bayou Teche on the south side of Red River.

Much has been written about the suffering of the emigrant Indians who were driven from their homes east of the Mississippi River, but it is doubtful if there is a more pathetic chapter in the annals of history than that relating to the suffering of the Quapaw. The Caddo assigned them some overflow land that they themselves could not use. Here the Indians planted three times the first year; the first two plantings were flooded out, and the third died from want of moisture. The Quapaw then applied to the Caddo to assign them other land, which the latter refused. In consequence of these crop failures, they had no food except a meager supply of fish; and sixty of the tribe actually starved to death. Young women were discovered in the agonies of death, one with a child tugging at the breast and another lying dead beside her.

"The Quapaws are a peaceable tribe," said their agent, "and they would prefer to perish than to be united to the Caddos, who they say are thieves and murderers. They said that they transferred by treaty to the United States one of the most valuable tracts of land in the country," and they had left not enough land to bury one of their tribe. Many of them were in great distress, particularly the old and infirm. After losing the principal part of their property on Red River and one-fourth of their numbers, the wretched survivors, after four years of suffering, wandered back to their old homes along the Arkansas River, trying to sustain life on their ancestral domain, to the great displeasure of the whites. Suffered by the governor to remain there, they tried again to build homes and make little farms, but, having no title to the land, the whites destroyed or appropriated their improvements, burned their cabins, and stole or cheated them out of their horses, cattle, and hogs.[3]

The humane Governor Pope wrote to the War Department that the Quapaw chief, Saracen, "called on me and made, I believe, a very sincere and certainly a feeling representation of his sufferings and misfortunes in the Caddean country, and the desire of his tribe to remain here in peace with us on some inferior lands, and appealed in a very impressive manner to the justice and humanity of his great father, the President, and the white people whose blood his nation had never shed. They are a kind, inoffensive people, and aid the whites in picking out their cotton, furnishing them with game. I have heard but one sentiment expressed in this territory with regard to this tribe, that of kindness and a desire that they should be permitted to live among us. I would be particularly gratified to be authorized to assign them a township on this river in the vicinity of their permanent residence. The residue of this tribe are now on their return from the Caddean to join their friends here. They will all be united shortly on this river, and they would prefer death to be driven from the land of their fathers."[4]

Out of their meager annuity of $2,000 payable in 1830, they set aside enough to defray the expenses of their chief, Heckaton, to Washington, so that he could tell the President about their troubles and suffering. He related, too, the fraud that was committed on them in the execution of the treaty of 1824, which, they said, was made possible by the use of whiskey. They complained particularly of the provision of the treaty in which their funds were charged with a claim amounting to $7,500 in favor of a white man named Hewes Scull, to whom, they said, they did not owe in excess of $100.

The Quapaw afterward sent a long communication to the President, in which they said that their chief was accompanied to Washington by Ambrose H. Sevier, delegate from Arkansas Territory, and Wharton Rector and an interpreter; that in Washington, Sevier neglected them and left them to shift for themselves, so that they felt very much alone among the white people. They said that Sevier, on one occasion, got Heckaton drunk and induced him to agree to have Wharton Rector as their agent, though the tribe very much preferred Antoine Barraque, whom they knew and trusted. And they also accused Sevier of trying to get Heckaton to destroy the message of the Indians to the President, complaining of the fraud involved in the allowance of Scull's claim. Heckaton was outfitted for his trip to Washington by Barraque's partner, Frederick Notrebe, a merchant at Arkansas Post. Notrebe was an army officer in France during the revolution, but left when Napoleon became emperor and, prior to 1818, came to Arkansas, where he became a wealthy planter. Frenchmen had intermarried extensively in the Quapaw tribe.

The whites were opposed to giving back to the Quapaw any part of their original home. Instead of that, in 1833 another treaty[5] was made at New Gascony with Heckaton and other chiefs, in which the government promised the Quapaw one hundred and fifty sections west of Arkansas between the lands of the Seneca and Shawnee, in what later became northeastern Oklahoma.

Wharton Rector was appointed to remove them to their new home. He was thoroughly distrusted by the Indians and was able to enrol only about one hundred and sixty. The remainder, about three hundred, some of whom feared the Osage, who would be neighbors in their new home, and, unable to live longer on the Arkansas, wandered off toward Red River again. Rector, in 1834, located his contingent in the future Oklahoma. Ten years earlier some of the Quapaw asked the Osage to receive them in the tribe. Later, General Clark again mentioned it to the Osage, who replied that the proposition was agreeable if the government would restore to them some of the vast domain they had so improvidently ceded to the United States. This, of course, was not done.

In 1838, when the boundary lines were surveyed, it was discovered that Rector had located the Quapaw on the lands of the Seneca and Shawnee. Here they had been building their homes and making little farms, and the knowledge that they would again be dispossessed for reasons not of their making thoroughly demoralized and disheartened them. In this state of mind they wandered off again, and about two hundred and fifty established themselves in a village on the Canadian River, near the future Holdenville. Here, with the hunters—the Kickapoo, Delawares, and Shawnee—they acted as a buffer between the Creeks, on whose land they lived, and the Comanche and other wild tribes. These Indians raised corn on the Creek land and engaged in hunting and trading expeditions in the country of the plains Indians in western Indian Territory and Texas. After the Gold Rush in the early fifties, some of the Quapaw established a temporary village in the Wichita Mountains. They were regarded as a brave though not a warlike people.

Most of the tribe gravitated to their proper reservation where their annuity was paid, and in 1852 the agent reported 81 men, 84 women, and 149 children—a total of 314 persons.[6] During the previous winter and spring every member of the tribe had been afflicted with the measles, from which forty had died.

The Quapaw were not disposed to cultivate the soil. Their annuity having expired at the last payment, they were greatly alarmed about the future and began to wander away again. A school which bore the pretentious title of "Crawford Seminary," which had been conducted with indifferent success in the tribe for ten years, gave up the ghost and closed its doors. The Quapaw said that they were tired of it and wished it discontinued. In view of the termination of their annuity, they planned to leave and engage in hunting expeditions with the western Indians.

The Quapaw were considered a harmless, inoffensive, and indolent people. There were a few exceptions, however. Their head chief, War-to-she, was a good man and very industrious. He always raised sufficient food for his own family and divided with his people who were less fortunate. He had a reputation for honesty in all his dealings. The second chief, Joseph Vallier, his son Samuel Vallier, and a few others were industrious, good men. They had farms on which they raised a sufficiency for their families, which they divided with their indolent neighbors, in whom they tried to stimulate habits of industry with indifferent success.

Father John Bax had done some good work among the Quapaw and had won their friendship to such an extent that he induced a number to send their children to the Osage Manual Labor School conducted by the Jesuit, Father John Schoenmakers, across the line in Kansas. The first baptism of a Quapaw at that mission was performed on September 18, 1848. Fifty-three were baptized in 1850. The Quapaw chiefs asked Father Schoenmakers for the admission of their children to the school. The matter previously had been presented to the Osage chiefs in council, who gave their unanimous consent, and ten Quapaw children were admitted at that time. It was not supposed that so many would wish to attend a school sixty or seventy miles from their home, but the facilities of the mission made such an appeal that by May, 1853, there were seventeen boys and seven girls from the Quapaw tribe in attendance. It then became necessary to make some financial adjustments of the matter, and the Quapaw chiefs on May 23 signed a petition to Father Schoenmakers, making formal application for the admission of their children. The priest then submitted the matter to the Indian Department, with the request that $55 per pupil be allowed the school. When this was arranged, the education of the Quapaw youth in the Osage school continued.

In the spring of 1852 a Quapaw came to visit his children in the school; soon after his arrival he developed a case of measles. This started an epidemic which spread all over the Osage Nation. It was followed by typhoid fever, and within a few months there was entailed the appalling death toll of a thousand Osage, mostly children. Included among the dead were George Whitehair, the chief, a number of pupils in the school, and Father Bax himself.

In 1857 the agent reported the Quapaw tribe as numbering four hundred, only half of whom were living on their reservation, the remainder still living on the Canadian River, in the Creek country, where they were seen by Hitchcock in 1841.[7] At the outbreak of the Civil War, the Quapaw were driven from the Indian Territory and became refugees in Kansas, where they suffered the most desolating hardships and privations. However, they were loyal to the government, and it was said that a larger proportion of their warriors volunteered for service in the Union Army than from any other Indian tribe.

In the autumn of 1865 the Quapaw were returned to their reservation, now reduced to 56,000 acres. They were destitute of every comfort and for several years were in a state bordering on starvation. Demoralized by the flood of whiskey introduced by the people of Kansas, large numbers of them died from its effects and from disease. Their crops were meager; their hay was destroyed by prairie fires; and many of their horses starved to death. Their recovery from the shock of the war was slow, and in 1872 they numbered only two hundred and forty; in 1880, only two hundred. As the years passed, their number continued to decrease.

After the Civil War the Quapaw found it impossible to live on their reservation immediately adjoining the south Kansas line, because of the unrestrained introduction of whiskey by people of Kansas. Demoralized and almost ruined by this contact, the Quapaw looked for relief to their friends the Osage. In 1876 the Quapaw chief and some of his people removed to the Osage reservation. In the following March, William Nicholson, superintendent for the central superintendency at Lawrence, Kansas, ordered H. W. Jones, the local agent, to remove the Quapaw at once to the Osage reservation, in order to make room for the Ponca Indians on their vacated reservation. He was also to transfer to the agent for the Ponca the "agency buildings on the Quapaw reservation (formerly agency for the Captive Indians)."

By 1878 all the Quapaw tribe but thirty-five were living with the Osage. A few years later, because of ill treatment by the Osage, they began wandering back to their own country. But it was not until 1893 that they were all located on their reservation. After this absence of fifteen years they came to be known as the Osage band of Quapaw.

MODOC

The year 1873 witnessed the arrival of the Modoc Indians. They formerly lived on the beautiful lakes of southwestern Oregon. Frequently conflicts with white immigrants, in which both sides were guilty of many atrocities, had given the tribe an unfortunate reputation. In 1864 the Modoc joined the Klamath, with whom they were closely related, in ceding their territory to the United States, and removed to the Klamath reservation. They seemed never to have been contented, however, and made persistent efforts to return and occupy their former land on Lost River and its vicinity.

In 1870 a prominent chief named Kintpuash, commonly known to history as Captain Jack, led the most turbulent portion of the tribe back to the California border and obstinately refused to return to the reservation. The first attempt to bring back the runaways by force brought on the Modoc war of 1872–73. After some struggle, Kintpuash and his band retreated to the Lava Beds on the California frontier, and from January to April, 1873, successfully resisted the attempts of the troops to dislodge them. The progress of the war had been slow until April of that year, when two of the peace commissioners who had been sent to treat with the renegades were treacherously assassinated by them.[8] In this act Kintpuash played the chief part. The campaign was then pushed with vigor; the Modoc were finally dispersed and captured, and Kintpuash and five other leaders were hanged at Fort Klamath in October, 1873. The tribe was then divided, a part being sent to the Klamath reservation and the remainder to Fort McPherson, Nebraska .

Captain M. C. Wilkinson of the United States Army, commissioned for the purpose, departed from Fort McPherson with these Indians by train on November 14, 1873. With his Indians—39 men, 54 women, and 60 children, including the widows and children of men recently executed in California—he arrived at Baxter Springs, Kansas, on November 16, where he installed them in an old hotel building for a week, except for a "working party" he took with him to the vicinity of the Quapaw agency. Here, with the help of the Indians and some hastily assembled lumber, he whipped up a crude, barnlike shelter for his party.

Wilkinson reported that "on the cars, in the old hotel building used for them at Baxter Springs, I found them uniformly obedient, ready to work, cheerful in compliance with police regulations, each day proving over and over again that these Modocs only require *just* treatment executed with firmness and kindness, to make them a singuarly reliable people."[9]

They were temporarily camped on the lands of the Quapaw and on August 6, 1874, received from the Shawnee a lease of a tract two and a half miles square off the northeast corner of the Shawnee reserve. Here, in six years, 56 children were born; but 110 of the tribe died from change of climate, malaria, and consumption. A large percentage of the deaths were among children; but with the adults deaths were caused largely by the use of whiskey introduced by white men in the adjoining state of Missouri.[10]

Under the influence of the Indian agent, the Modoc, on June 3, 1874, entered into an agreement with the Eastern Shawnee for the purchase of a tract of 4,000 acres. By 1876 the 117 Modoc, under the leadership of Scarface Charley,[11] were industriously engaged in making a living from the soil, an accomplishment they were just beginning to acquire. The agent seldom missed an opportunity to pay tribute to the excellent qualities of the Modoc, their industry and reliability. Furnished with the necessary wagons and teams, they engaged for many years in doing all the teaming from the railroad at Seneca, Missouri, to the Quapaw agency.

From the arrival of the Modoc Indians in 1873, the units of tribes making up the Quapaw reservation were fairly constant; that is to say, there were representatives of the eight tribes: the Quapaw and Wyandots; the Seneca, who received a few accretions from the Cayuga tribe in New York; the United Peoria and Miami, the confederacy which had previously absorbed the Wea, Kaskaskia, and Piankashaw; the Ottawa and Modoc; and the Eastern Shawnee.

The Ponca Indians were brought to the reservation in July, 1877, and the Nez Percés a year later. While the arrival here of the latter was a matter of considerable interest at the time, it was only temporary, as these Indians were soon removed to a reservation farther west. However, the arrival of the Ponca injected a phase of confusion among the Quapaw, on whose land they were temporarily located. It was at this time that, owing to the intrusion of white people from Kansas, the Quapaw were so disturbed that they decided to remove to the Osage reservation. Consolidation with the Osage had been in their minds for years. It had been suggested by the federal officials at the time they made their treaty in 1833. They were urged to join the Osage on the ground that they were closely related and spoke a similar language.

NOTES

1. 7 *U.S. Stat.* 176.
2. *Ibid.*, p. 232.
3. Grant Foreman, *Indians and Pioneers*, pp. 210 ff.
4. *Ibid.*, p. 211.
5. 7 *U.S. Stat.* 424.
6. *Report of the Commissioner of Indian Affairs, 1852*, p. 394.
7. Grant Foreman, *A Traveler in Indian Territory*, pp. 247, 256.
8. One of these was General E. R. S. Canby, who, forty years before, had served in the Indian Territory in connection with the removal of the Indians (see Grant Foreman, *Indian Removal*).
9. *Report, 1875*, p. 82.
10. Quapaw-Seneca Agency Archives (Oklahoma Historical Society).
11. When Scarface Charley died, the Indians built a fire, around which they danced and rang bells for three days to drive away evil spirits that might interfere with his reaching the happy hunting grounds. They would not stop until the agent interfered ("Foreman Collection," XL, 369 [Oklahoma Historical Society]).

CHAPTER XIX

SMALL TRIBES

THE few remaining Indians discussed in this book occupy a position that sets them apart from the other tribes. Concerning the Catawba, Natchez, and Nez Percés, their connection with the body of Oklahoma Indians is of the most tenuous character, but as they do, in fact, enter briefly into the history of these Indians, and undoubtedly contributed in a measure to the blood stream of Oklahoma Indians, this account would not be complete without some mention of them. Catawba, Natchez, and Nez Percé Indians actually lived within the present boundaries of Oklahoma. The New York, Chippewa, Munsee, and Stockbridge were so identified with the Delaware Indians during their residence in Kansas that the blood of those tribes unquestionably survives in the Delaware and Cherokee nations.

CATAWBA

The Catawba are said to have been the most important of the western Siouan tribes.[1] They were at one time a powerful nation, living in

South Carolina. With the single exception of their alliance with the hostile Yamasi in 1719, they were uniformly friendly toward the English and afterward kept peace with the United States; but they were constantly at war with the Iroquois, Shawnee, Delaware, and other tribes of the Ohio Valley, as well as with the Cherokee. The Iroquois and the Lake Tribes made long journeys into South Carolina, and the Catawba retaliated by sending small scalping parties into Ohio and Pennsylvania. The losses of the Catawba from ceaseless attacks by their enemies reduced their numbers steadily, while disease and debauchery introduced by the whites so accelerated their destruction that before the close of the eighteenth century the great nation was reduced to a pitiful remnant.

They sent a large force to help the colonists in the Tuscarora War of 1711–13 and also aided in expeditions against the French and their Indian allies at Fort Duquesne and elsewhere during the French and Indian Wars. Later it was proposed to use them and the Cherokee against the Lake Tribes under Pontiac in 1763. The Catawba assisted the Americans also during the Revolutionary War in the defense of South Carolina against the British as well as in Williamson's expedition against the Cherokee.

In 1738 smallpox raged in South Carolina, working great destruction not only among the whites but also among the Catawba. In 1759 it reappeared, and this time it destroyed nearly half of the tribe.

At a conference at Albany, attended by delegates from the Six Nations and the Catawba, under the auspices of the Colonial governors, a treaty of peace was made by them. This peace was probably final as regards the Iroquois, but the western tribes continued their warfare against the Catawba, who were now so reduced in numbers that they could offer little effectual resistance. In 1762 a small party of Shawnee killed the noted chief of the tribe, Kuy Haiglar, near his own village. From this time on, the Catawba ceased to be of importance except in conjunction with the whites.

In 1763 they had confirmed to them a reservation, assigned a few years before, of fifteen miles square on each side of the Catawba River, within the present York and Lancaster counties, South Carolina. On the approach of the British troops in 1780, the Catawba withdrew temporarily into Virginia but returned after the Battle of Guilford Courthouse to establish themselves in two villages of a reservation known, respectively, as Newton, the principal village, and Turkeyhead, on opposite banks of the Catawba River. In 1826 nearly the whole of their reservation was leased to whites for a few thousand dollars, on which the few survivors chiefly depended. About 1842 they sold to the state all but a single square mile, on which some of them continued to live. About the same time a number of Catawba, dissatisfied with their condition among the whites, removed to the Eastern Cherokee in western North Carolina; but, finding their position among their old enemies equally unpleasant, all but one or two soon returned.

The Catawba were sedentary agriculturists and seemed to have differed but little in general customs from their neighbors. Their men were respected, brave, and honest, although lacking in energy, and were good hunters, while their women were noted pottery-makers and basket-weavers. By reason of their dominant position they gradually absorbed the broken tribes of South Carolina. In their early history their population was estimated at fifteen hundred warriors, or about forty-six hundred persons.

Because of their location among the white people, the Catawba tribe gradually became largely intermingled with the whites. In an effort to improve their condition and remove them from their white surroundings, Congress on July 29, 1848, appropriated $5,000 for the removal of the remnants of this tribe "now in the limits of the State of North Carolina" to the Indian Territory.[2] In his annual report for the following year the Commissioner of Indian Affairs stated that a home had not yet been found for the Catawba of North Carolina west of the Mississippi River. "They prefer a residence among the Chickasaws, to whom application was made to receive them, but to which there had been no final answer."[3] But the Commissioner said that every effort would be made to carry out the law providing for their removal.

At a special session of the Chickasaw council on September 4, 1850, it was resolved that the Chickasaw Nation decline to receive the Catawba whom the United States was trying to locate in their country.[4]

No organized removal of the tribe was undertaken by the government, but in December, 1851, a party of twenty-five Catawba Indians left South Carolina, and, after six had died on the way, the surviving nineteen arrived at the Choctaw agency (Scullyville), Indian Territory, in February, 1852; they were peaceable and inoffensive people and begged to be admitted into the Choctaw Nation.[5] On November 9 of the next year the Choctaw council passed the necessary legislation adopting into the tribe the fourteen Catawba then living in the Choctaw Nation, survivors of the recent emigration of twenty-five. Their names were William Morrison, Thomas Morrison, Sarah Jane Morrison, Molly Redhead, Betsey Heart, Rebecca Heart, Phillip Keggo and his infant child, Rosey Ayers, Betsey Ayers, Julian Ayers, Mary Ayers, Sopronia Ayers, and Sally Ayers.[6]

The next year Congress reappropriated the sum of $5,000 to effect the removal of the Catawba west of the Mississippi and to subsist them for a year thereafter. At this time it was assumed that the tribe numbered about eighty.

The Choctaw council passed another act on November 12, 1856, declaring that those fourteen who were adopted into the tribe in 1853 were "jointly entitled to a full participation in all funds arising under the treaty of 1855 between the Choctaws and the Government of the United States."[7]

By reason of their dispersed condition, and their neglect by the federal government, the Catawba in the West did not benefit by the so-called "Allotment Act of 1887" and became scattered in and about the future Oklahoma, living in the manner of white people, whose blood many of them possessed. In an effort to improve their condition, a convention of the Catawba was held in Fort Smith, Arkansas, on April 25, 1895, where efforts were made to organize and present to Congress their claims to allotments of lands. This convention was composed of representatives of 257 persons of Catawba blood living in the Creek and Choctaw nations of Oklahoma and throughout western Arkansas. Of those in attendance, 125 were from Arkansas. Greenwood in that state was the home of 44, the largest number from any town; of the 132 living in Indian Territory, 17 claimed Checotah as their post office; and Starr was the home of 34. Perhaps the most conspicuous of these Catawba was "Judge" Leblanche, who was among the Catawba Indians admitted into the Creek tribe and who became a prominent merchant and cattleman, living near Checotah, Indian Territory.

The Indians who assembled at Fort Smith set up a permanent organization, elected officers, and planned subordinate Catawba associations in respective localities of members.[8] The main convention adopted a preamble, resolutions, and by-laws. Under the name of the "Catawba and Nonreservation Indian Convention," with James Bain as chairman and George E. Williamson as secretary, the proceedings were incorporated in a memorial which was forwarded to Congress, whence in turn it was referred to the Secretary of the Interior for investigation and report. The Commissioner of Indian Affairs thereupon prepared the desired report, which the Senate, on February 23, 1897, order to be printed, and which became *Senate Document 144* (54th Cong., 2d sess.). This report is exhaustive and contains all the history of these Indians within the knowledge of the Office of Indian Affairs at that time.

The Commissioner of Indian Affairs stated in his report that "no action appears to have been taken by the government or any of the Indians on the question of their removal to the Choctaw or other country until 1872, when Hon. J. C. Harper of the House of Representatives from Georgia, brought to the attention of this office the question of the removal of certain Indians in North Carolina and Georgia. Presuming that they were Cherokees, this office requested him, on the 13th of June, 1872, to furnish a list of the names and ages of said Indians." In reporting the names, Mr. James McDowell of Fairmount, Georgia, in October, 1872, stated that the Indians referred to, and who were asking relief of the government, were Catawba and eighty-four in number. Of this number, sixty-nine were named Guy—descendants of William Guy of Granville, Georgia, who had served five years in the Revolutionary army, along with Simon Jeffers, another Catawba Indian.

The Catawba became widely dispersed, and on January 9, 1896, Senator H. M. Teller wrote the Commissioner of Indian Affairs and inclosed a letter from P. H. Head, a Catawba Indian of Sanford, Colorado, submitting a petition purporting to have been signed by himself and twenty-five others, embracing six Catawba families once resident in South Carolina but who were no longer recognized by that state, asking to be united with the Ute Indian tribe living on the Uintah reservation in Utah.[9]

NATCHEZ

The Natchez were a well-known tribe who formerly lived in and about St. Catherine's Creek, east and south of the present city of Natchez, Mississippi. The name, belonging to a single town, was extended to the tribe and an entire group of towns, which included also peoples of alien blood who had been conquered by the Natchez or had taken refuge with them. Iberville, on his ascent of the Mississippi in 1699, names in the Choctaw language the following eight towns exclusive of Natchez proper: Achougoulas, Cogoucoula, Ousagoucoula, Pochougoula, Thoucoue, Tougoulas, Yatanocas, and Ymacachas.

It is difficult to form an estimate of the numerical strength of this tribe, as the figures given vary widely. It is probable that in 1682, when first visited by the French, they numbered about six thousand and were able to put from a thousand to twelve hundred warriors in the field.[10]

The Natchez engaged in three wars with the French—in 1716, 1722, and 1729. The last, which proved fatal to their nation, was caused by the attempt of the French governor, Chopart, to occupy the site of their principal village as a plantation. It opened with a general massacre of the French at Fort Rosalie in 1716. In retaliation the French, with a strong force of Choctaw allies, attacked Natchez villages, and in 1730 the Natchez abandoned their villages, separating themselves into three bodies. A small section remained not far from their former home, and a second body fled to a point near Washita River, where they were attacked early in 1731 by the French, many of them being killed, and about 450 being captured and sold into slavery in Santo Domingo.[11] The third and most numerous division was received by the Chickasaw and built a village near them in northern Mississippi, called by Adair "Nanne Hamgah." In 1735 these refugees numbered 180 warriors, or a total of about 700. In this same year a body of Natchez refugees settled in South Carolina with the permission of the Colonial government, but some years later they moved up to the Cherokee country, where they retained their distinct town and language up to about the year 1800. The principal body of refugees, however, had settled on Tallahassee Creek, an affluent of Coosa River. Hawkins in 1799 estimated their rifle-men at about fifty. They occupied the whole of one town called Nauchee and part of Abikudshi.

The Natchez were therefore not exterminated by the French, as has frequently been stated, but, after suffering severe losses, were scattered far and wide among alien tribes. A few survivors who speak their own language still exist in Oklahoma, living with the Cherokee;[12] on the west side of the Illinois River about four miles above Gore, Oklahoma, in a little settlement called Notche Town, are about two hundred Natchez, all the known survivors of this tribe. A research student from the department of anthropology of the University of Chicago spent several weeks a few years ago at Braggs, Oklahoma, with Watt Sam, a member of this lonely clan, in an effort to learn and record the language of these people before it should be utterly lost and forgotten.

NEZ PERCÉS

One of the most romantic names in Indian literature is that of Chief Joseph of the Nez Percés Indians—a man whose character and military strategy have long been celebrated in the annals of the West, related around campfires, and recorded by army officers and other writers of history. The life of this chief and his followers as part of the immigrant Indian population of Oklahoma is little known.

These Indians were given the name Nez Percés (meaning "pierced noses") by the French, from the fact that in the early days they wore rings in their noses. When the white people of the United States began their association with them, they occupied a beautiful area in Idaho, Washington, and Oregon. As the whites began to penetrate their country, they were importuned by the government to cede their domain and remove to a reservation. The Indians stoutly opposed these efforts; valiant old Chief Joseph scorned the arguments and efforts of the white man, saying that the Nez Percés loved their country and would never consent to give it up. However, the white man was relentless in his efforts. Employing tactics that had been effective with other tribes, he induced some of the minor chiefs to enter into a pretended treaty on June 11, 1855, and again in 1863 and 1868, giving up all their domain except a small reservation in Idaho known as the Lapwai lands, upon which the Nez Percés were required to locate.

Chief Joseph was not a party to these treaties and refused to be bound by them. He was an old man and on his deathbed, taking the hand of his son, said to him: "My son, my body is returning to my mother earth, and my spirit is going very soon to see the Great Spirit Chief. When I am gone, think of your country. You are the chief of these people. They look to you to guide them. Always remember that your father never sold his country. You must stop your ears whenever you are asked to sign a treaty selling your home. A few years more, and white men will be all around you. They have their eyes on this land. My son, never forget my dying words. This country holds your father's body. Never sell the bones of your father and your mother." This son was also named Joseph, the great Chief Joseph of history. It is small wonder that the dying words of his father kindled in his mind the resolution to resist to the end the blandishments and intimidation of the white man.

Young Joseph was a man of fine presence and impressive features, one of the most remarkable in Indian history. The treaties by which the whites obtained the right to the Wallowa Valley, the ancient home of Joseph's band in northeastern Oregon, were ignored by Joseph and his Indian followers, who continued to dwell there in spite of collisions with the whites, which became more and more frequent.

However, the subject of removing these Indians to the Lapwai reservation in Idaho, after the failure of a commission the previous year, was proceeding to a peaceful settlement when the outrageous acts on the part of the white settlers caused the Nez Percés to attack the settlement. War was declared. After several engagements in which the whites lost severely, Joseph displayed remarkable generalship in a retreat worthy to be remembered with that of Xenophon's ten thousand. In spite of the fact that in front of him were the troops of Colonel Nelson A. Miles, at his rear, those of General O. O. Howard, and on his flank, those of Colonel Samuel D. Sturgis and his Indian scouts, Joseph brought his little band, burdened with women and children, to within fifty miles of the Canadian border, their objective point, before they were cut off by fresh troops in front and were forced to surrender on October 5, 1877. The conduct of the Nez Percés during this retreat of more than a thousand miles and the military and tactical skill displayed by their leader won unstinted praise from their conquerors.

The surrender by Joseph and his people was conditioned on their being allowed to return home and live on the Lapwai reservation. General Miles endeavored to have that condition complied with, but the lieutenant general of the army strongly objected, and an order was issued by the War Department in November, 1877, to send all the Nez Percés to the Missouri River. Accordingly, Colonel Miles reluctantly sent the whole band, numbering 431, as prisoners to Fort Leavenworth, Kansas, where they were delivered to the agent on December 21, 1877.

To their great disgust and sorrow they were given as a camping place a low river bottom with no water except river water for drinking and with which to cook. They had always lived in a healthy country where the mountains were high, the air fresh, and the water cold and clear. In the new and unfamiliar surroundings of their prison camp many of them sickened and died and were buried in the strange land. At one time 260 of them were prostrated by sickness, and within a few months they lost by death more than a fourth of their entire number, besides three children who died on the journey from their homes.

The Indian agent at the Quapaw agency, H. W. Jones, was instructed on July 14, 1878, to go to Fort Leavenworth and bring the

Nez Percés prisoners to the Indian Territory. After making the necessary arrangements, a week later the agent and Inspector McNeil placed the Nez Percés on the train and brought them to Baxter Springs, Kansas, the evening of the same day. The next day they and their belongings were loaded into wagons and moved onto the Modoc reservation (part of the Quapaw reservation) near the agency. A few weeks later the agent purchased from the Peoria and Miami Indians seven thousand acres of land as a home for Joseph and his band. On July 30 four more arrived who had been in Canada visiting some of the tribe who were with Sitting Bull.[13]

Chief Joseph continued bitter in his denunciation of the violation of the agreement under which he had surrendered, which, he said, contemplated return to his old home. He refused to commit himself to acceptance of the purchase of the land from the resident Indians and said that he and his people would never consent to live there. Much sickness continued among them from the malarial germs acquired in their camp on the Missouri River, and a number died, but their health gradually improved in their Indian Territory camps.

After the removal of the company with the prisoners who accompanied Chief Joseph, other detachments were brought from their old homes to join the exiles, who helped to recruit the ranks decimated by death. A muster roll of these unhappy Indians made on February 10, 1879, and now in the archives of the Oklahoma Historical Society, gives a total of three hundred and eighty-four members, including men, women, and boys and girls. The list is headed by Chief Joseph, whose family included four men and three women.

The location of these Indians at the Quapaw agency, so near to Baxter Springs, Kansas, was unfortunate. An Indian agent accompanied Chief Joseph to the west of the Arkansas River to find a permanent home for the band. They selected a tract of four townships on the Ponca reserve where the Chikaskia empties into Salt Fork of the Arkansas River. A bill was subsequently introduced in Congress, authorizing the purchase of this land for them, and orders were given to remove the Nez Percés to this place. Considerable preparation was necessary, including the purchase of horses, wagons, etc., with which to move, but a start was made on June 6, with thirty-nine teams in addition to those of the Indians'. The journey of 180 miles was accomplished in nine days, and the Indians delivered to the Ponca agent, W. H. Whiteman, on June 15, 1879.

Most of the Indians located on the west bank of Chikaskia River about two miles from its confluence with the Salt Fork. The agent reported that their health was as good as could be expected under the circumstances. Most of the young and able-bodied men and women had been engaged in the late war with the whites, and many of these had been killed and wounded, so a large proportion of those now in the Indian Territory were old people and children, among whom the rate of sickness and mortality had been very high. While many had died of malaria, other large numbers were dying from pneumonia.

The number of Nez Percés located on their new reservation was 370. The agent said that they were of small frame and sharp features. The women were far superior to the men, who were indolent, and, indeed, were superior to any Indians he had ever seen. They were intelligent, very clean in their habits, exceedingly expert with the needle, vivacious and friendly, and, contrary to all other Indian women he had known, always responded to a white man's salutation with a friendly nod and smile.

The next year (1880) the children of the Nez Percés began attending the day school opened among them, taught by James Reuben, a fullblood member of their tribe, who had received his education at the Nez Percés agency in Idaho. He was devoted to the best interests of his people, laboring among them as a missionary as well as teacher, and on the Sabbath he held religious services, which were well attended. They were a religious people, and under the intelligent teachings of Reuben they were strict observers of the Sabbath, refusing to perform any labor whatsoever on that day. Twice on Sunday they met to listen to their minister's preaching and to sing hymns, interspersed with an occasional prayer. Their services were conducted with perfect order, and the congregation was as much interested in the proceedings as the white people in any church in the country. In bad weather they held services in a large tent erected for the purpose in Husses-Knutte's camp, but in pleasant weather their meetings were held in the open air under a brush arbor. They desired a building erected for church purposes.

The agent said that these Nez Percés were an intelligent, religious, and industrious people, ready and willing to work and help themselves, and that if agricultural implements, draft animals, and seeds were furnished them, they would do much toward their self-support. With only twenty-three teams at their disposal, they had hauled all their supplies a hundred miles from a railroad terminal in Kansas, besides breaking a hundred acres of prairie land and hauling logs for houses. They had good gardens in which they raised melons, potatoes, and other vegetables. They were taking excellent care of the ninety-six head of cattle issued to them. The agent said that they appeared to be natural herders and that they showed better judgment in the management of their stock than any other Indians he had even seen.

In the autumn of 1881 the agent reported their number to be 328, but much sickness and many deaths continued among them during the year. This, from the fact, he said, that they had not become acclimated and were, to a great extent, compelled to live in tepees, the cloth of which had become so rotten from long wear and the effects of the weather as to be no longer capable of keeping out the rain, which soaked the occupants and made them miserable. At the rate that they were dying, the agent said, they would soon become extinct unless something was done for them.[14]

Of all the Indians within his acquaintance, the agent said, they appeared to him as the most intelligent, truthful, and truly religious under their pastor, the Reverend Archie Lawyer, a full-blood Nez Percés Indian. One hundred and twenty-four of the tribe had joined the Presbyterian church organized among them during the year by the synod of Kansas. The piety, the universal attendance, the attention, and the general good conduct of these people elevated them much above their more favored white brethren. Poor as they were, they contributed $45 with which to buy the lumber and other material necessary to build a house for the pastor.[15]

These things, however, could not beguile the unhappy expatriates from their grief at separation from their own land. Love of country, as in all brave people, said their agent, was largely developed in this tribe, and they longed for the mountains and the valleys, the streams and the clear springs, of their old home. They were cleanly to a fault, and most of them had adopted the dress and, as far as possible, the habits of the white men.

The females outnumbered the males by more than a hundred. This surplus was represented by the widows of the warriors who fell during the war. These poor women were longing to go to Idaho to their friends and relatives, and the sympathetic agent urged the Indian Department to grant their prayer. Said he: "So brave, good and generous a people deserve well of their government, and I can only express the hope that such action will be taken at the coming congress in their behalf as may enable the department to furnish them with the horses and implements which they so much need. Such a people should not be allowed to perish, and this great government can afford to be generous and just."[16]

For some unaccountable reason the government had not provided for them so that they might make themselves independent by their own industry, and the Indians continued year after year in a state of suspense and uncertainty. During all the time since their surrender these people had exhibited a quiet and unmurmuring submission to the inevitable and had manifested a desire to obey all laws and regulations provided for their government; yet from time to time numerous petitions, urgent requests, and pathetic appeals had come from them praying to be returned to their old home and relatives. Thomas J. Jordan, the agent who assumed the office at the Ponca agency in 1882, said that these Indians were brave, energetic, exemplary, and faithful. "Their history from the earliest times of which we have any record is one of wonderful interest. Never large in numbers, the natural enemy of the Sioux, the Blackfeet, the Flatheads and the Crows, they maintained their position amidst a host of surrounding enemies and drove from their soil all intruders.

"Filled with a love of country—almost worshipping the high mountains, bright flashing streams, and rich fertile valleys of Idaho—they have inherited and transmitted to their children a name for bravery, truthfulness and honor of which they may indeed be proud.

"The unfortunate war into which they were driven in 1877 with the United States is far from being a blot on their escutcheon, and all brave, high minded people the world over will honor them for their gallant defense of their homes, their families, and their hunting ground. When they surrendered to superior force they did it in the most solemn manner and under the most solemn promises of protection and a return to their own country. That that promise has not been kept is an historical fact and has never been explained. Might never made right, and the power to punish can never excuse its exercise wrongfully. As the years go by the eyes of this people are turned to the northwest, and their yearning hearts pulsate naught but Idaho."[17]

The prayers of the Indians and the recommendation of their agent finally prevailed, and, when Reuben closed another successful school year at the end of May, 1883, by permission of the Indian Department and at an expense of $1,625, which Jordan himself advanced, he started for Idaho with twenty-nine Nez Percés, mostly widows and orphans of warriors killed during the war. The joy and anticipation of these poor people at the prospect of again seeing the mountains and streams they loved and of rejoining their relatives and friends in their old homes was very touching and must have brought a glow to the heart of the agent who was responsible for bringing it about. The Indians who remained in the Indian Territory continued industrious and faithful to their church, still in charge of the Reverend Archie Lawyer. They were fairly industrious, and, with the meager equipment furnished them by the government, they supported themselves by the cultivation of the soil;; they also obtained considerable cash from the manufacture and sale of Indian curiosities and trinkets, such as bows and arrows, moccasins and gloves, which they made in a tasteful manner.

These Nez Percés in the Indian Territory continued to improve and conduct themselves in an exemplary manner. Their agent reported in 1884: "They receive what is provided for them with apparent thankfulness, ask for nothing more and give no trouble whatever. They are extremely anxious to return to their own country. They regard themselves as exiles. The climate does not seem to agree with them, many of them have died, and there is a tinge of melancholy in their bearing and conversation that is truly pathetic. I think they should be sent back, as it seems clear they will never take root and prosper in this locality.

"The longing to return to their old homes and the unsettled feeling it naturally produces have no doubt interfered with their progress in farming and improving their lands. Nevertheless many of them have made very creditable progress, and have provided themselves with cozy and comfortable homes, and all seem inclined to work more or less. They are naturally, I think, more industrious than most Indians. The women especially are bright and active and exceedingly ingenious in the way of needlework, embroidery, etc. They manufacture a number of useful articles in a beautiful and tasteful manner, from the sale of which they realize a considerable income during the year."[18]

General Nelson A. Miles was a friend of the Nez Percés and a warm admirer of Chief Joseph. Though he was in command of the military expedition that resulted in the capture of these unhappy Indians, he sympathized with them in their misfortune and "frequently and persistently for seven long years," he said, after their capture, urged the War Department to return them to their home in Idaho. But it was not until 1884, when he was in command of the Department of the Columbia, did he succeed "in having them returned west of the mountains to near their own country, where they have remained in peace ever since."[19]

During the year 1884 these poor people were agitated over the subject of returning to their western home and confidently expected to go in the autumn. But the authorities neglected and disappointed them. Under this state of suspense they did not accomplish much in the way of industry and improvement, though they did continue to send their children regularly to the day school at Chilocco.

The Indians passed the winter in excited and pathetic anticipation of departing in the spring. Finally, in May, 1885, through the intercession of General Miles, Chief Joseph and his people were allowed to depart. The Indians were the possessors of coffee-boilers and cups. The agent purchased for them 2,000 pounds of bread, 2,498 pounds of beef, 140 pounds of coffee, and 163 pounds of sugar. Loading these supplies and their personal effects in wagons, thirty-five teams were employed to haul them to the railroad at Arkansas City, Kansas. On May 21, with eager anticipation, these expatriates left the agency and on the following day arrived at Arkansas City. Here they were joined by their children, who had been brought from school at Chilocco. They were then all placed on a special train of seven passenger cars. Of this company, 180 arrived at Lapwai, Idaho, on June 1, and reported to the agent. They were immediately taken to the hearts and homes of their friends.

Under the leader, Chief Joseph, the remainder, numbering 118, who were considered the leaders in the hostilities of 1877, were not allowed to return to Idaho but were taken to the beautiful Colville Indian reservation in Washington Territory. Before they were turned loose, however, the stern Indian agent had the long locks of the warriors cut. In their new location Chief Joseph proved himself a wise and capable leader under whom his people soon adjusted themselves to their new surroundings, built homes, and cultivated the fertile land on which they were located.

For twelve years Chief Joseph lived quietly on this reservation; but in 1897, becoming alarmed by renewed encroachments of the whites, he again took up the defense of his people, this time going to Washington and pleading with President McKinley. Again it was General Miles, the only white man whom he believed and trusted, who promised him that his people would not be molested in the lands they now occupied.

Returning to the reservation, he settled down to enjoy the peace and quiet of old age, making only one more trip, this time a friendly visit to President Roosevelt and to his old friend, General Miles. During this journey he took part in "Cummings' Indian Congress and Life on the Plains" while that show was exhibiting at Madison Square Garden. A year after this trip he dropped dead in front of his tepee, on September 22, 1904—a peaceful ending for "the Indian Xenophon, the Red Napoleon of the West."[20]

NEW YORK INDIANS

At an early date the New York Indians became involved with a corporation of white men, known as the "Ogden Land Company," which swindled them out of their land by a series of complicated transactions achieved by bribing some of the chiefs and securing their signatures after getting them drunk.[21] An interesting phase of the subject is the fact that, in order to promote their plans, the Ogden company employed the Reverend Eleazer Williams, a half-breed St. Regis Indian serving as a missionary, who figured in the famous hoax that identified him as the "Lost Dauphin" of France, and who aided the company in getting the Indians to consider a location far to the west.[22] A deal had been entered into with the Winnebago and Menominee Indians for certain territorial rights, but, for want of correct mutual understanding as to the terms, much controversy resulted, which was finally settled by a treaty between the Menominee and the United States, concluded in February, 1831,[23] to which the New York Indians gave their assent on October 17, 1832. In this treaty 500,000 acres of the Menominee reservation on Green Bay were secured to the New York Indians of the Six Nations and to the St. Regis tribe as a future home, on condition that they remove to it within three years, or in such reasonable time as the President should indicate.

The New York Indians were divided on the subject of emigration and took no steps to that end. On the contrary, the faction opposed to removal, who seemed to be in the majority, convened a council and ordained that "the Chiefs and Headmen of the Seneca Nation of Indians being assembled on the 29th day of July A.D. 1833, convened at the council house at the Buffalo Creek Reservation in the State of New York do ordain and establish this constitution for the Seneca Nation," in which it was declared that any chief or headman who should drink any rum, brandy, gin, or other ardent spirits should be deposed from his office and that any headman or chief "otherwise than a majority of chiefs, transacting business in the name of the Seneca Nation, respecting enrolling their names in favor of removing from their lands or using their influence to persuade the chiefs to sell, exchange or in any way to dispose of their lands to the whites, should be no longer a chief of the nation." This was signed by fifty-eight chiefs taking part in the council.[24]

After three years had passed and the Indians indicated no intention to remove, James Stryker was sent to confer with them on the subject. Accordingly, a council of the Indians was convened at Buffalo Creek Reservation; it was composed of two chiefs from each reservation, one of whom was from the Pagan party, opposed to emigration, and the other from the faction favorable to removal.[25]

The Indians held another meeting on October 15, 1833, when they agreed on a memorial to the President, in which they said that "after mature reflection and patiently discussing . . . . a matter so momentous to us as a people [they decided not] to part with more of our territory." This was signed by Big Kettle, Daniel Two Guns, Little Johnson, and White Seneca.[26] No decision was reached, but a delegation of six Seneca from the faction favorable to removal was selected to explore the western country. They departed under the conduct of H. P. Wilcox, who reported their arrival at Louisville on December 3, 1834.[27]

They explored the country in the northeastern part of Oklahoma, conferred with their kinsmen already located there, and after suffering great hardship from fatigue, cold, and sickness, turned their faces homeward. On February 22, 1835, they had progressed as far as Little Rock, whence they continued on to their eastern home.[28]

With a view to escaping the continuing sharp practices and other impositions of the white people in New York, the Indians decided to investigate further whether they might better their condition by joining their kinsmen in the West. Accordingly, under the direction of their agent, James Stryker of Buffalo, who reported progress on arrival at Louisville, Kentucky, they sent a committee to examine the country west of Missouri with a view to finding a location suitable for a new home.[29] This exploring party was composed of White Seneca and five other Seneca and Cayuga chiefs. They reached the Osage River on October 1, 1837, passed Harmony Mission, and on the fifth crossed the state line into the Cherokee Nation. On December 26 they made a detailed report of their explorations.

It later appeared that some of the Indians preferred to remove at once to the Indian Territory, which they were persuaded was the only permanent and peaceable home for all the Indians (at least that is the language employed by the scrivener in preparing the subsequent treaty the Indians were induced to sign). These Indians, therefore, asked the President to take back the Green Bay lands and to provide them a home in the Indian Territory instead.

Pursuant to the wishes of the Indians as expressed in the treaty, a new, long, and complicated treaty was executed at Buffalo Creek, New York, on January 15, 1838,[30] in which the several tribes of New York Indians relinquished to the United States all their land at Green Bay ceded to them by the Menominee treaty of 1831,[31] save a small reservation where some of their tribesmen had already located.

Article 2 of this treaty recited that in consideration of said cession, "in order to manifest the deep interest of the United States in the future peace and prosperity of the New York Indians, the United States agree to set apart .... as a permanent home for all the New York Indians now residing in the state of New York or in Wisconsin or elsewhere in the United States who have no permanent home, a tract of country within the present Eastern Kansas amounting to 1,824,000 acres, being 320 acres for each of said Indians." This area was a strip about twenty miles wide, extending west from the Missouri line, and included Fort Scott, Iola, Center, and Eureka, and ending just east of Eldorado. It was to be divided among the Indians, according to their numbers, as shown in the accompanying table.[32]

On the Seneca reservation:

Seneca	2,309
Onondaga	194
Cayuga	130
Total	2,633
Onondaga at Onondaga	300
Tuscarora	273
St. Regis in New York	350
Oneida at Green Bay	600
Oneida in New York	620
Stockbridge	217
Munsee	132
Brothertown	300
Grand total	5,425

The treaty contained a number of special provisions to adjust incidental questions of ownership and others that arose in connection with the affairs of the Indians. This treaty was signed by representatives of the Seneca, Tuscarora, Oneida, St. Regis, Onondaga, and Cayuga tribes who undertook to cede to the United States, with certain exceptions, all their interests in lands at Green Bay, secured to them by the Menominee treaty of 1831.

But still the Indians could not bring themselves to leave their old home, and it was necessary to negotiate another treaty on May 20, 1842, with the Seneca Indians to effectuate a deal with the Ogden Land Company.[33] This treaty undertook to settle questions then pending, as well as others involved with the emigration of the Indians to the West, though no obligations were assumed by the Indians or by the federal government in connection with the emigration.

Removal of these reluctant Indians was slow, and it was not until 1846 that anything like organized emigration was undertaken. The War Department had notified the Indians that it would not undertake to care for the emigration of less than a party of 250 Indians, on the ground that it would be too expensive to conduct them in smaller parties.

One Dr. Abraham Hogebloom was commissioned to act as removal agent for the Indians, with instructions that stressed particularly the minimum number to be removed with whom he was to proceed to their western home in the autumn of 1845. A delegation of Indians, anxious to be on the way to their new home, came to Washington in September, 1845, and reported that 260 were ready to start. Authority was then given to the emigrating agent to proceed. However, the requisite number still could not be organized, and such confusion attended the undertaking that the coming of cold weather made it necessary to postpone removal.

The next spring Hogebloom renewed his undertaking, but in spite of his efforts and those of the Indians who were desirous of going west, 250 Indians could not be enrolled for the adventure; disregarding his instructions, Hogebloom departed in June with only 213 Indians and had proceeded beyond the reach of the War Department before his violation of orders was known. Of his party, 62 deserted and departed for Canada instead of going west. A great deal of confusion resulted.[34]

Having left New York without due preparation for the comfort and health of the emigrants, much suffering and many deaths resulted. The flies became so bad, as they neared the Indian Territory, that they could travel only at night. The Tuscarora Indians in the party accepted the invitation of the hospitable Shawnee in Kansas to abide for a time with them until they should regain their health, which was greatly impaired by the hardships of the journey.[35]

The survivors of the expedition undertook to open up little farms; but, incapacitated by sickness and reduced in numbers by the mounting death rate, they made slight progress. Eighty-two of them died in the West, and, discouraged and impoverished by their experiences, ninety-four started back to New York the next year, leaving ten who were sick to follow after they should have gathered and disposed of their little crops. They went by way of St. Louis, and, in August, forty-five of them reached Buffalo on the steamboat *Buffalo*, in charge of Doctor Peter Wilson, an intelligent, educated Indian chief, who has been deputed for the purpose. "About thirty more are on the way and will arrive in a few days. These, with the exception of some six or seven who remain a short time to dispose of the few effects of the tribe, are all that survive out of 213 reported by the agent as having been removed. The story of their suffering, were it not borne out by the frightful mortality that has prevailed, and the sickly and emaciated countenances of the survivors, would appear incredible. In many instances both parents and children, after a delirium of several days found themselves childless or orphans, the parent or child having been consigned to their mother earth during their delirium. The government made no provision for their comfort, and the rations distributed among them were in many instances of inferior quality. The annuity due them in 1846 has been withheld and has not been paid them to this day.

"Soon after their arrival in the west, where they had been seduced by cunningly devised tales, pathetic appeals were made by them to their friends in New York for aid to return. Application was made both to the national and state governments without success, when the necessary amount obtained by individual contributions, mostly from their devoted and steadfast Quaker friends in Baltimore, Philadelphia, and N. York. When Dr. W[ilson] appeared among them like Moses among the Israelites, he was regarded as their deliverer, and although many were in feeble health, they eagerly embraced the opportunity to return at the risk of their lives. Two died on the way. We shall have more to say on the subject."[36]

The Indians who wandered back to New York destitute were quartered with some of their friends and relatives.[37] In 1852 thirty-six more of the "Six Nations or New York Indians" arrived at the Osage River agency in Kansas. They had contracted disease on the journey west and were dependent on charity. They planned, when able to travel, to join their brethren on their lands south and contiguous to that of the Miami.[38] The Commissioner of Indian Affairs, in 1857, recommended the area set apart for the New York Indians and not occupied by them should be allotted in part so that the few who had emigrated should receive their share and that the remainder of the land be put on the market for sale.[39]

The Kansas reservation set apart for the New York Indians was soon overrun by white people, making the situation of the Indians acute.[40] It was reported by the Commissioner of Indian Affairs that in 1860 thirty-two New York Indians had taken allotments on their reservation in Kansas and that the remainder of the reserve had been surveyed for entry by white settlers.[41] The next year it was reported that the New York Indians who for many years had been living on the lands of the Delawares, with their permission, desired an adjustment of their affairs so that they could remove onto lands of their own to make their homes. The superintendent strongly urged that this measure of relief be provided for.[42] After this tract was set apart, the Indians, with few exceptions, refused to remove to and occupy it. The Tonawanda band of Seneca released all their claim to it by treaty of 1857. After remaining unoccupied for many years, the Indians' right was declared forfeited and the tract restored to the public domain, except in the case of 10,215.63 acres in the northeastern corner of the present Bourbon County, which were allotted to thirty-two of the New York Indians who had removed to and settled upon the reserve. The occupancy by these thirty-two Indians was not, however, permanent, and by act of Congress of February 19, 1873, provision was made for the sale of these allotments to white settlers, the proceeds to be paid to the allottees or to their heirs.[43]

A number of these so-called New York Indians were living in Canada subject to the supervision of the Canadian Indian Office at Brantford. On January 27, 1881, Canadian Indian Superintendent I. V. Gilkison at Brantford wrote the Quapaw Indian agent, inquiring about a band of his (Cayuga) Indians who had left Canada to join the others of their tribe in the Indian Territory, who were said to have agreed to receive these Cayuga and adopt them into the Seneca tribe. The United States Commissioner of Indian Affairs, on August 10, 1881, wrote D. B. Dyer, agent at the Quapaw agency, to notify these Seneca chiefs that they had no right to receive foreign Indians among them without consent of the Department of the Interior. Notwithstanding this, forty more Cayuga arrived about the first of November, 1881, and the Indian agent was perplexed by the problem of caring for them.

An interminable amount of correspondence resulted between Canada and the United States. Notwithstanding the objections made by the Indian officials, thirty-two more came early in December, 1881—twenty-six from Canada and six from New York. The Indian agent at the Quapaw agency was ordered by the Commissioner not to enter the names of these Indians on the annuity rolls at the Quapaw agency. The new arrivals were said to be the most ignorant and worthless Indians of the tribe, and their presence promised to be a detriment to the western Indians. The Canadian agent, on January 9, 1882, wrote to the Quapaw agency, making inquiries about the Canadian Indians, their number, the names of those who had died, the condition of the living, their disposition as to returning to Canada, and the amount of railway fare by way of Buffalo to Caledonia, sixty miles beyond.

It developed that the earlier Cayuga arrivals were adopted by the Seneca Indians at the Quapaw agency, and those who followed hoped to be similarly favored. Having discovered their mistake, a number of the disillusioned Cayuga started to walk back to Canada. One, David Sandy, on his return reported that thirteen of his friends had died.

On April 26, 1882, Canadian Indian Superintendent I. V. Gilkison sent a draft for $550 to D. B. Dyer, Quapaw Indian agent, to pay for the return of the Cayuga to Canada. However, only eleven adults, with two children, availed themselves of the opportunity to return to their old homes.

The result is that, while the name "Cayuga" does not appear among the names of tribes recognized in Oklahoma, the tribe is certainly represented through the admixture of blood with the Seneca Indians.

STOCKBRIDGE AND MUNSEE

Stockbridge Indians with a number of Munsee fled to Canada during the War of 1812. From there they removed to Ohio and later, with the addition of a few Oneida Indians, to a tract of land at the head of Green Bay, Wisconsin, which had been purchased from the Menominee. Schoolcraft relates in his memoirs that on August 12, 1837, a party of 202 Munsee and Delaware Indians from the River Thames in Upper Canada reached his agency at Mackinac in a vessel bound for Green Bay, Wisconsin. With 68 others who were traveling by land, they were on the way to visit the Stockbridge at Green Bay and then continue on to join their Delaware kindred in Kansas. With their conductor, the Reverend Mr. Vogel, some of them came ashore at Mackinac to visit the agency and gratify their curiosity concerning the island.

Before the Munsee left Green Bay for Kansas they were incorporated with the Stockbridge, with whom they thereafter existed as one tribe. In 1839 the combined tribe, then numbering about 400, sold half of their reservation in Wisconsin on the east side of Lake Winnebago and agreed to remove to lands assigned them on the Kansas River. One party of 169 of them removed by way of Prairie du Chien down the Mississippi and up the Missouri to Fort Leavenworth. They themselves arranged their passage by steamboat down the Mississippi for which they paid $4,488. About seven miles below Fort Leavenworth they located on the lands of the Delaware Indians. They were good citizens, industrious and enterprising, built log cabins of hewn logs, and cultivated small farms on which they raised corn and vegetables, setting a good example for other Indians. They were subsequently reported as part of the Delaware tribe,[44] and in 1848 the agent said that the Munsee were amalgamated with their brethren, the Delawares, and that they were properly considered as part of that tribe.[45] However, in 1849, the Delawares objected to the presence of these Indians on their land without compensation, and the agent recommended that part of the Delaware land be purchased for them.

In 1851 the agent spoke of them as an educated people, but said that they had become much addicted to drunkenness. During that summer about forty Delawares, Shawnee, Maumee, and Stockbridge died from cholera, and thirty-two from whiskey and disease. Their number was steadily diminishing, and in 1853 the agent reported that there were only eighteen or twenty remaining, including but three men among them. From their addiction to whiskey introduced by the white man, they had become destitute and were suffering for food. But in 1854, in the treaty with the Delawares, provision was made whereby the latter conveyed to them four sections of land occupied by them for $2.50 an acre.[46] Three years later these Indians, still living seven miles below Leavenworth, Kansas, finding themselves surrounded and pressed upon by white people, were induced to sell their four sections of land to A. J. Isaacs for $43,400, and it is now occupied by the Old Soldiers' Home and Muncie Cemetery.[47]

The "Munsee or Christian Indians" were confederated with the Swan Creek and Black River bands of Chippewa Indians in Kansas, under the stipulations of the treaty of July 16, 1859.[48] During the days of reconstruction, while the Cherokee themselves were still in a distracted condition from the ravages of war, they took pity on the Munsee Indians and, observing their identification with the Delawares, entered into a compact with the survivors of that tribe on December 6, 1867, in which it was recited that, "actuated by motives of humanity and sincere desire to do good to all civilized Indians," they agreed to receive the Munsee or Christian Indians into the Cherokee Nation and to confer upon them all the rights and privileges of Cherokee citizenship.

The Munsee were to conform to and obey the laws of the Cherokee Nation and to pay to said nation the sum of four thousand dollars,[49] which was a small fraction of the consideration required from the Delaware and Shawnee nations for similar privileges. Definite information as to the extent to which this contract was executed is not available to the author. But from data at hand it can be said with confidence that some members of this fast-disappearing tribe actually removed from Kansas and located in the Indian Territory with the Cherokee and intermingled their blood.[50]

NOTES

1. *Handbook*, I, 213; reference is made to this authority for an extended account of Catawba history.

2. 9 *U.S. Stat.* 264.

3. *Report of the Commissioner of Indian Affairs, 1848*, p. 949.

4. Grant Foreman, *The Five Civilized Tribes*, p. 122.

5. *Ibid.*, p. 76.

6. *Choctaw Laws* (1869 ed.), p. 125.

7. *Ibid.*, p. 153.

8. They had previously met at Rocky Ridge and Ault's Mill, Arkansas (*Fort Smith Elevator*, August 16, 1839, p. 3, col. 6).

9. These were probably part of a delegation that removed to Colorado and New Mexico in 1890, some of whom joined the Mormon church. See an interesting article, "The Catawba Nation and Its Neighbors," *North Carolina Historical Review*, Vol. XVI, No. 4.

10. Le Page du Pratz, *Histoire de la Louisiane*, III, 218.

11. Carolyn Thomas Foreman, *Indians Abroad*, p. 57.

12. *Handbook*, II, 35. For an account of the few survivors in Indian Territory of this now extinct tribe of Indians see John R. Swanton, *Indian Tribes of the Lower Mississippi Valley*, p. 256.

13. *Report*, 1878, p. 67.

14. Agent to Commissioner of Indian Affairs, September 5, 1881, Ponca Letter Press Book (Oklahoma Historical Society); *Report, 1881*, p. 94.

15. *Report, 1881*, p. 94.

16. *Ibid.*

17. *Report, 1882*, p. 76.

18. *Report, 1884*, p. 89.

19. *Report, 1885*, p. 96; General Nelson A. Miles, *Personal Recollections and*

Observations, p. 415. General Miles doubtless secured authority for their removal in 1884, though they did not actually leave until the next May.

20. Miles, *op. cit.*, p. 415.

21. For further details of these Indians see *Report of Special Committee To Investigate the Indian Problem of the State of New York, Appointed by the Assembly of 1888, Transmitted to the Legislature of February 1, 1889* (Albany: Troy Press Co., 1889).

22. *University of Michigan Alumnus Quarterly Review*, XLIX (December 19, 1942), 59.

23. 7 *U.S. Stat.* 342.

24. See "Documents and Memorials" (National Archives), Tray 264, "Senecas (Emigration)."

25. *Ibid.*

26. *Ibid.*

27. *Ibid.*

28. *Ibid.*, Tray 293.

29. *Ibid.*, Tray 264.

30. 7 *U.S. Stat.* 550, 551

31. *Ibid.*, pp. 342, 551.

32. "Indian Land Cessions," *Eighteenth Annual Report of the Bureau of American Ethnology, 1896–1897*, p. 771.

33. 7 *U.S. Stat.* 586.

34. *Report, 1846*, pp. 214–15. See also *Friends' Review*, Vol. I, No. 40, p. 24; *Report, 1848*, p. 665.

35. *Report, 1846*, pp. 233, 234, 235.

36. Account in *Buffalo Advertiser*, reprinted in *Niles' Register*, August 21, 1847, p. 389; see same account in *New York Weekly Tribune*, August 4, 1847, p. 5, col. 6.

37. *Report, 1847*, pp. 890–92.

38. *Report, 1852*, p. 388.

39. *Report, 1857*, p. 296.

40. *Report, 1853*, p. 137. Before 1860 the lands of the Shawnee, Miami, Confederated Bands of Kaskaskia, Peoria, and Wea and Piankashaw had been allotted to the individuals in severalty. These Indians were thus scattered among the white settlements, exposed to all the evils resulting from unrestrained intercourse with the whites, and the Commissioner of Indian Affairs urged their removal from Kansas, with the observation that this action would "open to settlement some of the richest and most productive lands in Kansas" (*Report, 1860*, p. 37). "About 100 New York Indians made themselves comfortable homes but when the lands were thrown open to white settlement, they were compelled by the lawless violence of the citizens to abandon them" (*Report, 1867*, p. 18).

41. *Report, 1860*, pp. 238–344.

42. *Report, 1861*, p. 12.

43. See also acts of June 23, 1874, and April 17, 1878.

44. *Report, 1843*, p. 411.

45. *Report, 1848*, p. 445.

46. 10 *U.S. Stat.* 1051.

47. The sale was ratified by Congress the following year (11 *U.S. Stat.* 312).

48. Kappler (ed.), *Laws and Treaties*, II, 601; 12 *U.S. Stat.* 1105.

49. *Laws of the Cherokee Nation* (1868 ed.), p. 169.

50. In this connection it is interesting to know that on November 9, 1866, the Cherokee council considered a petition submitted by delegates of a band of Iroquois Indians living at Caughnawaga, Canada, seeking the privilege of citizenship in the Cherokee Nation. The council granted the petition on prescribed terms and gave directions for the execution of the necessary contract (*ibid.*, p. 89). On November 17, 1869, the Cherokee council and chief admitted to membership in the tribe I. Newton Parker of New York, a member of the Tonawanda band of Seneca Indians (*ibid.* [1871 ed]).

CHAPTER XX

THE QUAPAW AGENCY

AT THE present stage of the book it is appropriate to consider, collectively and finally, remnants of the eight immigrant tribes located in the northeastern two hundred thousand acres of Oklahoma, under the jurisdiction of one agency now called the Quapaw agency.

The Kaskaskia, Peoria, and Wea and Piankashaw, reduced from their former great population to 259 individuals, in order to increase their strength organized themselves into a confederacy in 1854, and from that time the government treated them as such. They suffered greatly from the depredations of their rapidly increasing white neighbors in Kansas. Their lands, allotted under the act of 1854, were taxed and sold by the state authorities in violation of law. At the beginning of the Civil War the Indians of this confederacy had begun to drift south from the reservation in Kansas and settle on the Quapaw reservation near their friends, the Seneca and Shawnee. Accompanying them were a few Miami Indians who had become disheartened and demoralized by the intrusion of white people on their lands and who left the reservation in the hope of finding a more congenial home in the Indian Territory.

In 1861 some of the Miami and the Confederated Peoria, Wea and Piankashaw, and Kaskaskia met in council and agreed to consolidate as one nation in order to increase their strength and ability to resist the aggressions of the whites. Later, after they had disposed of most of their land to the whites, they yielded to pressure of the latter, removed down into the Indian Territory, and located on the north half of the Seneca and Shawnee reservation. This location was confirmed to the confederacy in their treaty of February 23, 1867, which incorporated also the Miami Indians, now reduced to 92 from their total of 193 in 1854. Already living with the confederacy were 40 Miami who had yielded to white pressure and had left Kansas. Then the Indian Department encouraged the removal of the remainder of the tribe from that state. This was the customary solution of disputes between the whites and the Indians. White people in Kansas were not only cutting the timber on the lands of the Indians but opening farms, driving the Indians away from their homes, and refusing to believe that the red man could conceivably have any rights worthy of respect. The government not only did nothing adequate to prevent these outrages but, on the contrary, urged the Indians into measures of compliance and surrender.

A bill which seemed to offer a measure of relief for the oppressed Indians was introduced in Congress in 1870. It hung fire several years, however, while the white people were profiting by their illegal acts and possession of the land of the Indians and the latter were suffering accordingly.

The compact of union between the so-called "confederated bands" of Peoria, Kaskaskia, Wea and Piankashaw, and the Miami tribe of Indians on January 16, 1872, was reduced to writing. By this engagement the confederated bands were to convey for a stated consideration part of their 72,000-acre reservation in the Indian Territory to the Miami Indians.

The bill long pending in Congress was enacted into law on March 3, 1873;[1] it formally validated the act of union, the tribal relations of the Miami were abolished, and provision was made for such as chose to do so to remove from Kansas to the Indian Territory and unite with the "United Peoria and Miami" and for the remainder to renounce their Indian status and become citizens of the United States. The whites in Kansas were enabled by this act of Congress to buy the unallotted lands of the Indians practically on their own terms for a grossly inadequate consideration, as already explained.

Of the total Miami population, reduced from five hundred in 1846, thirty-four elected, under the act, to become citizens of the United States and seventy-two to remain Indians as members of the confederacy.

A detailed analysis of the area occupied by the eight small tribes in the northeastern corner of Oklahoma would be too complicated to attempt here. Suffice it to repeat that the first assignment to an immigrant tribe was that of 67,000 acres in 1832, at what was called the Seneca agency, on the west side of the Neosho River next to the Kansas line, to the Seneca Indians recently removed from Ohio. As previously related, when the Indians arrived they did not like the land assigned them, and accepted in exchange 60,000 acres immediately on the east side of the river and adjoining the Missouri line. The north half of this area was granted, December 29, 1832, to the Mixed Band of Seneca and Shawnee of Ohio; and the south 30,000 acres to the Seneca from Sandusky.

On May 13, 1833, by their treaty of that date, the Quapaw received from the United States, in exchange for lands elsewhere, a tract lying immediately south of the lands previously allotted to the Seneca and Shawnee, and north of the Cherokee Nation, comprising 150 sections or 96,000 acres. This area, for a long time untenanted by the Quapaw, stood thus until parts of it, by the Seneca, Shawnee, and Quapaw, were assigned to the Ottawa and Peoria confederacy. These arrangements were confirmed by the "Omnibus Treaty" of general readjustment of February 23, 1867. By this treaty the Seneca and Shawnee ceded part of the north 30,000 acres to the Ottawa Indians, the Quapaw and Peoria retaining part for themselves; and the Seneca and Shawnee confederacy was dissolved. This treaty was a complicated engagement by which each of the small tribes ceded its interest in a portion of the land held by it and passed title to others in certain designated areas.

By the same treaty the south 30,000 acres was divided between the Seneca from Sandusky and the Wyandots. Until 1870–71 this was known as the Neosho Agency.[2] The Indians then belonging to this agency were Seneca, Eastern Shawnee, Quapaw, Confederated Peoria, Kaskaskia, Piankashaw and Wea, Ottawa of Blanchard's Fork, and the Ottawa of Roche de Boeuf.

In 1870 Enoch Hoag, superintendent of Indian affairs at Lawrence, Kansas, reported that all the Indians of the Osage River agency had removed to the Indian Territory except the Miami.[3] These included, of course, the Peoria confederacy who were living within the jurisdiction of the Osage River agency, along with the Miami; but within the next year or two they also removed to join the Seneca and Shawnee in the Indian Territory.

About 1870, when the name "Shawnee Agency" attached to this jurisdiction, a permanent character of the much-reduced Indian units belatedly began to form. The "citizen" and Indian members of the Wyandot tribe began to unite. The Mixed Seneca, formerly connected with the Shawnee, were moving down and locating on the Seneca reserve and busying themselves with the erection of houses. Some of the Quapaw were locating on their reservation but were not doing too well.

Hopeful that this was to be their permanent home, but doubtless, in view of recent history, skeptical about it, the more progressive Indians tentatively addressed themselves to the establishment of homes and farms, and others responded halfheartedly to the urgings of the Indian agents. A few schools were started, but the response was meager. The most progressive of the Indians were the Wyandots, who had been badly abused in Kansas and who were quick to realize the advantage of a home far removed from the scene of their former mistreatment. The "Omnibus Treaty" having made the necessary provision, a commission appraised the amount of taxes unlawfully extorted from them by the authorities of Kansas, and Congress, on May 29, 1872, appropriated $11,703.56 to reimburse them for these losses,[4] besides $5,000 to help them get established. At the same time $20,000 was appropriated to enable the Peoria confederacy to locate on their reservation of 72,000 acres.

The subsequent career of the reservation was uneventful, though there was considerable coming and going of Indians, and consequently much confusion and little opportunity for any of the Indians to take root and improve their condition. During the uprising of hostile Indians in western Oklahoma in 1874, several thousand Kiowa, Comanche, and Cheyenne Indian captives were concentrated at Fort Sill. While the government was trying to decide on measures to deal with these Indians, Congress made an appropriation with which to purchase land from the Quapaw and on this tract locate these Indian prisoners to carry out some vague plans for civilizing them. Acting under orders of the Office of Indian Affairs, on March 26, 1875, Special Agent C. F. Larrabee arranged for the purchase of 40,000 acres of land from the Quapaw, erected a stone house 100 by 30 feet, broke out the sod of 270 acres, planted it to corn, fenced 400 acres of land—all with the expectation that the wild Indians would be induced to cultivate the land and produce corn for their food. By reason of these activities the agency was known for some time as the "Agency of the Captive Indians in the Indian Territory." When the commission appointed for the purpose was about ready to begin the removal of the prisoners, army officers objected, and the plans were suspended and were never carried out.

On July 15, 1878, H. W. Jones and Inspector McNeil went to Fort Leavenworth to receive the Nez Percés captives. After making necessary arrangements, they placed them in railroad passenger cars, on July 21, and took them to Baxter Springs, Kansas. The next day they were removed in wagons to the Quapaw agency.[5]

Concerning the Modoc Indians, Quapaw Agent H. W. Jones reported on September 21, 1874, that the 120 Indians of that tribe were turned over to him on November 22, 1873, by Special Commissioner

Captain M. C. Wilkinson. Jones proceeded to care for them in a camp near the agency. The Indians were delivered to him with no financial provision for their subsistence, and he did the best he could to help them make a crop. He had twenty acres of land plowed and then furnished the Indians with hoes, with which they planted corn, potatoes, melons, and garden vegetables. The Indians were deeply interested in this novel undertaking and watched their crops grow with absorbing solicitude. They succeeded in raising a few early vegetables, but, because of a drought, their other crops were a failure. The agent was particularly grieved over the loss of four acres of potatoes, of which the Indians were very fond, and which were scarce and expensive in the country. This agent and others invariably entertained the highest opinion of the character of the Modoc Indians, who were tractable, obedient, and persevering in their efforts to improve.[6]

Congress, in 1870, in inaugurating a new Indian policy after the Civil War, appropriated $100,000 to provide schools for the Indians, and efforts were made to interest the tribes under the Quapaw agency in enrolling their children. The response of the Wyandots was quite satisfactory, but it was several years before the other tribes could be induced to take more than a reluctant interest in the project. A significant phase developed from the fact that the Modoc Indians, who, on their arrival, were the most backward of any of the tribes, were much concerned not only in their schools but in every effort planned for their advancement. So interested were they in education that from time to time some of the adults of the tribe attended school to enjoy a privilege unknown to them in their western home. They were thrifty and enterprising, built good log cabins, tilled the soil, and did all the teaming of supplies from the railroad at Seneca, Missouri, to the agency for a wage that contributed measurably to their welfare.

However, they never ceased to grieve for their mountain home in Oregon. The agent related that they would come to him in tears, pleading for the privilege of returning to their old home or of sending someone who could bring back news of their relatives and friends.

In their new home the Modoc developed much tuberculosis, and, being sure that a return to the West would cure the victims, six consumptives and a nurse at last secured permission to go to Klamath agency in Oregon; one of them died, but the others, greatly benefited, returned to bring cheer to the exiles in the Indian Territory, nearly all of whom clamored to be allowed to go to Oregon. The doctor on the reservation, with deep sympathy for their feelings, said: "It would seem an act of mercy to allow them this one chance for life." The Modoc complained that they could not raise babies in their new home. Babies all died, which the agent attributed in part to the syphilis that prevailed among the Modoc.

It is an interesting fact that the Seneca and Shawnee, who had come direct from Ohio to their Indian Territory home in 1831, were the most backward of all the eight tribes, clinging most tenaciously to their old customs. As late as 1882 they still danced around a fire to drive away sickness and held their yearly green-corn feast, said their agent, though he marveled at their improvement since the days when they were ignorant, ill-fed savages living in huts of bark and wigwams of skins and hunting game for subsistence.

The Eastern Shawnee had dwindled to seventy-two in number. They were grieving for the death of their chief, John Jackson, a valuable man whom they could ill afford to lose. Of these Indians the agent said: "I know of no tribe who possess more kindly feelings; as a rule they are honest and industrious, but do not appreciate school privileges." They had just been saved from great suffering with an appropriation by Congress of $2,000 of their own funds to relieve them from the results of the loss of their crops by the preceding year's drought.

All the tribes on the reservation showed signs of gradual improvement. Outstanding among them were the Wyandots, who were enterprising and who built good homes and improvements on their farms. Only a small part of the total area under the Quapaw agency was cultivated. The remainder, which was principally rough timberland, was illegally appropriated by white people for grazing herds of Texas cattle.

In 1872 Quapaw Indian Agent Hiram W. Jones caused to be erected a school and boarding-house for the use of the Seneca, Shawnee, and Wyandots. This school was opened on June 1, 1872, and the following year the Wyandots, at their national council, donated funds for fencing 160 acres for a mission farm at the school.

The whites of adjoining Missouri and Kansas caused the Indians great annoyance and trouble. Some of them were convinced that they could safely trespass on the Indians' lands as the whites had done in Kansas and that the government would not intervene. In the late seventies, however, federal troops ejected some of these trespassers across the line. In spite of this, white people, to the great alarm and anxiety of the Indians, would slip in at night and mark trees to indicate claims which they imagined would be validated if they returned to renew their marks and thus keep their supposed claims alive, whereby their theft of Indian lands would accrue to them as farms, as had been customary in Kansas. The agent reported that in the spring of 1879 these white people were nervously waiting on the Kansas line while they contemplated a raid in force upon the Quapaw and Peoria lands, which they had been led to believe they would be permitted to effectuate.[7]

The death rate among some of the tribes exceeded the birth rate, but in the whole population this was somewhat compensated for by intermarriage with neighboring whites who were admitted into the tribal membership. In 1880 the population was as follows: Wyandots, 260; Ottawa, 114; United Peoria and Miami, 218; Quapaw, 200 (all on the Osage reservation but 35); Eastern Shawnee, 75; Seneca, 230; Modoc, 99; besides these, for a few years there were 25 Potawatomi and 27 "Cherokee Shawnee," drunken intruders, living on the reservation.

By 1885 it was said by the agent that the Indians under his supervision were all civilized. They were so intermarried with their white neighbors that in some of the tribes white blood predominated. The Quapaw and Modoc, however, were exceptions, the former having traditional laws against intermarriage with the whites.

Two years later the agent reported that sixty white persons had been admitted into the Quapaw and Miami tribes during the year with the approval of the Department of the Interior, which, he thought, was a mistaken policy. The Indians were so intermarried with their white neighbors that it was said that the Peoria, Miami, Wyandots, and Ottawa were practically a white people and that their Indian blood was scarcely perceptible.

The general allotment act of 1887 did not apply to the Five Civilized Tribes, Osage, Sauk and Foxes, and United Peoria and Miami Confederacy. But under authority of Congress, James R. Howard, special Indian agent, in the spring of 1888 made allotments of their land to 150 Wyandots, 130 Seneca, and 16 Eastern Shawnee; and allotments to all but the Quapaw were completed by 1893. Plans to authorize allotments of eighty acres to each Quapaw were objected to by the Indians of that tribe who insisted that their domain was large enough to yield two hundred to each. The Indians repeatedly sent delegations to Washington to secure a compliance with their wishes. After four years of rebuffs and disappointment, the Indians did something that was unique in Indian history—they took matters into their own hands and made their own allotments.

They met in council March 23, 1893, and passed necessary acts and resolutions to initiate the undertaking. Under this authority enacted by themselves, they allotted to each of 214 members of the tribe 200 acres of land. Only two refused to accept allotments. The allotting committee at their own expense had allotment certificates, record books, and complete plats printed, and then reported their acts to the council. The proceedings were then transmitted to the Office of Indian Affairs in Washington, where they were finally approved on April 7, 1893; and on March 2, 1896, Congress formally placed its stamp of approval on the proceedings of the Quapaw council.[8]

In the early eighties the fragments of the eight tribes represented in the Quapaw agency had so completely lost their separate identity, and even had so obscured their identity as Indians by white blood, that the Indian Department ceased to consider them in the category of separate Indian tribes. From this time on, the reports of the agents referred to them merely as "Indians of the Quapaw agency," though their vested rights to individual tracts of land were in no wise impaired.

Said their agent: "The Miami, Peoria, Ottawa and Wyandot Indians have for many years closely associated themselves with and intermarried amongst their white neighbors, and in consequence the Indian in his accepted sense has almost entirely disappeared from these tribes, leaving in his stead a race in which the white blood predominates, and a people having nothing in common with the Indian, and everything in common with the whites. The majority are intelligent and educated, and thoroughly understand and pursue agriculture and other civilized pursuits."[9]

The Miami Town Company, a Kansas corporation, was authorized by Congress in 1891[10] to purchase from the Ottawa Indians 557 acres of land at ten dollars per acre on which to lay out a town on the banks of the Neosho River, twenty miles northwest of the Quapaw agency, which became the present city of Miami, Oklahoma.[11]

The year 1901 was memorable at the Quapaw agency for two events. The first was the death of Indian Agent Goldberg and Mrs. Goldberg from eating poisonous toadstools by mistake for mushrooms. The second, a result of the first, was the abolishment of the

Quapaw agency and the changing of the management from the Indian agent and two school superintendents to a superintendent of the Seneca school.

While in the administration of the agency, tribal distinctions had ceased to be a matter of importance, Agent Goldberg's last report in 1900 showed the following census: Wyandots, 339; Seneca, 337; Quapaw, 251; Peoria, 175; Miami, 101; Ottawa, 170; Eastern Shawnee, 93; Modoc, 49.

From 1901 on, the reports from the Quapaw agency appeared as the "Report of School Superintendent in Charge of Quapaw Agency" from the "Seneca Training School, Quapaw Agency, Ind. T., Wyandotte, Ind. T." The superintendency was concerned principally with the supervision of the sale of inherited Indian lands.

In 1906 the superintendent reported a population within his jurisdiction of 1,730 Indians, 332 of whom did not live on the reservation. Besides these, there were 8,000 white persons. The land of the Indians had been allotted and much of it sold. The Indians were now thoroughly amalgamated with the whites, whose characteristics prevailed on the reservation where Indian laws and customs were wholly superseded by the laws enacted for the government of the whites.[12]

NOTES

1. 17 *U.S. Stat.* 633.

2. *Report of the Commissioner of Indian Affairs, 1871,* p. 499. Before the Civil War the Neosho agency was conducted at Crawford Seminary on the Quapaw reservation; but the agent, from fear of menacing Rebel marauders, removed his agency in September, 1861, to Fort Scott, Kansas, which became its temporary location. When, after the war, the agency was returned to its location in the Indian Territory, by order from Washington of March 1, 1871, it was thereafter to be known as the "Quapaw Special Agency" (Commissioner of Indian Affairs to Hoag, March 1, 1871, "Quapaw–Removal" [Oklahoma Historical Society]). In the report of Special Agent George Mitchell, and thereafter it was "Quapaw Agency" (*Report, 1871,* p. 499).

3. *Report, 1870,* p. 253.

4. 17 *U.S. Stat.* 189.

5. *Report, 1878,* p. 67

6. *Report, 1874,* p. 230. Bogus Charley, one of the last survivors of the Modoc removal to Indian Territory, died in 1881 at La Grande while on a visit to his sister at Walla Walla.

7. *Report, 1879,* p. 78.

8. *Report, 1893,* p. 141; 28 *U.S. Stat.* 907.

9. *Report, 1886,* p. 139

10. 26 *U.S. Stat.* 1010.

11. *Report, 1896,* p. 149.

12. *Report, 1906,* p. 218.

CHAPTER XXI

SUMMARY

THIS study may prompt speculation as to what has become of the Indian blood introduced into the present state of Oklahoma by Indians whose migrations have been described. As Indian tribes some of them have become extinct, and only their names survive as historical landmarks. An answer to the question as to what has become of their Indian blood is almost impossible, as officials of the government have never undertaken to pursue the subject to that conclusion, nor has sufficient information been compiled from which deductions can be made. It may be said that generalities are all that can be offered on the subject.

It is a safe generality to say that the persistence of Indian blood in each tribe is probably different from that in any other. It is also safe to paraphrase generally the statement of the agent for the Quapaw agency, wherein he said that some of the Indians in that jurisdiction have so intermarried with the whites that, at the time he wrote, it was impossible to distinguish a man of Indian blood from a white man, though he was carried on the rolls as an Indian. The other extreme is to be found in some of the native tribes of western Oklahoma, among whom today the full-blood predominates and little white blood is to be found.

This variation is noticeable among the Five Civilized Tribes, where the final rolls showed that the percentage of full-blood Indians varied from 40 per cent among the Seminole, 36 per cent among the Creeks, 31 per cent among the Choctaw, and 20 per cent in the Cherokee tribe to 14 per cent in the Chickasaw tribe, where the percentage of white blood is comparatively high.

If this study were supplemented by a table of statistics, interesting deductions might appear which a lack of applicable data renders impossible. Outstanding would be startling figures on the steady and rapid decline of Indian population since Indian removal from the East was inaugurated. Indian administrators occasionally called attention to this condition and to the reason for it: the diseases introduced among them by the white man—smallpox, measles, cholera, syphilis. Cholera, introduced by the emigrants during the Gold Rush, accounted for an accelerated death rate among the Indians. Thousands of western Indians died in 1837–38 from smallpox introduced by the white man. A few years earlier the Reverend Mr. McCoy observed the great loss of life from this dread disease among the Indians, as noted at an earlier stage of this book.

D. D. Mitchell, the intelligent superintendent of Indian affairs at St. Louis, reported in 1842 that the appalling loss of life among the Indians caused by smallpox, "which was brought over from the northern Mexican province about the year 1786, almost depopulated the country. There are many Indians now living who bear its marks, and retain a vivid recollection of its horrible ravages. Again, in 1838, the same disease swept off at least one-half the prairie tribes; hence the scanty population which seems almost lost in the vast expanse of prairie by which they are surrounded."[1]

Impressed by the rapid diminution of the American Indians, Congress, on March 3, 1865, by joint resolution authorized an inquiry into the cause by a joint special committee. This committee made an interesting report on January 26, 1867. Army officers, Indian agents, missionaries, and many others gave testimony. It was the consensus of these witnesses that the Indians were rapidly dying off from wars, change of climate, and diseases unknown to them until recently— smallpox, measles, and cholera. General John T. Sprague, who had assisted in the emigration to Indian Territory of thousands of Indians of the Five Civilized Tribes, testified to the almost universal prevalence of prostitution among the Indians. "The children die rapidly and suddenly from dysentery and measles, and from neglect and exposure to the weather. The adults die from fevers, small-pox, drunkenness, and diseases engendered from sexual intercourse. These diseases are among the men and women in the most malignant form, as the Indian doctors are unable to manage them. Indulgence in liquor, exposure, and the absence of remedies aggravate the disease. In this, striking at the very basis of procreation, is to be found the active cause of the destruction of the Indian race."[2]

Agents frequently attributed the growing death rate in part to the stubborn opposition of the ignorant Indian medicine man, who resisted the innovations of trained doctors employed to look after the Indians, because they robbed him of his influence in the tribe, and to the equally ignorant Indians, who were persuaded to shun skilled medical advisers.

At his office in Atchison, Kansas, in October, 1868, Thomas Murphy, superintendent of Indian affairs for the central superintendency, spoke on this subject with much feeling: "The Indian tribes of this superintendency, once so numerous and powerful, are rapidly fading away, and are destined at no distant period to be known only in history. Humanity demands for this unfortunate race that their journey to the land of shadows be smoothed by the tender care of a magnanimous government. How rapidly they are passing away will appear from the following facts:

"In 1854 the Kaskaskias, Peorias, Weas and Piankashaws were confederated, and their number at that time was 259; their present number is 179, showing a decrease of 80 in 14 years. In 1854 the Miamies numbered 198; they now number 92, a decrease of 106 in 14 years. In 1846 the Sacs and Foxes of the Mississippi numbered 2,478; they now number 957, including those in Iowa, a decrease of 1,521 in 22 years. In 1830 the Ottawas of Blanchard's Fork and Roche de Boeuf numbered 400; their present number is 151, a decrease of 249 in 38 years. In 1847 the Kansas or Kaw Indians numbered 1,500; their present number is 620, a decrease of 880 in 21 years. In 1848 the Pottawatomies numbered 3,235; their present number is 2,025, showing a decrease of 1,210 in 20 years. In 1839 the Shawnee numbered 963; their present number is 649, a decrease of 314 in 29 years. In 1862 the Kickapoos numbered 409; their present number is 269, showing a decrease of 140 in six years."[3]

The question is frequently asked: How many Indians are there in the United States and are they increasing or decreasing in number? This author does not attempt to answer these questions; the subject is discussed in an interesting but not definitive manner in the report of the Commissioner of Indian Affairs for 1877, where are compiled figures of "Estimates of Indian Population at Various Periods":

"Imlay, in his Topographical Description of the Western Territory, published in London in 1797, estimates the number of Indians 'who inhabit the country from the Gulf of Mexico on both sides of the Mississippi to the Gulf of St. Lawrence, and as far west as the country has been explored, that is, to the headwaters of the Mississippi, and from thence to the Missouri (I do not mean the head of it), and between that river and Santa Fe,' at 'less than 60,000.' "[4]

To the author this study demonstrates that the appalling destruction of the immigrant Indian tribes has been due largely to disease and other natural causes, but, more than all others, to the introduction among them of intoxicants by predatory white men utterly devoid of conscience or principle, who for sordid gain made a business of preying on the weakness, ignorance, and folly of helpless Indians. In an effort to correct this evil, Secretary of War Marcy, on April 13, 1847, addressed a circular letter to the governors of Missouri, Arkansas, and Iowa, in which he said: "I would respectfully, but earnestly, invoke the aid of the executive and other authorities of Missouri, Arkansas and Iowa, in the efforts which this department is now making, to suppress the traffic with the Indians in ardent spirits. The most stringent laws have been passed by Congress for this purpose, but as these are operative only in the Indian country, they fail to reach the most prolific source of this great evil, which is within the limits of the States adjoining our Indian Territory.

"It would be a useless task to depict to you the extent of the injuries which this instrument of evil has inflicted upon the red race of this continent. They are well known to you in common with the whole country. There can be no doubt that to it more than to any other agency is to be attributed the rapid decline of that race in morals as well as in numbers.

"While the Indians remained in the States, surrounded by, and intermixed with a vicious white population, who preyed upon them by corrupting their morals and taking advantage of their weaknesses, there was but little, if any, chance to interpose with any effect to shield them from the debasing influence of ardent spirits; but, now that they have been removed entirely beyond our white settlements, and no one is permitted to enter their country without permission from the proper authorities of the United States, the hope is entertained that, with the co-operation of the States along whose borders they are located, this evil may be materially checked, if not entirely overcome."[5]

This interesting letter continued with convincing demonstrations of the wrongs committed on the Indians by whiskey dealers in those states and concluded with a request that the governors invoke legislation in their states that would prevent the sale of liquor to the Indians across the line. The reply of the governor of Arkansas is the only on available to the author. Apparently the Secretary had sent him a second letter, dated July 14, 1847; to this Governor Thomas Drew of Arkansas wrote that he had sent to the legislature a special message on the subject, which was ignored, but he said that he planned to persevere.[6]

In modern times more enlightened and humane concepts of Indian administration improved the service and marked the end of the rapid decline in Indian population. This great reform had its inception in a suddenly awakened interest by eastern philanthropists, which first found expression in the creation by Congress and President Grant of the Board of Indian Commissioners, a body of persons of standing and influence, who served without pay as observers, conscience, and advisers to the President and the Office of Indian Affairs.

The influence of missionaries on the morals of the Indians,[7] along with education in the field of proper living, sanitation, substitution of medical care for incantations of medicine men, enactment and enforcement of laws against the introduction of whiskey—all tended to place the Indians' health on a par with that of the white man and to arrest the rapid death rate among them, until now, under the present enlightened Indian administration, the norm of the Indian's birth and death rate is very similar to that of his white brother.

NOTES

1. *Report of the Commissioner of Indian Affairs, 1842,* p. 426.
2. *Senate Report 156* (39th Cong., 2d sess.), pp. 424 ff.
3. *Report, 1868,* pp. 259 ff.
4. *Report, 1877,* pp. 487 ff. Imlay's tabulation is as follows:
   "P. 489

Morse's Estimate,	1820–21	of Indian	population		471,036
T. L. McKenney estimate,	1825	"	"		129,366
P. B. Porter	"	1829	"	"	312,930
Gen. Cass	"	1834	"	"	312,610
C. A. Harris	"	1836	"	"	253,464
Schoolcraft	"	1837	"	"	302,498

   "P. 491

Census	"	1850	"	"	388,229

   "P. 492

Commissioner of Indian Affairs	"	1855	"	"	314,622
Schoolcraft	"	1857	"	"	379,264
Indian Office	"	1860	"	"	254,300

   "P. 493

Commissioner of Indian Affairs	"	1865	"	"	295,774
Gen. F. A. Walker	"	1870	"	"	383,712
Commissioner of Indian Affairs	"	1875–6	"	"	{ 305,068 { 291,882"

5. *Report, 1847,* p. 767.
6. *Ibid.,* p. 769.
7. *Report, 1877,* p. 9.

TRIBES WHOSE BLOOD IS REPRESENTED IN OKLAHOMA

Anadarko
Apache
Arapaho

Caddo (Kadohadache)
Cahokia
Catawba
Cayuga
Cherokee
Cheyenne
Chickasaw
Chippewa (Ojibwa)
Choctaw
Comanche (Paduca)
Creeks (Muskogee)

Delawares

Eel River (Miami)

Foxes

Hainai (Ioni, Ironeyes)

Illinois
Ioni (Hainai)
Iowa

Kansas (Kaw)
Kaskaskia
Katakas (Kiowa Apache)
Kaw (Kansas)
Kichai (Kitsash)
Kickapoo
Kiowa

Lipan

Miami
Michigamea
Missouri
Modoc
Moingwena
Munsee

Natchez
Nez Percés

Osage
Oto
Ottawa

Pawnee
Peoria
Piankashaw
Ponca
Potawatomi

Quapaw

Sauk (Sac)
Seminole
Seneca
Shawnee
Skidi (Wolf Pawnee, Pawnee Loup)
Stockbridge

Tamaroa
Tawakoni
Tonkawa
Tuscarora

Waco
Wea
Wichita (Pani Pique, Towehash)
Wyandots (Huron)

BIBLIOGRAPHY

ALFORD, THOMAS WILDCAT. *Civilization*. Norman: University of Oklahoma Press, 1936.

American State Papers: Documents, Legislative and Executive, of the Congress of the United States, Class II: "Indian Affairs," Vols. IV, V, VI, and VII. Washington, 1832–60.

American State Papers: "Foreign Affairs," Vol. III. Washington, 1832.

American State Papers: "Public Lands, Vol. II. Washington, 1834.

Annual Reports of the Commissioner of Indian Affairs, 1824–1907. Washington, 1824––. [From 1824 to 1848, these reports were published with the reports of the War Department as a part of the documents (annual departmental reports) accompanying the *Message from the President of the United States to Both Houses of Congress at the Commencement of the Session of Congress*, which usually issued a numbered document of both the House and the Senate. Reports were also issued separately during this period, the earliest such report in the Library of Congress being for the year 1837–38. Thus for this early period there were at least three prints or editions. After 1848 these reports appeared in editions that varied at different times, the imprints usually bearing the dates of the reports, sometimes as part of the *Report of the Secretary of the Interior*, sometimes as separates, having no relation to any other report.]

CATON, JOHN DEAN. *The Last of the Indians and a Sketch of the Pottawatomies.* Chicago: Chicago Historical Society, 1870.

Constitution and Laws of the Cherokee Nation. St. Louis, 1875.

DALE, EDWARD EVERETT, and LITTON, GASTON. *Cherokee Cavaliers.* Norman: University of Oklahoma Press, 1939.

DE SMET, REV. P. J. *Western Missions and Missionaries.* New York, 1881.

DORSEY, GEORGE A., and MURIE, JAMES R. "Notes on Skidi Pawnee Society." Prepared for publication by ALEXANDER SPOEHR. University of Chicago. (MS.)

FARNHAM'S TRAVELS. "Thwaite's Western Travels." Cleveland, 1905.

FLINT, TIMOTHY. *Recollections of the Last Ten Years*. Boston, 1826

FOREMAN, CAROLYN THOMAS. *Oklahoma Imprints*. Norman: University of Oklahoma Press, 1936.

––––. *Indians Abroad*. Norman: University of Oklahoma Press, 1944.

FOREMAN, GRANT. *Pioneer Days in the Early Southwest*. Cleveland, 1926.

––––. *Indians and Pioneers*. New Haven, 1930; Norman, 1936.

––––. *Indian Removal: The Emigration of the Five Civilized Tribes*. Norman: University of Oklahoma Press, 1932.

––––. *The Five Civilized Tribes*. Norman: University of Oklahoma Press, 1934.

––––. *Adventure on Red River*. Norman: University of Oklahoma Press, 1937.

––––. *Marcy and the Gold Seekers*. Norman: University of Oklahoma Press, 1939.

––––. *Illinois and Her Indians*. ("Papers in Illinois History.") Springfield: Illinois State Historical Society, 1940.

––––. *A Pathfinder in the Southwest*. Norman: University of Oklahoma Press, 1941.

––––. *A History of Oklahoma*. Norman: University of Oklahoma Press, 1942.

GITTINGER, ROY. *The Formation of the State of Oklahoma*. Berkeley, Calif., 1917; Norman, 1939.

HODGE, FREDERICK W. (ed.). *Handbook of American Indians North of Mexico.* Washington: Bureau of American Ethnology, 1912.

IRVING, JOHN T. *Indian Sketches, Taken during an Expedition to the Pawnee and Other Tribes of American Indians.* London, 1835.

JEWELL, HORACE. *History of Methodism in Arkansas.* Little Rock, 1892.

JOHNSTON, JOHN. *Recollections of Sixty Years.* Dayton, Ohio, 1915.

KANSAS HISTORICAL SOCIETY, TOPEKA. "Clark Papers."

KAPPLER, CHARLES J. (ed.). *Laws and Treaties.* ("Indian Affairs.") Washington, 1903.

LATROBE, CHARLES JOSEPH. *The Rambler in North America.* New York, 1835.

Laws of the Cherokee Nation. St. Louis, 1868.

Laws of the Choctaw Nation. New York, 1869.

Laws and Joint Resolutions of the National Council. Tahlequah, I.T., 1871.

LE PAGE DU PRATZ, ANTOINE S. *Histoire de la Louisiane.* Paris, 1758.

MCCOY, ISAAC. *History of Baptist Indian Missions.* New York, 1840.

MANYPENNY, GEORGE W. *Our Indian Wards.* Cincinnati, 1880.

Maximilian's Travels. "Thwaite's Western Travels." Cleveland, 1905.

MILES, GENERAL NELSON A. *Personal Recollections and Observations.* Chicago and New York, 1897.

MISSOURI HISTORICAL SOCIETY, ST. LOUIS. "Frost Papers."

———. "Graham Papers."

———. *Publications.* October–December, 1940.

MORSE, JEDIDIAH. *A Report on Indian Affairs.* New Haven, 1822.

NATIONAL ARCHIVES, WASHINGTON. *Documents and Memorials.* Washington.

———. Department of the Interior, Office of Indian Affairs, "Ancient and Miscellaneous Surveys," Vol. IV: 'Notes' by A. Chouteau, 1804."

———. Report of Chouteau to Calhoun (Records of War Department, Office of Secretary of War).

———. Chouteau, Auguste, to Secretary of War, September 11, 1820.

———. Chouteau, P. L., to Clark, 1826.

———. "1829 Delaware and Senecas in Ohio (Emigration) Gov. Lewis Cass" (Office of Indian Affairs).

———. "Indian Office Files."

———. "St. Louis (Emig.) Gen Wm. Clark" (Mosely to Clark, July 4, 1838).

———. "Kaskaskia (Sub-agency)" (Office of Indian Affairs).

NYE, CAPTAIN W. S. *Carbine and Lance.* Norman: University of Oklahoma Press, 1937.

OKLAHOMA HISTORICAL SOCIETY. "Foreman Collection." Indian Archives.

———. "Kiowa Agent's Reports."

———. "Ponca Letter Press Book."

———. "Quapaw–Removal."

———. "Quapaw–Seneca Agency Archives."

———. "Sauk and Fox (Agent's Report)."

———. "Sac and Fox Letter Press Book."

———. "Wichita Agency."

Report of Indians Taxed and Indians Not Taxed in the United States: Eleventh Census, 1890. Washington, 1894.

RICHARDSON, JAMES D. *Messages of the Presidents.* New York, 1903.

ROYCE, CHARLES C. (comp.). *The Cherokee Nation of Indians: Fifth Annual Report of the Bureau of American Ethnology.* Washington, 1887.

———. *Indian Land Cessions in the United States: Eighteenth Annual Report of the Bureau of American Ethnology.* Washington, 1899.

SCHOOLCRAFT, HENRY R. *Journal of a Tour of the Interior of Missouri and Arkansas in 1818 and 1819.* London, 1821.

——. *Thirty Years with the Indian Tribes.* Philadelphia, 1851.

——. *Historical and Statistical Information Respecting the History, Conditions and Prospects of the Indian Tribes of the United States,* Vol. III. Philadelphia, 1853.

SHEA, JOHN GILMARY. *The Catholic Church in Colonial Days.* New York, 1886.

Speeches on the Passage of the Bill for the Removal of the Indians, Delivered in the Congress of the United States, April and May. Boston, 1830.

The Territorial Papers of the United States, Vol. X. Washington, 1942.

UNITED STATES HOUSE OF REPRESENTATIVES. *Document 233* (20th Cong., 1st sess.).

——. *Document 171* (22d Cong., 1st sess.).

——. *Executive Document 1* (30th Cong., 2d sess.).

——. *Executive Document 97* (40th Cong., 2d sess.) ("Report of Indian Peace Commission").

——. *Executive Document 153* (40th Cong., 2d sess.).

——. *Report 51* (19th Cong., 2d sess.).

——. *Report 87* (20th Cong., 2d sess.).

——. *Report 474* (23d Cong., 1st sess.).

——. *Report 188* (45th Cong., 3d sess.).

UNITED STATES SENATE. *Document 512* (23d Cong., 1st sess.).

——. *Document 1* (25th Cong., 2d sess.).

——. *Executive Document 1* (36th Cong., 2d sess.).

——. *Executive Document 78* (51st Cong., 1st sess.).

——. *Miscellaneous Document 23* (45th Cong., 2d sess.).

——. *Report 211* (18th Cong., 1st sess.).

——. *Condition of the Indian Tribes. Report 156* (39th Cong., 2d sess.). Washington, 1867.

United States Statutes. "Indian Land Cessions."

United States Statutes at Large.

WISCONSIN HISTORICAL SOCIETY, MADISON. "Draper Manuscripts."

MAGAZINES

Annals of Iowa (Des Moines)
Army and Navy Chronicle (Washington, D.C.)
Army and Navy Chronicle and Scientific Repository (Washington, D.C.) (successor to *Army and Navy Chronicle*)
Chronicles of Oklahoma (Oklahoma City, Okla.)
Indiana Magazine of History (Bloomington, Ind.)
Missouri Historical Society Publications (St. Louis, Mo.)
Nebraska History Magazine (Lincoln, Neb.)
Niles' Weekly Register (Baltimore, Md.)
North Carolina Historical Review (Raleigh, N.C.)
North Dakota Historical Quarterly (Bismarck)
University of Michigan Alumnus Quarterly Review (Ann Arbor, Mich.)

NEWSPAPERS

Arkansas Gazette (Little Rock)
Buffalo Advertiser
Cherokee Advocate (Tahlequah, I.T.)
Cincinnati (Ohio) *Enquirer*

Cincinnati (Ohio) *Gazette*
Columbus (Ohio) *Sentinel*
Daily National Journal (Washington, D.C.)
Edwardsville (Ill.) *Spectator*
Fort Smith (Ark.) *Elevator*
Fort Smith Herald
Indianapolis (Ind.) *Democrat*
Kansas Daily Commonwealth (Topeka)

Missouri Intelligencer (Franklin)
Missouri Republican (St. Louis)
Natchitoches (La.) *Courier*
National Intelligencer (Washington, D.C.)
New York Weekly Tribune
Ottawa (Kan.) *Journal*
St. Louis (Mo.) *Beacon*
Saint Louis Daily Union
Washington Daily Union (Washington, D.C.)

INDEX

Bax, Father John, influence of, on Quapaw, 312

Baxter Springs (Kan.), 250–51; Modoc Indians in, 315; Nez Percés pass through, 322

Beach, John (Sauk and Fox agent), appraisal of Indians by, 153; estimate of Sauk and Foxes, 147–58; locates agency at home of Baptiste Peoria, 151; reports on condition of Indians, 142–43

Bean, Agent J. L., 137

Beatrice (Neb.), 249

Beaver, Pond; see Castor Pond

Belleville (Ind.), 79

Ben Franklin (steamboat), carries emigrants down Ohio River, 67–68

Bennett, Agent Leo E., 200

Benton, Senator Thomas H., appraisal of Indian situation, 52, 53

"Big Bottom" (Ill.), 53

Big Jim (Wapameepto), "Absentee Shawnee" leader, 181

Big Kettle (New York chief), 331

Big Snake (Ponca Indian), 252

Big Spring (Ohio), 93

Black Beaver (Delaware guide), 43, 207

Black Bob's Band of Shawnee (Missouri Shawnee), 54; condition of, 177; in Kansas, 169; leave Kansas and join those on Canadian River, 170–71; looted by Quantrell's raiders, 173; memorialize President, 60; moving about in Arkansas and Missouri, 60; object to Ohio immigrants in Kansas, 170–71; opposed to joining other factions of Shawnee, 60; removal hindered by whites, 176; at St. Louis, 60; treaty to remove from Cape Girardeau, 63; whites object to, 60

Black Hawk (Black Sparrow Hawk or Makataimeshekiakiah) (Sauk Indian), 123; 139; band crosses Mississippi in 1832, 139; a prisoner, 139; two sons of, 146

Black Hawk War, 74, 139

Black Hoof (Shawnee chief), 31

Black River, 52

Black River Band (Chippewa), confederate with Munsee, 337

Black Sparrow Hawk; see Black Hawk

Blain, Agent S. A., 282–83

Blanchard's Fork: Ottawa Indians on, 72, 190; Ottawa lands on, ceded, 72

Blue Eyes (Waw-pee-ko-ny-a) (Kickapoo chief), 39, 40

Blue River, Potawatomi camp on, 117

Board of Indian Commissioners, 353

Bogus Charley (Modoc warrior), 348

Bond County (Ill.), 81

Boone, Colonel Albert Gallatin (Indian agent), 298, 304

Boundaries, 23

Bounty claims on Illinois lands, 36

Brandt, Joseph, translator of Book of Common Prayer, 166

Brazos River, 293

Briggs, Benjamin, assists Shawnee emigration, 73

Bright Eyes; see Susette

Brish, Henry C., 70, 76, 80; conductor of Ohio Indians, 67, 68, 69, 70

British: administration of Indian affairs by, 5; influence of, 86, 87

British traders: influence of, 87; influence on Kickapoo, 41; responsible for Indian participation in War of 1812, 30

Brothertown Indians, 332

Bryan, John A., 93

Buffalo, profits from, 267

Buffalo Creek Reservation (N.Y.), 330–33

Buffalo hunt: last by Pawnee, 243; by Oto, 265

Bureau of American Ethnology, 8, 15

Burial customs, of Sauk and Foxes, 156, 157

Butler, Pierce M., Indian council of 1843, 162

Cabeza (Cabeca) de Vaca, 292

Cache Creek (I.T.), 290

Caddo (Indians), 284–85, 286, 300; act as guides for Dragoon Expedition, 295; with Creeks, 164; Delawares merged with, 189, 295; disintegration of, 293; friendly to French, 292; habitat of, 292; Ioni and Delaware union, 284–85; land of, allotted, 294; location in Texas, 293; raided by Comanche, 294; removed to Indian Territory, 294; statistics, 285; treatment of, in Texas, 293; welcomed by Choctaw, 295

Caddo Confederacy, 291

Caddo County (Okla.), 302

Cadue, Peter (interpreter), 42, 46

Cahokia (Indians), 19, 21, 31; cede Illinois lands, 37; in Kansas, 204; take refuge in southern Illinois, 20

Caldwell, Billy (Potawatomi chief), 122

Calhoun, Secretary of War John C., 51

California emigrants: introduce cholera, 264; in Potawatomi country, 121

Camp Leavenworth (Kan.), 54

Camp Supply (Kan.), 300

"Camp Wichita" (Fort Sill), 298, 300, 304

Canada: Delawares in, requested to join